British Philosophers and Theologians of the 17th & 18th Centuries

A Collection of 101 Volumes

Edited by

René Wellek

Peter Browne

THE
PROCEDURE, EXTENT
AND LIMITS
OF HUMAN UNDERSTANDING
1728

Garland Publishing, Inc., New York & London

1976

Bibliographical note:

this facsimile has been made from a copy in the
Yale University Library
(K8.B81.d728)

Library of Congress Cataloging in Publication Data

Browne, Peter, Bp. of Cork and Ross, d. 1735.
    The procedure, extent, and limits of human under-
standing, 1728.

    (British philosophers and theologians of the 17th &
18th centuries ; no. 8)
    Reprint of the 1728 ed. printed for W. Innys, London.
    1. Knowledge, Theory of. I. Title. II. Series.
B1361.P8 1976   121   75-11201
ISBN 0-8240-1757-9

Printed in the United States of America

THE

PROCEDURE,

EXTENT,

AND

LIMITS

OF

Human Underſtanding.

ISAIAH lv. 9.

As the Heavens *are higher than the* Earth, *ſo are* my Ways *higher than* your Ways ; *and* my Thoughts *than* your Thoughts.

LONDON:

Printed for WILLIAM INNYS, at the Weſt End of St. *Paul's.* MDCCXXVIII.

CONTENTS.

A   CHAP.

CONTENTS.

CHAP.

CONTENTS.

CHAP.

CONTENTS.

THE

INTRODUCTION

TO THE

WHOLE DESIGN.

SOME years paſt a ſmall Treatiſe was publiſh'd with this Title, *A Letter in anſwer to a Book, entitled, Chriſtianity not myſterious ; as alſo to all thoſe who ſet up for Reaſon and Evidence, in oppoſition to Revelation and Myſteries.* It plainly appears to have been written in haſte, and with the incorrectneſs of a youthful and as yet unformed ſtile ; but the Foundation the Author all along proceeds upon, for the confutation of his Adverſary ; and for laying open the fallacy of mens Arguments againſt Divine Revelation and our Chriſtian Myſteries, drawn from the Topics of ſtrict Reaſon, Certainty, and Evidence ſeems to be ſolid and juſt ;

B　　　　　and

and indeed the only one upon which such a firm and unshaken Superstructure can be rais'd, as may be Proof against all the Arguments and Objections of Unbelievers.

THAT Letter proceeds intirely upon a Distinction at first laid down between a *Proper* and *Immediate* Idea or Conception of a Thing; such as we have of the things of this world, which are the proper and immediate Objects of our Senses and our Reason; and that Idea or Conception which is *Mediate* only and *Improper*, such as we necessarily form of the things of another world. It is there asserted as a sure and incontestable Truth, that we have no immediate proper Idea at all of God, or any of his Attributes as they are in themselves; or of any thing else in another world: and consequently, that we are under a necessity of conceiving all things supernatural by *Analogy*; that is, by the Mediation and Substitution of those Ideas we have of our selves, and of all other things of Nature.

THIS

THIS Diſtinction is there affirmed to be abſolutely neceſſary, for the aſcertaining and ſettling the Bounds and Meaſure of our Knowledge; for ſhewing the true Limits, and utmoſt Extent of human Underſtanding, that we may clearly and diſtinctly apprehend where mere *Knowledge* ends, and *Faith* begins: where it is they meet again, and inſeparably combine together for the inlargement of our Underſtanding vaſtly beyond its native ſphere; for opening to the Mind a new and immenſe ſcene of things otherwiſe imperceptible; and for a rational well-grounded Aſſent to ſuch Truths concerning them, as are a ſolid Foundation for all Religion Natural and Revealed.

THE nature of this *Analogy* the Author explains by a ſimilitude in this following Paragraph.

" AND thus it is plain, that tho' we
" may be ſaid to have Ideas of God and
" Divine things, yet they are not imme-
" diate or proper ones, but a ſort of Com-
" poſition we make up from our Ideas of

" worldly

" worldly Objects; which at the utmost
" amounts to no more than a Type or
" Figure, by which something in ano-
" ther world is signified, of which we
" have no more notion than a blind man
" hath of Light. And now that I am
" fallen into this Similitude, which seems
" well to explain the nature of the thing,
" let us pursue it a little ; and suppose,
" that to a Man who had never seen or
" heard any thing of it, it were to be re-
" veal'd that there was such a thing as
" Light.   This Man as yet hath neither
" a Name nor a Notion for it, nor any
" Capacity of conceiving what it is in
" it self. 'Tis plain therefore God would
" not reveal this to him by the name of
" Light, a word wholly unknown to
" him ; nor by stamping on his Mind
" any immediate Idea of the thing it
" self: for then it were utterly impos-
" sible for him to communicate this Re-
" velation to others as blind as himself;
" since nothing but the same Almighty
" Impression cou'd do that ; so that this
" Revelation must be made by Words
                              " and

" and Notions which are already in him.
" And accordingly when he is told, that
" it is a thing which can diffuse it felf in
" an inftant many thoufands of miles
" round; and enable him to know in
" a moment in what Order all things lay
" at a great diftance from him, and
" what Proportion they bore one to ano-
" ther; nay, that it could make him
" know where the Heavens lay; and
" that by the help of this he fhou'd there
" difcern at once, a vaft and almoft in-
" finite number of very pleafant Bodies;
" and, in fhort, that without the help
" of his Stick or his Hand he fhou'd
" know every thing that lay before him :
" After all, 'tis plain this Man wou'd
" form to himfelf an Idea of Light from
" his Touch; he wou'd think it very
" like Feeling, and perhaps call it by
" that name; becaufe this was the beft
" way he had of diftinguifhing one
" thing from another; and therefore
" wou'd conclude, that thofe Bodies he
" heard of muft needs be wondrous foft
" and fmooth. Juft thus do we con-

B 3   " ceive

" ceive the things of another World ; ſo
" that we may rack our Invention, and
" turn and wind all thoſe Ideas we have
" into ten thouſand different ſhapes, and
" yet never make up any true likeneſs
" or ſimilitude of the *Real* Nature of
" thoſe Objects of another World.

FROM hence the Author proceeds to
the application of this Diſtinction to the
Points in controverſy between him and
that famed Unbeliever he had to deal
with ; and particularly to the explaining the true manner of our conceiving
the Myſteries of Chriſtianity, and that
of the ever bleſſed Trinity in particular.

Now tho' the proceeding upon this
foot of *Analogy* may ſeem ſomething
ſtrange and new, yet it is as old as the
earlieſt Fathers of the Church ; who did
not indeed expreſsly lay down this Diſtinction, and purſue it Logically thro'
all the particulars of our knowledge human and divine ; or apply it to the exact
ſtating the Limits and Extent of human
underſtanding in general. But however
the ſum and ſubſtance of all their Anſwers

fwers to the Arguments and Objections of Heretics and Unbelievers might be refolved into this, *That the true and real Nature of God and his Attributes, and of all things in another World were utterly incomprehenfible and ineffable ; and confequently that all mens Reafonings from the Real Nature of things in this world, to the* Real true *ftate and condition of things Supernatural, were precarious and inconclufive.*

IT is now upwards of twenty-five years fince that Treatife was publifhed; and confidering it underwent feveral Editions; that it met with the approbation of fome men of greateft note, and higheft ftation in the Church; and never was anfwered any otherwife than by fome perfonal Reflections in a Pamphlet againft the Author; but chiefly confidering of what univerfal ufe and application the above-mentioned Diftinction is in all our Controverfies with Arians, and Socinians, and Deifts; how neceffary it is for reducing all matters in debate between them and us, to a Point under

B 4   every

every head, ſo that they may admit of
a clear and eaſy ſolution.   It cannot be
ſufficiently admired, that in this inter-
val (wherein ſo much hath been written on all ſides concerning Revelation
and Myſtery, and the Doctrine of the
Holy Trinity) the many pious and learned Defenders of our Faith have either
intirely declined proceeding upon the
foundation there laid ; or have given only ſome general, ſhort, and imperfect
Hints of this Analogy.   Inſomuch that
our Adverſaries have not yet found themſelves under a neceſſity of joining iſſue
upon that foot ;   and conſequently
obliged either flatly to deny and diſ-
prove our Conceptions of God, and his
Attributes, and of all things in another
World to be Analogous ; or to acknow-
ledge that all their Inferences and Concluſions drawn from the Nature of Man
and Things material, to the *Real* internal Nature of God and Things ſuper-
natural, are falſe and deceitful.

BUT our wonder will ceaſe, when we
conſider the no ſmall difficulty of ap-

plying

plying this Diftinction between proper and improper Ideas to the Myfteries of Chriftianity; and to the feveral difficulties and objections which have been raifed concerning them, even after it is allowed and throughly digefted ; befides the great danger of purfuing it thro' all the inftances which will every where occur: For without a judicious and cautious application of *Analogy*, men will be apt to miftake it for pure *Metaphor*, and by that means refolve all Religion into nothing more than mere Figure and Allufion.

THAT which makes the Danger of infifting upon this manner of conceiving God and his Attributes by Analogy yet greater, is the general prevailing prejudice againft it, from the exprefs Declarations of fome late Writers of great note; who have rejected utterly, and even exploded it by fuch pofitive Affertions as thefe, which will be throughly confidered in their due place. *If the Reafons of Juft and Good are the fame in refpect of God and Man ; then muft the Actions proceeding*

ing from them be of the same Kind. Again, *If the moral Attributes in God were not the same in* Kind *with those in Man, we cou'd have no knowledge at all of them ; nor cou'd we reason at all about them.* And again, *It is foolish for any man to pretend, that he cannot know what Goodness, and Justice, and Truth in God are ; for on that supposition God would be an unintelligible Being ; and Religion, which consists in the Imitation of Him, wou'd be utterly lost.* Again, *That Cogitation or Thought, Self-motion, Free-will, and Reflection which is implied in Self-consciousness, are in God Almighty the same in Kind* [with what they are in us] *tho' infinitely superior in Degree, is as demonstrable as either his Existence, or any other of either his moral or natural Attributes ; these being primary Attributes common to all Intelligences.* Others argue strenuously against this Analogy from that very Topic in the other extreme which makes it absolutely necessary, namely, the *Infinite Nature of God ;* by saying, *There can*
be

be no Proportion *or* Similitude *between Finite and Infinite, and confequently no Analogy.* The weight and authority of thefe great Writers hath probably deterred others from publicly attempting any thing this way ; otherwife than by fome general Hints, purfued perhaps only thro' one or two Paragraphs ; and hath occafioned their running rather into any other way of accounting for themanner of our conceiving God and Things immaterial ; fuch as by the common Deduction of Reafon ; by their Effects only ; by the Relation they bear to us ; or by Intellectual Ideas, and Metapyfical Abftractions.

ABOUT ten years after that Letter had appeared in Print, an eminent and truly learned Prelate ventured (in a Sermon preached and publifhed in 1709) to fhew the *Confiftency of Predeftination and Foreknowledge with the Freedom of Man's Will,* upon the fame foundation of Analogy (as his Grace intended) upon which the Letter had proceeded for the defence of our Chriftian Myfteries ; which is the only Difcourfe upon

that

that foot deferving the Reader's particular notice. In that Sermon his Grace
very juftly and truly afferts, with the
Author of the Letter, *That we have no
direct or proper Notion or Conception of
God and his Attributes, or of any other
Things of another World ; That they are
all defcribed and fpoke of in the language
of Revelation by way of Analogy and
Accommodation to our capacities ; That
we want faculties to difcern them ; That
the Words and Names by which we exprefs them are not to be taken literaly.*
He obferves, *that our Conceptions of God
and his Attributes, as far as they can
go, may be faid to correfpond to the Wifdom, Goodnefs, Holinefs, Juftice, Will,
and Foreknowledge of God.* And hath
this excellent Paragraph to that purpofe,
which I fhall here tranfcribe, only leaving out a few words, which have given
an handle for exception.

" I f we wou'd fpeak the truth, thofe
" Powers, Properties, and Operations,
" the names of which we transfer to
" God, are but faint Shadows and Refemblances

" femblances of the Divine Attributes.
" Whereas his Attributes are the Ori-
" ginals, the true real Things; of a
" nature fo infinitely fuperior, and dif-
" ferent from any thing we difcern in
" his Creatures, or that can be concei-
" ved by finite Underftandings, that we
" can't with reafon pretend to make any
" other Deductions, from the Nature of
" one to that of the others, than thofe
" he hath allowed us to make; or ex-
" tend the Parallel any farther than that
" very Inftance which the Refemblance
" was defigned to teach us.

Tho' his Grace thus rightly lays down
Analogy for the foundation of his Difcourfe; yet for want of having throughly weighed and digefted it, and by word-
ing himfelf incautioufly, he feems intirely to deftroy the nature of it; infomuch that whilft he rejects the ftrict
Propriety of our Conceptions and Words,
on the one hand; he appears to his An-
tagonifts to run into an extreme even
below *Metaphor*, on the other. His
greateft miftake is, that thro' his Dif-

courfe

courfe he fuppofes the Members and Actions of an human Body, which we attribute to God in a pure Metaphor, to be equaly upon the fame foot of Analogy with the *Paffions* of an human Soul, which are attributed to him in a lower and more imperfect degree of Analogy; and even with the *Operations* and Perfections of the pure Mind or *Intellect*, which are attributed to him in a yet higher and more complete degree. In purfuance of this overfight, he exprefsly afferts Love, and Anger, Wifdom, and Goodnefs, and Knowledge, and Foreknowledge, and all the other Divine Attributes to be fpoke of God as improperly as *Eyes* or *Ears*; That there is no more likenefs between thefe things in the Divine Nature and in ours, than there is between our *Hand* and God's *Power*; and that they are not to be taken in the fame Senfe. *That becaufe we do not know what his Faculties are in themfelves, we give them the names of thofe Powers that we find wou'd be neceffary to us in order to produce fuch Effects,*

Effects, (as we obferve in the world) *and call them Wifdom, Underflanding, Foreknowledge, &c. Becaufe he hath all the Advantages thefe Powers or Faculties can give him if he had them.* And again, *That he acts as if he had them. That we fpeak of him as if he had the like; as if there were fome fuch things in God; and becaufe we muft refemble him to fomething we do know and are acquainted with.*

AGREEABLY to this incautious and indiftinct manner of treating a Subject curious and difficult, he hath unwarily drop'd fome fuch fhocking Expreffions as thefe, *The beft Reprefentations we can make of God are infinitely fhort of* TRUTH. Which God forbid, in the Senfe his Adverfaries take it; for then all our Reafonings concerning him wou'd be groundlefs and falfe: But the Saying is evidently true in a favourable and qualified fenfe and meaning; namely, that they are infinitely fhort of the real, true, internal Nature of God as he is in himfelf. Again, *That they are Emblems*

blems indeed and *Parabolical Figures of the Divine Attributes, which they are design'd to signify* ; as if they were Signs or Figures of our own, altogether precarious and arbitrary ; and without any real and true foundation of Analogy between them in the Nature of either God or Man ; and accordingly he unhappily defcribes the Knowledge we have of God and his Attributes by the Notion we form of a ftrange Country by a *Map*, which is only *Paper* and *Ink, Strokes* and *Lines.*

NOTWITHSTANDING the main fcope and defign of his Grace's Sermon is juft; and that by any candid Reader he muft be however allowed to fuppofe that Goodnefs, and Mercy, and Juftice, and Wifdom, and Knowledge do exprefs fome real Perfections in God *Anfwerable* and *Correfpondent* (as he himfelf expreffeth it) to what they fignify in human Nature : And notwithftanding that the foundation of Analogy, upon which he builds, (if rightly explained and duly applied,) is folid and firm ; yet his
Anta-

Antagonists overlook all this, and lay the whole stress of their Answers upon those Errors he hath committed in the Superstructure. They take advantage only of his mistaken way of treating the Subject, and inadvertent manner of expressing himself. They do not answer him, by directly shewing the Foundation of Analogy upon which he argues to be false and groundless; and that our Ideas and Conceptions of God and his Attributes, obscure and imperfect as they are, must be however direct and immediate; and our Words as literal and proper in that case, as when we apply them to Things natural and human. No, they have not attempted this; but they do most injuriously represent his Grace's Opinion and Doctrine to be, That those Operations and Perfections of a human Mind, which we attribute to God, do signify nothing true and real in the Divine Nature: Whereas that great Prelate in some places expressly asserts the contrary, that they signify *more valuable Perfections and infinitely supe-*

C *rior*

rior to what they are in us ; and again, that his *Attributes are the Originals and true real Things.* And his Oppofers take this for granted ; that if thofe Attributes are in any fence *Analogous,* they can mean nothing true and *real* in the Divine Nature.

FROM thence they draw many formidable confequences, all which muft be allowed to be true, upon thofe falfe fuppofitions of their own. As, that his Grace's Principle of Analogy, which is call'd a *Paradox, renders the Gofpel Patchwork* ; *and all the Divine Attributes, together with all the great Doctrines of Chriftianity infignificant, ufelefs, and precarious* ; *and that thereby all Virtue and moral Practice falls to the ground. That by it his Grace hath banifh'd Truth quite out of the world* ; *and that it is all loft by his unexampled Theology. That by this the Scriptures are reprefented obfcure, ambiguous, dark, perplexed, entangled* ; *and contradictions rais'd in the Divine Nature and Attributes. That it makes way for all the er-*

4 *roneous*

roneous Suggestions of Enthusiastick Spirits ; for subverting all Christianity ; for sapping its Foundations ; and that it turns all its Doctrines into Banter, Ridicule, and Contradiction. That upon his Principle of Analogy, *they are all groundless, wild, and erroneous Notions ; Dreams, Whimsies, Improprieties, calculated for people's Fancies ; mere Fictions, Chimeras, and chimerical Conceits, and Compliances with false Images in the heads of the Vulgar. That his Grace hath outdone the Rehearser, who in effect impiously says, St.* Paul *and the other Apostles confound all with their improper way of talking ; that his Sermon hath done a great deal of Hurt and Disservice to the Church of Christ ; That a man might as well have performed what his Grace hath done by the subterraneous World, by the Philosopher's Stone, by Magic, and occult Qualities ; and that upon his Principle Ministers are not to trouble themselves, whether the Doctrine they preach be true or false.*

Out of a Pamphlet, the Author of which ftiles himfelf *a Profelyte to plain Dealing*, I have collected thefe few from many fuch like expreffions of a feverifh burning Zeal, and not *according to knowledge* for the Doctrines of the Gofpel; which are all however fafe upon his Grace's main Principle rightly underftood and candidly interpreted.

Another anonymous and much clofer Antagonift, who writes with lefs fhew of Zeal indeed for the Caufe of Chriftianity, but with better colour of Reafon; is no lefs fevere and injurious in his Cenfures of the main Principle upon which his Grace proceeds. He afferts with an air of great Pofitivenefs, that upon his Principle, *God is a Being without Wifdom, Goodnefs, Juftice, and Mercy, Knowledge and Holinefs. That all the moral and natural Attributes of God are indefenfible. That all the Arguments for God's Government of the World; and for rewarding and punifhing Men in a future State, which are drawn from the Divine Attributes taken*

4   *in*

*in a strict and literal Sense, are given
up ; and that we can never from thence
infer any Obligation to Duty. That thus
it is a Matter of no great consequence,
what Notions Men have of God. That
by consequence from his Principles God
must be without Distinction of Persons,
as well as without Parts and Passions ;
and that his Grace hath given up the
Cause to the Unitarians. That his Grace
owns, that God is neither Good nor Wise ;
and that according to him, the Scripture
Text,* Be ye holy as I am holy, *is as
unintelligible, as* Be ye holy as I am
Rabba. *That if his Grace meant to make
all our Notions of God pass for Riddles
in Divinity not to be understood, little
Credit will be gain'd by it to Religion.
That thus the Unity of God would be only something* AS GOOD *as but one God.*
The Author asks, *How can Men know
God's Will, when he hath no Will?*
And, *How can we imitate the Holiness
of God, unless it be of the same nature
with that Quality in us ?* And again,
Whither will Matters run ? Whither in-

C 3   *deed !*

deed ! when one may not so much as say, God knows whither. And he makes this Remark upon the whole, *That the World had been as wise and as quiet, if their ordinary Notions of God's Attributes had never been disturbed.*

I HAVE troubled the Reader with these empty Outcries and Sarcasms here, in order to prevent this loose and unreasoning way of speaking upon this Subject for the future ; and that I may prevail upon those Authors to think the Matter over again in cool Blood : And to consider, that they are the very Men who are justly liable and obnoxious to all those hard Speeches and frightful Imputations of sapping and subverting Christianity, which they so wrongfully charge upon the great and learned Prelate. Because they all along so strenuously maintain, *That if the Doctrines of the Gospel, God, and his Attributes, are by us conceived Analogicaly, there can be nothing of Truth and Reality in them.* And *that upon the Supposition of such Analogy, we cou'd have no Knowledge at all*

of

of them, but what is purely Figurative and Metaphorical. Two of the moſt deſperate and univerſaly pernicious Poſitions, that were ever openly and publickly maintain'd ; being by direct and immediate conſequence utterly deſtructive of all Religion Natural and Revealed : And which, if they were true, wou'd ſupport and confirm all the Arguments of Arians, Socinians, and Deiſts againſt the Chriſtian Revelation and Myſteries. To convince them effectualy that they are fundamentaly wrong, let them but ſingle out any one Idea or Conception, together with the Word by which we expreſs it ; and revolve it in their mind, and try whether they can transfer it to the Divine Being and the Things of another World, in the ſame ſtrict and literal Propriety with which they apply it to Man : And if they find this in fact not practicable, then let them ſuſpend all further Oppoſition to the Doctrine of Analogy, till the Nature of it is more fully and rightly explained, and the true Uſe of

it

it in Religion fhewn; together with the application of it to the Defence of the Truths and Myfteries of the Gofpel; and to the Confutation of Herefy and Infidelity.

SUCH Objections as have any weight or colour of Reafon in them may, God willing, be throughly confidered here-after. But by the way, it is conveni-ent to obviate and remove one popular Prejudice againft the enlarging upon this Subject of Analogy. What occafion or neceffity is there for it at this time, more than ever? Wou'd not the world have been as wife, and as good, and as holy, if Men's ordinary Notions of God and his Attributes, and of all things elfe fupernatural had never been difturb-ed? Yes it wou'd; and it cannot be fufficiently lamented, that they have been fo difturbed. But who are the Difturb-ers? The Arians, Socinians, and Deifts; who, by turning all the Words and Lan-guage of the Gofpel either into mere Figure and Metaphor on one hand, have argued away the whole Subftance of our
Faith;

Faith; and refolved all Chriftian Myfteries into nothing : Or by wrefting all the
Terms and Expreffions we have for them
to ftrictly literal and proper Acceptations on the other hand, have from thence
charged our Faith of the Gofpel and its
Myfteries with Inconfiftencies, Abfurdities, and Contradictions ? Or are they
the Difturbers, who undertake to fhew,
that thofe Gofpel Terms are to be underftood neither in a fence purely Figurative and Metaphorical, nor yet in their
ftrict and literal Propriety; and who by
that means lay open the Fallacy of all
thofe men's Reafonings from the Nature of Things known, to the real internal Nature of Things unknown ?

THE defign of the Scriptures indeed
is, that we fhould take both the moral
and natural Attributes of God, and all
things fpoke in them of another World
fo far literaly, as to give our Affent to
them all as to things true and real, upon
the Teftimony of God; without med-
dling with their Nature as they are in
themfelves, which is incomprehenfible.
But

But when Men will deviate from that Defign, and pervert this common, and familiar, and literal Acceptation, which would fully have anfwered all the Ends of Religion; and will raife their Obje-ctions from thence againft the Scriptures themfelves, and the Myfteries revealed in them: Then, when the Enemies of Revelation and Myftery make a bad ufe of it, by mifreprefenting and mifapply-ing this Analogy; it becomes abfolute-ly neceffary for the Orthodox to make a good ufe of it; to explain it truly, and apply it rightly; to diftinguifh the Nature of it with greater nicety, and fhew how it differs from Figure and bare Allufion.

THE fundamental Doctrine revealed in Scripture, and ever maintained by the Church, but denied by the Arians is, that God is *Truly* a Father; that Chrift is his *True* and *Genuine* Son, and *Actualy begotten* of the Father in his own *Divine* Nature and Perfections. The Ground of the Arian Scheme is, that the words *Father*, and *Son*, and
Begotten

Begotten cannot be underſtood literaly
and properly of God; therefore they
are to be taken *Improperly* and figura-
tively; namely, that Chriſt was *Made*
or *Created*, or ſome way *Produced* by
the Will and Power of God; and conſequently cou'd not be equal in Nature
and Perfections, nor co-eternal with him.
From hence they branch out into a large
Hypotheſis full of Blaſphemy againſt
God as a *True* Father; and againſt Chriſt
as *Truly* a Son, in the received ſence of
the words as they are commonly applied
to God and to Chriſt. For us to undertake to prove in the other extreme, that
thoſe Terms are to be underſtood *literaly*
and in their ſtrict *Propriety* of God and
Chriſt, is an impoſſible task; and thus
they will be ſurely too hard for us in
every point of Controverſy. But if we
take the middle way, and ſhew thoſe
Terms not to be taken in their *Firſt*,
and *Strict*, and literal Propriety; nor in
a mere and empty *Figure*, but *Analogicaly* thus: That Chriſt, in his Divine
pre-exiſtent Nature, is as *Truly*, and *Realy*,

aly, and *Actualy* the Son of God in a
supernatural incomprehensible manner,
begotten in his own Nature and full Perfections, as if he were literaly so; and
as *Truly* as a human Child is the Son
of his Father in the way of Nature;
then we bring the Controversy upon the
right foot; and they must stumble at
every step they take to confute us.

THE Dilemma the Socinians reduce
us to, and push us with at every turn
is this. All the words of Scripture, in
which the Mysteries of Christianity are
revealed, are to be understood either *literaly* or *metaphoricaly*. But you must
grant, say they to us, that they cannot
be taken properly and literaly; therefore they are to be taken Metaphoricaly; and consequently they are all nothing more than mere Figure and bare
Allusion: And accordingly they are so
full of this, that *Socinus* himself, speaking of the Gospel, hath this saying, *Tota
Redemptionis nostræ per Christum Me-
taphora.* The true Answer to them is,
that those words are to be understood
                                neither

neither in a ftrictly proper fence, nor in a fence purely Metaphorical, but Analogicaly; in which acceptation they contain and exhibit to us as much Truth and *Reality*, as they do when taken in their moft ftrict and literal Propriety.

THE whole fum and fubftance of the Deift's and Freethinker's reafoning may be refolved into this. You muft grant, fay they, that we can neither know nor believe any thing but what we have fome Idea of: And you muft grant likewife, that the Chriftian Myfteries are incomprehenfible, that is, that we have no Idea at all of them; therefore we can neither know nor believe them. And purfuant to this, they every where oppofe the Certainty and Evidence of Senfe and Reafon, and the clear and diftinct knowledge we have of *Their* proper Objects; to the Uncertainty, and Obfcurity, and Unconceivablenefs of Revelation and Myftery. Now we are under a neceffity of making them both thofe Conceffions thus *Separated* by them,

them, and yet their confequence is abfolutely falfe: But if you put them both together, they will make one Pofition abfolutely true; namely, that Propofitions, made up of Terms and Ideas ftrictly literal and proper; firft underftood and apprehended thus literaly, and then transferred by Analogy to things Divine and Incomprehenfible, do contain and exprefs as much folid and fubftantial Truth and Reality, as when they are applied only to things corporeal and human.

Nay, the Atheifts themfelves find their account in laying afide and confounding this Analogy; for thus they argue. If God is Infinite, no finite human Underftanding can have any Knowledge at all of him. It can't know him in the *Whole*, becaufe nothing finite can comprehend Infinity; nor can it know any *Part* of him, there being no part of Infinity. To which I return the Apoftle's Anfwer, that tho' we can't be faid to know any *Part* of him; yet we are truly faid to know him *in part*, as

we

we fee the reflection of a fubftance in a looking-glafs; that is, by Analogy with thofe Perfections we obferve in our felves, and in the things of Nature; the brighteft Mirrour in which we now behold him. But they urge, there can be no *Proportion* or Similitude between *Finite* and *Infinite*, and confequently there can be no Analogy. That there can be no fuch Proportion or Similitude as there is between finite created Beings is granted; or as there is between any material fubftance and its Refemblance in the glafs: and therefore wherein the *Real Ground* of this Analogy confifts, and what the Degrees of it are, is as incomprehenfible as the real Nature of God. But it is fuch an Analogy as he himfelf hath adapted to our Intellect, and made ufe of in his Revelations; and therefore we are fure it hath fuch a foundation in the Nature both of God and Man, as renders our *Moral* Reafonings concerning him and his Attributes folid, and juft, and true.

I MUST not now stay to enlarge upon these things, and shall here only give some account of my Design and Method in the further prosecution of this Subject.

THE great Genius of the last Century, under the head of Revelation and the Mysteries of Religion, observes how *God hath vouchsafed to let himself down to our Capacities; so unfolding his Mysteries as that they may be best or most aptly perceived by us; and, as it were, grafting or inoculating his Revelations into those Notions and Conceptions of Reason which are already in us.* After which, he reckons a Treatise of Logic calculated for this very purpose, among his *Desiderata. Itaque nobis res salubris videtur & imprimis utilis, si Tractatus instituatur sobrius & diligens, qui de usu Rationis humanæ in Theologicis utiliter præcipiat, tanquam Divina quædam Dialectica. Utpote quæ futura sit instar opiatæ cujusdam medicinæ; quæ non modo speculationum, quibus schola interdum laborat, inania consopiat; verum etiam contro-*

controverfiarum Furores, quæ in Ecclefiâ
tumultus cient, nonnihil mitiget. Ejuf-
modi Tractatum inter Defiderata poni-
mus; & Sophronem, five de legitimo ufu
Rationis humanæ in Divinis nominamus.

Now this is the very thing I aim at,
and what I endeavour by this firft Treatife to perform in fome degree. In
which I propofe rightly to ftate the whole
Extent and Limits of human Underftanding; to trace out the feveral fteps and
degrees of its Procedure from our firft
and fimple Perception of fenfible Objects, thro' the feveral operations of the
pure Intellect upon them, till i grows up
to its full Proportion of Nature : And to
fhew, how all our Conceptions of things
fupernatural are then *grafted* on it by A-
nalogy ; and how from thence it extends
it felf immenfely into all the Branches
of Divine and Heavenly Knowledge.

Some Treatife of this kind I forefaw
was neceffary to be premifed, before I
cou'd proceed to the application of this
Analogy to any of our Controverfies in
Religion ; becaufe of that ftrong Preju-

dice

dice againſt it, from an opinion that it ultimately reſolves all Religion into mere Figure and Alluſion, and conſequently brings it to nothing ; and becauſe of the many Errors and Prepoſſeſſions in the generality of young Students, taken up from falſe and pernicious Principles in ſome of our modern Writers of Logic and Metaphyſics. In order to obviate and remove theſe, I was to begin with the firſt Rudiments of our Knowledge ; to explain the ſeveral Properties of thoſe Ideas of Senſation, which are the only Materials the Mind of Man hath to work upon ; to lay open the true nature of *Divine* Analogy, how it differs from *human* Analogy, and how both differ from pure Metaphor : To ſhew, how we neceſſarily apply it to the conceiving the Divine Being and his Attributes ; of what univerſal advantage it is in directing us to the right uſe of Reaſon in Religion ; in enabling us to ſtate the true manner of apprehending the Myſteries of Chriſtianity ; and to judge, when it is that our Reaſonings upon them are

juſt,

juſt, and ſolid, and clear; and when they are confuſed, precarious, and falſe.

I HOPE the ingenuous Reader will ſuſpend any Indignation and Cenſure, which may ariſe from his Zeal for the Truth and Safety of Religion, till he can ſee the whole Deſign together in one view. For my Intention is (if God permit) in ſome of the following Tracts to proceed to our Controverſy with ſuch as are *declared* and *profeſſed* Arians, whether ancient or modern. When the way is thus far prepared, I purpoſe to lay open the deep Diſſimulation of all thoſe who have no other colour or pretence to renounce that name and Character, unleſs it be becauſe they rigorouſly maintain the rankeſt of *their* Heretical Opinions not *expreſsly*; but by *direct*, *immediate*, and *neceſſary* conſequence. The conſideration of the Socinian *Poſtulata*, and that groſs and complicated Scheme of Hereſy deduced from them with much Subtilty and Artifice, I leave to the laſt.

THE Sabellians began early in the Church to deſtroy the very Subſtance

of Chriftianity, and give an intire turn
to the whole Tenor of the Gofpel, and
the Reality of our Salvation by the Merits and Mediation of a Saviour: And
that, by arguing the words *Father* and
Son to be purely figurative, and confequently to denote only one and the
fame Divine Perfon; and thus they formed their Herefy upon the foot of *Metaphor*.

THE Arians afterwards, tho' they ran
into the quite contrary Extreme, yet argued from the very fame Topic of Figure and Metaphor; concluding juft as
the Sabellians did, that *Father* and *Son*
were Terms altogether *improper*, and
utterly unworthy the Divine Nature in
their literal and proper acceptation. But
they made a quite contrary ufe of this;
not only to prove them two diftinct and
different Perfons; but to prove the Son
to be of a different and fubordinate Nature, neither coeternal nor coequal with
the Father: and it was by this Artifice,
they endeavoured to obviate and inva-
lidate all the Arguments of the Orthodox,

dox, drawn from the real import and true acceptation of thofe words in the Gofpel.

THE Socinians agree with the Arians in allowing Chrift to be God in the moft elevated fence, and to all intents and purpofes that a made or created Perfon *can* be fuch; but that it is ftill in a figurative only, and not in the fame ftrictly proper acceptation in which it is attributed to the Father. And they differ from them in thefe two material Points, That whereas the Arians allow Chrift a pre-exiftent, tho' a made or created Nature; the Socinians will have him originaly a mere Man, and not in being till born of the Virgin *Mary*. And fecondly, Whereas the Arians, by holding Chrift to be God in a Figure only, do intirely take away all the real and truly divine virtue and efficacy of his Merits and whole Mediation for us; yet they do this by direct and immediate confequence only; and leave the Myfteries of Chriftianity in their full force and efficacy with fuch as do not difcern this ne-

ceffary

ceffary confequence. But the Socinians do exprefsly and profeffedly turn them all into pure Metaphor, and bare Allufion only to what was enjoined and practifed under the legal Difpenfation. So that they hold Chrift to be a *Figurative* Saviour, a figurative Prieft, a figurative Mediator; they refolve his Merits and Satisfaction, with the words *Price, Purchafe, Redemption, Wafhing* and *Cleanfing* of his Blood, all into mere Figure; and in fhort, turn our whole Chriftianity into a Metaphorical Religion.

THE Deifts and Freethinkers of all ranks and degrees, who build upon their Principles, have but one ftep farther to go, and do make this Inference, which is obvious and rational upon the Socinian Hypothefis; That if all thofe things are to be underftood in Figure and Metaphor only, then they can have nothing of Reality and folid Truth at the bottom. By the fame fatal Delufion with the Socinians, they utterly reject all *Analogy* in Religion as well as *Metaphor*; and therefore fet up for the belief of one only
Divine

Divine Perfon ;. and for fuch Principles of Morality as are deduceable only from the Light of Reafon, as they imagine, without the help of that Revelation, to which even they themfelves owe their beft and moft exalted Notions of it. They rigoroufly confine the Underftanding within the narrow bounds of *direct* and *immediate* objects of Senfe and Reafon; and will not fuffer the Mind of Man in any one Inftance to reach above the ftrictly literal and immediate acceptation of Words; fo as to transfer them and their Ideas Analogicaly with the leaft Truth and Reality to things incorporeal, and otherwife inconceivable and ineffable.

THE Progrefs from thence into fpe-culative Atheifm is fhort and eafy. For if all Revealed Religion is to be reject-ed as merely figurative, and metaphori-cal ; then all Natural Religion is to be likewife rejected ; becaufe all the Ideas and Conceptions we can have of God and his Attributes from the light of Reafon muft be equaly figurative and metapho-rical; and therefore we have no *Real* true

Know-

Knowledge at all of them ; and confequently can never prove the Exiftence of a Being whereof we have no true Conception or Knowledge.

I LOOK upon *Socinianifm*, together with the modern *Clandeftine Arianifm* which is moftly built upon it, to be in all probability the laft great Effort of the Devil againft Chriftianity ; which will then fhine out to the world in its full Luftre and Glory, whenever this thick Cloud is fully removed and diffipated, which he hath interpofed to obfcure and darken its Rays. Our modern Deifts, and Freethinkers, and Atheifts of all forts and fizes are likewife the natural Growth and Offspring of Socinianifm : They are as fo many Heads daily fprouting up from that figurative *Metaphorical Monfter*; each of which multiplies by being cut off, and they increafe their number by being as daily confuted. Nor can they ever be totaly deftroyed, till they are all ftruck off together at one Blow, skilfully levelled at the common Neck from whence they rife; which I am

per-

perfuaded can never be otherwife performed, than by a dexterous application
of that true Analogy (which hath a folid Foundation in the Nature of things,
and ever carries in it a fure, and certain,
and confiftent *Parity of Reafon*) to all
thofe Arguments and Objections raifed
againft Revelation, from men's blending
and confounding it with pure Metaphor,
a Creature only of the *Imagination*.

THE abfolute neceffity of anfwering
the Enemies of Revelation and Myftery upon fome other than the common
footing, is apparent; not only from the
daily increafing number of their Profe-
lytes, but from their boafted Triumphs
over the Orthodox; whom they pretend to have greatly diftreffed and
ftreightened, by reducing them to a neceffity of proving all the Scripture Terms,
wherein our Chriftian Myfteries are revealed, to be taken in their ftrictly literal and proper acceptation. This they
plainly difcern to be an impoffible task
to us; and therefore whilft the Cham-
pions

pions for the Cause of God and Religion are labouring and toiling up this Precipice; and ever bend all their force and strength to attack them in that part of their Hypothesis, in which alone they are impregnable; they, from the opposite side, never fail to ply them at every turn with Figure, and Metaphor, and Allusion. From hence it is, that their greatest Advantages are gained; and tho' they can never hope to obtain any intire Victory from thence, yet this serves to raise a Mist before men's eyes; to perplex and darken the whole controversy; and to render every material point of it confused and indistinct, so that it cannot be brought to a certain and determinate Conclusion. All this difficulty and obscurity, as I conceive, may be effectually removed by rightly stating the true nature of that Analogy which runs thro' our Conceptions of Things divine. For then the only Objection left to the Adversaries of Revelation will be; that *Granting* all we contend for, yet

Analogy

Analogy at beſt is ſtill but *Figure* ; and therefore that by this method of proceeding, we make that very Conceſſion which gives up the Subſtance and Reality of Myſtery. To which the Anſwer is obvious, That if they will take the word *Figure* in *General*, and in a great latitude, as it is oppoſed to the ſtrictly *Literal* Propriety of thoſe Scripture Terms, in which our Chriſtian Myſteries are delivered ; and muſt and *will* call them ſuch ; there is no danger in a *Word*, ſo they allow the *Thing :* And will afterwards fairly diſtinguiſh between that which is *Purely Figure*, and ſerves only for a mere Elegance and Ornament of *Speech* ; and that which hath as ſolid a Meaning and as ſubſtantial a Ground in the very *Nature* of things, as if it cou'd be expreſs'd in Terms ſtrictly literal and proper.

THIS I apprehend is to be no otherwiſe performed, than by rightly explaining the Nature of that true and *Neceſſary* Analogy, which runs thro' all our

Con-

Conceptions and Language of Things divine. And furely there cannot be a better Teft, that this is the true Meafure and certain Rule in thinking and fpeaking of things otherwife imperceptible and ineffable, than its being univerfaly applicable to fo many different Subjects and Controverfies ; and yet never once giving juft occafion for a Sufpicion of its failing in the Trial : efpecialy if it is all along found confiftent with it felf under fo many various ufes ; beginning in our moft natural Conceptions of the Attributes of God, and ending in the moft fublime Myfteries of Chriftianity.

My Defign in each of the following Tracts is, not to calculate them for an Anfwer to any particular Book or Author, but to the whole Caufe in controverfy with Arians and Socinians ; and other Unbelievers who build upon them, and do from their Hypothefes argue againft all Revealed Religion, with better colour of Reafon, than thofe Hereticks do againft the Truth and Reality

of

of our Chriſtian Myſteries. My Purpoſe is to lay a Foundation for anſwering, not only what hath been already offered by them; but what may be advanced upon the like erroneous Principles for the future. In order to which, I am not to expatiate into any great variety of Matters ſubordinate, and of leſs moment; or to apply Arguments or Solutions to each man's peculiar way of Reaſoning: But to make a juſt and impartial Repreſentation of their Doctrine and Principles; to ſtate rightly the fundamental Queſtions in debate; that the whole Controverſy may be brought upon the right foot, and the material Branches of it reduced to the utmoſt point of Deciſion. To ſingle out ſuch of their Arguments as are the main Pillars and Support of their whole Scheme of Religion; none of which I think to paſs over or conceal; but to propoſe them in their full Strength and Force, and in the ſhorteſt and cleareſt Light, as I have collected them out of their beſt and moſt valua-

ble

ble Authors. And laftly, fo to adapt my
Anfwers to them, that in reading any
of their Works, with a continual eye to
the diftinction between Metaphor and
the true Divine Analogy, the main Delufion and Fallacy which runs thro' them
all, may lie open to every difcerning and
unprejudiced Perfon.

I HAVE endeavoured to be very exact
and juft in my Quotations, tho' I name
none but the Antients; and even out of
thefe I decline, as much as may be, ci-
ting either the Place or Page from
whence the Quotations are taken. The
few Paffages cited for their Authority
only, are to be met with in moft Books
upon the Subject; and as for the reft,
whether from the Antients or Moderns,
I leave them to pafs according to their
own intrinfick worth and value, without
the additional weight of great Names.
The world is already filled with that kind
of Learning, which confifts in tedious
Differtations concerning what fuch and
fuch men's thoughts and opinions were,

in

in Matters plainly to be decided by Reaſon and Scripture; when the main Queſtion is, what Opinions they *Ought* to be of; and who gives the beſt and moſt convincing Reaſons for what he ſays? Truth will ever ſtand upright alone; but Error is tottering, and falls to the ground when its Props are removed; and every thing merely human is to be eſteemed, not according to the Perſon who ſaid it, but according to the intrinſic weight of what is ſaid.

Tho' I may commit many miſtakes and overſights in the courſe of my Performance; (and who is intirely free from them?) yet that ought to be no Prejudice againſt the main Foundation I have laid, and do all along proceed upon. If it is falſe and imaginary, and a groundleſs Invention of Man, it will come to nought; and I pray God it may do ſo ſpeedily, that the Fallacy may be laid open to his Glory, and to my own Shame; who have been ſo deeply engaged in dangerous Error and Miſtake: But if the Foundation

is

is good, and agreeable to the Light both of Nature and Revelation, as I truſt it will be found, then it is *of God*; it will ſtand ſure ; and all Contradiction and Oppoſition given to it, will tend only to its farther Eſtabliſhment ; and to the Strength and Confirmation of that whole Superſtructure which is raiſed upon it.

A N

THE

PROCEDURE,

EXTENT

AND

LIMITS

OF

Human Understanding.

BOOK I.

CHAP. I.

NO Affertion whatfoever feems more agreeable to Reafon, than that Things *Human* and *Divine*, *Natural* and *Supernatural*, are not perceived by the Mind of Man after the fame manner. Every one at firft Hearing will be apt to think this a true Propofition; and on fecond Thoughts will look upon it as Matter of greateft Confe-quence in Religion, that it be throughly weighed and confidered: And yet by fome

ftrange

ftrange unaccountable Unhappinefs, it hath fo
fallen out, that nothing hath been more overlooked than this fignal and important *Difference*; and lefs attended to in moft of thofe
Controverfies, which have all along difturbed
the quiet and peaceable Courfe of the Gofpel.

THIS Overfight hath been equaly the
Caufe of all the Errors of *Enthufiafts* on the
one hand; and of the pretended *Votaries* to
ftricteft *Reafon* and *Evidence* on the other. For
tho' thefe two feem to be in contrary Extremes,
and to run as far from one another as they can;
yet they both fet out at firft with the fame fatal Delufion; they meet again at length in
one common *Error*, and proceed in all their
Notions and Arguments upon the fame grofs
Suppofition, That *Human* and *Divine* Things are
alike the *Direct* and *Immediate* Objects of our
Underftanding.

UPON this very Miftake it is, that on one
fide Men will not ftoop fo *Low* as Reafon; and
that on the other, they will not venture to rife
Above it. While *Enthufiafts* afpire to a more
direct and immediate View of Things, which
are not in fuch a Degree difcernible either by
Senfe or Reafon, their Notions muft of Neceffity be all fencelefs and irrational: And while
the Boafters of *Reafon* and Evidence acquiefce
intirely in the immediate Objects of our underftanding Faculties, and will not fuffer the
Mind

Mind to launch out beyond them, they by directly Confequence deſtroy all Religion, as well *Natural* as *Revealed*.

MY Deſign being to lay a Foundation for the clear and effectual Confutation of moſt Errors of both kinds, but eſpecially thoſe of the *Arians,* and *Socinians*, and *Deiſts*, and *Freethinkers* of all Sorts; againſt whom the following Diſcourſes are more directly levelled; I foreſee it neceſſary, that the *Firſt* of them ſhould be taken up in tracing out the *Bounds* and *Limits* of Human Underſtanding. The exact Deſcription of theſe, with ſuch Plainneſs and Perſpicuity, that Men may know how to *Stop* when they come to the full Extent and *Natural* Compaſs of it; and then to *Pauſe* a while, 'till they are ſenſible how the Mind muſt *Begin a-new* for the Apprehenſion of Things *Supernatural*, and intirely immaterial; ſeems to me the greateſt Service which can be done to all Religion in general, in this notional and ſceptical Age. For as the miſtaking of theſe Bounds hath been the Cauſe and Occaſion of moſt *Deluſion* and *Error*; ſo the having a proper Recourſe to them, is become the only effectual Way of forming diſtinct and ſatisfactory *Anſwers*, to moſt of thoſe Difficulties and Objections which have been raiſed againſt the Truths of Religion.

THE

THE Bounds set out to our Understanding by nature, are not very extensive; for the Mind hath originaly no larger a Sphere of its Activity than this visible Frame of material Objects, that seems to be shut in by the fix'd Stars; which intire Space we may conceive to be but as a *Point* to the Universe; and yet all Things beyond them, with respect to any *Direct* or *Immediate* Perception of our Faculties, are as if they had no Being: Insomuch, that if Men were resolved never to concern themselves with any Exercise and Application of their *Knowledge* and Assent, farther than the direct and immediate Objects of their Senses and their Reason, they must necessarily cut off all Intercourse and Commerce with Heaven; and there could be no such Thing as any true Religion in the World.

AND therefore now we are to consider after what manner it is, that the Mind of Man dilates and extends itself beyond its native Bounds; how it supplies the want of *Direct* and *Proper* Ideas of the things of another World; raising up *Within* it self *Secondary* Images of them, where it receives no *Immediate* Impression or Idea from *Without*. How the vast and boundless extent of the *Universe*, with the great and glorious Variety of heavenly things, the World of *Spirits*, and even *God* himself and his *Attributes*; together with all the Sacred *Mysteries* of Christianity become the Objects of our

4   Reason

Reaſon and Underſtanding: Inſomuch, that Things *Otherwiſe imperceptible* grow *Familiar* and *Eaſy*; and how we are able to meditate and diſcourſe, to debate and argue, to infer and conclude concerning the nature of thoſe things, whereof we have not the leaſt direct Perception or Idea.

BEFORE I proceed to this, I ſhall premiſe it as a ſure and unconteſted Truth; That we have no other *Faculties* of perceiving or knowing any thing divine or human but our *Five Senſes*, and our *Reaſon*. The Contexture of our Frame is ſo various and complicated, that it is no eaſy matter nicely to diſtinguiſh our underſtanding Faculties from one another; and Men who would appear more ſharp-ſighted than others, and pry farther into this matter than there is occaſion, may increaſe the number of thoſe Faculties: But they will be all comprehended under *Senſe*, by which the Ideas of external ſenſible Objects are firſt conveyed into the *Imagination*; and *Reaſon* or the pure Intellect, which operates upon thoſe Ideas, and upon them, *Only* after they are ſo lodged in that common Receptacle.

As this firſt Volume relates to Knowledge in general, and is chiefly Logical, and preparatory only to what is intended ſhould follow; ſo I have been more large and particular in thoſe parts of it which eſpecially regard my

main

main Defign. But the touching upon fome collateral Points that fell in my way, was almoft unavoidable ; the placing of which in a true Light might prove of confiderable Service to thofe who have been mifled by fome late Authors of Vogue and Authority. Whether thefe incidental Subjects are truly determined here, or not ; I defire it may be obferved, that this will not any way affect the main Doctrine, nor alter the principal Foundation laid, in relation to our manner of conceiving the things of another World.

I LAY no greater a ftrefs upon any of thofe Points, than as being matter of highly probable Conjecture only, and as what appears to me to be Truth ; and do accordingly leave them to ftand or fall, as they fhall be found more or lefs agreeable to the natural Sentiments of any Reader who is yet free to judge for himfelf, and unbiaffed from the Weight of great Names. This previous Caution I would have extended particularly to what is faid concerning the Souls of Brutes ; the degree of our Knowledge in natural Caufes and Effects ; the Nature and Ufefulnefs of Syllogifm ; to my conjectural Obfervations, at the latter End of the fecond Book, upon that Scripture Diftinction of *Spirit*, and *Soul*, and *Body* ; as well as to all other matters which have not a direct tendency to eftablifh the main Doctrine of *Divine Analogy*.

CHAP.

CHAP. II.

Of Sense, and the Ideas of Sensation.

OUR five *Senses*, tho' common to us with Brutes, are however the only *Source* and Inlets of those Ideas, which are the intire *Groundwork* of all our Knowledge both *Human* and *Divine*. Without Ideas of some sort or other, we could have no Knowledge at all; for to know a thing, is to have some *Representation* of it in the Mind; but we cannot think, or be conscious of thinking, 'till we have some Idea or Semblance of an Object to think upon; and without our Senses, we could not have one internal Idea or Semblance of any thing without us. Insomuch that in our very Entrance into the large and capacious Field of Argument which is before us, we must lay down that Maxim of the Schools as universaly true without any Restriction or Limitation, *Nihil est in Intellectu quod non prius fuit in Sensu*; or, as a certain Philosopher expresseth it with more Softness, *Nescio an quicquam Intellectus moliri possit, nisi ab Imaginatione lacessitus.*

THE Imagination is the common Storehouse and Receptacle of all those Images, which are transmitted thro' the Senses; and till this is furnished in some degree, the Soul, while it is in the Body, is a still, unactive Principle;

E 4

ciple; and then only begins to operate and first exert itself, when it is supplied by Sensation with Materials to work upon : So that the most abstracted spiritual Knowledge we have, as will hereafter abundantly appear, takes its first Rise from those Sensations; and hath all along a necessary dependence upon them.

I am not unaware, how much this positive Assertion will at first startle and surprize all those, who have hitherto fancied they could abstract intirely from all Ideas of Sensation; and that by the help of such as are *Purely Intellectual* they could think altogether independently of them. And the thought which naturally arises in their Mind on this occasion is this; That if this kind of Abstraction is utterly impracticable, what then will become of all our Knowledge of the Things of another World? Of all *Reveal'd Religion*, and the Truths of *Morality*, and the *Mysteries* of Christianity? They are all, I trust in God, very safe; and will become the more so when this Assertion is fully laid open, rightly explain'd, and universaly acknowledged to be true.

The Question is not, what the *Consequences* may be of enlarging upon this *Principle*, and pursuing that *Analogy*, by which alone our natural Ideas and Conceptions become subservient to the conceiving and apprehending things supernatural? But whether the Principle is true?

For

For there is a mutual Sympathy and faſt Connection between the Truths of *Nature*, and
thoſe of *Religion* ; they fall in together, and
cloſe whenever they meet, ſo as to communicate Light and Strength to each other. This
Opinion, as every thing elſe which is agreeable
to Reaſon, will I hope be of no ſmall Advantage to true Religion ; for I doubt not but the
Effect of putting it in a right Light will be,
that *Enthuſiaſm*, in all the great Variety of
Shape in which it ſhews itſelf, will fall to the
Ground at once ; and all thoſe Objections a-
gainſt Revelation and Myſtery will be removed, which proceed upon their being *Ab-
ſtruſe*, *Unintelligible*, and *Contradictory* ; and thoſe
who expoſe our Chriſtian Myſteries, or explain
them away under Pretence and Colour of adhering to ſtrict Reaſon and Evidence, will be
under a neceſſity of finding out new Topicks.
So that, tho' we thus ſtoop as *Low* as the *Earth*,
yet it is that from thence we may with more
Vigour take our Flight even to *Heaven* itſelf,
for the Contemplation of all the glorious Objects of another World.

BEFORE I ſpeak of the particular Properties of theſe Ideas of Senſation, it will be
convenient to obſerve theſe three things in general concerning them.

1. THAT it is no way to the Purpoſe of
the following Diſcourſe to decide here, whether

all fenfitive Perception be performed by any
Actual Impreffion of the Thing itfelf upon our
Senfes? Or by any *Operation* of the Senfe upon
the Object? Whatever the Quality in fenfible
Objects is, which enables them to imprint fome
Reprefentation or *Character* of themfelves upon
us; or whatever that Frame and Contexture of
the Organs is, which difpofeth them either to
receive that Impreffion, or to take the Like-
nefs of thofe external Objects by any intrinfick
Virtue and Power of their own; it is certain
that all fuch Perception neceffarily requires the
Prefence of the Object; with an immediate
actual Operation either of the Object upon our
Organs, or of our Organs upon the Object.
The Effect and Confequence is the fame, as
when we apply the Wax to the Seal, or the
Seal to the Wax; there follows fome fort of
Reprefentation of the Object and its Qualities.
This is the Cafe of all thofe material external
Objects, which by their Prefence have left any
Footftep or Character of themfelves upon our
Senfes; and this Reprefentation or Likenefs of
the Object being tranfmitted from thence to
the Imagination, and lodged there for the
View and Obfervation of the pure Intellect, is
aptly and properly called its *Idea.*

I F any one, not yet fatisfied, fhall ask farther what an Idea is? I fhall defire him to look
upon a *Tree*, and then immediately to fhut his
Eyes, and try whether he retains any Similitude

tude or Refemblance of what he faw; and if he finds any fuch within him, let him call that an Idea, till a better Word can be found; and thus he will have a more exact Knowledge of what an Idea is, than he could attain to by any Defcription or Definition of it. Thus it is that all the great *Variety* of Objects in the vifible Creation is let in upon the Mind thro' the Senfes; as all the Parts of a delightful and fpacious Landfchape are contracted, and conveyed into a dark Chamber by a little artificial Eye in the Wall; and fo become confpicuous and diftinguifhable in Miniature.

I KNOW there are fome who will allow nothing to be called an *Idea* but what we have from our Senfe of Seeing; tho' at the fame time they give us no other Word for the Senfations of the other four Senfes: But the Perceptions of the other four are truly and properly Ideas; for otherwife a blind Man, tho' he was born with all his other Senfes, could have no Impreffion of any Object conveyed to his Imagination which might be an Idea or Reprefentation of it; and confequently he could have no Knowledge, no not fo much as any irrational Animal. It is eafily owned that the Ideas of Sight are more numerous, and more vivid, and diftinct than thofe of the other Senfes; and more clear and lafting Reprefentations of external Objects: And therefore becaufe the Sight is the nobleft and moft extenfive of them,

I gene-

I generaly take my Inftances and Similitudes
from thence; not but that I comprehend all
other Senfations under it.

2. N o r Secondly, doth it make any alteration in the Foundation upon which I build,
whether the Ideas of fenfible Objects exhibit to
us a true Image of their *Real* Nature, as they
are in themfelves; or whether the Objects be
only the *Occafions* of producing them; or whether we perceive them only by their *Effects*, or
Adjuncts, or *Circumftances*, or *Qualities*: As Heat
may be no true Image of Fire; nor Light of
the Sun; nor Colour of the Superficies; nor
Sweetnefs of Sugar. For whatever Impreffion
external fenfible Objects make upon us, this we
call their Idea; becaufe it is the only Perception of them we are capable of, and the
only way we have of knowing them. Which
Idea, tho' it fhould be fuppofed to exhibit to
us no more of the true and intrinfick Nature
of the Object, than the Impreffion on the Wax
doth of the real true Nature of the Stone or
the Steel which made it: Yet the Object leaves
behind it fuch a Similitude and Refemblance
of it felf upon the Senfes, as anfwers all the
Ends of Knowledge in this Life; and lays a
Groundwork fufficient to build all that Knowledge upon, which is neceffary in order to another, whether in refpect of natural or revealed
Religion.

THAT our Ideas or Perceptions of fenfible Objects do not exhibit to us their whole intrinfick Nature, fo as to afford us a complete and *Adequate* Knowledge of their intire Effence; together with the inward Configuration and Difpofition of all their Parts, is eafily granted: But that they are agreeable to the true Nature of the Things perceived, as far as they go; that there is fuch an exact Correfpondence between thefe and their Ideas, that what Knowledge we have of the Objects is *True* and *Real*, and not feign'd or *Imaginary*, is more than probable: Our Knowledge falls fhort indeed, but it fails in Degree only; and tho' it is *Imperfect*, yet it is not *Falfe* or delufive.

Now that the Nature, and Attributes, and intrinfick *Qualities* of fenfible Objects are thus far intirely agreeable to that external Appearance they make to us by the Mediation of our Ideas, is fufficiently evident from this plain Reafon: Becaufe it was as eafy to the *Power* and *Wifdom* of God, to have contrived all our Organs of Senfation for a juft and exact Perception of their real true Nature; as for what is *Feign'd* only and *Delufive*, which is in truth no real Perception of them at all. He could as well have adapted all our Faculties to the real Nature of Things as they *Are* in themfelves, as to what they are *Not*; and we may reafonably conclude, that this is more agreeable
able

able to the *Truth* and Veracity of the Divine Nature, than to have made us altogether for Delusion ; and put such an invincible *Deceit* upon all the Powers and Faculties of Perception which he gave us, that we should have no *Real true* Knowledge of any of their proper Objects, but be deceived in every thing about us.

NOTHING can be more absurd than this Opinion, according to which external Objects are only the *Occasional Causes* of such Affections in us as the Objects themselves have no Similitude of, nor any natural Relation to. For no Thought is more obvious than that every thing should act according to its respective Nature ; and if so, then they must operate upon our Senses according to their own intrinsick Qualities ; and our Sensations of them, as far as they reach, must be just, and agreeable to what the Objects are in themselves. But this Opinion must suppose that God *Suspends* the real Nature and intrinsick Powers of every Agent, and miraculously interposes in every act of theirs, to alter those Effects which they are naturaly disposed to produce, into some others quite different from them, or above their Power of Acting. Thus all Objects without us must operate upon us by Qualities and Attributes quite different from what they are realy endued with ; they must affect us in a manner beyond or beside any Power of Acting

ing

ing that is in them; and we may as well suppose that nothing may act upon something.

HOWEVER Persons may for Argument sake, or out of any Affectation of Singularity, abet this Error; yet they can't forbear suspecting it to be such when they consider, that all external sensible Objects have universaly the same uniform Effects upon all Men's Senses, and at all times, when they are equaly disposed: This must incline them to believe, that as far as external Objects do affect us, they do it truly according to their own intrinsick Nature and our's; and that if our Organs were more nicely disposed, and our Faculties more curious and perfect, all farther Impressions of external Objects upon us, would be just and real; and still more exact and complete Representations of their true Nature and Essence.

3. A THIRD thing necessary to be premised, and of no small Consequence towards removing infinite Confusion out of our way of *Thinking*; and towards a clear and distinct Procedure of our Understanding in the attainment of true Knowledge is; that the Word *Idea*, according to its genuine and proper Signification, should be limited and confined to our simple Sensations only, and to the various Alterations and Combinations of them by the pure Intellect. Whenever the Word is apply'd to the Operations of our Mind; or to these considered

4   in

in Conjunction with any of thofe Ideas of Senfation on which they operate, it is ufed in a very *Loofe* and *Improper* Manner; and the calling them all Ideas indifferently, and in the fame propriety and ftrictnefs of Speech without diftinction, hath evidently tended to the amufing and perplexing the Underftanding; and no way contributed to the improvement and enlargement of our Knowledge.

THUS the laying down the Ideas of *Senfation* and *Reflection* to be *Alike* the *Original* Sources and Foundation of all our Knowledge, is one great and fundamental Error which runs thro' moft of the Difcourfes and Effays of our modern Writers of Logicks and Metaphyficks. Nothing is more true in Fact, than that we have no Ideas but of fenfible Objects; upon thefe it is that the Mind begins to exert all its *Operations*; of which we have a *Confcioufnefs* indeed; but cannot frame to our felves the leaft Idea or Refemblance of them, abftractedly from thofe Objects upon which they operate. We are *Confcious* to our felves of the two chief Operations of the Mind, Thinking and Willing; as alfo of the feveral Modes of them, *Remembrance, Difcerning, Reafoning, Judging, Knowledge, Faith,* &c. But let any Man look into himfelf, and try whether he can find there any Idea of *Thinking* or *Willing* intirely feparate and abftracted from any thing to be thought of or willed; or fuch as he doth of a *Tree* or an *Horfe*; and

and he will soon be convinced of the miftake of expreffing all thefe Operations by the Word *Idea.*

It is plain that *Thinking* and *Willing*, with all the various Modes of them, are not Ideas; but the *Actions* and *Workings* of the Intellect upon *Ideas*, firft lodged in the Imagination for that purpofe; and neceffarily to be confidered as antecedent to any fuch Operations. When thefe are firft laid down as the only Ground-work and Materials of all our Knowledge, then the various Operations of the Mind upon them come naturaly to be confidered; but not as a new Set of *Ideas*, as if the Operations of the Mind were to be their own Ideas, and exercifed up-on *Themfelves:* And that likewife not imme-diately, but by the Mediation of Ideas, as it is in fenfible Objects, which is grofly abfurd. Nothing is properly an *Idea* but what ftands in the Mind for an Image or Reprefentation of fomething which is not in it; the thing muft be without us; and becaufe it cannot itfelf enter, the *Likenefs* of it only is conveyed thro' the Senfes into the Imagination; which is by Nature difpofed for receiving and retaining the Impreffion. But it is not fo with the Ope-rations of the Mind, which are themfelves within us originaly; and are not known merely by any Similitude or Reprefentation of them in the Imagination.

F   This

THIS is inftead of many Arguments to fhew the great miftake and abfurdity of that Expreffion *Ideas of Reflection*; fince we neither have nor can have Ideas, pertinently fpeaking, of any thing but what is external to the Mind'; and which can enter into it no other way than by Similitude only, or Reprefentation of itfelf. So that nothing is plainer than that we do not conceive the Operations of our Minds by the Help or Mediation of any Ideas which are fubftituted in their ftead; but that we have an immediate *Confcioufnefs* of the Operations themfelves; as being already within us, and effentialy belonging to our very Make and Frame.

BUT if Men muft have all the Operations of our Minds to be *Ideas*, and will right or wrong call them by that Name; yet 'tis plain they would be neither *Direct*, nor *Simple*, nor *Immediate*, nor *Original*. The very Word *Reflection* would even thus fpeak them to be only *Secondary* Ideas; for the Truth is this: Firft there is a direct and immediate *View* of the Intellect upon the Ideas of Senfation; from thence, by an immediate Confcioufnefs, it obferves its own *Motions* and *Actions* and Manner of operating upon thofe Ideas; then forms to itfelf the beft *Conceptions* it can of thofe Operations; not *Abftractedly*, but in *Conjunction* with thofe

Objects,

Objects, or rather Ideas of them, which its O-
perations were exercised upon.

So that all the Operations of the Mind necessarily presuppose Ideas of Sensation as prior
Materials for them to work upon; and without which the Mind could not have operated
at all; no, nor have had even a Consciousness
of itself, or of its own Being: Insomuch that
it never could have exerted one Act of Thinking, if it had not been first provided with some
of these to think upon; and this the compound
Word *Consciousness* plainly imports. As we
could have had no Notion of *Sight*, without
some outward Object to exercise the Eye upon; so the pure Intellect could have no Notion or Consciousness of any one of its Operations, without some precedent Idea in the
Imagination for it to work upon. And again,
as the Eye can survey the whole beautiful
Range of visible Beings, but hath no Power
to cast one direct Glance upon itself; so the
Soul of Man can take a View of all the inex-
haustible Store of Ideas treasured up in the
Imagination, by a *Direct* Act; but cannot have
the least direct or reflex Idea of itself, or
any of its Operations. I might add to this,
that we are so far from having any *Immediate*,
Simple, or *Original* Ideas of the Operations of
our Mind, that all the *Ideas* we attempt to
form of the Manner of its Acting, and the
Expressions we use for it are borrowed from
Sensation;

Senfation ; as will more fully appear hereafter.

As the Mind can have no *Direct* and *Immediate* View of its own Operations, fo neither
can it have any *True* and *Proper* Ideas of them ;
and the Affectation of calling thefe by the name
Ideas, and holding them to be equaly fimple
and original with thofe of Senfation, is the firft
fatal Step which is ufualy made out of the way,
to miflead the Underftanding in its fearch after
Truth ; and from that time forward Men wander up and down in a *Labyrinth* of Ideas without the leaft Progrefs towards the Attainment
of any folid and fubftantial Knowledge.

When the Ideas of Senfation and Reflec-
tion are firft laid down indifferently for the
Groundwork, then Men run endlefs Divifions
upon them ; then come on *Compound* Ideas of
both together ; Ideas of *Simple Modes* ; Ideas of
Mix'd Modes ; Ideas of *Primary* and *Secondary
Qualities* ; Ideas of *Relations* ; Ideas of *Paffions* ;
Ideas of *Power* ; Ideas of *Caufes* and *Effects* ;
Ideas of *Virtues* and *Vices* ; in fhort every thing
muft be ranged under fome Head or other of
Ideas : Tho' it be a *Scheme* as precarious and as
void of any Foundation in Nature as *Ariftotle's*
Predicaments, but much more perplexed and
confounding ; and thus they go on till their
Heads are fo fill'd and impregnated with them,
that they turn every thing into Ideas that

4   comes

comes in their way, infomuch that they can neither think nor fpeak without them.

TAKE a Sample of this profound *Ideal* Wifdom out of one of the moft celebrated Authors of this Strain; Would you know what *Power* is? The Anfwer is, *That it is a compound Idea in the Mind which it hath received both from Senfation and Reflection*; that is to fay in plain Language, it is fomething we know by our *Senfes* and our *Reafon*. But how comes any thing like it into the Mind at all? Thus; *The Mind being every Day informed, by the Senfes, of the Alterations of thofe fimple Ideas it obferves in things without; and taking notice how one comes to an end, and ceafes to be, and another begins to exift, which was not before; reflecting alfo on what paffes within itfelf, and obferving a conftant Change of its Ideas, fometimes by the Impreffion of outward Objects on the Senfes, and fometimes by the Determination of its own Choice; and concluding from what it hath fo conftantly obferved to have been, that the like Changes will for the future be made, in the fame things, by like Agents, and by the like Ways; confiders in one thing the Poffibility of having any of its fimple Ideas changed, and in another the Poffibility of making that Change; and fo comes by that Idea we call Power.*

WHAT a Treafure of Wifdom is here unlocked, and laid open to the View of ignorant

Novices!

Novices! After reading that long Description, let any Man look into his own Mind and observe whether he doth not know as little of the true Nature of Power as he did before; besides that it all along grosly supposes Ideas to be in the Things *Without* us, which are only in our selves, and not in the Objects. There is no more in it all than this in plain Language; because we observe the things without us change, and we find the Mind changes; therefore we infer, there must be something able to make and to suffer that Change; and thus, says he, we conceive *Power*, which is an Idea of *Sensation* and *Reflection*. Whereas realy nothing can carry the Mind farther from a true Notion of Power, and particularly from the infinite Power of God, with whom there is no *Variableness or Shadow of Change.*

IF it be replied, that we form an Idea even of the Power of God, as is above described; then I ask, what becomes of the greatest Instance of his Power, that of *Creation*, which is no *Change* but a Production out of Nothing? Upon that refined and abstracted Notion of Power we must ridiculously suppose, that there was a *Passive* Power in the Creature to be made before it had a Being; and an *Active* Power in the Creator to make it: And in short that God hath no Power at all of *Creation*, and can only change all which *Before* had a Being, and a
passive

paffive Power in them to be changed. It is
not ftrange that young Students fhould be
amufed and dazzled with fuch paint and glit-
tering outfide of Knowledge; but it may juftly
be wondered at, that Men of Progrefs in Years
and Learning fhould be fo pleas'd and delighted
with this empty Noife and gingling of Ideas;
that they cannot be too lavifh in their Admi-
ration, and Praifes, and Recommendation of
fuch Syftems as draw them out into great
lengths, without any real and folid Improvement of human Underftanding at the bottom.

No R laftly have we, properly fpeaking,
any Idea of *Pain* as our moft celebrated Idealifts affert we have; for if we had, we fhould
not difcern the Pain *Itfelf* either of Body or
Mind, but the *Idea* of it: It is enough and
too much that we have an immediate internal *Senfation* or *Feeling* of bodily Pain, and a
Confcioufnefs of Anguifh or Pain in the Mind;
and confequently the moft apt way of expreffing it is that by which we find it affect
us. The very fame may be faid of *Pleafure*
both of Body and Mind; for if we had the
Idea only of Pleafure within us, we could not
have the Subftance or *Reality* of it; becaufe
Both could not be within us at the fame time
(as I have before obferved concerning the O-
perations of the Mind) and thus our Happinefs would not be true and real, but falfe and
delufive. Therefore it is better to lay afide

F 4   that

that affected way of expreffing thefe by the Word *Idea*, and fpeak of them as of internal Senfations or Affections of the Body or Mind, which we perceive and are *Confcious* of without the Mediation of any Ideas.

I MIGHT thus run thro' all thofe things which Men affect to exprefs by *Ideas*, beyond thofe of Senfation, and fhew how very unaptly and improperly the Word is apply'd to them; not without great Confufion and Detriment to the Progrefs of our Underftanding in the Purfuit of Knowledge.   After all, we have no Idea of any thing but of external fenfible Objects; and when once we pafs the Ideas of Senfation, the Word is ever after Equivocal, and of an uncertain Meaning.   And therefore it were well that we could fix it here once for all; and never apply it to other things, but rather exprefs them by thofe Words which obtained in the World, before the Word Idea ufurped upon them, and thruft them out of ufe; fuch as *Notion*, or *Conception*, or *Apprehenfion*, or *Confcioufnefs*, or by fome other Term of this Sort, which may diftinguifh this Kind of Knowledge from that which we have of external Objects by their internal Ideas.

CHAP.

C H A P. III.

Of our Idea of Spirit, and of God in particular.

I AM now come to what is a yet greater Refinement of this Ideal Knowledge; namely, That we have the cleareſt Idea of active Power from our Idea of *Spirit*, and not from Matter; becauſe Matter hath only a *Paſſive* Power, that is a Power not of Acting itſelf, but of ſuffering the active Power. This Spirit, according to the Standard and Oracle of Ideas in our Age, is a *Thinking Subſtance*; which he labours to ſhew may be *Matter* for ought we know; ſo that according to him we have our Idea of active Power from ſpiritual Matter, or from a *Material Spirit:* Thus hath he confounded the Uſe of Words and the received Way of Thinking and Speaking; ſince by *Spirit* is ever underſtood ſomething that is not Matter.

As ſhameful an Abſurdity, and palpable Contradiction as this appears at firſt Sight, yet it is plain to be ſeen in that Author, and open to every conſidering Reader. It is impoſſible for us to have an *Idea* of *Active* Power in any Degree, if we muſt have it only from an *Immaterial* Subſtance, of which we have no *Idea* at all; nor indeed a Conception of any one Operation of it independent of Matter or material Organs; in Conjunction with which the Spirit of Man exerts all its Operations. The truth is thus; we obferve fuch Effects with regard to things material and fenfible, as we conclude cannot proceed from any inherent Power in themfelves; and therefore we rightly infer there muft be fome other Beings *Not material* which have the Power of producing fuch Effects; tho' fuch Beings are utterly imperceptible to us, and we have no *Idea* of them properly fpeaking. So that we come to our Knowledge of Power, not from any *Direct* Knowledge or Idea we have of Spirit; but intirely from our Reafoning upon fenfible Objects.

In purfuance of a long Chain of Ideas, Men have prefumed in the Face of common Senfe and Reafon, to lay down this monftrous Pofition magifterialy and with great Pofitivenefs. *That we have as clear and diftinct an Idea of Spirit, as we have of Body.* The fhorteft way to confute this Abfurdity is, what the Philofopher took, with him who denied there was any fuch thing as Motion; by rifing up and walking before him. So I would place a human Body before the Eyes of any one who maintains this Affertion, and then require him to place a Spirit before my Eyes.

BUT

BUT instead of this, by the magical Virtue of Ideas, he will cast a Mist before you, and say, That you can conceive *Thinking* and *Willing* as easily as you do *Extension* and the *Cohesion* of the solid Parts in Matter. Suppose this true, which is absolutely false, That we have as clear and distinct *Ideas* of Thinking or Willing (which are each of them in Man, one and the same united Act of a material and immaterial Substance in *Conjunction*) as we have of Extension and Cohesion: Yet how doth this give us any Idea of the Operations of a *Pure Spirit*, acting intirely independent of and separate from Matter? No doubt a pure Spirit hath *Perfections* answerable to that *Thinking* and *Willing* in us, which are performed by the Help of material Organs; but we can no way discern of what kind they are in themselves.

GRANT it to be true, *That we perceive not the Nature of* EXTENSION *clearer than we do that of* THINKING; yet we do not perceive the *Knowledge* of a *Spirit* so clearly as we do that of *Thinking*, which is *Our* way of Knowledge: Nay we do not *Perceive* it at all, and that is the Reason why we *Conceive* it and speak of it by that Thinking and Willing we find in our selves.

THE Ground of the Fallacy which deceives in all this reasoning is, that *Thinking*, which expresses what we know by a consciousness of it in our selves, is every where confounded with the *Knowledge* of a pure Spirit, of which we have no direct immediate *Idea* or consciousness at all: And the Inference made is this; Because we perceive *Thinking* as clearly as we do *Extension*, therefore we conceive what *Knowledge* is in a pure Spirit, as clearly as we do Extension. Whereas, we are sure that whatever the manner of knowing is in pure Spirits, it is no more performed by Thinking, than their Motion is by Walking, or Running, or Flying. Their way of Knowledge cannot be of the same kind with our Thinking, which is successive, and by the concurrence of material Organs; and is accordingly ever performed to more or less Advantage, as these Organs are better or worse disposed: They are soon relaxed and tired by the labour of Thought and Attention, and must be constantly wound up a-new by Rest or Sleep; a Distemper puts the whole Machine out of frame, and so ruffles, and even overturns it, as to spoil all our sober Thinking, and change it into Raving and Madness; and if the fibres and vessels of the Brain are intirely obstructed, as in an apoplectick Fit, we cannot think at all.

WHAT an extravagant Thought is it then to imagine that a pure Spirit *Thinks?* It

Knows

Knows indeed, but we know not *How* ; to be sure not by playing upon a set of material Strings, exquisitely contrived and wrought up into a curious Contexture of bodily Parts for that purpose ; according to the prevailing mistaken conception of the manner of our Spirit's Thinking within us; that is, only *In* the Body, and not by a necessary *Co-operation* with it ; as if *Matter* were not as *Essential* to our manner of Knowledge by Thinking, as *Spirit*.

THE same Argument for the proof of that ridiculous Position, *That we have as clear and distinct an Idea of Spirit as we have of Body*, is varied thus ; *A solid extended Substance is as hard to be conceived, as a thinking immaterial Substance*, say the Asserters of it. How great a Solecism and Contradiction a *Thinking Immaterial Substance* is, we have already seen ; but letting that pass, sure we know more of bodily Substance, than we do of spiritual. For we know by a *Direct* and proper Idea, that Extension is a Quality essential to Body ; but we are so far from knowing whether a pure Spirit be *Extended* or no, that there is no one essential Quality of it which we do know by any *Direct* and *Proper Idea* at all, or by any *Conception* whatsoever, as it is *In its own Nature*. There is an ambiguity in the Word *Substance*, which they overlook ; the Word is applied to a pure Spirit *Indirectly* only ; and if we would express ourselves in strict propriety when we speak of

Spirit,

Spirit, we muſt lay aſide that Word, and ſub-
ſtitute the Word *Being* inſtead of it.

IT is granted that we have no clear Idea
of bodily Subſtance ; but ſurely there is a great
difference between having no *Clear* Idea of a
thing, and having no direct proper Idea *At all*
of it, in any degree. We have no clear Idea
of Spirit, ſay they ; but have they any Idea at
all of it but what is borrow'd, and what we
are compell'd to place *Inſtead* of it ? When we
attempt to frame to our ſelves any *Poſitive Idea*
of Spirit, we do it from matter refin'd and exalted to the greateſt degree that falls within the
compaſs of our Obſervation ; which yet hath
no more in it of the *Real Nature* of a pure Spirit, than a lump of Led, or than Thinking
hath of its way and manner of Knowing.

COMMON Senſe and Reaſon, to thoſe
who will uſe them in a plain way, make it evident, that we have no *Immediate* or *Direct*
Idea or Perception of Spirit, or any of its Operations, as we have of Body and its Qualities.
And becauſe we are ſure we can have no ſuch
Idea of it in this Life ; therefore we are naturaly led to expreſs it by a *Negative*, and call it
an Immaterial Subſtance ; that is, ſomething
which hath a *Being*, but is not Matter ; ſomething that *Is*, but is not any thing we directly
know ; and for want of any direct and poſitive
Idea of it, we conceive and expreſs it after the

beft manner we can; faying it is *Something* which *Thinks* and *Wills*, becaufe we obferve thefe to be the Operations of an united Body and Spirit in our felves, and the greateft Perfections of our reafonable Nature; and confequently, the fitteft to reprefent the inconceivable Operations of a Being which is all Spirit: Tho' nothing is plainer, than that it neither thinks or wills as we do; and that thefe are in themfelves as unapt to exhibit to us the *Real Manner* of Knowledge in a pure Spirit, as an human Body is to reprefent its Subftance.

C o u l d any one have imagined, that by a dextrous jumble of Ideas, Men fhould go about to make us believe, that *We have as clear and diftinct an Idea of God, as we have of Man*; and that *We are as ignorant of the Effence of a Pebble or a Fly, as we are of the Effence of God?* Do we not know by direct and proper Ideas, that it is of the Effence of a Pebble, to be *Extended, Hard,* and *Heavy?* And of a Fly, to have a fort of animal Life and Motion by the fluttering of its Wings? And do we know fo much of the Effence of God by any direct Idea or Knowledge whatever? And will any Man affert we are as ignorant of the *Effence* of a Thing, of which we know many effential Properties by *Direct* Ideas; as we are of the Effence of a Being, none of whofe effential Properties we are able to obtain any Idea of, as they are in their own Nature; and of which we can form

Analo-

Analogical Conceptions only? Again, Do we
not know it to be of the *Essence* of a Man to
be composed of Soul and Body, and to Think
by the operation of these two essential Parts in
conjunction? And have we any direct Notion
or Idea of the Essence of God, how it differs
from Matter; and after what manner his
Knowledge is performed? Do we not know
that it is essential to a Man, a Fly, and a
Pebble to be *Finite* ; and have we not a direct,
and immediate, and clear Idea of this Finite-
ness? But have we any *Actual Idea* of Infinity
at all? We have no positive Idea of Infinity,
and therefore we express it by a negative, *Without End*; tho' what it is to be without Beginning and End we know not : We never can
enlarge our Thoughts so far, but we may carry
them farther; and therefore can never reach
Infinity, which hath no bounds; when we have
enlarged our Thoughts to the utmost of our
Capacity, we are as far from any *Actual Positive*
Idea of Infinity, as when we first began.

I F it is here objected, That in the above Assertion by *Essence* is not meant the *Essential Properties*, but the *Intima Substantia* or *Substratum*
of those Properties ; I answer, that as far as we
directly know the essential Properties of any
Substance, so far we have a direct knowledge
of the Substance *Itself :* And if we had a direct
knowledge of *All* the essential Properties of any
Substance, we should have an *Adequate* knowledge

ledge of that Subſtance; for ſurely if there be
any meaning in Words, the knowing any of
the eſſential Properties of a Thing, is knowing
So much of its very Subſtance or Eſſence.

ALL that I obſerved of Spirit in general,
muſt be true of the Divine Nature in a more
eminent degree. Thoſe Attributes and Perfections in God which we are now under a neceſſity
of conceiving by that *Thinking* and *Willing* in us,
and by the various modes of them, which are
all performed by help of material Organs, do
vaſtly more tranſcend the greateſt Perfections
in the higheſt Order of created Beings; than
theirs do thoſe that are in Man. And if we do
but conſider how far even thoſe Angelic Perfections are probably removed from all communication with Matter, or dependence upon
it; we ſhall then perceive that our *Thinking*
and *Willing*, performed in eſſential Conjunction
with Matter, are but a very feint and diſtant
Analogy, for conceiving the *Otherwiſe* utterly
inconceivable and *Correſpondent* Perfections of
God.

PROPERLY ſpeaking, we have no *Idea* of
God; inſomuch that we come to the knowledge of his very *Exiſtence*, not from any Idea
we have of him, or from any direct *Intuition*
of the Intellect; but from the obſervation
and reaſoning of the Mind upon the Ideas
of Senſation; that is, from our reaſoning upon

G   the

the works of this visible Creation; and for want of any *Simple* and *Direct Idea* of him, we from thence form to our selves an indirect, *Analogous*, and very complex Notion of Him.

GOD is in himself *Simple* and *Uncompounded*, and if we had any direct and positive *Idea* of him, this would be so likewise; and therefore when Men *Attempt* to form any *Simple* Idea of him, they do it by a figurative one of transcendent *Light*, or visible Glory of the *Sun*: But because we have no Idea of him, as he is in his own uncompounded Essence, we conceive him the best we can by a very complex *Notion*; by removing from him all the Imperfections of the Creatures; and attributing to him all their Perfections, and more especialy those of our own Minds. Not by adding *Infinity* to each of them, as some assert, which is itself a *Negative*, and therefore can make up no *Positive Idea* of the supreme incomprehensible Being; and if it could, yet would be far from exhibiting to us any thing of his true Nature and Essence, as he is *In Himself*. For the greatest Perfections of those Creatures which fall within our observation, and those we find in our selves particularly, are realy but so many *Imperfections* when referr'd or attributed to the Divine Nature as it is in itself; even with the most exalted meaning we can annex to them in their *Literal* and proper Acceptation.

A 3

As for inftance, the knowledge or confcioufnefs we have of our own *Exiftence* may convince us, that it is a manner of Exiftence altogether unworthy of an *Immaterial* Subftance,
and much more of the Divine Being : Let the
nature and manner of his Exiftence be what it
will, to be fure he doth not exift according to
any fuch grofs Idea at all as we have of Exiftence; fo that when we attribute to God *Infinite Exiftence*, we fpeak without *Ideas*; for
we have no actual Idea of exifting infinitely.
So when we attribute *Duration* to God, which
in our notion of it neceffarily includes *Succeffion*, we attribute another Imperfection of
the Creature to him; and when we *Enlarge*
that Duration in our Thoughts as far as we
are able, by *Infinity* added to it, we are in
truth but multiplying and increafing fo many
Minutes, and *Hours*, and *Months*, and *Years*
for the Divine Being to laft. Again, All the
Direct Idea or Conception we have of *Power* is
that which one *Body* hath over another, or at
beft that of a Spirit and Body *United* and
acting in Conjunction; the greateft and moft
exalted Operations of which are nothing but
Weaknefs and Imperfection when *Literaly* attributed to God.

AND thus it is with *Pleafure* and *Happinefs*;
the greateft and moft refined Pleafure we are
capable of in this Life, either in Body or Mind,
and which we can have any *Proper* and *Direct*

Con-

Conception of, is altogether unworthy of God's *Real Nature*: And when we add *Infinity* to any of our Pleasures; or to speak with a plain meaning, when we magnify them as far as our Imagination can reach; we are but enlarging and extending the Imperfections of a Creature to a monstrous and boundless Size, in order to work them up into an Idea of him, who is the inconceivable Fountain of all Perfection. If it is said here that we attribute all these to God in the *Abstract* only, and not as they are in *Us*, the Observation is very just; but then it is saying in other Words, That they are all of a quite different *Kind* and in a different *Manner* in God, from what they are in the Creature; and *In Him*, such as we have no *Proper* Conception or Idea of.

THAT there are *Incomprehensible Perfections* in the Divine Nature *Answerable* to what *Power*, and *Wisdom*, and *Goodness* are in us; and whereof these things in us are but the distant only, and feint, tho' *True* Resemblances, is natural and easy to conceive; and no way unbecoming the Divine Nature, or any way injurious to it. But that his *Power* should be conceived as an ability to *Change* things infinitely, or by any other direct Idea we have of Power; That his *Wisdom* should be *Infinite Thinking*, which is perform'd not without the labour and working of our Brain; that his *Goodness* should be conceiv'd by adding Infinity
to

to our moft commendable *Paffions* or *Affec-tions*; which are all of them fo many different movements only of our bodily Organs in con-junction with the Soul ; or by infinite *Regula-tion* of like Paffions with ours. I fay, the ad-ding *Infinity* to thefe, or to any other *Terms* which exprefs Perfections of ours, natural or moral, in their *Literal* Sence; or the multiply-ing or *Enlarging* of thofe Perfections of ours in number, or *Degree* only to the utmoft ftretch of our Capacity and Underftanding, and the attributing them *So* enlarged to God; is in truth and ftrictnefs no more than raifing up to our felves an immenfe and *Unwieldy Idol* of our own Imagination, which has no Founda-tion in *Reafon* or the *Nature* of Things.

Nothing is more evident, than that we have no *Idea* of God, as he is in himfelf; and it is for want of fuch an Idea, that we frame to our felves the moft excellent *Conception* of him we can, by putting together into one, the greateft Perfections we obferve in the Creatures, and particularly in our own reafonable Nature, to ftand for his Perfections. Not moft grofly arguing and inferring, that God is (in Effect and Confequence) fuch an one as our felves, only infinitely enlarged and *Improved* in all our natural Powers and Faculties; but conclu-ding, That our greateft Excellencies are the beft, and apteft, and moft correfpondent *Re-prefentations* only of his incomprehenfible Per-

fections;

fections; which infinitely tranfcend the moft exalted of what are in any *Created* Beings, and are far above out of the reach of all human Imagination.

I HAD not been fo exprefs and particular upon this head, were it not for the mifchievous confequences of that vain affectation both to Religion and Learning in general, of confining all our Knowledge to *Direct* and *Immediate Ideas* only. For the Men of this ftrain ever lay it down for a fure Principle they never recede from, *That we can have no Knowledge without Ideas*, which is certainly true; and even without Ideas of *Senfation*, which are indeed the groundwork and rough materials of all the moft refin'd and abftracted Knowledge we are capable of. But then the Inference they make from hence at every turn, when they venture to fpeak plain is, *That therefore we can have no Knowledge of any thing* BEYOND *them* ; or that we have no Knowledge of any thing *But* what we have an *Immediate* and *Proper* Idea of; and fince we can have no immediate and proper Idea but of fenfibleObjects, that Confequence of theirs is directly deftructive of all Religion as well *Natural* as *Reveal'd*. Thus do thefe Idealifts, firft make the Word too *General* and indeterminate, comprehending under it *All* forts of Perceptions, and all kinds of Knowledge whatfoever ; and then to ferve a Turn, *Confine* it to that Knowledge which we have only by *Proper* and *Immediate* Ideas.

NOR

NOR is this Affectation lefs injurious to the Underftanding in general; for it comprehends things of *All Kinds* under one and the *Same* Word, by that means blending and confounding their true Diftinctions. Infomuch that after ringing the *Changes* upon *Ideas* thro' whole Volumes together, the Authors leave the Reader in a fort of a Maze, with a long *Chain* of them *Ratling* in his Head; and without any other real and fubftantial Knowledge than what he got from that part of them which treats of Ideas of Senfation. Thus far it muft be confeffed they have treated of them ufefully and commendably; but all beyond this is fpecious *Trifling*, and nothing more than an empty Shew of great Exactnefs and Accuracy.

C H A P. IV.

The feveral Properties of Ideas of Senfation.

SINCE then it appears the Ideas of Senfation are the only fubject matter which the Mind hath to work upon, provided by God and Nature for the exercife of all its Powers and Faculties; and fince they are the foundation and rough materials of all our moft *Abftracted* Knowledge; out of which each Man raifes a fuperftructure according to the different

Turn

Turn of thofe Organs which are more immediately fubfervient to the Operations of the pure Intellect; and according to the various ways and methods he takes of exercifing thofe Operations upon them, it will be convenient to fay fomething concerning the feveral *Properties* of thofe Ideas.

I. ACCORDINGLY the firft Property of them is, that they are *Original*. By which is meant, not only that they are the *Firft* Ideas the Mind receives; as if it afterwards received Ideas of a *Different* Nature, and *Equaly Original* in their Kind; or as if the Imagination was firft ftock'd with Ideas of Senfation, and the Mind was afterwards fome other way fupplied with a *New* Sett of Ideas *Independent* of them: But they are fo call'd becaufe we receive them, from our firft coming into the World, without any *Immediate* concurrence of the pure Intellect; being altogether antecedent to any of its Operations; infomuch that the Soul, before there is fome *Impreffion* of outward Objects upon the Senfes, is a *Still* unactive Principle, unable to exert itfelf in any degree; it cannot form one Thought, nor have the leaft confcioufnefs even of its own *Being*. Thefe Ideas are, in refpect of all our *Notions*, and *Conceptions*, and *Reafonings*, in this one inftance like the firft particles of Matter in refpect to all the Subftances that are compounded out of them; namely, that they run thro' an
infinite

infinite variety of *Changes* from the Operations of the Mind upon them; but do in themselves remain the same and unchangeable. As all our *Compounded* Ideas are made out of These alone, and as even our most abstract *Complex Notions* take their first *Rise* from them; so is our *Knowledge* of all Things, whereof we have complex Notions or Conceptions, *Ultimately* resolvable into these Ideas only ; and not indifferently and promiscuously into simple Ideas of *Sensation* and *Reflection* as *Equaly* original. By this Property they are distinguished,

1*st.* FROM such Ideas as are supposed to be *Innate*, such as we are by some imagined to be born with, and are so interwoven with our frame, that they necessarily grow up within us; and would be in our Mind, if there were no impression from outward Objects upon the Senses. That which gave *Rise* to this Opinion of *Innate* Ideas was, the loss Men found themselves at in solving the Manner of our conceiving *Immaterial* and heavenly Things; they would not give way to such a Thought, as that we should conceive them by the help and *Intervention* of any things in *This* World, there appearing no Congruity or Proportion between them; and therefore they had recourse to innate Ideas for that purpose, which should be the Objects of the *Pure Intellect* independent of all Sensation. But let any Man, if he is able, abstract from all Sensation or Impression of material

terial Objects, and look inward, and try whether he can find one *Simple Idea* independent of it for the Mind to exercife any of its Operations upon ; and if any fuch inftance is pretended to be offer'd, it will be eafy to fhew the neceffary connexion it hath with *Senfation*, and the *Dependence* it hath upon it.

THAT we have no *Innate Ideas* is fufficiently evident from hence (which is the *Common* Argument againft that Opinion) that there is no *Occafion* at all for them; and that they are altogether fuperfluous and unneceffary. There is no occafion for innate Ideas of *Senfible* Objects, becaufe there is an eafy obvious way of attaining them by the Senfes; and if *Some* Ideas of them are innate, it is hard to give a reafon why they fhould not *All* be fo. So that if there be any Ideas innate, it muft be of *Immaterial Objects*; but with regard to the Knowledge we have of fpiritual Things, as it cannot be accounted for from any innate Ideas of them, fo our Conceptions of them are eafily explain'd by the mediation of Ideas of *Senfation*, confider'd together with the *Operations* of the Mind upon them. The *Rife* and whole extent of all our Knowledge of them is plainly accounted for from the Ideas of *Senfible Objects*; the neceffary Confequence we draw from *Their* Exiftence to the Exiftence of things *Not Senfible*; and from that *Manner* of conceiving thefe, which we afterwards naturaly fall into, by the

help

help and *Mediation* of such Things as are with-in the compass of our present Sphere.

THUS for instance, we conceive the *Knowledge* of a Spirit by the mediation of our *Thinking*, and the various modes of it exercised on Ideas of Sensation ; its *Moral* Perfections by our *Willing*, and *Passions*, and *Affections*. So we make up the best Conception we can of the Divine Nature and Attributes, by putting together the greatest Perfections we find in our own, to stand for and represent them. If we had any *Innate* Ideas of those spiritual Things, they would be as *Direct* and *Immediate* as the Ideas of sensible Objects are ; they would be *True* and *Proper Representations* of those Things as they are *In Themselves*, and no way *Analogical* as they now are : We should think of them as directly, and speak of them as properly as we do of the most familiar Objects of Sense ; and not by any Words or Ideas or Conceptions *First* apply'd to the Things of *This* World, and then transferred by Analogy to the Things of *Another* ; as it is evident we always do, whenever we think or speak of them.

2*dly*. THAT property of Ideas of Sensation that they are *Original*, distinguisheth them from such Ideas as, tho' they may not be *Innate* and born with us like the former ; yet, according to a very common and most erroneous Opinion,

are

are acquired by, and seated in the pure Intellect *Alone*; and are answerable to the Ideas of sensible Objects lodged in the Imagination; in order to be the materials of our Knowledge of *Spiritual* Things, as those in the Imagination are of Things *Material.* But if there are any such purely Intellectual Spiritual Ideas, we must come by them one of these three ways; either

1. BY the *Presence* of the Object, and an immediate Impression of it upon some Faculty in the Mind which is disposed to receive that Impression, and to retain it. But every one that considers impartialy will be sufficiently conscious to himself, that no immaterial Object was ever present to any Faculty of his Mind; or ever made any Impression upon it, so as to leave behind it any *Just* and real *Similitude* or *Resemblance* of itself. If it were so, we should distinguish *Immaterial* Objects, by their *Ideas*, not only from *Material* ones and their Ideas; but also with as great *Exactness* from *Each Other* as we now do material Objects: The Ideas of them would be as clear and *Distinct*, as those we have of sensible Objects; we should as readily conceive and describe them; and we should have as few doubtful Disputations about the Idea of a *Spirit*, as about that of a *Tree* or an *Horse.* We should then have as clear and distinct an Idea of spiritual, as we have of bodily *Substance* (which,

as

as I have shewn, we have not) and of its Way of *Knowing*, as we have of *Thinking*; of its Way of *Communicating* its Knowledge, as we have of *Speaking*; we should have *Proper* Words for all these, and think of them and express them in a Manner and Language quite different from what we now do.

2. OR Secondly, These supposed Ideas of the pure Intellect must proceed from the *Immediate* Power of God, who may, according to this Opinion, impregnate the Mind with true and *Direct* Ideas of spiritual Things, which were never present to any of our Faculties, and therefore could make no Impression upon them. The Power of God is never to be disputed, but the Question is, Whether he actualy *Doth* so? If ever he doth so, it is by some *Miraculous Supernatural* Act; whereas we are now speaking of what our Perceptions are in the *Ordinary* way of Nature and Grace. God may communicate to the Mind of Man who never had his Eyes open an Idea of *Light*; but it is not probable he ever did so. He hath indeed *Opened* the Eyes of those who were born blind, that they might see the Light; and he will open the Eyes of our Understanding in the next World for the *Contemplation* of immaterial Objects, with the same ease that we now behold material; but whenever that is done, we shall have the same manifest, and perspicuous, and *Direct* view of them, that we now have of

3 the

the Objects of Senfation. If God did imprint upon our mind any *Direct* Idea of himfelf, tho' it were not very *Clear* and *Diftinct*; all *Arguments* for the Proof of his *Exiftence* would be as needlefs, as thofe we fhould ufe to prove the Exiftence of a Man who ftood before our Eyes: We fhould then think and fpeak of him according to that *Proper Idea*; and not as having *Reafon*, and the *Operations* and *Affections* of an human Soul.

3. OR laftly, The Mind muft have an *Inherent* Power of raifing up to *Itfelf* fimple Ideas of things whereof it can have no actual View or Intuition; of Objects which in themfelves have no fuch Intercourfe or Communication with any of our Faculties. But if the Mind could not frame to itfelf one Idea of any fenfible *Material* Object without its immediate *Prefence*, or the actual Impreffion of it; much lefs can we fuppofe this poffible to us with refpect to purely *Spiritual* and *Immaterial* Objects; which can have no conceivable way of leaving any Characters or Ideas of themfelves upon the human Soul, in its prefent ftate, but by fuppofing fome Impreffion upon thofe bodily Organs by which it performs all its Operations. There can be no direct Perception but by the application of the Object to our Faculties, or of fome of our Faculties to the Object; where neither of thefe is done, it is as abfurd to fay the pure Intellect can fupply *Itfelf* with
Ideas,

Ideas, as to say it can think, when it hath nothing to think of.

PERHAPS this Power of raising up to itself *Ideas*, without the presence or impression of *Any* Object whatsoever, is a *Privilege* of the Divine Intellect alone; and answerable to the Almighty Power of Creation, or producing a Thing out of Nothing. But the power of the Mind in our little World, is much the same with that of the whole Man in the greater; it is as impossible for it to raise up to itself any simple Idea intirely *New* and independent of all Sensation, as it is for a Man to add one Particle to the common *Mass* of Matter; tho' it must be confessed to have a wonderful Sagacity in working upon what it finds already stored up in the Imagination. So that the five Senses are as so many Windows thro' which the Mind takes in a prospect of the whole visible Creation; and if these were from the first stopped up and closed, it would be always involved in thick *Darkness*: And even now, with all our Senses, we have no more *Direct* Perception of any thing beyond the fix'd Stars by the *Eye* of the Intellect, than by that of the Body.

MENS endeavouring to abstract the Intellect from all Objects of Sense, so as to take a *Direct View* of spiritual things; and working up their Minds to an opinion and belief that they have some degree of *Intuitive Direct* know-

knowledge of them tho' *Imperfect* and obscure, hath proved a fatal Delusion, and never served any real and substantial *End* of Religion. I believe I may safely appeal to the Experience of the best of Men, whether they ever found any the least *Glimmerings* of such celestial Light in their most exalted Contemplations? Many who never aspired to this *Immediate* and familiar Intercourse with heavenly Objects, have arrived to great degrees of habitual Virtue and Holiness; whereas the contrary Opinion doth but puff Men up with spiritual Pride; and too often ends in rank *Enthusiasm.*

3. THIRDLY, by that property of Ideas of Sensation, their being *Original*, they are distinguished from such as are called Ideas of *Reflection*, or such as we are supposed to have of the Operations of our own Minds. But these Operations cannot be discerned by the means and intervention of any *Ideas*; for then we should have no Perception or even Consciousness of the Operations *Themselves*; but of those Characters only and *Representations* of them, which would stand in the Mind instead of the Operations; as the Idea of a *Tree* stands in the Mind for the Tree itself, and is the immediate Object of Thought. And since there neither is nor can be an *Idea* of what is *Itself* actualy in the Mind already, those Operations can be perceived no other way than by a *Self-consciousness.* The Eye of the Mind,

as

as I said before, cannot take a view either of its own Subſtance or Eſſence, or of its own Properties or Qualities by any *Reflex* Act: It doth not come to the knowledge of its own Faculties by any ſuch unnatural *Squint*, or diſtorted *Turn* upon itſelf; but by an immediate *Conſciouſneſs* of the ſeveral different ways of its own working upon thoſe Ideas of Senſation lodged in the Imagination.

We have not even the leaſt *Direct Idea* or Perception of the purely ſpiritual Part of us; nor do we diſcern any more of its *Real Subſtance* than we do that of an Angel. We are ſo far from an exact view or intuitive knowledge of it, that we are forced to argue and infer its very *Exiſtence* from our Obſervation only of ſuch Operations as we conclude could not proceed from mere Matter; and becauſe we have no direct Idea of it, we expreſs the *Nature* of it, as we do that of Spirit in general, by the negative Word *Immaterial*. And as we cannot form one Thought of our Spirit, otherwiſe than as it is in conjunction with the Body; ſo neither can we conceive any of its Operations but as performed together with bodily Organs: And therefore it is that we are under a neceſſity of expreſſing the *Modus* of them all in Words borrowed from Senſation and bodily Actions. Thus we ſay the Mind *Diſcerns, Apprehends, Diſtinguiſheth,* or *Separates* one thing from another; it *Draws* one

thing

thing out of another, which is a *Confequence* or one thing *Following* from another. Nay, when we would *Attempt* to form *Ideas* of *Thinking* and all the various Modes of it, they are imagin'd to be so many *Motions* or Agitations of the Soul, in conjunction with the moft refin'd and fpirituous Parts of the Body, about the Ideas of fenfible Objects, and the *Notions* formed partly out of them : And when from the Exiftence of thefe fenfible things it infers the Being or Exiftence of things fpiritual and imperceptible, and exercifes thofe *Motions* or Operations upon them, as *Reprefented* by their Subftitutes; that is properly meditating upon the things of another World.

AND thus it is with all the Paffions of the Mind, *Love, Defire, Joy, Sorrow, Hope, Fear, Anger*; when we attempt to form *Ideas* of them, we do it by conceiving them as fo many *Motions* or Agitations of the fineft and moft curious Parts in the frame of an Human Body, in conjunction with the purely fpiritual Part of us, about Objects of Senfation or their *Ideas*, or about our complex *Conceptions* : And when thofe Motions are, by the *Mediation* of thefe Ideas and Conceptions exercifed upon Objects out of the reach of all our Perception, fuch as God and *Heavenly Things*, and upon fuch Things of this World as have a more immediate relation to them, that is *Religion*. This is drawing the Mind off from the things of this World, and fetting our Affections on things above; and the more habitualy

all

all those *Motions* of the Soul are imployed that way, to the greater degrees of true Devotion, and Piety, and Holiness do Men arrive.

CHAP. V.

A second Property of Ideas of Sensation, that they are Simple.

A SECOND Property of an Idea of Sensation is that it is *Simple*; that is, an *Uniform Uncompounded* Appearance, which cannot be resolved into more Ideas than one of the *Same Kind*; and is the Effect and Consequence of one single individual *Sensation.* So that this Property is applicable only to our *First* Sensations or Perceptions of Things, consider'd antecedently to any Act or Operation of the Intellect; excepting only that of a bare *View* and merely intuitive Knowledge of them, in the same Order and Figure they lie ranged in the Imagination; before it makes any *Composition*, or *Alteration*, or *Comparison*; and before it forms any *Judgment* upon them; or draws any *Consequences* whatsoever in relation to them.

THE Notion of *Simple* Ideas I think ought not to be reduced to such a narrow compass as they generaly are by Logicians; as if the Ideas of *Sounds*, and *Tastes*, and *Smells*, and *Colours*, and *Tangible Qualities* only were *Simple*; and as if the Ideas of single separate *Bodies* were all *Compound-*

ed.

ed. Surely we fhould include into our Notion of *Simple* Ideas all that ftrikes the Senfe at once ; as when we fee the *Sun* or *Moon*, an human *Body* or an *Horfe* ; thefe and all fuch like are properly *Simple* Ideas ; for it is the *Intellect*, and not the *Senfes*, which fub-divides them in-to more Ideas than one, by directing the Senfe or Imagination to furvey the Parts, or Quali-ties, or Accidents fucceffively : The Senfation is *One* only at firft ; it is but one *Single Act* of Perception ; for you cannot divide the Idea of an human Body into the Ideas of *More* Bodies, nor that of an *Houfe* into Ideas of more Houfes. And therefore once for all, by a *Simple* Idea I mean, all that *Refemblance* or Similitude of the external Object, which the Organ of Senfation is capable of receiving in one diftinct Percep-tion ; as the Idea of an *Human Body :* Tho' it may be fubdivided into many other Ideas ; as into the Ideas of all the different *Parts* of that Body ; and tho' thefe again may be divided into Ideas of ftill leffer Parts ; fo that fimple Ideas may be thus multiplied, as far as it is within the Power of Senfe to diftinguifh.

1. B Y this Property, Ideas of Senfation are diftinguifhed, Firft from the various Alterations and *Combinations* made of them by the Mind. As thefe fimple Ideas came into the Imagina-tion without the Concurrence of the Intel-lect, fo neither can it deftroy any one of them ; but all beyond thefe are the *Creatures*

of

of the Intellect, which hath a sovereign Sway and arbitrary Power over those *Ideas :* It alters, and *Enlargeth,* or *Diminisheth* them in any Proportion ; it *Separates* and *Transposes* ; it turns and winds them at pleasure : and thus raiseth up to itself a new Set of *Compounded* Ideas with which the Imagination is furnished by it from *Within,* as those which were *Simple* and *Original* enter thither from *Without.* Thus the Ideas of many Men may be put together into one Idea of an *Army* ; many Sheep to make the Idea of a *Flock* ; many Houses into one Idea of a *City* ; and thus also the Idea of *One* Man is by the Intellect made to stand for all Mankind, which is then called an *Universal* Idea.

2. THE Ideas of Sensation are by this Property distinguished from all those *Notions* or *Conceptions* which are Compositions only of the Intellect out of our simple and compound *Ideas* of Sensation, consider'd together with the various *Operations* of the Mind upon them. Such is the Notion we form of *Charity,* which is made up of the Ideas of a *Man* in Misery, of the Money or other *Relief* that is given him ; and also by adjoining the several Operations of the Mind upon them, such as *Pain* of Mind for his Misery, a Sence of Duty to God, and *Compassion* for a fellow Creature. And thus it is with all *Virtues* and *Vices,* of which properly speaking we have no *Ideas Simple* or *Compound-*

ed ;

ed; but each of them is apprehended by Ideas of Senfation, and the Motions or Operations of the Intellect upon them, put together into one complex *Notion* or Conception; and comprehended under one Name or *Term*, which is of a Signification fo complex or general, that it always imports a Combination of feveral different Conceptions and Ideas.

AFTER the fame manner the Intellect raifes up to itfelf a Conception of *Spirit*; becaufe it finds neither a fimple nor a compound *Idea* thereof within itfelf, it makes up a fort of complex notion or *Conception* of it, by firft adding together the Operations of our Mind, fuch as *Thinking* and *Willing* and the feveral Modes of them; and then *Subflituting* them fo combined, to reprefent the Perfections of a *Being* or *Subflance* of which we have no *Proper Idea*; and of which we form the beft Idea we *Can* from that of the moft fpiritious part of material Subftance. And this is the way the Mind fupplies the intire want of *Simple Ideas* for the Things of another World, whereof it hath not any, even in the moft obfcure and imperfect degree; fo that it may be truly faid, our *Simple* and *Compound* Ideas of Senfation, together with the various Operations of the Mind upon them, do comprehend the full extent of all our Knowledge: But to lay down Ideas of *Reflection* together with thofe of *Senfation* as *Equaly* the *Ground-work* of our Knowledge,

ledge, is confounding the *Workman* with his *Materials*; and the Skill and Manner of exercising his Art, with the Stuff he works upon.

C H A P. VI.

A Third Property that they are Immediate.

ANOTHER thing peculiar to Ideas of Sensation is that they are *Immediate*. The original and simple Ideas of Sensation when they are *First* obtained, necessarily presuppose the Presence of the Object, and some real actual Impression of it upon the Organs of Sense; there is an *Immediate* and direct Representation of the Object, and it is perceived without the mediation or *Intervention* of any other Object or Idea whatsoever. Thus the Ideas of a *Man*, and a *Tree*, could never have come into the Mind, if they had never been present to the Sense, and the Eye had not actualy seen them. Nor was it possible for us to have had an Idea of a Trumpet's *Sound*, unless the Collision of the Air had been once so near that some of the Undulations of it could strike upon the Sense of Hearing. So that by this Property they are distinguished,

1. FROM the Ideas we have of absent Objects of the same kind, but such as were never

Actualy

Actualy perceived ; thus the Idea of a Man we *Have* feen, ftands for the Idea of any other Man we *Never* faw. The Mind hath no other way of conceiving a Man or an Horfe which was never prefent to the Senfes nor actually perceived, but by fubftituting the Idea of a Man or an Horfe which was fo.

I f the Intellect could dilate itfelf no farther than the very particular or individual Objects which have been *Prefent* to the Senfes and actualy perceived, its Sphere of Activity would be very fcanty, and all our Knowledge confin'd within a very narrow Compafs: And yet this muft be fo, if Men refolved neither to *Know* or *Believe* the Exiftence of any thing but what is or hath been prefent to fome of their Faculties, and thus actualy perceived by them ; they muft not believe that there is a Man, or a City, or a Country in the World they never faw. We readily yield our firm affent to the *Being* even of fenfible Things which we never perceived, and do reafon and difcourfe of them under borrowed and *Subftituted* Ideas ; and we efteem our Knowledge of them to be *Real*, and *True*, and *Solid*, tho' we never had any actual Perception of them. And yet that Knowledge muft be owned to be in fome Meafure imperfect, becaufe no two Individuals of a like kind are intirely and *Exactly* the fame in all particular Refpects ; and therefore the Idea of one muft reprefent the other but imperfectly.

perfectly. All the *Men* and all the *Cities* we have not seen, somewhat differ from any we have seen; the Men have different Features, and Shapes, and Colours perhaps, and the Cities differently-dispos'd Streets and Houses; and yet notwithstanding their many *Unlikenesses* to that Idea by which we conceive them, we cannot say they are altogether *Unknown* to us.

2dly. *I*DEAS of Sensation are by this Property distinguished from all *Ideas* or *Conceptions* of things which are purely Figurative and *Metaphorical*. Of these there are two Sorts; one of which may be distinguished by the Name of *Human*, and the other of *Divine Metaphor*: But the latter being chiefly to my purpose, I shall take more particular Notice of that only here.

*D*IVINE Metaphor is the substituting our Ideas of *Sensation* (which are *Direct* and *Immediate*) as well as the *Words* belonging to them, to express the invisible and immaterial Things of Heaven, of which we can have no direct Ideas, nor any *Immediate* Knowledge or Conception; as when God's *Knowledge* is express'd by his *Eyes* being in *Every Place*; his *Goodness* in granting our Petitions, by his *Ear* not being *Heavy*; his *Power* by a *Strong Hand*; and many others of this kind used in Scripture to express his Attributes, and other heavenly Things
with

with an Emphafis, and in a Figure and Allufion only, *Without any correfpondent Reality or
Refemblance* between the Things compared.

BOTH Human and Divine Metaphor agree
in this, That the figurative Words, and Ideas,
and Conceptions, are us'd without any *Real
Similitude* or *Proportion*, or *Correfpondent Refem-
blance* in the things compared. The Compari-
fon is not founded in the *Real Nature* of the
Things, but is a pure Invention of the Mind
and intirely *Arbitrary*. There is for Inftance
no Similitude or real Correfpondence in the
Nature of Things between the *Verdure* of a
Field and *Smileing* ; between a *Faculty* of our
Soul in diftinguifhing Beauties and Defects in
Writing, and Painting, and Mufick, and the
Tafte of the Palate ; between the *Roughnefs* of the
Sea, and the *Anger* of a Man ; and fo likewife be-
tween *Hands*, and *Eyes*, and *Ears*, and God's in-
conceivable, tho' *Real* fupernatural *Perfections*.

2. THEY agree in this likewife, That neither of them are abfolutely *Neceffary* to a *True*
and *Real* Knowledge of the Things defigned to
be expreffed or conceived by the fubftituted
Ideas. They would both be intirely ufelefs,
were not thofe Things known otherwife more
Immediately and *Directly*, or at leaft more *Exactly Before*, after another manner.

AND they differ in this, That in Human
Metaphor, the Ideas or Conceptions *Defigned*

to

to be expres'd, are or may be as *Directly* known and as *Immediate*, as the Ideas and Conceptions placed in their *Stead*. But in Divine Metaphor the *Substituted* Ideas are *Immediately* and *Directly* known, but what is designed to be expres'd and convey'd to us thus, is no way conceivable by any *Direct* and *Immediate* Idea, Conception, or Notion.

3dly. The Ideas of Sensation are by this Property distinguish'd from all Ideas or rather *Conceptions* and Notions which are purely *Analogical*. That is, when the Conceptions and *Complex Notions* we already have of Things *Directly* or *Immediately* known, are made use of and substituted to represent, *With some Resemblance, or correspondent Reality and Proportion,* Divine things whereof we can have no *Direct* and *Proper* Idea, or *Immediate* Conception or Notion at all. As when our Conception of *Human Wisdom*, which consists in Thinking and Reason, is substituted to represent an *Inconceivable* but *Correspondent* Perfection of the Divine Nature. This I call *Divine Analogy*, to distinguish it from that *Human* Analogy which is used to conceive things in this World; as when we conceive the various Operations of *Instinct* in Brutes, by Analogy with those of *Reason* in Men.

THIS Divine Analogy is universaly us'd with respect to all *Immaterial* or purely spiritual

tual

tual Things of another World, when we wou'd apprehend them with any degree of *Real*, or *True*, or *Useful Knowledge*. For since there can be no actual *Idea* or immediate *Conception* or *Confcioufnefs* of what is purely fpiritual, by any of our Faculties of Body or Mind, or of both together; confequently there is a neceffity for thus making other Conceptions and Notions which are familiar to us, and direct, and immediate, to *Stand* for them in the Mind; that by their *Mediation* we may think and fpeak of what is otherwife inconceivable and unutterable with any Degree of correfpondent Exactnefs and Proportion. Thus we conceive the *Knowledge* of purely fpiritual Beings by our *Thinking*, and apply the various Modes of it to them; nay, we thus conceive God himfelf and all his Attributes, and fpeak of them by the mediation of the Operations of our own Mind, and of the more commendable Paffions and Affections of an Human Soul.

C H A P. VII.

That they are Direct.

A FOURTH Property of Ideas of Senfation, which I fhall affign, is that they are *Direct*; by which they are not oppofed to fuch as arife from any *Reflex* Act of the Mind upon itfelf. The Mind or fpiritual Part of us cannot look upon or into itfelf, by either a direct
rect

rect or reflex Act, any more than it can difcern
a Soul in its State of Separation from the Body: We have no Knowledge of our own Spirit, or of any of its Faculties, but from a confcious Experience of its feveral Ways of Acting upon the Ideas of Senfation, or the Objects
of the vifible Creation; which tho' it be neither a direct nor reflex View, yet is a *Knowledge* of the Operations of our Mind, as *Immediate* as the View it hath of thofe Ideas of external Objects upon which it operates. But
they are by this Property oppos'd not only to
all *Indirect Ideas*, but to our indirect *Conceptions* and Notions alfo; which Oppofition may
be illuftrated in general by this Similitude.
When we look ftrait in a Man's Face, this
gives us a *Direct* Idea of it; but if we had never feen that Face but in a Glafs, it would have
given us an *Indirect Idea*, or bare Refemblance
of it: So that an indirect Idea or Conception is when we have never difcerned the thing
Itfelf, but either a mere *Shadow*; or elfe a more
perfect Similitude or *Refemblance* of it in fomething elfe.

1. THUS then they are by this Property oppofed Firft, to thofe *Metaphorical* Ideas, or
mere *Shadows* only and Allufions, made ufe of
to conceive the Objects of another World. For
inftance, the Idea of the *Sun* or a refplendent
material *Light* is *Direct*; I do not difcern it by
the Intervention of any other Idea: But when

4   this

this Idea is put for the *Glory* of God or of Heaven, it becomes *Indirect*. I can have no *Direct* Intuition or Idea of the Glory of Heaven in any degree, and therefore I view it as well as I can *Indirectly* in that of Light. And thus I conceive God's Power by a *Mighty Arm*; and the *Motion* of Angels by *Flying*.

WHAT Idea I have of *Material Substance* is in every Respect a *Direct* one. My Senses have a direct Perception of its Bulk, Extension, Figure, and Solidity. But when this Idea of Substance is applied to conceive the Substance or Essence of Matter and Spirit in strict Conjunction, it is *Indirect*; and much more so when 'tis used for purely immaterial Substance; for then it can import nothing but *Being* in general.

2dly. THEY are by this Property oppos'd to those Types only, or bare *Resemblances* of God and the Things of another World, which for want of any *Direct* View or Knowledge of them, are in a good Measure render'd intelligible, and become conspicuous by a kind of *Reflection* only from our direct Conceptions of Things in this World; as the Likeness of a Body is from a Mirrour or Looking-Glass. For our *Conceptions* and Notions may be *Direct* or *Indirect*, as well as our *Ideas*. When they stand in the Mind for their proper and *Original* Objects, and when the Words that express them

them are taken *Literaly* for such Objects, they are *Direct*; we have a direct Knowledge of the things they stand for. But when they are *Substituted* to conceive, and do *Stand for* Divine Immaterial Things, then they become *Indirect* and *Analogical*. Thus the Conception I have of *Thinking* in its most perfect Degree, is from an *Immediate* Consciousness within me; and may be called so far a *Direct* Conception, because it needs not the Intervention of any other Conception by which to know it. But when I place this to *Represent* and *Stand for* the Knowledge of a pure Spirit, it becomes an *Indirect* and *Analogical Conception*.

AND thus it is with God and his Attributes; I can have no *Direct* View or Intuition by the Eye either of Body or Mind, of any thing in the divine Nature; therefore there is no other way of beholding him but in the *Mirrour* of the visible Creation, and particularly in our selves: So we behold his *Wisdom* in our *Thinking* and Reasoning; his *Power* in our worldly Dominion and Power; his *Goodness* in the Rectitude of our most commendable Passions and Affections. Not by adding *Infinity* to each of these, as some have grosly mistaken, so as to stretch our Imagination as far as we can to *Infinite Thinking*; *Infinite Strength*; *Infinite Rectitude* of *Passions and Affections:* But by adding Infinity to those *Incomprehensible Perfections* in the divine Nature of which we have not the

4   least

leaft *Direct* Glimpfe or Knowledge ; and therefore do conceive them *Indirectly* in thofe *Refemblances* of them which are difcernible in the moft perfect Works of the vifible Creation. Thus, as in a Mirrour, we *See him who is invifible* ; and inftead of *Seeing all things in God*, as fome have *Enthufiafticaly* fancied, we fee God in his Creatures; and the *Invifible things of him are known, by the things that are made*.

THE true Nature and Manner of the *Prefent* Knowledge we have of the things of another World, is, by the Apoftle, very aptly defcribed by our *Seeing thro'*, or rather *In a Glafs darkly* ; and our *Future* Knowledge of them by our feeing *Face to Face* ; that is *Directly*, and not by any *Reflection* either of mere *Shadows* only, or *Refemblances*, as it is now with us. The Word Ἐσόπτρα in the Original of that Paffage is not a *Perfpective*, but a *Mirrour* or Looking-Glafs; and the true rendering of it is *In a Mirrour or Looking-Glafs*, as the Words join'd with it are Ἐν αἰνίγματι, *In* an obfcure Reprefentation; this is evident from the Oppofition in the following Words, *Then Face to Face*. To fhew the great Aptitude and Significancy of that Similitude of our *Seeing in a Glafs darkly*, I fhall obferve thefe two things.

1. THAT a Glafs or Mirrour exhibits to us nothing of the *Reality* and *Subftance* of the thing reprefented in it ; the Similitude form'd by the

Reflection

Reflection of the Object hath no more of the true *Essence* and Properties of the thing itself, which it exhibits, than a mere *Shadow*; and is nothing more than an *Appearance* which perisheth with the Removal of the Object. And yet we cannot say but that there is a Representation, and a true one; but that there is a *Real Likeness* of the Substance in that airy Form; and that there is however such a *Proportion* between them, that the Idea of a Face we never saw but in a Glass is a just one, and may be well *Substituted* in the Mind for the Face itself, and that it gives us some *Real* and true Knowledge of it.

THUS it is with those *Conceptions* which stand in our Minds to represent God and Spiritual Things. Tho' the things they are substituted for, are of a quite different *Kind*, and tho' these *Substitutes* are no more in respect of them, than a fleeting transient Appearance only in the Glass, is to the Man himself whom we see in it; yet there may be such a Likeness or Proportion and *Analogy* between them, as may render our natural and familiar Conceptions of worldly Things apt and just Representations of things *Supernatural*, and particularly of the Divine Nature: Insomuch that the Knowledge we have of them by that Analogy, tho' *Imperfect*, shall be however *True* and *Real*; and all our just Thoughts and Reasonings upon them shall be solid and substantial; that is,

I   while

while they are kept within the due **Compaſs** of thoſe Similitudes and Repreſentations of them. For then it is that Men run into Soleciſm and Abſurdity, into Error and Confuſion concerning God and ſpiritual Things ; when they, not contented with this imperfect degree of Knowledge by Repreſentation only and *Analogy*, will argue from Things merely *Natural*, to the *Real Intrinſic* Nature of thoſe Things which now we can know no other way but by that *Similitude*, or *Correſpondency*, or *Proportion* they, bear to our natural Ideas and Conceptions: And when they proceed upon this falſe Suppoſition, that what can be affirmed of theſe Repreſentations only, muſt be ſtrictly and literaly true with reſpect to the *Real Nature* and Subſtance of the Things they repreſent.

U P O N this very miſtake it is that our modern clandeſtine *Arians* argue Chriſt to be a *Separate*, *Inferior* Divine Perſon ; *Subject* and *Sent*, and doing the *Will* of another, in as ſtrict and *Literal* a Sence as one Man can be ſaid to be the Meſſenger of another, and to perform his Will, and to be ſeparate from him : Tho' this be as abſurd as to argue that the Reflection and Image of a Man in the Glaſs, is a true and *Real* human Body and Perſon, in all reſpects like one of our ſelves. Again, Theſe very Men at another time run into a quite *Contrary* Extreme and Abſurdity ; and, like the *Socinians*, turn this *Analogy* into mere

mere *Metaphor* and *Allufion* only. Thus they
argue that *Son* and *Begotten* when fpoke of
Chrift, are only a *Figure* for a more tranfcendent Act of *Creation* ; which is as groundlefs as
afferting the Image in the Glafs to be no more
than a metaphorical Allufion only, without any
correfpondent *Refemblance* or Analogy at all to
the Man reflected from it. And thus the Socinians will have the Blood of Chrift to be no
Price, Purchafe or *Redemption*, becaufe there can
be no proper and literal *Price, Purchafe* or *Redemption* in the Cafe.

I·N fhort, moft of the Arguments by which
the *Socinians* bring all the Myfteries of Chriftianity to *Nothing* ; as well as thofe of all the
Deifts and Freethinkers of this unbelieving
Age who owe all their Infidelity to the Socinian
Hypothefis, are built upon this fandy Foundation. Accordingly when we come to confider
them more particularly, we fhall find that their
Reafonings and Inferences are as abfurd, as
thofe would be which we fhould make from
the *Likenefs* of a Man in the Glafs, to his *Real
Nature* : As if we fhould from thence argue
with great acutenefs, that a Man himfelf could
have neither a *Body* nor *Solidity*, nor *Spirit*,
nor *Life*, nor *Reafon* ; that he had neither *Senfation* nor *Speech* ; nay, that he was nothing
but a mere Shadow or Appearance, and had
no *Being* but in our Imagination alone.

2. THE

2. T H E fecond thing I fhall obferve concerning that Similitude of the Apoftle's is, that in all Inftances univerfaly we ufe the *Same* Words and Expreffions for the *Similitudes* and *Appearances* of Things in the Glafs, by which we exprefs the Things *Themfelves*; and indeed this is the moft juft and proper way we have of fpeaking of them: For tho' there is nothing of the *Real Nature* of the Objects reprefented, in thofe Appearances; yet there is fuch a Correfpondency and *Proportion* between them, that the fame Words aptly ferve for both. Thus we fay we *See* a *Man* in a Glafs, when we fee no fuch thing; for the Appearance hath nothing of the real Nature of Man in it: And thus we fay we fee the Sun, Moon, and Stars in the Water, when there is no fuch thing there. And yet it would be abfolutely falfe to fay we do *Not* fee any thing at all of them in the Glafs, or in the Water; becaufe there is fuch a *Similitude* and *Proportion* between the Objects and thofe Reprefentations of them, as would give us fome imperfect Idea or Notion of the Things themfelves, tho' we had never feen them but in a *Glafs*, or in the *Water*.

ACCORDINGLY then if we could but make the Suppofition that there were a Perfon who never faw the Face of any other Man but in a Glafs, nor *Sun*, *Moon*, or *Stars* but in the Water; how imperfectly would he think and

2   fpeak

speak of the Things themselves represented to
him by those Adumbrations and faint Appearances? I shall only observe in short that he
would not be able from thence to know exactly any one particular with respect to their *Real
Nature*; and every Inference he made from
those Images to the *Intrinsick Substance* or Essence and *True Properties* of the things signified,
would be full of Absurdity and Solecism. One
of the last things he could infer would be, that
any of them had *Solidity* and a *Body*; or that
the human Appearance could have *Sense*, and
Reason, and *Understanding*, and *Will:* And
in such a Case as this, all the *Names*, and
Words, and *Expressions* he used for those *Similitudes* only, he would substitute for speaking of the Things themselves; and would not
invent *New* Terms and a *New* Language, for
Things whereof he had no Idea or Conception
as they were in their own Nature.

It is this kind of Analogy which runs thro'
all our *Expressions* of spiritual and immaterial
Objects. As we have no *Idea* or *Conception*
of their real and true Nature, so neither can
we invent any *Words* or Expressions which
shall be peculiar and proper to them; nor indeed can any Words *Express* what is *Inexpres-
sible*: Therefore we are under a necessity to
Speak of them after the same manner we *Conceive them*; and apply those Words and Phrases
to them by which, in their first Propriety, we

I 3 express

exprefs the Ideas or Conceptions which ftand for them in our Minds. Thus the Word *Spirit* in its firft Propriety is ufed to fignify the moft volatile and exalted Parts of *Matter* ; and is from thence taken to exprefs an human Soul in *Conjunction* with Matter ; and from thence again transferr'd to reprefent a purely *Immaterial* Subftance by Analogy. The Word *Wifdom* fignifies primarily the moft advantageous and dextrous management of our Thinking or Reafon, to obtain a commendable end ; and is from thence apply'd to an *Inconceivable Perfection* in the Divine Nature: So *Goodnefs* which is firft apply'd to the regulating our Paffions and Affections with regard to other rational Creatures, is attributed to God; and ferves to exprefs fome incomprehenfible Perfection in him, for which we have neither a *Proper* Word, Idea, or Conception; and fo it is in all other Inftances. Thus the fame Words and Phrafes ferve to exprefs the things whereof we have *Direct* and *Immediate* Ideas and Conceptions, and thofe things whereof we have *None* fuch; they equaly fignify fomething *Real* and fubftantial, whether they are apply'd to one or the other : Only when they are apply'd to the latter, they are always taken in a more *Elevated* and *Exalted* Sence ; to denote Things which fo far tranfcend all our Capacities, that we have no other way of thinking or fpeaking of them, but by fuch Words and Conceptions as are common and familiar to us.

CHAP.

C H A P. VIII.

A fifth Property, that they are Clear and Diſtinct.

THE laſt Property of Ideas of Senſation is, That of their being *Clear* and *Diſtinct*; which is meant only of thoſe that are *Simple* and *Original*; the Impreſſions made by parti-cular ſenſible Objects upon any of our Organs of Senſation ; which have ever a greater or leſs Degree of Perſpicuity in Proportion to that Strength, and Firmneſs, and Frequency with which the Object ſtrikes upon the Senſe ; and to the Vigour of the Imagination in receiv-ing and retaining them. Then an Idea is at the Height of Perſpicuity when it is ſo evi-dently and plainly diſcerned by the Mind, that it can be diſtinguiſhed from all other Ideas at one *View* of the Intellect ; without farther Ob-ſervation or Reaſoning, to ſeparate it from o-thers that have any Likeneſs or Reſemblance of it ; and then it is that it removes all Doubt, and compels our Aſſent to the Truth and Ex-iſtence of the Object it repreſents. Now by this Property theſe Ideas are diſtinguiſhed,

1. FROM all Deluſions of the Senſes. There is ever more or leſs Obſcurity and Confuſion in our Ideas according to the preſent Temper

of

of the Organ of Senfation, the Diftance of the Object, and the Quality of the Medium which interpofes: Thefe being rightly and duly difpofed, every original Idea which is made by one and the fame Object, and at the fame time is not only *Diftinct*, and *Clear*, and *Adequate*, but *Simple* too; as the Impreffion of a Seal is but one Figure and Similitude, tho' it confifts of feveral different Parts. Thus the Idea caufed in the Mind by our looking on a Man, or an Horfe, or a Tree is a fimple Idea; and is diftinct, and clear, and adequate; and the Reafon is plain, becaufe fuch an Idea contains all that the Object is naturaly difpofed to imprint upon the Senfe *At once*, and all that the Senfe is framed and contrived by the Author of Nature to take in or receive at *One* Act of Senfation.

OF this Kind are all our Ideas of every fingle and particular Subftance; for tho' when I look upon it, I do not fee into the inward *Effence* and Configuration of all its Parts; nor difcern all its primary and fecundary Qualities; nor *How* they fubfift in it; nor can view it fo as to take in all its Powers active and paffive: Yet the Idea comprehends all that the Object is naturaly difpofed to Imprefs upon the Senfe at once; and all that either the Senfe or the *Imagination* is capable of receiving from one fingle View. Whatfoever is beyond this is the Object of more *Particular* Senfations, or rather of Reafon and Obfervation; and not of one fingle single Act of Sensation. And sure it must be absurd to say, that an Idea of Sensation is either *Obscure* and *Indistinct*, or *Inadequate* because it doth not contain what the Object cannot communicate to the Sense, nor the Sense is any way capable of perceiving.

FROM hence we see how fanciful and precarious that Opinion is, which asserts our Ideas of all, even single and particular Substances, to be *Complex*, and *Indistinct*, and obscure, or *Inadequate*; because we do not discern the inward Configuration of all their Parts, together with all their essential Qualities and Powers by any Act of Sensation; whereas for the same Reason there could be no such thing as a clear and distinct Idea of *Any* Object whatsoever. Thus you shall have no clear and distinct Idea of *Sound*, because in one and the same Sensation we do not perrceive that Commotion or Concussion of the Air which causes it; and those Undulations which gradualy flowing from thence do at length strike upon the Organ of Hearing: Nor can the Ideas of *Taste* be *Simple* or *Clear*, because we have no Gust or Sensation of the exact Figure and Conformation of those minute Particles of Matter which affect the Tongue or Palate; neither thus are our Ideas of Colours *Simple*, or *Clear*, or *Distinct*, or *Adequate*; because the Eye doth not discern that peculiar Texture of those Particles in the Superficies of Bodies, which Reflects the Light so as to give it that Appearance,

ance, rather than any other. This abſurd Opinion was invented and tedioufly purſued, only for the Support of that bold and irrational Poſition, *That we have as clear and diftinɑ an Idea of the Subftance of a Spirit, as we have of bodily Subftance:* Whereas, were this true, we ſhould from thence have as *Direɑ*, and *Clear* and diftinɑ, and *Adequate* a Knowledge of all created Spirits, and as clear and direɑ Evidence of their *Exiftence* and true Properties, as we have of Body.

2. B Y this Property the *Simple*, original Ideas of Senſation are diftinguiſhed from all the *Alterations* made in them afterwards by enlarging or diminiſhing; and by the various *Combinations* they undergo at the Will and Pleaſure of the pure Intelleɑ. Thus the Mind may alter the whole Face of Nature, and ſome way or other change every Objeɑ from what it realy appears to the Senſes; and raiſe up to itſelf ſuch new Ideas out of thoſe which are ſimple and original, as have no Being but in the Intelleɑ alone; ſuch as thoſe of *Pigmies*, *Fairies*, and *Centaurs*. Theſe do all go under the Denomination of Ideas of Senſation, tho' not occaſioned by the Preſence or Impreſſion of any external Objeɑ: Becauſe as they are formed by the Intelleɑ in the Imagination out of our ſimple Ideas, ſo they remain there and become new and further Materials for the Mind to exerciſe its Operations upon; and they have

2   **greater**

greater or less Degrees of Distinctness and Perspicuity, as they are more or less alter'd and compounded.

I WOULD observe here that when any particular simple Idea is rendered *Specific*, then from being *Clear* and distinct it becomes more *Obscure* and confus'd. In order to understand which it must be consider'd, that we do not form specific or universal Ideas, or Notions, by collecting all the Powers and Qualities observed in the Particulars of every kind; and then putting them together to make up one Idea or Notion to stand for them all, and which is supposed to be formed by *Abstracting* from all the *Individuals*. But what is quite the reverse, all our specific or universal Ideas and Conceptions are formed thus; the Mind substitutes the Idea or Conception it has already obtained of some one Individual, to stand for and represent all the Individuals of the same Kind. As for instance, when I would form an *Universal* Notion of *Mankind*, I do not first collect all the Powers and Qualities I observe common to all particular Men, and then put them together into one abstract Notion of Mankind, to include all the Individuals: But on the quite contrary, having obtained the clearest *Complex* Notion I can of one individual Man, the Intellect makes that a Representative of all the Men in the World; and thus renders it *General* in its *Signification*, and consequently

more

more obfcure. Whereas were all the Individuals of each Kind exactly the fame in all refpects, as they differ in many ; the Idea or Notion when it became thus Specific or General, would be as clear and diftinct as when it ftood for one Individual.

3. BUT laftly, the fimple Ideas of Senfation, together with thofe compounded out of them, are by this Property diftinguifhed, as I may fo fay, even from *Themfelves* in a *Secondary* Acceptation and Application of them ; that is when they are taken in Conjunction with the Operations of the Intellect, and thus are *Subftituted* for the Reprefentation of things of the *Real True* Nature of which we can have no Notion or Idea at all, that is for the things of another World ; which for greater Clearnefs and Brevity it will be convenient hereafter to denote by the Name of the *Antitypes*, and thofe Ideas or Notions which reprefent them by that of the *Types*. As when *Begetting* is put for the *Supernatural Generation* of the Son from the Father ; *Father* and *Son*, for the *Relation* between the two firft Perfons in the Trinity ; our human *Spirit*, or rather *Soul*, for a Being purely *Immaterial*, and particularly for the *Third* Perfon in the divine Nature ; *Price*, *Purchafe*, *Ranfom*, for the *Merits* of Chrift's Death, and the *Value* and *Power* of his Sacrifice with God ; *Mediation* and *Interceffion* among Men, for the *Inconceivable* Manner

ner of his *Reconciling* us to God. I might thus
run thro' all our Conceptions and Words for
the things of another World, which in their
firſt and ſtrictly *Proper* Signification are diſtinct
and *Clear* ; but then are commonly ſuppoſed to become more confuſed and *Obſcure*,
when they are transferred from their natural
Import and Signification to things Supernatural, and therefore otherwiſe utterly inconceivable.

AND thus it is likewiſe with all thoſe *Complex Notions* and *Conceptions* which are made
up of our *Simple* and *Compounded* Ideas of Senſation, in Conjunction with the *Operations* of
our Mind upon them. The more of theſe are
accumulated to make up one Conception or
Repreſentation, the more confuſed and indiſtinct it is. As when we put together the Ideas
of a *Man*, of *Want* or *Miſery*, of an *Alms*, the
Notion in general of our *Duty* to God, of *Humanity* towards our fellow Creatures, and of the
Reward of another World to make up a complex Notion of *Charity*. And thus it is alſo in
the complex Notions we form to our ſelves of
Immaterial Beings, and of all things *Relating* to
them ; as when to the Word *Subſtance* and our
Idea of it we add *Thinking* and *Willing*, together with the various *Modes* of them, to make
up an *Analogical* complex Notion of *Spiritual*
Being in general : And when again we carry
on that very Conception and render it yet more
com-

complex by adding to it all other the greateſt Perfections natural or *Moral* we are capable of obſerving in rational Agents; which Conception becomes yet leſs clear and diſtinct by removing from it all the *Imperfections* of the Creatures within our view, for a Repreſentation of the divine Nature. All thoſe Ideas and Notions which go to make up theſe Compoſitions, are, when conſidered ſingly and ſeparately, plain and obvious, clear and diſtinct, both in their *Firſt* and *Analogical* Acceptation; but when they are united into *One Complex* Conception which ſtands in the Mind to ſupply the Place of one *Simple* uncompounded *Idea*, which we ſhould have of that Thing if we had Capacities or Faculties for a *Direct* or immediate Perception of it; then they become more confus'd and obſcure.

BUT then it ought to be well conſidered, that whatever there is of ſuppoſed Obſcurity and Confuſion in thoſe Analogical complex Notions ſo form'd, and then ſubſtituted for the Repreſentation of heavenly Things; it does not proceed merely from their being *So Complicated*, (in which inſtance they are only on an equal Foot with all other very complex Notions) nor does it proceed from the nature of the Things thus *Repreſented*, they being in their *Own Nature* very clearly intelligible had we Capacities ſo to apprehend them: But from a prevailing erroneous Opinion, that we have *Direct* and *Proper,*

per, tho' indiſtinct and confuſed *Ideas* of thoſe things, whereof in Reality we have no other than *Indirect* and *Analogical* Conceptions; and from a miſtaken Imagination that theſe Analogical Conceptions give us ſome imperfect Degrees of *Direct Perception* where we have none at all. In order to the right apprehending of which I ſhall propoſe theſe two things to be conſidered.

1. THAT in Reſpect of *Immaterial* Beings, and of all things relating to the *Real True* Nature of them as they are in themſelves, we are as a Man born *Blind* in Reſpect of Light or Colours; and not as a Man who hath a very *Dim* Sight, or who can diſcern *Direct*, tho' *Faint* Glimmerings of Light; and hath ſome *Immediate*, tho' no more than *Confuſed* and imperfect Views of viſible Objects. We can have no Ideas of immaterial Beings from our Senſes; nor have we any Ideas of them that are purely *Intellectual* and intirely independent of Ideas of Senſation; we have not the leaſt Spark of Light, or ſmalleſt Glimpſe, whereby to diſcern their *Real* Nature or Eſſence, or any Part of it; ſo that thus far it is not an indiſtinct or *Obſcure* Perception, but *No* Perception at all. When Men are fully appriſed of this they will find,

2. THAT all thoſe Conceptions which *Stand* in the mind for ſpiritual Things, and thoſe Words

Words and Expreſſions which we uſe for them, are in themſelves, at leaſt *As clear* and diſtinct when they are apply'd to this ſecondary and *Analogical* Sence, as when they are apply'd to what they import in their firſt and *Proper* Signification; that is, *As far as we can have any Knowledge at all of thoſe Things of another World, or are obliged to give any Aſſent to them.* As for Inſtance, The Conceptions of *Father, Son,* and *Spirit* are clear and diſtinct enough in their firſt and proper Acceptation; the *Relation* between *Father* and *Son* among us is clear and diſtinct; and ſo are thoſe Properties of a *Human Spirit,* which we have from *Self-conſciouſneſs.* Now when theſe are *Transferred* from their firſt and proper Signification to the Perſons in the Bleſſed *Trinity,* they are no leſs diſtinct and *Clear* than before, as far as we are *Obliged* to *Underſtand* that Diſtinction in the Divine Nature, or to *Believe* it. For the *True* and *Real Nature* of the Father, Son, or Holy Spirit is no Object either of our *Underſtanding* or *Faith*; any farther than to underſtand and believe that the Diſtinction is *Real,* as it is *Incomprehenſible. How* and after what exact manner the firſt is a Father, *How* the ſecond a Son, and *How* the third a Spirit differing from either, is likewiſe no Object of our Chriſtian *Faith,* becauſe it is no Object of our *Underſtanding*; and becauſe we can *Believe* nothing but *What* we firſt *Underſtand* diſtinctly and clearly, and as *Far* only as we underſtand it.

IF

IF we underftood the real manner of Diftinction in the Divine Nature *Confufedly* and
Indiftinctly, our *Affent* would be fo likewife:
No, what we are to believe is, that we conceive nothing of the *Real Nature* of Father,
Son, and Spirit, nor of the *Manner* of that
Diftinction. But we are bound to believe what
we *Do* underftand, namely that there *Is* a *Real*
and true Diftinction, and a *Perfonal* one likewife in the Divine Nature; as there is a real
and perfonal Diftinction between the *Father* and the *Son* among *Men*, and as there is
a real and perfonal Diftinction between one
Human Spirit and another; but *What* they are
in *Themfelves*, and *How* they are *One* or how
they are *Three*, we have not fo much as a
Confufed and *Obfcure* Perception of.

So again, the Idea and Word *Begotten*,
when apply'd to the Communication of the
Divine Nature to the Son, is as clear and diftinct as when apply'd to *Human Generation*.
As for the true and *Real Manner* and Nature
of the Divine Generation, it is true we cannot
have the leaft Idea or Conception of it; and
accordingly we cannot give our *Affent* to
what we do *Not* at all apprehend. But we
know clearly and diftinctly that the Son is faid
to have been begotten of the Father; and
whatfoever *Incomprehenfible Manner* of Production is meant by the Word, we are to underftand

K

derstand and believe what is clearly and distinctly expressed by that Term ; that Christ is the Son of God by a supernatural Generation in as *True* and *Real* a Sence, as one Man is the Son of another in the way of Nature: **And** that the Divine *Generation* differs as *Essentialy* from all manner of *Creation*, as a Man's begetting a Son differs from his making a Statue ; and the not giving our Assent to what *Is* so clearly and distinctly revealed is *Infidelity*.

Thus it is with the Conceptions and **Terms,** *Price*, and *Purchase*, and *Ransom*. As far as we are obliged either to know or believe that the Blood of Christ is such, we have as clear and distinct Ideas of them when apply'd to it, as when they are used in the common **Affairs** of Life ; insomuch that we can know clearly and distinctly, and give a firm unshaken Assent to this Proposition, That the Blood of Christ was a *Real* and *True Price, Purchase*, or *Ransom* for us; tho' we are utterly ignorant of the *Nature* and *Degrees*, of the Virtue and Merit of his Sacrifice with **God,** which are no Objects either of our Understanding or Assent: As we might know and believe that a Price and Ransom was paid for the Redemption of a *Captive*, tho' we know neither the *Kind* nor the *Value* of the Price by which he was redeemed.

And

AND laſtly, thus it is with the Conception and the Word *Interceſſion*. How and after what real *Manner* Chriſt intercedes for us, ſo as to prevail with God in our behalf; and how he pleads the Virtue and Merit of his Sacrifice, can't be ſaid to be *Obſcurely* and *Indiſtinctly* known, but totaly and intirely *Unknown*; as it is not at all revealed, ſo it is no Article or Part of our Chriſtian Faith: But that he doth make a *Real* and true Interceſſion for us, is revealed; and this is clear and diſtinct, and accordingly the proper Object of our Knowledge and Aſſent; and all that we are to believe of the *Real Nature* of that Interceſſion is, that we neither *Have* nor *Can* have any Knowledge of it in this World, and therefore ought to acquieſce therein till we come to another. In the mean time we are to *Believe* as *Far* as we can *Know* clearly and perfectly; that Chriſt intercedes for us; as we might believe that the Son of a Prince intercedes to his Father in behalf of a Captive; tho' we may be utterly ignorant after what manner he performs it, and what Motives or Arguments he makes uſe of to obtain that Pardon and Redemption.

I MIGHT here run thro' all the *Attributes* of God, and *Myſteries* of the Goſpel, and ſhew how the Ideas and Conceptions which are ſubſtituted for them in the Mind, and the Terms by which we expreſs them, are as *Clear* and *Di-*

K 2   *ſtinct*

ſtinct when attributed or apply'd to thoſe *Heavenly* things (as far as we are obliged to believe them) as when they are taken in their *Firſt* and ſtrictly proper Signification ; and how what is *Unknown* of them is no direct or immediate Object either of *Reaſon* or *Faith*. As alſo how all our *Moral* Reaſonings upon the *Types* hold true in reſpect of the *Antitypes* ; and then only are dubious or falſe when we attempt to reaſon from the *Real Nature* and Subſtance of the Types, to the real true Nature of the Antitypes whereof we are utterly ignorant. But all this will be fully conſider'd when I come to lay open the Nature of *Analogy* in a following Treatiſe, together with the manifold Uſe of it in Religion.

C H A P. IX.

The Difference between Divine Metaphor and Divine Analogy.

FRO M what I have already ſaid in Chapter the Sixth, Metaphor in *General* may be eaſily and widely diſtinguiſhed from all Analogy : But becauſe the Diſtinction is of great and important Moment, I ſhall more particularly place the difference between *Divine Metaphor* and *Divine Analogy* in a clear and oppoſite Light here ; theſe two being moſt liable to be confounded and miſtaken. But before
I en-

I enter upon the Explication of this material Difference, I must desire the Reader to recollect what I have already said of the proper Use of the Word *Idea*, and that I think it ought to be confined intirely to our simple and compound Ideas of *Sensation*, in Distinction from all the *Operations* and Affections of the *Mind*, of which we have an immediate *Consciousness* without the Intervention of any Idea; and from all those complex *Notions* or *Conceptions* form'd by the Mind out of its own Operations and the Ideas of Sensation. Thus we have an *Idea* of an House, a *Consciousness* of Thinking or Grief, and a *Complex Notion* of Justice, Mercy, and Charity. If this be observed, the following Distinctions will be clearly and fully apprehended.

1. FIRST then, Divine Metaphor is intirely *Arbitrary*; and no way absolutely *Necessary* towards our conceiving or expressing the Nature of purely spiritual Things or their Properties. But Divine Analogy is, in our present Circumstances, absolutely necessary both to our conceiving and speaking of immaterial Things; when we would think of them with any degree of *Exact Knowledge* at all, or express any *Correspondent* Reality in those Things: Because, as I said, we can neither know them by immediate *Ideas*, or by *Consciousness*, or by any *Direct* Perception or *Notion*. In short, we can neither conceive them

K 3 *Of*

Of our Selves; nor can any thing intirely *New* concerning them be *Reveal'd* to us, as our Faculties now are, without the Mediation of this Analogy. But 'tis quite otherwise with Divine Metaphor; This is never us'd but to express something *Already* known and conceived by the Light of Nature, or revealed by God with more Exactness thro' the Mediation of *Analogy*.

WERE we capable of forming no other than *Merely Metaphorical* Ideas or Conceptions of God and heavenly Things; and were no other also made use of in a Revelation of Doctrines intirely new concerning them ; such merely figurative Ideas or Conceptions could never have answered the necessary Ends either of natural or revealed Religion. For as they would then be mere Figure and *Allusion* only, without conveying a Notion or Conception of any thing *Correspondent* or *Answerable* in the very intrinsick Nature of the Divine Things; we never cou'd have *Argued* from them with *Justness* and *Certainty* , or without perpetual Mistake and fatal Error : All our Reasonings upon them would be precarious, and without any solid Foundation in the *Nature* of the Things ; and in short we should have nothing more than a *Merely Figurative,* that is, no *Real,* and *True,* and *Exact* Knowledge of them at all.

Now this Obfervation can no way depre-
ciate the Excellency of *Scripture Metaphor*;
becaufe this always fuppofes us furnifhed before-
hand with more exact, and complete, and *Correfpondent* Notions of God, and other heavenly Things from natural Reafon or Revelation, by Analogy.   And therefore 'tis that the
Holy Spirit has given us, not merely figurative and Metaphorical Ideas *Only* but Analogical Conceptions and Terms for all the things of
another World which were neceffary for us to
have any true and undoubted Knowledge of;
particularly of God and his Attributes, the
Myfteries of Chriftianity, and the future State
of Rewards and Punifhments.   And tho' we
read of the *Hand*, and *Eye*, and *Face*, and *Arm* of
God, yet we are fuppofed to have had Notions
of his *Power*, and *Wifdom*, and *Goodnefs* before;
or this Metaphorical Manner *Alone* could never
have given us any ufeful Notice or real Knowledge of thofe his inconceivable Perfections.

It no way debafes Scripture Metaphor to
fay, that it anfwers not an End for which common Senfe will tell us it was never *Intended*
by the Holy Spirit.   When it is ufed in Scripture to exprefs heavenly Beings, it is not defigned to defcribe any thing really Correfpondent and *Truly Anfwerable* in thofe Beings, as
Analogy is: But rather to *Exprefs* more
Emphaticaly, what we *Know* already more
K 4   *Exactly*

Exactly by Analogy. Then indeed the Metaphorical Images in Scripture serve to excellent Purposes; namely to illustrate what was *Otherwise* known and conceived; to awaken and exalt the Mind; to strike it with greater Awe and Surprise; and to move all our religious Passions and Affections; which is the proper use of all Figure. Even *Human* Metaphor, were it used to express or conceive any thing which we never could have had any Idea, or Consciousness, or Notion of, but merely from that Metaphor *Alone*, would convey to us no *Real* or true Knowledge; and much more would this be true of *Divine* Metaphor, if it was the only Method we had of conceiving and expressing the imperceptible things of God and another World : For what real or *True* Knowledge could we possibly have of the *Infinite Power* of God for instance, by the merely figurative Idea and Expression of a *Strong Hand*, or *Mighty Arm*, if we could never have known it more exactly some other way ?

FOR these Reasons it is, as I observ'd, that wherever God is pleased to reveal any thing intirely new concerning heavenly Things, he always does it by Analogy with the things of this World, and not by Metaphor only ; in such Instances we always find Analogy us'd to *Inform* the *Understanding*, as Metaphor and other Figures are, to *Affect* the *Imagination*. And there is so little danger of mistaking one for
the

the other in Scripture, that no Perfon who will ufe his common Senfe without prejudice, can ever confound them. For who, could otherwife than wilfully, miftake the *Analogy* in the Words *Son* and *Begotten* when applied to Chrift, for pure *Metaphor* and Figure only; or the Words *Door*, and *Way*, and *Vine*, and *Light of the World*, when fpoke of him, for an Analogy as compleat and perfect as the former; without the utmoft Violence to his Underftanding? And yet as plain and obvious as this is, the not duly confidering this material Difference between Divine Metaphor and Divine Analogy has been the Occafion of numberlefs and *Fatal* Errors in Religion.

2. THE fecond Difference is this. In Divine Metaphor the Refemblance, or Proportion, or Correfpondency is *Imaginary*; 'tis pure Invention and mere Allufion alone, and no way founded in the *Real Nature* of the things compared. But in Divine Analogy the Refemblance, or at leaft the *Correfpondency* and *Proportion* is *Real*, and built on the very *Nature* of Things on both fides of the Comparifon. There is fomething realy correfpondent and anfwerable and proportionable in heavenly and fpiritual Beings, to thofe Conceptions which are juftly fubftituted to reprefent them. As for inftance, there is certainly fome inconceivable *Perfection* in God anfwerable to *Human Knowledge*; which is obtained by the

2   Labour

Labour of Thinking, and the Operation of Matter and Spirit in essential Conjunction : *Goodness* in God is an inconceivable Excellency of his Nature correspondent to what we conceive and express by the same Word in human Nature ; And the *Similis Ratio* or *Proportion* runs thus, *What* Knowledge and Goodness are in the Nature of *Man*, *That* some inconceivable but correspondent Perfections are in the Nature of *God*. And so 'tis in all the other Attributes, which tho' totaly different in *Kind* from those Properties in us bearing the same Name, yet are thus very usefully and truly represented to our Mind, so as to answer all the purposes of substantial Knowledge and Religion.

3dly. WHAT yet more widens the difference between Divine Metaphor and Divine Analogy is this. Divine Metaphor expresses immaterial Things by our *Ideas of Sensation only*. But Divine Analogy furnishes us with a Knowledge of the same Objects by substituting the *Conceptions* or *Complex Notions* of our Mind to represent them. Thus when the *Glory* of God is expressed by the resplendent *Light* of the Sun, even this is nothing more than mere Metaphor ; tho' indeed it must be confess'd that a more noble and exalted one cannot enter into the Mind of Man. But when we represent the *Knowledge* of God by *Our* Knowledge, and the *Goodness* of God by the Good-

3   ness

ness of a *Man* (which are the only *Direct* Notions we can have of either Knowledge or Goodness) this is true Analogy. When the Joys of Heaven are called a *Crown* of Righteousness, and Heaven itself described as a New *Jerusalem* , these are mere Metaphors borrow'd from Ideas of Sensation; but when 'tis said that the Righteous shall obtain *Joy and Gladness*, and *Pleasures for evermore*, this is an Analogical Conception; and represents an *Inconceivable* future Bliss *Correspondent* and *Answerable* to the best Conception we are able to form of Joy and Pleasure here, in the Gratification of all our reasonable Affections.

THE Ground and Reason of this last Distinction between Divine Metaphor and Divine Analogy will appear very obvious if we consider, that there can be no *Real Resemblance* or true Correspondency, between mere Objects of *Sense* or their Ideas, and *Immaterial* heavenly Beings. But there may be a real *Resemblance*, or at least a true Correspondency and *Proportion*, between the *Operations* of our *Mind* (as well as our *Complex Notions* formed partly out of them) on one Side of the Comparison; and the immaterial Things they are substituted to represent on the other. For as we are made in some Measure after the *Image of God*, especialy in our spiritual Part, this serves to render all the Analogy rationaly built on such Conceptions and Notions, *Real* and *Just* with

with refpect to him and his Attributes; as well
as to other purely fpiritual Beings who are
created in a yet *Nearer* Likenefs to him. And
therefore his *Natural* or rather *Supernatural* Attributes we conceive by Analogy with the Operations and *Properties* of our own *Minds*; and
what we call his *Moral* Attributes, we conceive
by Analogy with our complex Notions of
human *Virtues* and moral Excellencies.

Now therefore to prevent any Miftake
hereafter in relation to thofe Inftances which
may be given of Analogy, I muft obferve that
tho' *Light*, in its greateft Refplendency is *Material*, and an Object of Senfation; and therefore cannot be transferr'd to God otherwife
than *Metaphoricaly*; there being nothing in
his purely fpiritual Nature correfpondent or
anfwerable to Matter: Yet as *Intellectual Light*
is ufed for *Knowledge*, and becomes expreffive
of the moft noble Faculty or Perfection of the
human Mind, it carries in it fo much of the
Nature of the true Analogy; and therefore
whenever I ufe it as an inftance of fuch, I take
it in that Sence, and as it excludes all Materiality.

Again, The Idea of *Subftance* is an Idea
altogether of Senfation, as it includes Length,
Breadth, and Thicknefs; and therefore cannot be transferr'd to God in this Sence, otherwife than by pure Metaphor; and this preca-
rioufly

riouſly too, ſince it is no Scripture Metaphor.
And therefore whenever I mention our conceiving the Subſtance of God by Analogy with
material Subſtance, I ever mean as it imports
the Notion of *Being* in general only.

So again, *Wind* or *Breath* are Ideas of Senſation, and cannot be transferr'd to the Holy
Ghoſt otherwiſe than Metaphoricaly: But as
Wind or Breath from its firſt Propriety comes
to ſignify *Animal Life* both in Man and Beaſt,
and from thence is uſed to expreſs the immaterial *Spirit of a Man*, which is a Notion
complex enough to take in all the Operations
of an human Mind; then 'tis pure Analogy,
us'd to conceive the Incomprehenſible and
Holy Spirit.

To ſum up the Difference then between
Divine Metaphor and Divine Analogy in full.
Metaphor expreſſes only an *Imaginary* Reſemblance or Correſpondency; Analogy conveys
the Conception of a *Correſpondent Reality* or *Reſemblance*. Metaphor is rather an *Alluſion*,
than a real *Subſtitution* of Ideas; Analogy a
proper Subſtitution of Notions and Conceptions. Metaphor at beſt is but the uſing a
very remote and foreign Idea to expreſs ſomething *Already* ſuppoſed to be more exactly
known; Analogy conveys ſomething correſpondent and anſwerable, which could be
No otherwiſe uſefully and realy known
with-

without it. Metaphor is moftly in Words, and is a Figure of *Speech* ; Analogy a *Similis Ratio* or Proportion of *Things*, and an excellent and necef-fary Method or Means of *Reafon* and *Knowledge.* Metaphor ufes Ideas of *Senfation* to exprefs immaterial and heavenly Objects, to which they can bear *No Real* Refemblance or Proportion ; Analogy fubftitutes the Operations of our *Soul*, and Notions moftly formed out of them, to reprefent Divine Things to which they bear a *Real* tho' *Unknown* Correfpondency and Pro-portion. In fhort, Metaphor has *No* real Foun-dation in the *Nature* of the Things compared ; Analogy is founded in the *Very Nature* of the Things on both Sides of the Comparifon : And the Correfpondency or Refemblance is certain-ly *Real*, tho' we don't know the exact *Nature*, or *Manner*, or *Degree* of it ; at leaft we may fafely prefume this from the Truth and Vera-city of God, who has thus made his Revela-tions to Mankind under the Analogical Con-ceptions and Language of this World.

THO' nothing is more plain and evident than this *Analogy*, which runs thro' all our Conceptions and Reafonings upon the Things of another World, when we come to reflect and confider the Matter clofely ; yet we fall into it fo naturaly, and are fo ufed to it from the firft, that we are generaly infenfible of it ; and apt to take it for granted that thofe Con-ceptions are as *Direct* and *Immediate*, and our

Lan-

Language for them as ftrictly proper, as when they are applied to the Things of this World. And indeed there would have been no harm in leaving the World to continue in that Opinion; there would have been no Occafion for unde-ceiving Men, nor for putting them upon di-ftinguifhing fo nicely the nature of *Metaphor* and *Analogy*, if there had been any other ef-fectual way of clearly and fatisfactorily obvia-ting the many dangerous Miftakes, and even fatal Errors prevailing in this Age, which ftrike at the very root of Chriftianity. It is now become abfolutely neceffary to put this matter into a *Glaring* Light, fince the whole *Socinian* Syftem, and all that Infidelity which is the Effect and Confequence of it; as well as fome more *Modern* Syftems which are in no fmall degree built upon its general Principles, turn upon refolving all Revelation and the Myfte-ries of Chriftianity into mere *Metaphor* and *Allufion only*: And upon their ever confound-ing this with the true Analogy, which is of a quite different kind; which is founded in the very *Nature* of Things, and is abfolutely ne-ceffary even to our *Thinking* of heavenly Ob-jects, tho' we fhould never exprefs our Thoughts by Words.

HAVING thus ftated the wide Diftinction be-tween Divine Metaphor and Divine Analogy, as far as was neceffary here; I fhall only take notice of one Objection againft this Diftinction
which

which may be made by those who always find their Account in *Confounding* them.

PERHAPS they will say, that by their resolving several Things in the Gospel Mysteries into Metaphor, they do not intend to reduce them to *Mere Figure* only, and so bring them to *Nothing* as I insinuate: But on the contrary they will affirm, that they intend to understand by those *Metaphors* something as *Real*, and *Solid*, and *True* with regard to spiritual Things, as I wou'd make this *Analogical* Sence of them to signify.

Now to this I answer, That tho' the Gospel Terms, when applied to Things of another World, should be *Intended* by them to mean *Something* true, and real, and solid (as indeed all Metaphor is intended to do) yet if they be taken as *Mere Metaphor*, they cannot express or convey any thing of a *Correspondent Reality* in those Divine Things; or any thing which has a *Real* and *True* Proportion or *Resemblance* in the *Very Nature* of those spiritual Objects. And therefore, however they may *Intend* it, it cannot thus signify as much *Real* and *Solid Truth* with regard to the Mysteries of the Gospel and heavenly Things, as *Analogy* does; because this not only expresses *Somewhat Real*, and *Solid*, and *True*; but *Correspondent* also, and *Proportionable*, and *Answerable* in the *Very Natures* of the Things compared.

EVEN

EVEN in thofe Expreffions of Scripture which are allowed on all hands to be pure Metaphor, tho' *Some* Truth and Reality be certainly meant by them, yet are they widely different from Analogy. As for inftance; when God is faid to have a *Mighty Arm*, it means fomething as real and true, as when it is faid God is *Powerful:* And yet there can be nothing *Correfpondent* and *Anfwerable* to a great Arm of Flefh, in God. Whereas when God is faid to be powerful, and wife, and good, we don't only mean fomething true, and folid, and real; but alfo inconceivable Perfections in his real Nature *Correfpondent* and anfwerable to Power, and Wifdom, and Goodnefs in us. And again, to make this yet plainer; when *Generation* is made a mere Metaphor for a tranfcendent Act of *Creation*, it may indeed be *Intended* to fignify fomewhat real, and folid, and true; but can mean nothing in the Divine Nature fo correfpondent and proportionable to human Generation, as that Chrift fhould be in as much Truth and Reality the Son of God by fupernatural Generation, as one Man is the Son of another in the ordinary way of Nature; which is the true and analogical Acceptation of the Term *Begotten.* And for thefe Reafons it is, and in this Sence, that we juftly charge our modern Arians with bringing the Myfteries of the Gofpel to *Nothing* by their unwarrantable and metaphorical Interpretations.

L   BUT

But if, after all this, they should allow the Terms in which the Gospel Mysteries are expressed, to signify not only something *Real* in spiritual Things, but also somewhat *Correspondent* and *Proportionable* to the Things of this World substituted for them; and yet will still call this *Metaphor:* They are then grosly guilty of confounding two Things totaly different, by perversely giving them the same *Name* to serve a vile Turn; and also make a Conceffion which at once renders them shamefully inconfistent with themselves, and overturns all their Schemes of Divinity.

BOOK

BOOK II.

CHAP. I.

Of the Pure Intellect.

HAVING in the first Book consider'd the Ideas of *Senfation* as the only *Materials* which the active and busie Mind of Man hath to work upon; and as the fole Groundwork or Foundation for the whole Superstructure of human Knowledge; I come in this fecond to treat of the PURE INTELLECT. By which I would have it obferved here, once for all, that by this I do not mean that immortal immaterial Part of us, denoted in Scripture by the Word Πνεῦμα or *Spirit*; nor do I mean any the moft refined and exquifite parts of the Body, or animal Spirits, which are more immediately fubfervient to the intellectual Operations of that Spirit; but by the *Pure Intellect* I always underftand *Both* thefe operating together in effential Union and Conjunction; fo that all *Thinking* or *Reafoning* is a mix'd and compound Act of both Matter and Spirit. *Thinking* is by a general Miftake attributed to the *Pure* Spirit, exclufively of thofe material Organs without which it cannot exert one *Thought*; and in a neceffary Conjunction with which, it performs all its Operations.

THIS

T H I S will be yet clearer, if we diftinguifh thefe following Words of a near Signification; and which have therefore been ufed promif-cuoufly.

T H E *Spirit* is the purely immaterial Part of our Compofition, which is capable of Sepa-ration from the Body, and can then exift and operate independently of Matter: This is of-ten by miftake call'd the *Soul*, in a vulgar and more indiftinct way of fpeaking; but is di-ftinguifh'd in the Scripture by the Word Πνεῦ-μα *Spiritus.*

T H E *Soul*, or rather inferior Soul, as it is ufed to be called in Diftinction from that which is pure Spirit; is a Principle refulting from an effential Union of the pure Spirit with our ma-terial Frame; and it is in Scripture denoted by the Word Ψυχὴ *Anima,* or *Soul.*

T H E *Mind*, in a common and more indi-ftinct Acceptation, is Synonimous with *Soul*; but is in truth a more general and complex Term, and includes the pure *Spirit*, together with the *Intellect*, the *Will*, and *Memory*, and all the *Paffions* and *Affections* of the infe-rior Soul; and is properly Νᾶς *Animus,* or *Mind.*

T H E

THE Pure Intellect taken in Diftinction from thofe three, is properly the pure Spirit or immaterial Part of us, as acting in effential Union and Conjunction particularly with thofe animal Spirits and remote imperceptible Fibres of the Brain, which are more immediately fubfervient to *Thinking* or Knowledge, and all the Operations of the Underftanding. This is call'd Νόησις *Intellectus*, or the *Pure Intellect*.

IT hath been the occafion of numberlefs *Errors* and *Miftakes* in Religion, and too many of them fatal; that Men have been ufed to think and fpeak of the pure Spirit, or fuperior Soul, as if its Operations were *Now* in all refpects the fame, and as intirely independent of Matter, as they will be when it is in a ftate of *Separation*. Men commonly fpeak of it as of fomething *Within* us, and not *Of* us; as if it thought and reafoned *In* the Body, and not together *With* any part of it; as if the Body were a mere *Box*, or *Cafe*, or *Place* of Refidence for it. Not confidering that there is as much Truth in faying, that the Body is in the Spirit, as in faying that the Spirit is only *In* the Body; tho' this founds odly to a vulgar Ear; or indeed to any one who is not capable of underftanding, that thefe two different Principles could not conftitute one and the fame Individual Man, unlefs both were intimately united in Operation and Effence.

IT

IT muft be allow'd we can form no other Notion of *Knowledge* in an Angel or feparate Spirit except by that of *Thinking*; but this is no more than an *Analogical* Conception, which the Mind fubftitutes inftead of the real true manner and kind of Knowledge in Angels which we are utterly ignorant of: and which is as imperfectly reprefented by Thinking, as their Motion is by the moving of our Feet. All their Knowledge, as far as we can apprehend it, muft be *Intuitive* and *Inftantaneous*; whereas ours at the beft is fucceffive, and gradualy perform'd by the concurrent Motion of fome bodily Parts within us; which is the Caufe of that *Labour* and *Wearinefs* we experience in the Act of Thinking. If the pure Spirit within us cou'd think and reafon *Independently* of all material and bodily Organs, we fhould never be tired with thinking; but on the contrary we feel it to be a *Labour* of the Brain, and we find our felves as much wearied with intenfe Thought, as with hard bodily Labour. If it were not thus, the Body would be *Poffefs'd* only of a Spirit, and not a *Partaker* with it; and Thought would not be an Operation of the *Man*, but of fomething *Within* him.

I CANNOT forbear again remarking here the fhameful Inconfiftency of thofe Men, who maintain that we have as clear and diftinct an Idea of *Spirit* as we have of *Body*; for this rea-

fon,

fon, becaufe we have as clear and diftinct an Idea of *Thinking*, as we have of *Extenfion* or *Solidity* : And who at the fame time argue the Soul may be material, becaufe God can fuperadd to Matter the Power of Thinking. For is not *Thinking* and *Willing* even in their Hypothefis, oppos'd to *Extenfion* and *Solidity*, as *Effential* Properties utterly incompatible in the fame Being ; fo that Body and Spirit are by thefe Properties effentialy diftinguifhed from one another, as well as in our Ideas or Concep-tions of them ? And how then can Thinking be fuperadded to Matter, without making it a Spirit? If we have a clear Idea of Spirit from *Thinking*, and of Body from *Extenfion* and *Solidity* ; then, whenever Matter is made to think of itfelf, without the Concurrence of fpiritual Subftance, all our Ideas are changed and confounded ; then it might be faid we have a clear Idea of *Matter* from *Thinking* ; and we muft look out for fome other effential Property to give us a clear Idea of *Spirit*. To which I fhall add, that one and the fame Pro-perty of *Thinking* cannot be *Effential* to one fort of Being, and *Superadded* only and merely *Ac-cidental* to another ; wherever it is, it muft be an original effential Property ; fo that the Re-moval of it will make a Thing ceafe to be what it is ; as the fuperadding it will make a Thing what it was not in its own Nature be-fore. It is even ridiculous to fay, that tho' Thinking is not originaly effential to Matter,

yet

yet it may be made to Think by accident, fo as that Thinking may be a new and adventitious Quality of it. For it muft be granted, that whenever *Thinking* goes together with *Extenfion* or *Solidity* in the fame Body even by Accident, they will each of them ceafe to be any Marks of Diftinction between Body and Spirit.

BESIDES, if the Soul may be material, and Thinking is fuperadded to it; fure this can give no Idea of the manner of Knowledge in a Being altogether immaterial, and which hath Knowledge not fuperadded, but originaly in its own Nature and Effence. If they fay that a material and immaterial Subftance may both of them *Think*, tho' after a different *Manner*; this is playing upon the Word *Thinking*, and taking it for *Knowledge* which is a general Word, and includes the Knowledge of God and Angels; whereas the proper Acceptation of it, is for the particular way of Knowledge in Man. But call the Knowledge of God and Angels by what Name you will, nay call it *Thinking* it will end in the fame thing; for the *Manner* of it in God, and Angels, and Man muft be allow'd as effentialy different as their Nature; fo that *Thinking* in Man can give us no *Direct* Conception of Thinking in a pure Spirit.

BY the *Pure Intellect* cannot be underftood a fpiritual Subftance within us acting of itfelf,

2   and

and intirely free; as if the Spirit were only included and confined *Within* the Body, and refided there as in a Habitation. Nor muft it be confider'd as a Being *Disjoined* and *Separate* and acting by the help of bodily Organs, as fo many mere *Inftruments*, by which it performs all its Operations; for in truth and Reality the Body is no more a mere *Inftrument* to the Soul, than the Soul is to the Body. Tho' this is a plain Truth and will be eafily granted, yet it is generaly overlooked by the Writers of Logic and Metaphyfics; and whoever obferves it, will find a grofs Mifapprehenfion of this fundamental Point run thro' all the Language of moft of thofe who have treated of human Underftanding. They proceed upon a Suppofition that the Mind acts as if the Man were *All* Spirit; or as if all the Organs of the Body were fo many Inftruments at beft, which are neceffary to exert thofe Powers and Faculties *Inherent* in *Itfelf alone*, independently of Matter; and confider'd abftractedly from its clofe Conjunction and effential Union with the Body. Thus they fuppofe *Thinking* with all the Modes of it, and *Willing* to be Actions purely fpiritual, as if they had no Dependence upon Matter; and even all the *Paffions* in human Nature are fpoke of by them, as fo many Motions or Affections of the *Soul* only, as if it were in actual Separation from all Matter; and exerted its Operations only *In* the Body, and not in any Conjunction or Co-operation

With

With it. This hath been the occasion of so many grievous *Mistakes*, and even pernicious *Errors* that it would be endless to recount them ; many of them I shall have occasion to speak of in the Sequel of these Discourses : And by digesting this throughly, that the purely spiritual part of us never acts at present but in essential Union and necessary Concurrence with Matter ; the Reader will be able to see thro' the rest whenever they occur.

AFTER what *Manner* the *Spirit* of Man may act in a State of Separation we are utterly ignorant ; it is in itself altogether Immaterial, and we know as little of it considered in that State, as we know of the Nature of Angels : Nor can we in the least conceive how things Material do affect a pure Spirit ; but this we know, that while it is united to the Body it can exert no Act of its own intirely distinct and independent of it. Its most *Refined* Reasonings, and most *Abstracted* Speculations are performed in Conjunction with those animal *Spirits* and imperceptible *Fibres* of the Brain, which lie far out of the reach of all human View; even by the Help of Glasses which magnify to the largest Size. For which Reason, the Mind cannot have an actual Perception of any thing *Without* it, but as the Object first affects some of our Senses, and then a *Likeness* of some sort, or *Representation* of it is conveyed inwardly to the Imagination. So
that

that we are to confider the pure Intellect and Mind as a *Compofition* of Spirit and Matter, in ftrict and effential Union with one another; infomuch that all their Operations are the joint and infeparable Acts of both together; fuch as could not proceed from Matter, or Spirit alone; and fuch as would be Operations of a quite different Kind, if the fpiritual Part of us were to act by itfelf. Having premifed this, I fhall proceed to confider the feveral different *Operations* of the Intellect upon thofe Ideas of Senfation, which are as it were ftored and layed up in the Imagination; I mean thofe Operations which neceffarily prefuppofe Senfation, and contain the whole Procefs and utmoft Extent of human Underftanding. Accordingly,

1. THE firft of thofe Operations of the pure Intellect is that of a *Simple View*, or Survey of thofe Ideas of Senfation, in the very Order and Condition they lie in the Imagination, without *Altering* the Nature or Situation of any òne of them; without paffing any *Judgment*, or making any *Inferences* with Relation to them. This the Logicians have rightly termed *Simple Apprehenfion*, but do unhappily always confound it with pure Senfation, and the mere *Mechanical* Perception of external Objects; by which means the firft and fundamental Diftinction between *Reafon* and the natural *Inftinct* of Brutes is loft.

THERE

THERE is an essential difference between a simple *Apprehension* of the Mind, and a simple *Perception* of the Sense; the Consequence of this is an *Idea* in the Imagination; the former frames or occasions no *New* simple Idea, and only apprehends one that is *Already* made and presented to its view: As when by looking upon a human Body, a Representation or Similitude of it is transmitted thro' the Eyes to the Imagination; this is the Cause of a *New* Idea, in which the pure Intellect hath no part; it contributes nothing to the Production of that Idea, and it is formed without the least Act or Concurrence of the Mind. In all Sensations the Imagination is purely *Passive*, disposed by Nature to *Receive* only, and *Retain* such Impressions as are made upon the Senses; so that there may be an immense Number of simple Ideas lodged there, before we need necessarily suppose one simple Act or Apprehension of the Intellect with relation to them, which must be an Act *Subsequent* to all Sensation whatsoever; and never to be considered in Conjunction with it, as if it were one and the same thing. The simple Apprehension I am now speaking of, is an Act or Operation of the *Mind*, and not of the *Senses*, which last is common to us with Brutes; but the first a Perfection and Excellency of an human Soul: Insomuch that it is the most noble and elevated Manner of Operation in the Intellect; and
that

that by which it comes neareſt to the Manner of Knowledge in Angels; *Præcipua*, ſays a great Philoſopher, *Intellectûs humani ſicut Angelorum functio videtur eſſe, ut ſit ex ſuâ naturâ intelligens; hoc eſt ſimplici Intuitu, non ratiocinatione cognoſcens.*

Now therefore antecedently to this ſimple Apprehenſion, or any other Act of the pure Intellect, we are to ſuppoſe the Imagination plentifully ſtored and furniſhed with Ideas of Senſation altogether without its Concurrence. They began to be tranſmitted inwardly thro' the Senſes from our *Infancy*; they daily multiply by *Experience* and our Converſation with external ſenſible Objects; and are increaſed to a prodigious *Number* before we are conſcious to our ſelves of any Operations of the pure Intellect upon them. In this common Storehouſe, and Receptacle, thoſe Ideas lie in *Confuſion* together, all disjoin'd and unranged; and in no other Order than that wherein they *Chance* to be firſt tranſmited. And were there no *Immaterial Principle* at all within us, they would always remain in the ſame diſorderly Condition, undiſturbed and unobſerved; and without any other *Alteration* than what would be made by the Acceſſion of *New* Ideas from Objects as yet unperceived; and by the reviving of thoſe that were defaced or obliterated, from the Repetition of ſuch Impreſſions as had been made before.

CHAP.

CHAP. II.

Of Instinct in Brutes.

THIS is the very State and Condition of *Brutes.* Tho' they are capable of all the Sensations that are in us and tho' the Senses of many of them are more *Acute* than those in man, and consequently more susceptible of quick and vigorous Impressions from sensible Objects; yet all this is no more in them, than the striking of one material Substance upon another; the Effect of which remains just as long as there is a Disposition in the animal Spirits to retain it : But for want of an higher and *Immaterial* Principle, when the Idea is once formed, they can take no *After View* or Notice of it distinct from the Sensation itself. This is the utmost Extent of all that Knowledge in Brutes, which we call by the Name of *Instinct*; and is realy no other than a Calculation or *Disposition* of their Senses by the Author of Nature, to excel in those particular Instances of Sensation, wherein the *Being* or *Preservation* of every Species is most concerned. They are never actuated or influenced by more than *One* simple Idea at a time; nor by that neither, but when there is some *Actual Impression* of the external Object to stir it up within them, or some *Remains* of the Impression con-

tinuing

tinuing in the Imagination and Brain ; and all they perform is at the *Impulfe* and *Inftigation* of particular Ideas of Senfation, which is the only *Direction* they have in all their Operations.

FOR this Reafon Brutes can have no fuch thing as *Memory* properly fo called ; for after the Impreffions are made, or the Ideas form'd, they lie in their Imagination (without any Notice or Obfervation) to fway and direct their Motions, as long as they laft : But their Ideas decay gradualy, fo as never to be revived again by any proper *Recollection*; and muft be renewed by a Repetition of the fame, or of a like Impreffion, from the Prefence of the Object ; which is as different from *Memory* as natural *Inftinct* is from *Reafon*. The bare receiving and retaining the Impreffions or Ideas of external Objects in the Imagination, is not *Memory* even in *Man* ; but an Ability or Faculty of *Viewing* them at Pleafure, in the Abfence of the Objects which they ftand for in the Mind ; of *Reviving* them again within us and *Clearing* them up after they have grown *Confufed* and *Obfcure*, without any *New* Impreffion from Abroad : And above all a Power in the Intellect of *Impregnating* the Imagination with all its own *Alterations* and *Combinations* of fimple original Ideas; together with a Faculty in the Mind of Retaining and Recollecting all its various *Complex Notions*

I and

and *Conceptions*, at its own Will and Pleasure; nothing of all which is in the Nature and Power of Brutes. It may seem indeed that a *Dog* can at once attend to the *Shape*, and *Smell*, and *Voice* of his Master; and put those Ideas together to make up one compounded Idea. But the Dog frames no Idea of his Master from them all at once; but ever distinguisheth him by some *One* of them at a time, and by them all successively. If he hears his Master's *Voice* he attends only to that; if he *Sees* him, all Attention to his Smell and Voice is lost; and when all these Ideas of the Master are in *Any Degree* defaced and impaired by Absence, there can be no renewal of them but by the *Approach* or *Presence* of the Master.

THE common Objection against what I have said of Brutes here is, that a Dog *Dreams*, and *Barks*, and *Moves* in his Sleep; that he is *Uneasy* in the Absence of his Master; distinguisheth the *Smell* of him among a thousand, and *Knows* him again when he sees him; that he will find the way *Home* again after being conveyed to great *Distances* from thence; which Operations could not possibly be performed without a Memory. But this Objection supposes me to have asserted, that Impressions made by external Objects upon the Senses and Imagination of Brutes, last no longer than the *Presence* of the Objects; that these being removed leave no Footsteps of themselves behind;

hind; and that all Ideas of them immediately vanish, when the Objects are withdrawn. Whereas I affert the quite contrary ; that external Objects do often leave behind them more *Deep* and *Lasting* original Impreffions upon the Imagination of Brutes, than they do upon that in Man (I mean exclufive of *Recollection* in us) and the Ideas remain there in the Abfence of the Objects, for a Principle of Operation in them ; and to direct, and actuate them and determine all their Motions.

I T is by thefe the Dog *Dreams* and *Barks* in his Sleep, diftinguifheth his Mafter in a Crowd from all other Men, and hath fuch a ftrong Propenfion towards home, that he will find the way to it from a great diftance before the Traces of the Road are worn out of his Brain. Nay I affert farther, that it is neceffary their mere Senfations, and the Ideas or firft Impreffions in their Imagination, fhould be more ftrong, and lively and durable, than they are in Man (as daily Obfervation fhews us they are) becaufe Brutes are altogether acted and governed by *Senfe*; and thofe ftronger and more vigorous Impreffions of fenfible Objects, and the more exquifite Difpofition of their Organs to receive them, is plainly defigned by the Author of Nature to fupply the want of *Reafon*, and of any immaterial Principle in their Compofition.

M   BUT

BUT then nothing of all this is truly *Memory*; tho' it is something Analogous to it, for which we have no distinct and proper Word, yet it is intirely different from it both in Kind and Degree. For as the Sensation or Idea grows languid and wears away, so doth it gradualy cease to influence or move the Brute; it cannot be continued at one stay, by any Attention or Advertency to one Idea more than another; it cannot be regain'd or reviv'd at Pleasure when it is become weak and feeble, by any voluntary Recollection from within, or any Hint or Intimation only from without, as in Man; nor can it ever be restor'd again, as I observ'd, but by a new Sensation from the Presence of the Object. Memory is not a bare *Retaining* simple Ideas in the *Absence* of the Objects they represent; but a Power of *Recollecting* them at Will; and of attending to one Idea more than another, without regard to the Strength and Acuteness of the Sensation.

ANOTHER Objection against the Opinion of Brutes having no Principle of Action in them above Matter is, that upon this Supposition they could not *Move themselves*. To which I answer, that they do not *Move themselves*, tho' they may be said to move *Of themselves*; as a *Clock* can't in any Propriety of Speech be said to move itself, tho' it moves of itself by the Force of Spring, or Weight, or Pendu-

Pendulum. And do we think that God cannot inconceivably form a piece of Clockwork which shall go of itself, and perform all its Motions (if I may be allow'd so distant a Comparison) for ten, or twenty, or thirty, or even an hundred Years together; unless some outward Violence or inward Failure of the Wheels or Springs occasions a stop of that Motion, which kindles and keeps up the animal Heat and Warmth, and preserves all parts of the admirable Machine from mouldering and Dissolution? And, to carry on the Similitude, would it come much short of Frenzy in Men to argue that a Clock must have some degree of *Reason* and *Memory*, and an *Immaterial* Principle in its Composition; because it moves of itself? Or, on the other hand, supposing the Clock to be *Mere Matter*, to dispute whether God cou'd not endue it with a Power of *Thinking* if he pleas'd?

BRUTES are moved by the *Internal* Impulse of those Ideas which they have got from the Impressions of outward Objects, while those Ideas last, tho' the Objects are *Absent*; as well as when they are *Present*: Just as the Motions of a *Watch* are not only varied immediately by the Finger from *Without*, while it actualy touches the Machine; but also by the Impression *Left* upon the Spring by the Hand, after 'tis removed. All the Actions of Brutes are from a Necessity of Nature; they

cannot

cannot act *Otherwife* than they do, in the fame Difpofition of the Parts whereof they are compounded, and under the fame Impreffions from external Objects. They ever yield to the moft *Powerful* Senfation, which remains as a ftrong and fure Byafs upon them, 'till the fenfitive Idea is defaced or worn out; or till fome other Rub in their way, or fome ftronger Impulfe or Impreffion diverts their Courfe, and gives the Motion a new Determination. They cannot be properly faid to *Intend* or *Defign* any Motion one Moment before they move; nor can they of *Themfelves* alter any particular Motion, or change it for another. And tho' they have a Propenfion and Tendency to many Things which are for their own Prefervation, and that of their Species; yet all this is from a certain *Neceffity*, and a wife Difpofition of the Parts of their Frame; from an *Aptitude* in them to be fo moved by the Temperature of the Air, the Seafons of the Year, and the various Impreffions of fuch external Objects as conduce to the Prefervation of their Being, and the Continuation of their Species.

Now fhould we ftop here, and cou'd fuppofe that Characters of all the *Objects* in Nature, with all the *Ideas* they have an aptitude to caufe in us, were ftamped on our Imagination; and painted in lively and lafting Colours, fo as to remain there diftinct and intire; yet this alone would not amount to the leaft degree

gree of *Reason*. An Imagination so furnished could be conceived as no other than a large and curious *Picture* of the whole Face of Nature, retaining the Similitudes of a vast Variety of Objects, in the very Order and Proportion they were delineated; and at the best preserving them in the same Rank and Form perhaps in which they were received thro' the Senses. All this being hitherto no more than the Impression of one *Material* Substance upon another, there it must remain intirely useless and in vain as to any true and *Proper Knowledge*; and altogether unseen and unobserved, without some higher and *Immaterial* Principle to take a Prospect of it in general, and a Survey of the several Parts of it successively. When the Mind proceeds no farther than a bare *View* of these Ideas, it may be called an *Intuitive* Knowledge; and even this *First* Step of real Knowledge we could not be capable of, if the Thinking Substance within us were altogether material.

THAT Question so much debated, and so tediously pursued by some, *Whether God by his Almighty Power cannot superad to our Idea of Matter a Faculty of Thinking?* is shamefully trifling and frivolous, unbecoming Men of common Sence; but much more Philosophers and Metaphysicians. The very Question supposes that Matter hath nothing of Thinking in its *Own Nature*, and this is readily owned

by

by them; becaufe of that plain Confequence, That if Thinking were *Natural* to Matter, then every *Particle* and every *Syftem* of it would Think: So that the Queftion can have no more Meaning in it than this, Whether God can *Alter* the very Nature of Matter, fo as that it fhall be Matter and not Matter at the fame time? Whether he can make the fame Thing to be a *Thinking*, and *Unthinking* Being at the fame time? To make the Queftion Sence it muft be, Whether God created Matter with an *Aptitude* and Capacity to Think in any *Particular Contexture*, or *Combination* of its Particles into any Syftem whatfoever; or by the Addition of any peculiar *Motion* added to it? But if fo, then Thinking would be a *Primary Effential* Quality of Matter, whenever it fubfifted under that particular requifite Difpofition or Motion of Parts; and then again do but *Change* this Difpofition of its Parts, and put them into *Another* Motion or Situation, which are things merely *Accidental* to it, then it lofes that effential Quality of Thinking: And thus the fame Faculty fhall be *Effential* and *Not effential*; *Accidental* and *Not accidental* to the fame thing. So that now the Doubt is neceffarily refolved into the firft Sencelefs Queftion again, Whether Almighty Power cannot fuperad to Matter an *Effential* Quality which is *Unnatural* to it?

I F

IF Men should give themselves up to the starting such Questions about every thing in Nature and Religion, Whether Almighty Power cannot alter every Thing from what it is, and make it something else; what Jargon would they make of Philosophy and Divinity? The true Question is, What Almighty Power *Hath* done, and not what it *Can* do? Sure they must be very zealous for the Materiality of the Soul who raise a Question, Whether God may not interpose his Almighty Power to work *Against* Nature, and alter the general Laws, and Properties, and Course of it in every Man that is born. To support the Affirmative of this Question they define a Spirit a *Thinking Substance*, designedly leaving a Fallacy in the Dubiousness of the Word *Substance*; and thereby disingenuously confounding all Distinction between *Material* and *Immaterial Being*, which is all we can mean by *Substance* when apply'd to Spirit. The *Tendency* of that way of arguing is, to *Conclude* our Souls material; for if it is as easy for God to superad to Matter a *Power* of Thinking, as to superad a spiritual *Substance* or Being; then the latter is altogether *Unnecessary*, and therefore *Improbable*.

IF it is here said, that since even *sensitive Perception* is not originaly *Essential* to Matter as such, it is as easy for us to imagine that

the

the almighty Power of **God** may fuperad
a *Property* of *Thinking* to **Matter**, as a Property of *Senfitive Perception*; **I** anfwer, that
no Man can with any Truth, or Juftice to his
own Mind fay, that it is as *Eafy* and *Natural*
for him to imagine the one as the other; or
that he conceives no greater **Abfurdity** and **In-**
confiftency in the former, than in the latter: **For**,
however unknown the *Reafon* may be, and
how little foever we are able to account for it,
the mind of Man cannot but furmife that
thefe two things are not equaly probable and
rational; fo that at firft fight the **Objection**
carries in it fomething of *Unfairnefs* and *Dif-
ingenuity*.

Bu**t** on the contrary, our **Reafon** and **Ima-**
gination do both of them readily fuggeft to us
this wide difference between *Thinking* and *Senfation*; that the firft, and not the latter, muft
be originaly an *Effential* **Quality** in whatever
Being it is found: For if we did not naturaly
conceive it as fuch, Men would never have
attributed it without **Scruple** to the *Effence*
of *Spirits* in general, and to *God* in particular;
to whom they never yet ventur'd to attribute fenfitive Perception, otherwife than in
pure Metaphor. So that we cannot imagine
Thinking to be fuperadded to mere *Matter*
under any Modification, or Contexture, or
Motion whatfoever, otherwife than as an *Effential* Q *uality*, not only *Above* the Nature of it;
but

but even so *Contrary* to it, that the superinducing of it upon mere Matter muft imply this Contradiction, that it fhall be Matter and not Matter at the fame time ; and muft confound all the commonly received Differences and fettled Diftinctions in the Mind, not only between the Nature of *Man* and that of all irrational *Animals*, but alfo between thefe and all purely *Spiritual Beings* ; nay, between thefe laft and the whole Race of *Infects*, even the very loweft of them that are endued with Life, or Senfe, or Motion.

IF it is further urged, that *Senfitive Perception* is effential to *Brutes* (which on my Suppofition are mere Matter) tho' not effential to the *Parts* of that *Matter* of which they are compos'd; and therefore the fuperadding even this effential Quality muft change the Nature of Matter, and make it quite another Thing from what it was before; fo that the fame Contradiction holds here as in the fuperadding of *Thinking* to it, namely that it fhall be Matter and not Matter at the fame time. The Anfwer is obvious, that fenfitive Perception is *Effential* to Brutes not as they are *Matter* ; but as they are a Syftem of Matter under a *Certain Modification*, and *Contexture*, and *Motion* of its Parts, by which they are adapted and difpofed to receive certain Impreffions from external Objects : But that all this is unravelled again, and intirely ceafeth
with

with the diffolution of the Frame; whereas
we neceffarily conceive *Thinking* not only original and effential to the Thinking *Subftance*,
but *Inseparable* from it.   *Senfitive Perception*
therefore cannot be called effential to Brutes,
in the fame Sence that we conceive *Thinking*
effential to the Soul of Man; nor can it be
faid to be *Superadded* to Matter, in the fame
Sence that fome Men fuppofe Thinking may
be fo: Nor can we fuppofe the Abfurdity and
Contradiction to be the fame in both Suppo-
fitions; there being no Propriety in that Phrafe
of *Senfitive Perception being fuperadded to Mat-*
ter; any more than in faying, that *Motion and*
Sound are fuperadded to the Matter of a Clock.
Motion and Sound are effential to a *Clock*, but
not to the *Matter* of it.

I AM aware of the laft great Objection
which lies againft this whole way of arguing;
that from thence it will be inferr'd, that all
Senfitive Perception in *Brutes* muft intirely differ from that which is *Human*, and be quite
of another *Kind*; fo as to be a refemblance only,
or a fort of Imitation of our Senfations.   I
fhall make no other reply to this, than to leave
the Objection as I find it.   For I don't know
why we may not allow *Senfitive Perception* in
Brutes, to be fomething correfpondent only
and *Analogous* to Senfation in Man, as natural
Inftinct is to *Reafon*.   Their Senfations may
be all as *Real* as ours, and yet be of a very
I   different

different *Kind*; and that they are fo, is more than probable, fince it is plain they can have no fuch *Confcioufnefs* of their own Senfations as we have of ours; nor have they any *Knowledge* of them properly fo call'd, as we have; nor have their Senfations any immediate effential Concurrence of *Spirit* as thofe which are human: So that fince this feems to be the Cafe, all the Impreffions made upon the Organs of Senfation in Brutes, and the Ideas confequent to thofe Impreffions are realy to be confidered as abftractedly and as much feparated from any Concurrence or Obfervation of a true Principle of *Reafon* and Underftanding, as the Sound and Motions of a *Clock*. And for this reafon I would have it remark'd here, that whenever I ufe the Words *Knowledge*, or *Difcerning*, or *Diftinguifhing*, or *Action*, as applied to Brutes; I don't mean that they have any fuch Powers properly fpeaking as thofe which are called by the fame Names in Mankind: But only that thefe are the beft *Analogous* Notions and Words we have, to reprefent thofe *Movements* of theirs which feem to *Mimick* the *Actions* and Faculties of Men.

BUT however this may be, yet the Obfervation arifing from thence is very natural; that thofe Men run into an unreafonable Extreme on the other hand, who to avoid the Souls of Brutes being immaterial, will have them to be no other than a more refin'd and
complicated

complicated fort of *Engines* or *Inftruments*; and call them mere *Machines*, or *Puppets*, or *Clock-work*; as if the Wifdom and Power of the great Creator in the Difpofition of Matter and Motion, were to be directed by the Rules of our Mechanics; and confined to obferve the Meafures of human Artifice and Contrivance. As if God could not, after an *Inconceivable* manner, work up a Syftem of mere Matter into a Brute; and by a curious Difpofition and Contexture of all its Parts, vaftly out of the reach of our Comprehenfion, could not render it in a peculiar manner fufceptible of fuch Motions and Impreffions from external material Objects, as may be the impulfive Caufe of all that variety of Actions we fee in them; and particularly of thofe which have fo near and lively a Refemblance of our human Senfations. So that all the Arguments to prove Brutes mere *Machines* and *Engines*, in the common Acceptation of thofe Terms, are precarious and imaginary; and the Words carry with them an odious tho' tacit Comparifon between the Art and Contrivance of Man, and the infinite Power and Wifdom of God, whenever they are ufed otherwife than as bare *Illuftrations* only of the Actions of Brutes; after which manner alone I would have them underftood wherever they occur in this part of my Difcourfe.

THEY who hold *Senſitive Perception* in Brutes to be an argument of the *Immateriality* of their Souls, find themſelves under a Neceſſity of allowing thoſe Souls to be *Naturaly Immortal* likewiſe; and they are ſo embaraſſed in thinking how to diſpoſe of thoſe *Irrational Immortal* Souls after the Diſſolution of their Bodies, and what ſort of Immortality to contrive for them, that they imagine them all to return into the great Soul or Spirit of the World; or by a *Metempſychoſis* to paſs into the Bodies of ſucceeding Animals; and then when they have done their Work, at the End of the World they are to be diſcharged out of Being, and again reduced to their primitive Nothing.

BUT if thoſe Souls are once granted to be *Immaterial,* it is utterly inconceivable that they ſhould not *Naturaly* have the ſame *Immortality* with thoſe which are Human; ſince we cannot with any Sence or Conſiſtency diſtinguiſh two *Different* Kinds of Immortality for created Spirits. If the Soul of Brutes is Immortal, *That* cannot, when ſeparated, be thought to remain altogether in a State of utter Inactivity and Inſenſibility, which communicated Senſe and Activity to Matter while in Conjunction with it. And if ſo, they muſt be ſenſible of *Happineſs* or *Miſery*; and in ſome Degree liable to Rewards and Puniſhments, as eternal as their Souls.

3 WHAT

WHAT heightens the Abfurdity of this Way of Thinking is, that in imagining the Souls of Brutes to be Immaterial, Men muſt necef-farily diſtinguiſh a great *Variety* of them both in Nature and Degree ; one ſort for *Birds*, an-other for *Beaſts*, and another for *Fiſhes*. And theſe muſt be all ſubdivided again into very different Species of immaterial Souls, according to the different Sorts there are under each of thoſe general Heads. Nay every *Fly* and *Inſect* muſt on this Suppoſition have ſome ſort of im-material Soul, even down to the *Cheeſe Mite*; and what is yet more abſurd is, that there muſt be an infinite Variety of *Immortalities* imagin'd to ſuit the Rank and Condition of every indivi-dual, living, ſenſible Creature.

I SHALL conclude this Head of the *Simple Apprehenſion* or intellectual *View* of the Mind which follows upon Senſation, when I obſerve that the Reaſon why the Intellect, which takes a clear and diſtinct View of ſuch numberleſs Objects of Senſe in their Ideas ; hath not how-ever the leaſt obſcure or indiſtinct direct Appre-henſion or ſimple Intuition of a *Pure Spirit* ; is, becauſe we neither have an immediate *Conſci-ouſneſs*, nor a *Direct* ſenſible *Perception* of any thing relating to the Nature of ſuch a Being ; nor can there be any *Idea* of it, to be view'd in the Imagination ; which is however Capa-cious enough to take in all viſible Nature, and
to

to ftore up an immenfe Number of Ideas of all Objects which occur to the Senfes. What an amazing Variety of them are daily conveyed in by that one Senfe of *Seeing*? to which if we add thofe of the other Senfes, we fhall render the Number inexhauftible; and yet nothing of all thefe is properly Knowledge, confider'd in themfelves, and abftractedly from that Intuition or *View* taken of them by the pure Intellect: They are only the rude and unwrought Materials, heaped together for that Superftructure which every Man is to raife according to the peculiar Difpofition of his natural Genius, the different Methods he purfues, and the Degrees of that Application of the Intellect which he ufes.

C H A P. III.

The fecond Operation of the pure Intellect, That of Judgment.

THE fecond Operation of the pure Intellect upon the Ideas of Senfation is commonly called the *Judgment* it paffes upon them. Becaufe my Purpofe is not to go thro' the Art of Logic in general, but to trace the Rife, and Progrefs, and Extent of our Knowledge, more efpecialy as it relates to *Religion* and the things of another World; I fhall not enlarge upon this Operation as far as the

Nature

Nature of it requires, nor am I willing wholy to pass it by.

THE great Variety of Ideas of Sensation which is conveyed to the Imagination and lodged there, is not for the sole guidance and direction of us, by any inward *Instinct*, or *Impulse* of theirs; and in order to remain there always unviewed and unobserved by any higher Principle; which is the Condition of Brutes. Nor are they there only for the naked View and *Simple Intuition* of the Mind which is its first Operation upon them; but as Subjects for the *Farther* Employment of our Understanding and Will; for Observation and Judgment; for all our Inferences, Discourses, and Reasonings; for the Exercise of all the Faculties of an human Soul; and for Ingredients which go into the Composition of all those *Complex Notions* and Conceptions which the Mind raises up to itself for its own use, and to supply the Want of *Simple* and *Original Ideas:* Insomuch that it hath an arbitrary Sway and sovereign Power over them; and they are subject to the Exercise of all its Operations at pleasure. Concerning these Ideas and the several Operations of the Mind upon them, these Mistakes are common among Logicians, and some Writers of Metaphysics.

THO' they rightly lay down *Ideas* as the only Materials for the Mind to work upon; yet

THE UNDERSTANDING. **177**

yet they do it in the *General,* without limiting
them to thofe of *Senfation* only ; and without
exploding and rejecting fuch as are falfly fuppofed to be *Purely Intellectual,* and equaly *O-
riginnl*; and which are imagined by fome to
come into the Mind another way than by Senfation or Reflection; all which are accordingly
thought to be (in common with thofe of Senfe)
the firft Ground-work and Materials of our
Knowledge. As thefe laft are not mentioned
in their Introductions to the Art of Reafoning,
which they muft and ought to be, if they believed there were any fuch Ideas; fo neither is
there any *Provifion* made for the real want of
thefe purely intellectual Ideas, thro' their whole
Syftems. This fure is an inexcufable Omiffion,
and a fundamental *Defect,* both in the old and
new Logic; that they make no Provifion for
explaining the true Manner of coming to the
moft excellent Part of our Knowledge, that
of things *Divine* and *Immaterial.* This muft
be either by Ideas of them *Purely Intellectual*;
or by Ideas of *Reflection*; or by the help of
thofe of Senfation formed into *Complex Notions,*
by confidering them together with the Operations of the Mind; and then fubftituting thefe
Notions *Analogicaly* to reprefent things Immaterial. Now the two firft of thefe Methods
are merely *Imaginary,* and have no Foundation in Nature or Reafon; and the laft is intirely omitted by the Writers of Logic; who
not knowing where to fix the *Rife* and true

N   *Manner*

Manner of our fpiritual Knowledge and Conceptions, have made it over to be treated of in *Metaphyfics,* under the firft mention'd Head of Ideas *Purely Spiritual* and *Intellectual*; with much Obfcurity and Confufion, and with very little, or no real Improvement of human Underftanding.

OTHERS confound thofe original Ideas of Senfation, with the Operations of the Mind upon them, fo far, that they fancifully lay down thofe Operations as a new Set of original Ideas for the Mind to work upon. What an aukward Abfurdity is this? The fame thing fhall be an *Idea,* and the *Operation* of the Mind upon an Idea at the fame time; and thus we muft have a new Idea for another fecond Operation, and fo on *In Infinitum.* And this new Set of Ideas is expreffed by a Term as abfurd, an *Idea of Reflection*; a hard Word without any real or determinate Meaning. If they had diftinguifhed them in plain Language, into Ideas of *Senfe,* and Ideas of *Reafon,* (which they might with equal good Senfe have done) all the Amufement would ceafe; becaufe every Body could then fee that *Reafon* is the Operating of the Mind upon our *Ideas*; and fome Ideas muft therefore neceffarily be *Prefuppofed,* either thofe of the pure Intellect, or of Senfation, or of both.

AND

AND laſtly, whereas this of *Judgment* is a very *Complicated* Operation, and conſiſts of many Particulars, which if enlarged upon and treated of with Diſtinctneſs and Perſpicuity, would contribute much to the Direction of our Underſtanding in the purſuit of Knowledge: Yet theſe are ſlightly paſſed over and reſolved immediately into *Propoſition* and *Enuntiation* ; whereas theſe latter ſhould be treated of ſeparately from Judgment, and under a diſtinct Head. For the Operations of the Mind compriſed under that of its Judgments, may be without any *Actual* Affirmation or Negation. If it is ſaid that Propoſitions are the Judgments of the *Mind* reduced to Sentences ; I grant it, but theſe are as *Accidental* to the *Inward* Judgments of the Intellect, as Words or Terms are to the Ideas in the Imagination, and ſhould be treated of with the ſame Diſtinction ; beſides that ſome of the Operations comprehended under that general Name, do not admit of any Affirmation or Negation. I ſhall inſtance in ſome of the chief of thoſe Operations of the pure Intellect upon our Ideas, which I include under this Head of Judgment.

1. THAT of *Separating* them from one another, and *Ranging* them into any order at Will. Our Ideas lie originaly in the Imagination, in the ſame confuſed and diſorderly Manner, in

which

which outward Objects from our Infancy happen to ftrike upon our Senfes; and would always continue in the very fame fituation, if they were not in the Power of the Intellect to difpofe and manage at pleafure: By *Singling* out one or more from the reft, for a more *Diftinct* and *Particular View* and Confideration; by *Sorting* and *Tranfpofing* them for any Purpofes of the Mind; and particularly *Ranging* them under feveral diftinct *Heads* or Kinds for the forming *Univerfal* Ideas; as when the Ideas of all Men we have, and have not feen, are reprefented by the Idea of *One* Man, which ftands for all *Mankind.*

THE Ideas of Senfation in Brutes lie within them unremoved, and their fituation is unchangeable; they cannot put them out of the order wherein they were tranfmitted thro' the Senfes; becaufe they are purely paffive, not only in the *Reception* of all their Ideas, as we are; but in that Inftigation and *Impulfe* of thofe Ideas which excites and prompts them to all their Operations. Their Ideas being, as ours are, the Impreffions only of one Part of *Matter* upon another; and there being no active immaterial Principle within them to change their Pofition, they muft neceffarily remain thus fix'd and *Unalterable* while they laft; as fo many Figures of a Seal impreffed upon Wax.

2. AN-

2. ANOTHER inftance is that of *Comparing* our Ideas one with another, to mark and obferve their *Agreements* and *Difagreements* in every particular, whether effential or accidental to them; as when the Idea of a *Tree* and that of an *Horfe* are compar'd in refpect of their *Vegetative* and *Animal* Life; in refpect of the *Circulation* of the *Sap* in one, and of the *Blood* and *Spirits* in the other. This Operation ought to be diftinguifhed from that of confidering the *Relations* they bear to one another, which is but one particular way of comparing them; the *Likenefs* and *Unlikenefs* of Ideas, their *Agreements* and *Difagreemnnts*, are things different from their mutual *Relations* in all other Inftances, and their *Dependences* upon one another; and therefore thefe are of a diftinct and feparate Confideration.

BRUTES do not *Compare* in any degree; for as they have a bare *Senfation* only of the Object, and not even a fimple *Apprehenfion* of its Idea within them, diftinct from that Senfation; fo they can never attend to more than *One* Idea at once; they muft necefFarily advert to their Ideas fuccefFively one after another, and feparately; but can never put two or more Ideas together to make a *Comparifon*. If they had any Power for fuch a Performance within them, we fhould fee them actualy put two or more outward *Objects* together;

gether, as we do, for their more convenient
and eafy diftinguifhing. Brutes may indeed
be *Said* to *Difcern* the difference between two
or more Objects which are prefent to their
Senfes; and to diftinguifh them in fome fenfible
Circumftances which immediately ftrike upon
them: But this is not *Comparing Ideas*, no
nor their *Objects*, even when they are *Prefent*;
nor is it any thing of the fame nature with
Difcerning in Man; for they diftinguifh thofe
Objects no otherwife than by being moft *In-
fluenc'd* and *Moved* by fuch of them as do
make the ftrongeft, and moft vigorous, or the
moft frequent and lafting Impreffions upon
their Senfes.

3. A THIRD inftance is that of the Intellect's *Enlarging* or *Diminifhing* thofe Ideas in
any Proportion whatfoever. When we have
looked upon a Tree we can fhut our Eyes,
and enlarge the Idea we have of it to any *Size*,
even to reach the Clouds; or diminifh it in
our Thoughts till we reduce it to what it was
in its firft Principle or Seed. This is what a
Brute can't do; it cannot enlarge or diminifh
the Idea of an Object which is even prefent to
the Senfe; fo far is it from being able to make
the Idea of it larger or fmaller, that it neceffarily retains it juft as it was received from the
Senfe. For *Mere Senfation* is but the *Action*
or *Impreffion* of material Objects, upon Organs
which are material; and the Ideas of Brutes

are

are caus'd only by the Impreſſion of the animal Spirits from thoſe Organs upon the Imagination; that is upon the moſt ſpirituous and
refin'd Parts of the animal Frame, diſpoſed by
Nature for the common Reception of thoſe
Impreſſions; and therefore a *Simple Idea* can
receive no Alteration whatſoever in Brutes but
what comes from the external Object; and
this can make no Impreſſion but according to
its own natural Bulk and Size.

So that in order to a Poſſibility of *Enlar-*
ging or *Diminiſhing* any one Idea, we muſt
neceſſarily ſuppoſe ſome *Principle* diſtinct from
Matter, and *Superior* to it; that is ſome immaterial Principle which hath a Power over
thoſe Ideas that mere *Matter* cannot have. If
a Brute could enlarge or diminiſh an Idea in
the leaſt degree, it is eaſy to conceive it muſt
be able to do ſo in any Proportion; for the
ſame Power or Faculty that enabled it to *Be-*
gin that Operation, muſt enable it to *Carry*
it *On* farther; the firſt Act of enlarging or diminiſhing being equaly, if not more difficult,
than a proceeding in it, and as intirely independent of all Matter and Senſation. To
which I ſhall add, that the Senſations of Brutes
are all the *Direction* they have for their Pre-
ſervation and Safety; and if they could thus
Diſguiſe them, by *Altering* the *Size* and *Pro-*
portion of their Ideas; thoſe Ideas would not

N 4   anſwer

anſwer the *Ends* of Nature, but *Miſguide* them in all their Operations.

4. ANOTHER Act of the pure Intellect comprehended under its judging of Ideas, is that of *Dividing* and *Compounding* them. A ſimple Idea, as hath been obſerved, is not that only which is intirely *Adequate* to what it repreſents, and *Indiviſible* into more Ideas of the *Same Kind*; but that which is taken in with any Diſtinctneſs by *One ſingle* Act or O-peration of one and the ſame Senſe; ſuch as that of an *Horſe* or a *Tree*; and this may be ſub-divided into more Ideas of the ſeveral *Parts* and the Idea of each Part may be viewed and conſider'd ſeparately by the Mind. This is utterly out of the Power of Brutes; a Dog which firſt hath had one view of his Maſter may, while he is preſent, look at his Face, and afterwards at his Feet, or at any other part of him ſucceſſively; but this is not *Subdividing* the *Idea* of an human Body into the Ideas of its Parts: For when the Dog's Eyes are ſhut, or the Man diſappears, he is utterly incapable of this Subdiviſion in the *Abſence* of the Object.

THE Power of the Intellect is no leſs in *Compounding* its Ideas either in the *Whole*, as when it compounds the Ideas of many Trees to make up a Wood; or of many Houſes to make up that of a City: Or in *Part*, when it ſeparates the Parts of different Ideas to frame

a new

a new *Compofition* out of them. And this is done either *According* to Nature, as when the Ideas of the Stem and many Branches are put together to make up that of a Tree ; or *Againft* Nature, as when part of an Horfe and part of an human Body are united into a Centaur ; which latter fort have been well called *Chimerical.*

BRUTES can no more *Compound* than they can *Divide* ; for all Senfation is of *Particulars* and therefore fo muft the Ideas be which are confequent to it. What is there in *Them* which fhould unite any of thofe Particulars into one *Compound* Idea ? Not the external *Objects,* which can each of them make but one fingle Impreffion of themfelves ; nor the *Organ* of Senfe, which receives the Impreffions fingly, and tranfmits them fo to the Imagination, which alfo being material retains them juft as they are tranfmitted from the Senfes. So that nothing can put two or more of them together into one compound Idea but fome Principle fuperior to Matter, and to all that the Object hath any Aptitude or Power to work either upon the Organ of Senfation, or upon the Imagination. It hath been urged that a Dog compounds the *Shape,* and *Smell,* and *Voice,* to make up a *Compound* Idea of its *Mafter* ; and that it knows him by all three at *Once,* which, as I have obferved, is not true : However were it fo, this would be a compounding

of

of inward Ideas only in the *Presence* of the outward Objects of them; so that unless the Dog could unite those three Ideas in the *Absence* of his Master to make up *One* Idea of him, it is not properly that compounding which is the Privilege and Power of an human Intellect.

CHAP. IV.

Of Abstraction.

ANOTHER Act of the pure Intellect in relation to the Ideas of Sensation commonly reduced to this head of Judgment is said to be *Abstraction*, which is usualy distinguished into two Sorts, and both of them equaly groundless.

I. THE first is a *Logical* Abstraction in order to form *General* Ideas; which is thought to be performed by withdrawing the Mind intirely from all the *Individuals*, and then forming one single Idea which shall represent the *Whole* Kind or Species at once; as when we remove our Thoughts intirely from all the Individuals of *Men*, and frame to our selves one general Idea distinct from them all to represent the whole Race. And these *General abstract* Ideas shall, in the modern refined Method of forming them, prove the strangest and most inconsistent confiftent *Monfters* in the World. Thus the *General abftract Idea* of *Man*, fhall not be of a black or white, fhort or tall, thick or flender Man; but fhall be *All* thefe and *None* of them at the *Same* time: The general abftract Idea of a Triangle fhall be neither of an *Equilateral*, nor *Equicrural*, nor *Scalenum*; neither *Oblique* nor *Rectangle*, but all and none of thefe at once:

Now this is utterly impracticable, and therefore Abftraction in this Sence is a hard Word and without any determinate Meaning; for if the Intellect abftracts from all the Ideas of every Individual, it can have no Idea at all left to operate upon. When we fay *Mankind*, it expreffeth no one *Diftinct*, *Abftract*, *General* Idea which ftands in the Mind for all the Individuals at once; but it fignifies the Idea of *One Individual*, which is no otherwife made general, than by our conceiving all the reft of the fame Kind *By* that one; fo that in truth it is the fingle Idea of any one Individual which is made to ftand for and reprefent the whole Species. There is no fuch thing in Nature as any *Univerfal* realy *Exifting*, either to ftrike upon our Senfes, or to be an Object of our Reafon; and confequently there can be no fuch general abftract Idea in the Mind. If there were any fuch, it would be equaly *Simple* and *Original* with that of one Individual; and, which is yet more abfurd, whether fuch an

Idea

Idea were fuppos'd to be from *Nature*, or from *Abftraction*, or *Creation* of the *Intellect*, it would neceffarily imply this plain Abfurdity, That it would not only be both a *Particular* and *Univerfal* Idea, as you differently *Confider'd* it, which is very allowable and may be true; but it would be actualy and *In itfelf* both a *Simple* and *Compounded* Idea at the *Same* time, which is downright Contradiction; *Simple*, as it reprefented the whole *Kind* at once, in one fimple Idea *abftracted* from all the Individuals; and *Compounded* as it *Included* them all.

AND now we may have leave to wonder at thofe Perfons, who fingle out this fort of *Imaginary Abftraction* for the only perfect Diftinction between *Men* and *Brutes*; and chufe to place the only Difference between them in that fort of Abftraction which one would think could never enter into the Head of *Man* or *Beaft*. Nay we may with good reafon fay, that of all the Operations of the pure Intellect they are leaft diftinguifhable in this of making the Idea of one Individual ftand for all of the fame Kind, which is the *True* Abftraction. When we have an Idea of one particular Man, this ferves us to diftinguifh the whole *Species* from any other: And thus far even Brutes feem to approach to this Power, namely, that the Idea of a *Particular Man* whom a Dog for inftance hath feen, ferves in his Imagination

where-

whereby to distinguish any *Individual* of the *Same* Species, (as often as it is excited again by the *Presence* of any other Man) from the Individuals of any *Other* Species.

IF Men had said that tho' Brutes distinguish every Individual as it is an *Outward Object*, and as it actualy presents itself to the *Sense*; yet this is not distinguishing *Ideas* in *The Absence* of all the Individuals, or making one Idea or Conception stand for the Ideas or Conceptions of them *All.* That they can't any way distinguish one whole *Species* from another; much less discern any determinate essential Property, wherein *All* the Individuals agree; as Rationality in Man. And lastly, that they cannot distinguish even between the *Individuals*, but in such Qualities as depend upon actual outward *Sensation*; whereas Men can distinguish between both the *Species* and *Individuals* in things intirely independent of all outward Sensation. If these things, I say, had been urged, they would indeed have made a perfect Distinction in this respect between Men and Brutes. But for Men to allow Brutes *Reason* in common with Mankind, that is, allow them to be reasonable Creatures; and yet afterwards to place the Distinction between them and us in a sort of Abstraction which is altogether *Irrational*; is no other than first *Raising* Brutes up to the Dignity of human Nature, and then *Degrading* Mankind below it.

4   I HOPE

I HOPE from what I have said it is reasonably plain how false and groundless that Opinion is, which afferts, that *Brutes do some of them reason in certain Inflances, as furely as they have Senfe. And, that if they have any Ideas at all, we cannot deny them to have fome Reafon.* But if *Some* Brutes reafon, why not *All* Brutes? Or which are thofe Brutes which do reafon, and which do not? Which are the rational Brutes, and which are irrational? Again, which are the certain Inftances in which they do reafon, and which are to be referr'd to pure Inftinct? Surely if fome of them have reafon, they all have more or lefs of it; it is fure they are all directed in their Operations by one common Principle, whether that be *Reafon* or *Inflinct*; which laft is no other than the prompting and Impulfe of Ideas from the Impreffion of outward Objects.

IF you grant they have *Some* degree of Reafon, it will be hard to tell why they have not a *Greater* degree of it; for they have as many Senfes as Men, and generaly more acute; and confcquently have all their Ideas more diftinct than we have. Ideas of Senfation are the only original Groundwork of all *Our* Knowledge; and if Brutes have all the *Materials* which we have, and can *Reafon* upon them, what fhould hinder them from attaining

taining to the fame degrees of *Knowledge* which we have? What trifling is it to fay they reafon but a *Little?* They compare their Ideas but a *Little?* They compound them but a *Little?* For fince material Objects can caufe Ideas by making Impreffions of themfelves, but no mere Matter can operate upon thofe Ideas after they are once form'd ; then the caufe that we reafon more, and Brutes lefs, muft be, either becaufe their *Organs* are not fo well difpofed to act in Conjunction with an immaterial Principle; or becaufe the immaterial Principle in them is of a very *Diminutive* Kind ; or not *Quite* fo immaterial perhaps as ours. They who ftretch their Zeal fo far for making *Men* of Brutes, are the very Perfons who labour to make *Brutes* of Men ; and will have the *Soul* of Man to be nothing but *Matter* with a Faculty of Thinking *Superadded* to it: And if fo, the Soul of a Brute, according to them, muft be Matter with *Reafon* fuperadded to it; for Thinking and Reafon fignify the fame thing.

I⊤ is confeffed then by thefe Men, that *Thinking* is a Faculty that is not originaly in the Nature of Matter, but *Superadded* ; and if fo then it is a Faculty *Above* the Nature of it, and therefore *Contrary* to the Nature of it. But it implies no Contradiction, fay they ; no more, fay we, than that God fhould make the fame thing to be *Matter*, and *No Matter* at

the

the fame time; no more than in fuppofing
that Almighty Power fhould take away *Know-*
ledge from a pure Spirit, and fuperad *Gravity*
or *Solidity* to is; that is fhould make it fomething elfe, and not Spirit. To which I may
add this Contradiction farther, That the fame
Faculty of Reafon fhall be *Effential* to a Syftem
of Matter, and yet only *Accidental* and *Super-*
added to that fame Syftem by almighty Power;
for that *Thinking* is *Effential* to *Man* I hope
will be allowed by thofe, who contend for the
Poffibility of its being *Superadded* to *Brutes.*

WHAT Extremes thefe Advocates for Brutes
run into? They attribute *Thinking* to Beings
purely *Immaterial*, to Angels, and to God
himfelf; whereas it is properly the joint Act
or Operation of pure Spirit and Matter in effential *Conjunction*; and on the other hand
they attribute Thinking or Reafon both to
Men and Brutes as *Mere Matter*, without any
Union with an immaterial Subftance; and
both with equal Abfurdity. That which deceives Men in this latter Opinion is, that in
all their Reafonings in favour of Brutes, they
ever confound the actual *Perception* thefe have
of outward *Objects*, with the Knowledge we
have of the *Ideas* of thofe Objects after they
are lodged in the Imagination: Whereas the
fimple *Apprehenfion* of the Mind; *Judging* in
all its Inftances; *Reafoning*, and all the Operations of the Intellect are moftly imploy'd
and

and exercifed immediately upon *Ideas*, and not upon their external Objects.

THIS it is which evidently fhews the Neceffity of an immaterial Principle in Man ; for the Action or Impreffion of Matter upon Matter, may occafion many, and very diftinct *Ideas* ; but thefe are as yet nothing more than fo many immediate fenfitive Perceptions of the outward Object conveyed to the Imagination ; which may from within prompt and excite Animals to many Operations : But being only confequent to the fimple Perceptions of the Objects, and not being any *New* Perception or Apprehenfion of the *Ideas* themfelves, it is a Degree of Knowledge which can receive no other Increafe than what proceeds from a Renewal or *Repetition* of the fame or like Impreffions ; unlefs there were a Principle above Matter to apprehend the Ideas themfelves, to judge of them, and to reafon upon them. Without this there can be nothing beyond a bare Perception or Idea of the Object, which is fooner or later worn out as there are new Impreffions of different Objects ; or according to the Difpofition of thofe refined and fpirituous Parts of the Frame which are more immediately fubfervient to the Imagination, the Seat of thofe Ideas.

ALL hitherto is but a naked Perception of the outward Object ; but when thefe Ideas are

once ftamp'd, what fhould begin *Anew* to operate upon them? To take a View of them; to
alter and tranfpofe them at pleafure; to enlarge and diminifh; to divide, compare, and
compound; to draw Inferences from them;
and weigh and confider all their mutual Relations and Dependencies? Surely not *Mere
Matter*, which could do no more than either
Leave Impreffions of itfelf, or *Retain* thofe Impreffions when they are made; and by that
means caufe a fimple bare Perception of the
external Object; but could not proceed one Step
farther towards any *Higher* Operation *Upon* that
Impreffion or Idea.

To clear up what hath been faid, and en-
force this Argument, I fhall reduce the difference between that *Knowledge* and Perfection
which is in us, and that *Perception* which is in
Brutes, to thefe few fhort Obfervations.

1. ALL Knowledge in Brutes is immediately
of the external *Objects* themfelves; but the *Ideas*
of them are the immediate Objects of the Intellect in Man. They have a bare naked Perception of the fenfible *Object* only; we have
a farther Perception or Apprehenfion of the *Idea*
itfelf in Diftinction from the Object and feparate from it. By the *Idea* they apprehend
the *Object*; by the *Intellect* we apprehend the
Idea.

2. THE

2. THE Knowledge of Brutes *Terminates* in Ideas; ours only *Begins* there.

3. THEIR simple Ideas of Senfation are the whole *Extent* of all their Knowledge; whereas they are only the *Groundwork* and firft Materials of ours.

4. IF their Ideas are ever fo little defaced or decayed, they can never be repaired but by a *New* Impreffion of the Object: Ours can be renewed and revived again, when faded, by voluntary Recollection *Without* the Object, which is truly and properly Memory.

5. THEY *Necessarily* follow the Inftinct and Prompting of their fenfitive Ideas in all their Operations; we can regulate all our Operations even in *Oppofition* and contrariety to them.

6. THEY cannot *Alter* the Nature, or Proportion, or Difpofition of any of their Ideas; we can *Tranfpofe*, and *Alter*, and *Compound* them even *Againft* Nature.

II. THE other fort of Abftraction is called *Metaphyfical*, and is faid to be perform'd by taking the Mind intirely off from all the Objects, or rather *Ideas* of Senfation, and all its Compofitions out of them; and from all thofe *Complex Notions* and Conceptions of things in

O 2   this

this World, which are made up of Ideas of
Senfe confidered together with the Mind's operations upon them; in order to form *Abftract*
Ideas of *Heavenly* Things and *Incorporeal* Beings.   But this is utterly impracticable in this
Life, as any one may find upon a Trial; after the utmoft Efforts of the pureft Intellect to
conceive or frame fuch an *Abftract* Idea, he will
find his Attempt vain and trifling.   If any one
fuch Idea could be affigned, and a proper Name
found out for it, we might the lefs wonder
how Men could purfue this Notion fo far as
they do, to the great Hinderance of true Knowledge, and Perplexity of human Underftanding.

IF we *Abftract* intirely from *Material* Subftance and its Properties, we fhould have no
Idea nor indeed Confcioufnefs of *Being* at all ;
for that could never enter into the Mind without the Idea of fomething actualy Exifting upon which to exercife our Thoughts; and fince
the Mind can directly perceive nothing actualy
exifting but what is Material, our very Idea of
Exiftence muft take its firft Rife from thence. If
we abftract totaly and intirely from *Thinking*,
we can have no Conception at all of the *Knowledge* of any *Incorporeal* Being ; therefore *Thinking*, which is the joint Operation of pure Spirit and Body united, is the beft Notion and *Reprefentation* we can have of that Knowledge,
which is performed without any Concurrence
or

or Communication with Matter. If we abstract, I say, intirely from our *Thinking*, which includes the Labour of the Brain; we could form no Notion or Conception of the *Wisdom* of Spirits in general, much less of the Wisdom of God; and therefore for *Want* of any such abstract Notion or Idea, which Men are pleas'd to speak so much of, we are forced to substitute that of our *Thinking*, to represent an inconceivable *Correspondent Perfection* which is in God. So if we totaly abstract from the Notion of *Power* in Man, we shall have neither a Word, Idea, or Notion left for that incomprehensible Perfection in God called by the same Name; and thus it is with his *Goodness*, and with all other Perfections which we attribute to him.

THE Case is the very same in the Mysteries of Christianity. If we totaly and intirely abstract from the Ideas or Notions we have of *Father*, *Son*, and *Spirit* in the strictly literal and proper Signification of the Words, when spoke of Men; we can have no Notion or Conception at all of any personal Distinction in the Divine Nature: And therefore it is that God, in Condescention to our only way of Knowledge by the Operations of the Intellect upon Ideas of Sensation, hath thus revealed that Mystery to us for which we could have had no such *Abstract* Notion or Idea; and consequently no Idea or Conception *At all*, if it were not to be conceived by the Mediation and *Substitution* of

such

such as were plain and familiar to us. If we abstract intirely from a *Price*, *Purchase*, or *Redemption* among *Men*; we could have no *Purely Intellectual* or *Abstract* Notion or Idea of the real worth and value of the Blood of Christ to obtain Salvation for us; and consequently no Notion or Idea at all of it: Therefore this Mystery is reveal'd to us under that Analogical or borrowed Conception among *Us*, which is most suitable and answerable to the Nature of that *Divine* Price or Purchase; to that Value and Merit which, as it is in its own Nature, is utterly incomprehensible to us. And lastly, should we abstract intirely from the Notion we have of a *Man's* interceding to a Prince, in behalf of a Criminal; we should have no Notion or Idea left in the Mind to represent that *Intercession*, which Christ makes in our behalf to God.

THUS I might run thro' all other Instances of Divine Things, and shew how we can form no Ideas or Conceptions of them intirely *Abstracted* from those of *Sensation*, and the *Operations* of our Minds upon them; and that when we *Attempt* to do so, we can neither think nor speak at all of them. The true *Abstraction* (if Men *Will* call it by that Name) consists, not in thus aspiring above the Power and Reach of all human Understanding, and hunting after Ideas or Conceptions of Divine Things and incorporeal Beings intirely abstracted from

all

all Senfation, and totaly independent of it: But in altogether laying afide that vain and fruitlefs Attempt, and in fubftituting the only Notions we have, and which are *Natural*, and *Eafy*, and *Familiar*, to *Reprefent* and *Stand For* thofe immaterial heavenly Things, of whofe real Nature and Properties we can otherwife obtain no Notion or Idea; and in raifing and transferring our Thoughts thus, from the *Literal Strict* Propriety of thofe Words and Phrafes, in which we exprefs them; to that *Analogical Import* and Signification of them, by which they are as it were fanctified and fpiritualized. That is, by confidering each of the Conceptions we thus fubftitute, as reprefenting a real and *Correfpondent*, but *Inconceivable* Nature or Perfection, of which we cannot in our prefent State form any *Abftract Idea* or Notion; or indeed any other Conception at all, than by Mediation of the Ideas and Notions of this World. This is the *True* and only *Abftraction* we are capable of with regard to Things fpiritual; which, we fee, is fo far from being intirely independent of all Ideas of *Senfation*, and the immediate Operations of the Intellect upon *Them* (as fome would have it) that we can no otherwife think and fpeak of fuch Objects than in thefe worldly and human Symbols; and that if we abftract from *Thefe*, we muft at the fame time abftract from *All* thought of heavenly and fupernatural Beings, and can have neither Names nor Ideas for them.

THUS

THUS might we reaffume all the foregoing Inftances, and fhew how we are capable of
no other abftract Notions of the Exiftence and
Attributes of God and pure Spirit, than fuch
analogical Reprefentations as I have defcribed;
unlefs Men will ftill call thefe *Abftract* and
purely *Intellectual Ideas*, becaufe they ftand in
the Mind for what is *Incomprehenfible*, and of
which we can have no proper abftract Ideas or
Notions at all. When we employ our Thoughts
on the Myftery of the *Trinity* for inftance, it
is not to be done by aiming at any *Abftract* intellectual Ideas of that incomprehenfible Unity
and Diftinction in the Divine Nature; which
can never be obtained: But by exercifing our
Mind on thofe *Subftituted Conceptions* in which
that Myftery is revealed to us; by confidering
the familiar Notions of a *Father* and *Son* by
Nature, together with the beft Conception we
can form of our own *Spirit* which is united to
Matter, as the only *Correfpondent* Reprefentations we can have of that Divine Diftinction;
and by taking thofe Terms in the Analogical
Sence, as being expreffive of what is *Anfwerable*, tho' *Still inconceivable* in the Divine Nature.

Now in proceeding thus we muft neceffarily infer, that if this Myftery is revealed to
us under fuch Analogical Refemblances as evidently imply a *Real* and even *Perfonal* Diftinction;

tion; we are to think and speak of it as such, or not think or speak of it at all. I here leave the Reader to run over all the other Mysteries of Christianity in his own Mind; as well as every thing in *Natural* Religion relating to the Nature of God, and the things of another World; and see whether this is not the *True* Abstraction? And whether any thing hath been of more fatal Consequence to Religion, than mistaking it for an airy fanciful Pursuit of *Abstract* Notions, and *Purely Intellectual* Ideas of things altogether imperceptible and inconceivable as they are *In themselves*, by the help of even the most exalted Notions we can form? I shall only give the Hint here, that this true Abstraction, or rather transferring of the Mind from our Ideas and Notions of things temporal, to those spiritual Things which are thus represented by them; holds not only with respect to the *Understanding*, but also the *Will* and *Affections* of an human Soul : Which are never by any *Direct* and *Immediate* Operation employed on *Abstract* intellectual Ideas of heavenly Things; but are then lifted up from Earth to Heaven when they are exercised on our common and natural Ideas or Notions considered as *Types*, which represent answerable inconceivable *Antitypes*. Thus are our *Love*, *Joy*, *Fear*, *Hope*, *Desire*, *Gratitude* employed, not *Immediately* upon any direct Ideas of the real Perfections of *God* or *Heavenly Bliss*, which are incomprehensible ; but upon the Analogous

4   Conceptions

Conceptions we form of the *Goodnefs* and *Power* of God, and of a *Future Blifs*, from the beft Notions of that Goodnefs, and Power, and Happinefs which we experience *Here* : That is in other Words, we employ our Affections on things inconceivable, in their correfpondent Subftitutes alone ; in which cafe the Ideas or Conceptions don't ftand for their *Proper origi-nal* Objects, but are us'd as *Reprefentations* of what is highly exalted above the Reach of all our Faculties. This is the only Method we can arrive to of fanctifying our Affections ; of removing them from things on Earth, and *Set-ting them on things above* ; things *Not feen*, and whereof we can have no *Direct* or *Abftract Ideas* at all.

W H A T hath been faid hitherto of the Ope-rations of the pure Intellect, relates to *Simple* Ideas of Senfation only ; and therefore it will be convenient to obferve here, That the fame Operations are likewife exercifed upon all thofe *Alterations* and *Compofitions* which the Mind raifes up to itfelf out of thofe fimple Ideas ; whether according to Nature, as the Idea of a *Wood* or an *Army* ; or againft Nature, as the Idea of a *Centaur*. When the Imagination is impregnated with thofe voluntary Alterations or Combinations of fimple Ideas, the Mind hath the fame full Power over them, which it had over fuch Ideas as were fimple and origi-nal ; as that of *Intuition* or fimple Apprehen-fion,

fion, and of *Judgment* in all its Inftances of *Comparing*, *Compounding*, *Enlarging*, *Diminifhing*, and *Dividing*. The Mind hath likewife the fame arbitrary Dominion and Sway over all the *Complex Notions* and *Conceptions* which are formed out of thofe fimple or compound Ideas, confidered in Conjunction with the Operations of the Intellect upon them ; fuch as our Notions of *Juftice* or *Charity*, and of all *Virtues* and *Vices*.

BUT what is more Material to be obferved is, that tho' we have no abftract and purely intellectual Ideas of celeftial and immaterial Beings for the Employment and Exercife of any Operations of the Mind : Yet that which fully compenfates the intire want of fuch fpiritual and intellectual Ideas, and ferves all the ends of *Reafon* and *Religion* in this Life is, that thefe Operations are employed and exercifed upon all our Conceptions and complex Notions, in the *Same Manner*, when they are *Symbols* only and *Reprefentations* of things purely fpiritual; as when they immediately reprefent things merely *Human* or *Temporal*. That is, the Mind exercifes all its Faculties and Operations upon its Notions and Conceptions, as well and *Eafily* when the Terms by which they are expreffed are taken in their *Analogical* Sence and Meaning; as when they are confidered in their *Firft* and ftrictly *Proper* Signification; the Mind is equaly converfant

fant with thefe Conceptions when they reprefent their Archetypes, as when it thinks of
them without any farther Reference or Relation to the things of another World. As for
Inftance, the fame Operations of the Intellect
are exercifed upon *Spirit* when it fignifies a
purely *Immaterial* Being, as when it is taken
in its more original Acceptation for our *Soul*,
which is Matter and Spirit in effential Union ;
upon *Knowledge* when it is ufed to reprefent a Perfection of *God*, as when it ftands in
the Mind for that which is *Human*, the only
Knowledge we have any direct or proper Conception of. And fo it is in all other Inftances ;
our intellectual and reafoning Faculties have
the fame full and free Scope and Liberty here;
in *Apprehending*, and *Judging*, and *Inferring*,
which they could have if there were no fecon-
dary or Analogical Acceptation of our Words
and Ideas ; as will more fully appear hereafter.

C H A P. IV.

Of Relation.

THE fixth Inftance of the Mind's Operation upon its Ideas refer'd to the
Head of its *Judgments* is, that of obferving
their mutual *Relations* and *Dependencies*. This
is *Comparing* indeed, but it is in one particular
Inftance

Inſtance only; not in the *Likeneſs* and *Unlikeneſs* of things, which is very different from *Relation* and *Dependency:* For there may be a *Similitude* where there is no *Relation*, and there may be a *Relation* or Dependence where there is no *Similitude*; as that between *God* and *Material Subſtance* which is referred to him as its Creator. I ſhall dwell no longer upon this Operation of the Intellect, than is neceſſary to ſhew the Method and Procedure of human Underſtanding in the Attainment of Knowledge.

1. FIRST then, when the Mind conſiders the mutual Relations and Dependencies between all its Ideas of ſenſible Objects as they are in their own Nature, without any reſpect which they bear to Man as a *Rational* intelligent Agent; from hence there opens a large and ſpacious Field of Knowledge: That of natural *Cauſes* and *Effects*; of the Manner of material Beings *Operating* upon, or *Suffering* from each other; of all their active and paſſive Powers, as ſome expreſs it; and in ſhort of their affecting and influencing one another in innumerable Inſtances; and this is called *Natural Philoſophy.*

BUT here it is worth obſerving, that all the real true Knowledge we have of Nature is intirely *Experimental*; inſomuch that, how ſtrange ſoever the Aſſertion ſeems, we may lay this
down

down as the first fundamental unerring Rule in Physics, *That it is not within the compass of human Understanding to assign a purely speculative Reason for any one Phænomenon in Nature*; as why Grass is green, or Snow is white? Why Fire burns, or Cold congeals? By a *Speculative Reason*, I mean, assigning the true and *Immediate efficient* Cause *A Priori*, together with the manner of its Operation, for any Effect whatsoever purely natural. We find indeed, by Observation and Experience, that such and such Effects *Are* produced; but when we attempt to think of the Reason *Why*, and the *Manner How* the Causes work those Effects, then we are at a Stand; and all our Reasoning is precarious, or at best but probable Conjecture.

I f any Man is surprized at this, let him instance in some speculative Reason he can give for any natural Phænomenon; and how plausible soever it appears to him at first, he will, upon weighing it thoroughly, find it at last resolv'd into nothing more than mere Observation and *Experiment*; and will perceive that those Expressions generaly used to describe the *Cause* or *Manner* of the Productions in Nature, do really signify nothing more than the *Effects*. The most plausible Reason which can in such Cases be assigned, will be found to amount to nothing beyond a bare Comparison or *Analogy* of some *Effects* with others;

as

as when Inferences are made from the Proportion of Velocity in other *Liquids* thro' *Tubes*
of certain Conical Figures, to the Circulation of
the *Blood* and *Spirits* in the *Arteries* and *Veins*
of an human Body. Now tho' this laſt ſhould
be allow'd a plauſible way of *Gueſſing* how far
the Effects may be *Similar* in both; yet what
Certain Scientific Concluſions can poſſibly be
drawn from it, when ſuch a Variety of Cir-
cumſtances, as occur in the complicated Frame
of an human Body, muſt join to render the
Caſes ſo widely *Different*? Or what can be
more groundleſs than to conclude, with a Phi-
loſophic Air of Poſitiveneſs, that becauſe
the ſmalleſt Particles of ſome Medicines which
we can diſcern with Microſcopes, ſeem, when
thus view'd, to reſemble *Wedges, Globes,* &c.
therefore the *Inviſible* Particles of which even
Theſe are compos'd, wou'd be found of the
ſame Figures, were the Cluſters diſſolved and
capable of being thus ſeen: And that conſequently when they are diſſolved in the Hu-
mours of our Body, they muſt act *Mechani-
caly* juſt as a Wedge or Globe, *&c.* does out of
it? All theſe Obſervations may with equal
Juſtice be extended to the Accounts given of
the Mechanical Cauſes and Manner of Motion
and Operation in the *Larger* Bodies of the U-
niverſe; whenever the Terms uſed in ſuch
Treatiſes are pretended to ſignify any thing beyond *Effects* known from Experiment.

FROM

FROM hence we may fee how little that abstracted and Mechanical way of reasoning from the Structure and *Configuration* of the minute Particles in *Medicines*, and of the Solids and Fluids in human Bodies, which obtains so much of late, is like to contribute to advance the Art of Healing ; since it is in Truth no other than running altogether into *Hypotheses*, tho' our modern Mechanical Reasoners profess, at the same time, to reject and explode them utterly. For however they may tell you plausibly in *General*, that the different *Species* and *Effects* of Bodies, with their specific *Qualities* and *Attributes*, proceed from nothing else but the different *Figure, Size, or Motion* of their minute Particles : Yet when you come to *Particular* Instances, and demand of them what that peculiar Configuration, Texture, Size, or Motion of the Particles, for instance, of Flower of *Sulphur*, or *Camphire*, or *Mercury* is, which renders them capable of *Operating* after such and such a manner, and producing such *Effects* in the Solids or Fluids of an human Body, and *How* they act ; you will find them utterly at a Loss. And whoever reads the Mechanical Reasonings of some of our best and most ingenious modern Physicians upon the Operations of those very Medicines, will find them all precarious *Conjecture* ; and nothing more than uncertain *Hypothesis*, dressed up in the Style and

and Form of *Certainty* and *Demonstration*. I cannot forbear therefore mentioning again this Fear and Jealousy of my own, which I am perfuaded is not altogether groundlefs; That there never will be any great and confiderable Advances made in the Art of *Healing*, till all Hypothesis and Mechanical Reafoning is out of Vogue; and till Men are come about again to the ancient Method of pure Experiment, and the common obvious Reafoning intirely from thence.

THUS fhort and imperfect is all our boafted Knowledge of Nature; we are intirely in the dark as to the inward Structure and Compofition of the minute Particles of all Bodies; and can with no degree of Certainty judge or determine any thing concerning them, but from their outward Appearances and fenfible Effects; when we attempt any thing beyond this, all our Reafonings are full of Confufion and Uncertainty. And yet even this purely *Experimental* Knowledge of Nature is however a Degree of it aptly fuited to our prefent State and Condition in this Life; it anfwers all the *Reafonable* Ends of our Well-being and Prefervation: And if we had Sagacity and Acutenefs of Senfe enough to penetrate into the very *Intimate Effences* of Things, and into the exact Configuration of the *Minuteft* Parts of Matter, it would perhaps anfwer no other end

P   but

but that of useless Speculation and Amusement.

2. FROM our Ideas of Sensation we infer the certain Existence of those external Objects which cause or occasion them in us; from the Existence of these again, we infer a first Cause of all things eternaly and necessarily existing; since nothing could produce itself, or act before it was: And from hence again proceeds the Knowledge of that Relation which he bears to us as our *Creator*, and *Preserver*. From hence again we infer the probable Existence of created immaterial Beings, which bear to us the relation of fellow Creatures; since we can set no Bounds to Space, nor to Almighty Power; which must be able to create Beings of Perfections vastly superior to those of Mankind; and free from those Weaknesses and Imperfections we labour under; and to whose unbounded Power and Majesty it seems most agreeable to have done so. From these Relations and Dependences flow all the Duties comprehended under Piety towards God, such as *Worship*, and *Prayers*; *Thanksgiving*, and *Praise*; *Reliance* upon his Providence, *Gratitude*, and *Fear*; as also Veneration and Honour towards those our fellow Creatures of so superior a Rank and Degree, that we can have no *Direct* or *Proper* Idea of them in this World.

AGAIN, when we come to confider the *Relation* we bear to our fellow Creatures of the fame Nature and Degree in this World, thence arife the Duties of Humanity and Juftice. And when we diftinguifh thefe by the feveral particular Relations of Confanguinity or Affinity, fuch as *Wife* or *Husband, Parent* or *Children*; or in any other Refpects more circumftantial or adventitious, fuch as that of *Mafter* or *Servant, Prince* or *Subjects*; from thence flow all the feveral refpective Duties and Obligations which unbiaffed Reafon and Experience teach us to be neceffary to the Benefit and Advantage of the whole Kind, and of every individual Man in particular; and are therefore to be difcharged to each other mutualy, according to the nearnefs or diftance of that Relation they bear to us.

LASTLY, When we come to confider the neareft of all Relations, that which we bear to our felves, the regard that every Man ought to have for his own Welfare and Happinefs; and the Relation which all *Other* vifible Creatures bear to him as a *Rational* Agent, thence arife all thofe Virtues and Duties which naturaly tend to promote the Good of Body and Mind, fuch as Sobriety, Temperance, Chaftity. And all comprehended under this fecond Head, is properly *Natural Religion* or *Morality*; for the Sanction of all the Rules and Precepts

whereof,

whereof, and to shew their tendency towards
our Happiness in another World, the Understanding proceeds thus: From the apparent unequal Distribution of Rewards to those who
observe them; and of Punishments to such a
transgress them in this Life, so plainly inconsistent with Goodness and Justice in a perfect
Being; we infer the Necessity of a future State
for a final Reward and Punishment; and consequently the Immortality of human Souls.

BEFORE I proceed to the next spacious
Scene which opens itself to human Understanding, it is worth observing here; that tho' all our
Knowledge of Nature consists either barely in
the mere Contemplation and *Simple Apprehension* of our Ideas of Sensation; or in *Experiment* and Observation of outward Appearances, and of the various ways of external Objects operating on one another; insomuch
that all the pretended Theory and *Speculation*
of natural Causes and Effects is precarious Conjecture: Yet when we proceed to Morality,
our Knowledge, tho' more truly *Speculative*,
is *Certain* and *Undoubted*, for the Regulation
of our Practice. We have a more evident, clear,
and distinct Knowledge of the Truths of natural Religion, than of the *Nature* or *Essence*
of any sensible Objects, on which their Properties and Effects depend. Material Bodies
strike upon the Organs of Sensation only by
their Qualities and Effects; and just as these
receive

receive the Impreffions, fo they are directly convey'd to the Imagination, but without any clear and *Adequate* Reprefentation of the intimate Effence of the Objects; and confequently we can know nothing more of them than from their fenfible Properties and Appearances, and from obferving how many different ways they influence and affect one another. But the Cafe is otherwife when the Intellect confiders the feveral *Relations* they bear to one another and to us, and their mutual Refpects and Dependences; here its Knowledge is *Clear* and *Adequate*; here it expatiates and exerts all its Powers; the Judgments it paffes upon thefe, without Partiality and Paffion, are *Certain*; its Deductions are *Undoubted*; its Conclufions without Confufion; and all the *Rules* and *Precepts* it forms concerning thofe Relations are of eternal Verity. And 'tis agreeable to the Wifdom and Goodnefs of God that the Cafe fhould be thus; fince even the *Experimental* Knowledge we have of natural Objects is perfectly fufficient for all the Ends of natural Religion and Morality; and as to any Other Ufe of it, ferves the Conveniences and Exigences of *This* Life only; whereas the Truths of Morality have a farther Refpect to *Eternity* and the Purpofes of another World.

C H A P.

CHAP. VI.

Of the different Kinds of Knowledge and Evidence.

IT being a Matter of no small Consequence to the Procedure of the Intellect in general, to state the several very different *Kinds* of Knowledge, as well as the *Degrees* of it in each Kind which admits of them; I shall observe that there are these six very distinct Sorts of *Knowledge* following, and as many very different Kinds of *Evidence* upon which they are founded.

I. THE first is that which we have from our *Senses*; and consists in an *Intellectual View* of all those *Ideas* which are thro' them conveyed inwardly to the Imagination. This is a Knowledge *Direct*, and *Immediate*, and *Intuitive*; utterly exclusive of all Reasoning and Argumentation: The View is *Simple*, and the Ideas hitherto uncompounded; and the Intellect is as yet no farther employ'd than in a bare *Contemplation* of the Ideas. It is this view of the Intellect which renders it properly *Knowledge*, and distinguishes it from *Natural Instinct* in Brutes, which are not capable of any such *View* of their Ideas. This carries in it the *Highest* Kind of *Evidence*, because it is so direct,

rect, and immediate, and simple, that it admits of no *Medius Terminus*, or common Measure, and consequently of no *Proof* or Evidence
at all from *Reason*; and all manner of Proof
or Evidence would, if *Attempted* here, have
less of Perspicuity and Certainty in it, than
that which it already contains in its own Nature. This is a Knowledge which admits of
no *Degrees* of Evidence, for *All* external Sensation is equaly certain and undoubted *In itself*;
and the Evidence of *One* Sense is equaly clear
with that of *Another*, in respect of their proper
and different Objects; and this Evidence can
be no otherwise varied than by the present Dif-
position of the *Organ* of Sensation; or of the
Medium; or by the different Degrees or Manner of *Impression* from the outward Object.
When the Sensation is regular and perfect, the
Assent of the Intellect naturaly and *Necessarily* follows all at once; but however is not
Extorted after the *Manner* it is in Demonstration, which compels by intermediate Proof and
Deduction. Wherefore it would be an odd
Affectation to call this sensitive Evidence by
the Name of *Demonstration*, merely because it
is obvious and natural, and not to be deny'd;
or because the contrary can be reduced to such
a Contradiction as this: As if a Man should
see a *Tree*, for instance, before his Eyes, and
should say, the Denial of it implies *That the
Tree should be there, and not there at the same time*;
or that he both sees and doth not see a Tree at the
center P 4
P 4   *same*

same time. Men may in *Words* indeed profess their Diffent from the Evidence of Senfe, and charge it home with Falfhood and Fraud; yet this is no other than giving themfelves the Lie: It is acting againft Nature, which will recoil with irrefiftible Force whenever the unnatural Reftraint is relaxed. When the Organ is rightly difpofed and exercifed upon its proper Object, in a juft Diftance and Medium, the cleareft and ftrongeft *Reafon* muft yield to its Evidence, and can never interpofe but when there is a reafonable Sufpicion of fome Failure in the *Act* of Senfation: Nor can it make any Inquiry whether the Evidence of Senfe is true? But only whether it is truly the Evidence of Senfe? So that for a Man to argue againft the plaineft Evidence of Senfe, is to oppofe the Evidence of *Reafon* to what in its own Nature admits of *No* Reafoning at all; or what is worfe, to lay afide both Senfe and Reafon, and form a Judgment upon any Inftance of Senfation without Regard to either of them.

I t will be proper to add thefe two Things farther concerning the Evidence of Senfe; firft, that it was *Neceffary* it fhould be fo direct and immediate, fo clear and undoubted; becaufe it is the *Firft Foundation* of all *Other* Knowledge of things Human and Divine. If the Truth of this Knowledge admitted of any *Doubt*, or were capable of any *Proof*, we fhould wander about in an everlafting *Scepticifm,*

ticifm, without the leaft Certainty in any thing:
For no Proof urged for it, can be plainer or
more evident than that which it is brought
to prove; and would therefore *Itfelf* require
another Proof, and fo on with endlefs Confufion. The other thing to be obferved is,
that all *Self-evident Propofitions*, and *Axioms*,
and *Poftulata*, are clear and evident in Proportion to their near Affinity to Senfation;
and owe their apparent Truth and Certainty
to a more *Immediate* Correfpondence with it.
As that *The Whole is greater than the Part*; *two
Things equal to a third are equal in themfelves*;
all which and fuch like are derived more directly from Senfation, and therefore have in
them a Degree of Evidence little inferior to it.

Now what I have faid of fenfitive Knowledge muft be underftood of the *Immediate* and
bare *Act* of Senfation only, or of the Idea confequent upon it; which the Intellect firft
takes for granted, and then makes its own
Remarks, together with all its Inferences and
Deductions from it. So that thus far only it
is properly *Knowledge*, or a *Neceffary Affent* of
the Mind to an evident Truth; and not *Faith*;
(for indeed *All* that is ftrictly and properly
Knowledge doth, as fuch, exclude all that is
properly *Believing*) and a Man is faid actualy
to *Know* and not to *Believe* what he truly
fees with his Eyes and hears with his Ears:
Faith may be *Confequent* to that Affent of the
Mind upon fenfitive Evidence, but cannot be

3   that

that *Very* Aſſent of the Mind which makes it *Knowledge.* Thus they who actualy ſaw *Lazarus* come out of his Grave at the call of *Jeſus*, could not be ſaid to *Believe* that they ſaw him riſe from the dead, but to *Know* that he did ſo. They who were Eye-witneſſes of Chriſt's Aſcenſion, could not be ſaid to *Believe* that they ſaw him aſcend; but to *Know* it. This Knowledge indeed and immediate Evidence of Senſe may be a good *Ground* and Foundation of ſuch *Truths* as are directly deduced from thence by moral Reaſoning and Deduction, and which may ſo become the Objects of our *Faith.* As the raiſing *Lazarus* from the dead was a ſenſible Evidence of a Divine *Almighty Power* in Chriſt; and his aſcending up into Heaven a ſenſible Evidence of the *Truth* of his *Doctrine*, and of his being the *Son* of *God* and the true *Meſſiah*, as he declared himſelf to be: The Spectators had a *Knowledge* of the *Facts*, and a *Faith* of thoſe *Truths* whereof they were intended as a *Proof* and Evidence.

So it was with *Thomas* the Apoſtle; he could not be ſaid to *Believe* that he felt the Print of the Nails in the Hands of Chriſt, and the Mark of the Wound in his Side; but that he actualy *Knew* them to be there: And from thence he *Neceſſarily* inferr'd the Truth of his Reſurrection, which was *Knowledge* ſtill; and upon this *Senſitive* and *Rational* Knowledge it

was

was that he founded that great Article of *Faith*, which he made open Profeſſion of by crying out *My Lord and My God*. The Saying of our Saviour upon that Confeſſion of his Faith was, *Bleſſed are they which believe and have not ſeen;* which is our Caſe who are now *Believers:* Not becauſe we believe without *Knowledge*; but becauſe our Faith is founded upon *Rational* only and *Moral*, and not upon any *Senſitive* Evidence of our own. We have firſt a Knowledge or moral Certainty of the Truth of the *Facts*, from their Teſtimony who had a ſenſitive Evidence of them; from the Hiſtory of the New Teſtament, and the rational Proofs of its being the Word of God: And it is upon this *Knowledge* we found our *Belief* of Chriſt's being the Son of God and true Meſſiah; of his having almighty Power; and of his being *Our Lord and our God.*

As it was neceſſary to diſtinguiſh theſe two things with ſome exactneſs, *Senſitive Evidence* and *Faith* properly ſo called, upon many Accounts; ſo eſpecialy was it requiſite in order to open the Fallacy of thoſe who inſiſt upon *Strict Evidence*, in oppoſition to *Revelation* and *Myſtery.* The Evidence of *Facts* related in Scripture, either *Senſitive* or *Rational*, is not properly *Faith*, but *Knowledge*; and the *Rational Knowledge* of ſuch Facts Men either have, or may have if they pleaſe, after the ſame Manner they now come by the *Knowledge* of other

Tranſ-

Tranfactions related in *Prophane* Hiftory. And as for thofe reveal'd *Truths* which are *Deduced* from them, and which are properly the Objects of our *Faith*, fuch as Chrift's being the *Son* of God and true *Meffiah*, his having almighty *Power*, and being truly our Lord and our *God*; it is plain they are of fuch a Nature as not to admit of any immediate *Senfitive* Evidence. Had thofe myfterious Doctrines and Truths been *In themfelves* capable of *Immediate fenfitive* Evidence either to the *Jews* or us, they would then become *Knowledge*, as was that of the Facts and Miracles; and fuch evident Knowledge as would neceffarily *Exclude* all *Faith*. So that tho' our modern Unbelievers had actualy *Seen* all the Miracles wrought by our Saviour, yet ftill upon their Principles they muft have continued void of all *Faith* in thofe *Myfterious Doctrines* to which the Miracles were defign'd to procure our affent. For Miracles are but a *Mediate external* Proof of the Truth of fuch Doctrines, and have no *Natural* and *Neceffary* Connection with the Propofitions reveal'd; and tho' an hundred of them were wrought for the procuring our Affent to *One* Myftery, it would ftill remain as *Incomprehenfible* as before. But thefe Men are not fatisfied with any thing fhort of a ftrict and *Immediate intrinfic* Evidence for the *Doctrines* themfelves; infomuch that their obftinate refufal of an Affent to thefe reveal'd Truths, upon fuch a Principle, is in this Refpect a Degree

of

of Perverſeneſs even beyond that of the har-
den'd Jews; who attributing Chriſt's Miracles
to the Power of Beelzebub, and no other than
giving Teſtimony to himſelf, required a Sign
from the Father in *Heaven*; and had this been
granted they were content to acquieſce in the
Belief of his *Doctrines*.

But our modern Unbelievers, if conſiſtent
with themſelves, muſt have rejected the Doctrines notwithſtanding their ſeeing even *Such* a
Miracle from *Heaven*: For this would be but
a *Mediate* Evidence ſtill of the Truth of thoſe
divine Doctrines our Saviour preach'd; ſome
of which would have continued, by their very
Nature, equaly Myſterious and Inconceivable
to them as before. And therefore *They* muſt
have called for either a *Direct ſenſitive Intuition*,
or an *Immediate Evidence* of the divine Truths
themſelves; ſuch as would give them a *Clear*
and *Adequate* Knowledge of the real *Intrinſic*
Nature of Things, which is incomprehenſible
either to Senſe or Reaſon: And upon a Re-
fuſal of this, they muſt intirely have declined
any *Faith* where they had no *Direct* Knowledge by *Ideas*, nor immediate Comprehenſion
of the incomprehenſible Myſtery *Itſelf*. Is it
not a monſtrous Inconſiſtency in our Oppoſers
of Revelation to profeſs themſelves willing to
become *Believers*, if all Points of the Chriſtian
Faith were put into ſuch a Light as that it
would be *Impoſſible to* BELIEVE them: For
whether

whether they had the immediate Evidence of *Sense*, or of strict *Demonstration* for them, it would be then all *Knowledge* or *Science*, and not *Faith*.

II. ANOTHER *Kind* of Knowledge is that which we have from *Self-Consciousness*. As we come to the Knowledge of things without us by the *Mediation* of their *Ideas*; so on the contrary we have an *Immediate* Feeling or *Consciousness* of what is transacted in our Mind, without the Intervention of any *Ideas* whatsoever. Thus we have a Knowledge of all the *Faculties* or Powers and Operations of the Soul; not only those of the *Intellect* and *Will*, together with all the various Modifications of them; but of all the *Passions* likewise and *Affections* of the *Inferior* Soul. This Kind of Perception some have not unaptly called *Internal Sensation*, in order to distinguish it from that Perception we have of *External* Objects by their Ideas, and which cannot otherwise be known than by some Representations or Characters of them lodged in the Imagination.

CONCERNING this Kind of Knowledge which we have of the Faculties of our own Minds, so very different from what we have by external Sensation; it will be necessary to observe, that we have no degree of it *Antecedent* to the *Actual Exercise* of those Faculties upon the Ideas of *Sensation*; as we should have had no Knowledge

ledge of any of our bodily Motions if the Parts were not actualy moved: Infomuch that it is from the internal Senfation or Confciouf-nefs of thofe *Operations* of the Powers of the Mind upon fuch Ideas, that we neceffarily infer its very *Exiftence*; and obtain the higheft moral Certainty of an immaterial Principle within us, endued with a Power of voluntary Motion or *Activity* in itfelf, and of communicating Motion at Will and Pleafure to the Parts of the Body. Thus we could have had no Con-fcioufnefs of *Thinking*, antecedently to, and ab-ftractedly from any Object or *Idea* actualy thought upon; or of *Willing* without fome-thing actualy Will'd or defired; nor of *Love*, *Hatred*, *Fear*, till thofe Paffions were *Exercifed* upon fome *Object* loved, or hated, or feared; and fo in all the other Faculties and Affections of the Mind.

Now fince we can have no Confcioufnefs of any of the Powers of our Minds before they actualy operate; and that their firft Operations muft neceffarily be upon Ideas of Senfation; it is plain we cannot have *Simple Ideas* of them, but are obliged to form to our felves *Complex Notions* of them, made up of thofe *Ideas* upon which they operate, together with the Man-ner of the Mind's operating upon them, and of its affecting the Body in thofe Operations.

THO'

THO' this Kind of Knowledge neceſſarily *Preſuppoſes* that which we have from external *Senſation*, and is of a more complex **Nature**; yet it is nothing inferior to it in Point of *Certainty* and Evidence. The *Neceſſary* Aſſent of the Mind doth not only follow of Courſe upon this Conſciouſneſs, as it is in the Caſe of external Senſation; but *Falls in* with it: They are ſo cloſely connected that the *Conſciouſneſs* is itſelf the *Immediate* Act of Aſſent or *Knowledge*; at leaſt they are ſo inſeparable that they cannot be diſtinguiſhed even in **Thought**. When this internal Senſation or Conſciouſneſs is truly natural, by means of a due **Tone and** Temper of the animal Spirits, and of the finer Parts of the Body which are the more immediate Inſtruments of thoſe mental Operations, we can never be *Deceived* in this Article of Knowledge. It is ſo *Sure* and obvious, ſo *Clear* and diſtinct that it admits of no Proof or *Farther* Evidence from Reaſon; and yet it would be perverting the true Procedure of human Underſtanding to confound this with *Demonſtration:* Since it is ſo *Immediate* and *Intimate* to us that there is no room for any Application of a *Common Meaſure* either to illuſtrate or increaſe its Evidence; or to diſcover the **Truth** or Falſhood, in any Inſtance, of thoſe Faculties and Operations whereof we have ſuch a real internal Feeling. So that for a **Man to** argue away any Inſtances of this *Knowledge*

we

we have from Self-Confcioufnefs, or deny their Certainty, would be no lefs abfurd than flatly to contradict the moft clear and diftinct Perception of *External* Senfe. Only it is to be obferved that all here faid of this Knowledge is to be underftood of the *Firft* and *Immediate* Perceptions of our mental Operations, and of their Reality and *Truth*; and not of any *Farther* Obfervations made upon them by the Intellect, or of any *Deductions* or Confequences afterwards drawn concerning the Nature or *Manner* of thofe Operations. To inftance in fome few Particulars of this Kind of Knowledge.

A MAN who by an immediate Confcioufnefs of what paffes within him doth not *Know certainly*, that he hath a Faculty of *Reafon* and Underftanding as well as of *Senfitive Perception*; and that thefe two are totaly different in *Kind*, and not in *Degree* only; is not capable of being altered in his Opinion by any *Argument* or Perfuafion: This Knowledge is fo immediate, that tho' many other Arguments may be offered to render that Point highly *Probable*; yet nothing can work a full *Conviction* of the Truth of it, but the Regard and Attention he hath to an inward *Feeling* and *Confcioufnefs* of fuch a reafoning Faculty within him. If by being Confcious to what is tranfacted in his own Mind, he doth not perceive fuch an *Effential* Difference between *Thinking* and *Senfitive*

Q   *Per-*

Perception, as is a sufficient *Ground* for these Consequences, *That Reason is a Faculty intirely different in* Kind *from that Instinct and sensitive Perception which he observes in Brutes*; and *That mere Matter is not capable of Thinking and Reason* ; no Evidence whatsoever built on any Foundation from *Without,* can add to the Truth and Perspicuity of those Conclusions, or raise them up to an higher Degree of Certainty in him.

AGAIN, we have an immediate Consciousness of a *Freedom of Will* within us; or of a Power to act or forbear to act, and to act this way or the quite contrary in all Matters of Duty, as well as in all things indifferent: From whence the natural Deduction of Reason is, that our Actions being *Free* and Voluntary they must be capable of being *Imputable* to us as moraly *Good* or *Bad,* and consequently liable to *Reward* or *Punishment* from Him who endued us with that Faculty. This free Principle within us is so *Self-evident,* that no Reason or Argument can render it more so; all attempt of *Proof* for the Corroboration of it is utterly needless, and serves only to perplex and confound the clearest Evidence the Mind is capable of for the Truth of any thing : So that in all Contention and Debate relating to this Point, as well as to what immediately depends on it, the last Appeal for a final Decision must be to the immediate *Consciousness* of the Mind ;
and

and he who would not determine against absolute *Decrees*, and unconditional *Predestination*, *Election* and *Reprobation*, from a *Discernment* of Freedom of Will within himself; must be a corrupt Judge and blinded with Prejudice; and is not capable of a full Conviction from any other Topic.

THUS again, we have an immediate Consciousness and internal Sensation of *Remorse* on the Committal of wicked Actions, and of a secret *Complacence* of Mind on the Performance of such as are moraly Good; and by the same Consciousness we perceive these to be immediate natural Spurs to one, and Determents from the other. And as we have an immediate Self-Consciousness of these *Passions*, so by an obvious Deduction of Reason, they become such a solid *Ground* of Evidence for the essential and eternal *Difference* between *Virtue* and *Vice*, that he who will not be convinced of this difference by Reasoning from such Consciousness, would be hardy enough to resist all Arguments built on any other Foundation. I do not say that these Passions of Pleasure and Pain naturaly consequent to our Actions, are *Themselves* an *Immediate* Evidence of the moral Good or Evil of Actions prior to any *Deduction* of Reason; or that we have an internal *Instinct* and *Moral Sense*, whereby we *Immediately* and *Intuitively difcern* the *Difference* of Virtue and Vice without any Inference of

Q 2   Reason,

Reafon, and previoufly to it, as fome ridicu-
loufly affert: Becaufe nothing can be plainer
than that the *Actions themfelves* muft be *Apprehended* as *Moraly* Good or Bad before fuch
Natural Pleafure or Pain can be caufed by them;
and confequently their moral Good or Evil
muft confift in fomething previous not only to
thofe *Paffions*, but alfo to *Any* Faculty *Whatever* that *Apprehends* it. But I fay there cannot be a furer *Ground* on which to build an
undoubted *Argument* for that real and unalterable Difference between Virtue and Vice,
which is antecedent in itfelf both to our *Perceiving* it, and being thus affected by it, after
Any manner.

NOR does it take off any thing from the
Certainty of this Knowledge I am fpeaking
of, or the Force of its Evidence, that fome
Men have little or no *Remorfe* in the Committal of habitual and known Sins. For it
was not fo with them at *Firft*; they are in an
Unnatural State, and have almoft quite defaced
and fmother'd one of the ftrongeft Paffions in
human Nature by inceffant Contradiction, and
offering it perpetual Violence, till they are almoft paft any *Feeling* or Confcioufnefs of it.
And when this genuine and proper Ground of
a reafonable and fatisfactory Proof of the *Difference* between Virtue and Vice, is rendered
weak and feeble in Men; then they become
clamorous in their Demands either for an
Inftinct

Inſtinct whereby to diſcern it *Immediately* and *Intuitively*; or for ſuch ſtrict *Demonſtration* as is quite beſide the Nature of Morality, as well as reveal'd Religion. And this unreaſonable Claim of theirs has put ſome well meaning Perſons upon abſurd and fruitleſs Endeavours to prove that ſuch an *Inſtinct* or *Senſe* is actualy implanted in human Nature; and others to prove that ſuch *Demonſtration* may be had in all the important Points of natural Religion.

So again, if from that immediate Conſciouſneſs Men have of the Operations of their own Minds, they are not convinced that their Knowledge is of the Operations *Themſelves*, and not of any *Reflex Ideas* within them of thoſe Operations; a ſtronger Argument cannot be offered for their Conviction.

Lastly, if a Man from the Obſervation of what paſſes within him is not Conſcious to himſelf that he hath no *Purely Intellectual*, or *Abſtract ſpiritual Ideas* for the Exerciſe of the Operations of his Mind, independently of all Ideas of *Senſation* (the *Neceſſary* rational Conſequence from which is, that he hath no way of conceiving things purely Spiritual and *Immaterial* but by *Analogy* with thoſe *Complex* Notions and *Conceptions*, form'd from thoſe Ideas conſidered together with the Operations of our Mind upon them) it will be in vain to offer

Q 3   many

many other things which may be said upon this
Point for farther Proof and Illustration.

THESE two forts of Knowledge are *Immediate*, and consequently a Sort of *Intuition* ; and
considered strictly in themselves, do exclude all
Reasoning and consequential *Deduction*, which,
as we have seen, are of an *After* Consideration.
And this leads us to another Kind of Knowledge or Evidence very different from either
of them, which is *Mediate* and altogether ac-
quir'd by Deduction and Consequence: That
is *Reason* ; which differs from the Understanding or *Intellect*, in that *This* is a more general
Term and denotes the very Power or *Faculty
itself* ; but the other expresseth an *Operation* of
that Faculty, and is limited to that one *Particular* Operation which consists in Illation or
Consequence. This therefore we are to distinguish into *Four* different Heads of Knowledge,
according to the different *Manner* of the Intellect's Procedure in making its Deductions and
Consequences, and according to the different
Kind of *Evidence* in each of them.

I. THE first Head of this Knowledge or Evidence is that of *Science* or *Demonstration* ; which
may be placed in the clearest Light at once
in the *Syllogistic* Form, or in what is reducible
to it, by the actual Application of a common
Measure, *Determinate* and *Certain*, to two Extremes which are *Infallibly* Commensurate with
it :

it: So that the Conclusion follows by an *Ab-solute Necessity*, and *Compels* the Assent of the Intellect to the Truth of it, even in Opposition to any Tendency of the *Will* to the contrary should it be *Attempted*; and the Knowledge is as infallible, as the direct and clear Perception of Sensation or Self-Consciousness. The Logicians confine Demonstration to *Causes* and *Effects*; and they make two sorts of it, that of proving the *Effect* from the immediate *Cause*, and that of proving the *Cause* from a remote *Effect*. The Mathematicians apply the demonstrative Form to Number, Extension and Figure; but with this difference, that tho' they make their *Inferences* expresly, yet they carry one of the *Premises* in their Mind. And from thence again the Name only, and empty Colour of it came to be introduced into *Ethics* and *Metaphysics*; not without a plausible Appearance of a great Improvement of them; but in Consequence and Reality, not without darkening and enervating all the Doctrines and Precepts of Morality and Natural Religion.

II. THE next Head of Knowledge which we have from Reason is, that of a *Moral Certainty*, the utmost Degree of which approaches next to what is Demonstrative. This Knowledge is acquired by such Proofs or Mediums as have an *Indubitable* Connection only with the two Extremes. The Force and Evidence of this a plain Understanding is capable of apprehendhending, and it rarely or never requires the *Syllogiſtic* Form for the Inſtruction of Perſons unprejudiced; tho' this is ſometimes neceſſary for the Confuting perverſe and groundleſs Oppoſition. The Arguments here are drawn from Topics of Reaſon in general, and the Evidences which go to make up a *Moral Certainty* may be a *Combination* of all Kinds of Knowledge, not excepting even that of Science or ſtrict *Demonſtration.* From thence indeed Arguments may be drawn in Natural Religion; as when we prove the Power, and Wiſdom, and Goodneſs of God from Aſtronomical Propoſitions already demonſtrated: But then the Moral Deductions made from thence are not *Themſelves* capable of the ſame demonſtrative Evidence; the Mathematical Propoſitions are taken for *Granted* here, and then Moral Arguments are built upon them, which conclude with a quite *Different* Kind of Certainty. The Aſſent of the Mind here is free and *Voluntary*, and follows by a *Moral Neceſſity* only; which obligeth every one not to oppoſe or contradict the common Sence and Reaſon of Mankind; and in *Religion* particularly (in Relation to which we have this moral Evidence more eſpecialy under Conſideration) the with-holding our Aſſent to it is ever utterly *Inexcuſable.* Thus as in Demonſtration the Aſſent of the Intellect is *Compel'd*, nay tho' it ſhould meet with the Oppoſition of the *Will*; ſo in Moral Evidence it is quite the *Reverſe*; for in this the Will hath a great Power and Influence

Influence in promoting or obstructing that Assent: And hence it comes that there is Room left for Passion and Prejudice of all Sorts to interpose here, and give a Byass to the Intellect contrary to its own natural Tendency; and to the Right it hath of judging and determining upon all Degrees of moral Reasoning according to the true Merits of the Cause.

We come to the Knowledge of every thing in Natural Religion for which we have a moral Certainty, by a long and imperceptible Series of Reasoning; and the Progress is flow from one Step to another, till at last the Mind forms to itself Propositions of clear and unquestionable Verity; which some Men are apt to look upon as so many *Axioms* and *First Principles* and *Postulata*, because they require no express and immediate Deduction of Reason for their Certainty and Evidence. Thus the *Evidences* of *Natural Religion* and *Morality* grow up with us from our tender Years, and receive a daily Increase of Strength, from continued Observation, and the habitual Exercise of Reason, according to the Advantages of Education: Insomuch that this Knowledge of the plainest and most obvious *Moral Truths* is gradualy obtain'd by Deduction and Consequence; such as, *There is a God. God is to be worshiped by Man. Every one ought to enjoy what is his own. Where there is no Property there is no Injustice.* The Procedure of the Intellect in

coming

coming to this Knowledge is by such insensible Degrees, that Men are sometimes apt to look upon these and such like Propositions as Sentiments purely natural and *Innate*; and a Sort of *Principles* congenial to the Mind, whereof they have a kind of *Intuitive* Knowledge, exclusive of all preceding Deduction, as being superfluous and unnecessary. Now tho' these plain Truths are so evident that they leave no room for *Doubt*, and that the contrary may be reduced to *Absurdity*, and a Contradiction to the common Sense and Reason of Mankind; it would however be very improper to call any Proofs and Reasons which may be offered for them by the Name of *Demonstration*, or to assert that they either have, or are capable of having *Mathematical Certainty*. This is no other than confounding two very different Kinds of Knowledge; which when rightly distinguished are both of them equaly true, and solid, and undeniable, and founded upon the strongest Evidence the Nature of either will admit of, and yet are not capable of the same kinds of Proof; and therefore the Absurdity of blending these together is the very same, as if we jumbled *Moral Certainty* and Evidence, with that we have purely from external *Sensation* or from *Self-Consciousness*.

Now because natural and reveal'd Religion are capable of no other than a *Moral Certainty*; and that to the great Disadvantage of both, this

this hath been confounded with *Demonftration* ; and becaufe fome Men have afferted that natural *Religion* or *Morality* is capable of *Mathematical* Certainty, and that others have in vain attempted to frame Syftems of Morality purfuant to that grofs Opinion ; I fhall diftinguifh the different Nature and Properties of thefe two kinds of *Evidence*, in oppofite Columns under two diftinct Propofitions, the one *Mathematical* and the other *Moral.*

Mathematical Certainty,	*Moral Certainty.*
As in this Propofition.	As in this Propofition.
The three Angles of a right lin'd Triangle are equal to two right ones.	*There is a God.*
HERE there is the utmoft Degree of *Abfolute* Certainty ; the Evidence is *Infallible*, and the Confequence follows by a *Natural* Neceffity.	ON this fide there is the utmoft Degree of *Moral* Certainty ; the Evidences for it are *Indubitable* , and the Confequences follow by a *Moral* Neceffity.
THE Demonftration, when underftood, *Compels* and *Extorts* the	THE Arguments on this fide *Ought* pofitively to *Determine* the Judg-

Assent of the Intellect.

Judgment; they *Demand* and *Require* the *Assent* of the Intellect.

IN this Point of Knowledge there is no Concurrence of the *Will*; it is the sole Operation of the *Intellect*, and no Prejudice or Passion can so interpose as to Sway or Influence its Judgment or Illation.

IN this Knowledge a Concurrence of the *Will* is requisite even to the Assent of the *Intellect*; and it hath a great Power and Influence in promoting or obstructing that Assent: So that a Man shall either give it, or with-hold it, as he is impartial and unprejudiced; or as he is blinded with Passion, or habitual Immorality.

ON this side there can be no *Degrees* of Evidence or *Certainty*; all Demonstrations are equaly certain; there can be no Proof but of one *Kind*; nor can there be any *Additional* Force of Arguments drawn from *Other* kinds of Knowledge.

THIS side admits of several *Degrees* of *Certainty*; it takes in *All Kinds* of Knowledge; and the Truths of Morality are *More* or *Less* evident according to the Strength and Perspicuity of the Arguments by which they are proved.

4

One

One Demonſtration amounts to the utmoſt *Infallible* Certainty; an hundred Demonſtrations of the ſame thing, would not *Increaſe* or confirm the Evidence, which neceſſarily excludes *All Poſſibility* of the things being otherwiſe; and every Proof but the *One ſhorteſt* and *Cleareſt* are ſuperfluous.

HERE *Many various Arguments* may concur to make up even the higheſt Degree of *Moral Certainty* for any one Point; and yet no *Two* Arguments be exactly of the ſame weight. This moral Certainty excludes all *Reaſonable Cauſe* of Doubting, tho' not a bare *Natural Poſſibility* of the things being otherwiſe for ought we know.

ON this ſide there is a Concurrence of *Senſation* by viſible Figures and Diagrams, to help the Mind in a ready apprehending and retaining a continued Chain of Deductions; the very thing which enables Men in Mathematics to proceed in a Series of *Enthymemes,* leaving out one Propoſition of the

HERE there is no *Viſible Clue* of that kind for the Procedure and Guidance of the Intellect; but all its Deductions are *Purely Rational,* and all its Reſolutions and Concluſions are intirely *Abſtracted* from any *Immediate Act* of *Senſation*; and therefore it is that in Matters of Difficulty here the Dialectical

Argument in the complete Form.

lectical Form of Syllogifm is moftly in Ufe, wherein the common Meafure is actualy apply'd to both Extremes.

HERE all the Contradictions and Abfurdities confequent upon a Denial of the Truth, are plainly difcernible in the *Very Nature* of the Things themfelves; they are in a great Meafure immediately evident to *Senfe*; and are therefore glaring and palpable; and follow with an abfolute and *Infallible* Certainty, like all other Conclufions which have *Mathematical* Evidence.

HERE the Contradictions and Abfurdities you are preffed with in Argument, are difcernible by the *Intellect* alone; they have a Refpect to our way of Thinking and Reafoning; and follow with a *Moral* Certainty only, upon a denial of the Truth, like all other Conclufions which have *Moral* Evidence only.

THIS takes Place in things *Natural*, and *Material*, and *Senfible*, fuch as Quantity, Figure and Extenfion; the Ideas of all which we have from *Direct*

THIS extends itfelf to things *Spiritual* and *Supernatural*, fuch as God and his Attributes, and all other *Immaterial* Beings; whereof we can have

4

no

and *Immediate* Sensation.

no *Direct* and *Immediate Ideas*; and which are therefore no otherwise conceivable, but by the *Mediation* of things natural. God and his Attributes are the *Immediate* Objects of our *Knowledge* and *Faith* in their Types and Representations only; and the *Mediate* Objects of both as to their *Real Incomprehensible* Nature and Substance.

ON this side the *Ideas* are *Simple* and *Determinate*, and concerning which there is a *General Consent*; and therefore all their *Agreements* and *Disagreements* may be render'd so distinct and manifest as to strike the Mind fully and irresistibly, at once.

OUR Reasonings on this side are all about *Notions* and *Conceptions*; which are not only very *Complex* in themselves, and each of them a Composition of many Ingredients; but wonderfully varied according to the different Sentiments of Men and their very opposite ways of Thinking; so that there is no small Difficulty in bringing Men to fix
and

and afcertain their moral Notions and Conceptions by the *True* Meafure or Standard.

THIS is ftrictly *Knowledge* or *Science*, and neceffarily excludes all *Belief* in general, and *Faith* properly fo call'd, and all Affent of the Mind upon the *Teftimony* of others.

HERE we may be faid both to *Know* and to *Believe* the fame Propofition, in natural or reveal'd Religion. To *Know* it upon the utmoft moral Proof and Evidence ; and to *Believe* it in general, becaufe the voluntary Concurrence of the *Will* is requifite to that Affent of the Mind, and it is not extorted. And it is alfo a *Religious Faith* when there is a full Concurrence of the *Will* and *Heart* to it, *Subfequent* to that Affent of the Intellect.

THIS Propofition contains Matter of pure Speculation or *Theory* only ; and it requires no Concurrence

AS there is a Concurrence of the *Will* requifite in order to influence the Affent of the Intellect to the
Truth

of the *Will* either *To* or after the Assent of the Intellect; so that the *Practical Uses* of it are merely accidental.

truth of this Proposition; so must it afterwards continue to *Close* with that Assent in order to regulate our *Practice*, and to sway and influence the Manners of Men, which is then a truly *Practical Faith*.

1. **FROM** the very different and even opposite Nature of *Moral Certainty*, and that which is strictly *Demonstrative* and *Mathematical* put into this Light; it must appear First, that there is as little room for the latter in *Morality* and *Natural Religion*, as in *Revelation*. To make this Point the more evident, I have taken for my instance the fundamental Truth of all *Natural* and *Revealed* Religion, and which of all others is presumed to be the most strictly demonstrable. The Proposition is undoubtedly and unquestionably true; it hath the highest kind of Evidence the nature of the thing will admit of: It is founded upon the plainest *Reason* and the utmost *Moral Certainty*; so as to *Demand* and *Claim* the Assent of the Intellect; and render its Dissent inexcusable *Partiality* and *Wickedness*. But that it is not strictly *Demonstrable* is plain from the very *Existence* of a Deity being revealed in Scripture by the name *I am*, which is in other Words, *I exist*; and from

R   that

that saying, *The Fool hath said in his Heart there is no God:* For if there were any *One* demonstrative Argument, or a Mathematical *Certainty* for it, this would render all *Other* Arguments either from *Scripture* or *Reason* intirely needless; and there could not be such a thing as a speculative Atheist in the World; whereas the Experience of all Ages hath shewn, that there are many such *Fools*, otherwise of great Learning and natural Sagacity, who have argued that there is no God. They have indeed varied much in their Manner of doing this; some who denied the *Existence* of a Deity, have however allowed a *First Cause*; others who allow'd a *First Canse*, have deny'd it to be an *Intelligent Agent*; others who allow him to be an *Intelligent Agent*, yet deny his *Providence*; and some who allow his *Providence*, have however corrupt Notions of his *Attributes*, and such as by immediate Consequence destroy his very Existence. And we are not without a lamentable Instance, even in our own times, of a *Person* of great natural Sagacity and close Application; who hath first undertaken to *Demonstrate* the Existence *of One God Only*, by a Chain of Metaphysical Deductions: And yet afterwards hath publish'd another Book of no small Bulk to demonstrate, by the same dint of Metaphysics, the Existence of *More* Gods than *One*; tho' if you strip both these Undertakings out of their Metaphysical Dress, the irreconcileable Inconsistency and Contradiction

between

between them will be evident to common Sence and Reafon; and nothing will appear plainer, than that there can be no *Demonftra-tion* for the Exiftence of *One God*, but what muft conclude as neceffarily againft the Exiftence of any *Other* God whatfoever, *Co-ordinate* or *Inferiour*.

WHEN the Reader's Aftonifhment is over, how this Palpable *Monftrous* Inconfiftency fhould pafs with fuch Currency and Smooth-nefs as it hath done, and without a general Ob-fervation and Abhorrence; I fhall go on to re-mark, that if there were any one clear de-monftrative Argument of apparent Mathema-tical Certainty for the Exiftence of a Deity and his Attributes, then all that Variety of Opinions would fall of Courfe; nor would there be any fuch thing as *Idolatry*, or worfhip-ping more Gods than one: And what is yet more ftrange, whofoever was capable of un-derftanding that Form of Demonftration might be faid indeed to *Know* there is a God; and yet not *Believe* in him, according to the proper Acceptation of a *Religious Faith*. Alas! no-thing is farther from the Nature of *Mathema-tical Certainty*, than *Metaphyfical Abftractions*; and Mankind would be in a defperate Con-dition indeed, if they were to depend upon fuch Abftractions for the fundamental Point of all Religion natural and reveal'd; and were to be conducted by a *Spider's Clue* thro' an

intricate

intricate *Maze* of nice and thinfpun notional
Abftractions, before they could arrive at this
Conclufion, *Therefore there is a God*; or which
is in Effect or Confequence the very fame,
Therefore there is but *One* God.

THAT Mathematical Certainty is not to
be had but in things Mathematical, and that
Demonftration properly fo call'd can have no
Place in *Morality* or *Natural Religion*, hath been
the general Opinion of the Wife and Learned;
accordingly it is a faying of *Jamblicus*, *That
Demonftrations are not to be expected in Matters
concerning God and things Divine.* And in an
excellent Treatife of natural Religion (which
went thro' the Hands of two great and Learned Prelates of our own ; and which hath more
Force of Argument and ftrict Reafoning in it,
than all the Abftracted and Metaphyfical
Tracts which have fince appeared upon that
Subject) there is another faying full to the fame
Purpofe. *Do Men expect Mathematical Proof
and Certainty in moral Things? Why, they may
as well expect to fee with their Ears, and hear
with their Eyes.*

THE endeavouring to gratify Men in that
unreafonable Expectation is not only *Abfurd*,
as being altogether impracticable; but hath
been of *Pernicious* Confequence in thefe two
Refpects. *Firft*, As the Writers in this way
have furnifhed the World with an handle for

2   think-

thinking that nothing in natural Religion is to be regarded as strictly *Obligatory*, farther than it is capable of such demonstrative Proof: And since the Nature of it will not admit this, the unavoidable Miscarriage of all who attempt it is of no small Prejudice to the Cause they would thus maintain by *A Zeal without Knowledge*. For I appeal to any observing Person, whether the Effect and Consequence of it hath not already been, the supporting and encouraging *Libertines* and *Unbelievers* in their Demands for *Demonstrative* Certainty and Evidence in every Point both of *Faith* and *Practice?* And whether every Thing now published in Religion is not too generaly look'd upon with Contempt, which hath not some Air and Appearance at least of demonstrative Certainty and Evidence? The discerning Men among Infidels, Freethinkers, and Libertines do well know that such Evidence is never to be obtained either for *Natural* or *Reveal'd* Religion; and that nothing can contribute more to the Advantage of their Cause, than thus drawing off their Antagonists from a truly rational and solid way of Argument, and putting them upon an impossible Task; wherein they must necessarily waste and consume all their Strength and Vigour in empty *Noise*, and *Flourish*, and *Beating* of the *Air*.

Secondly, As it is a direct *Insinuation* against all *Reveal'd Religion*; for if mere Morality is strictly *Demonstrable*, and Revelation is capable

of

of no more than *Moral Evidence*, then it can never be upon an equal Foot of *Certainty* and *Credibility* with natural Religion. This Confequence is fo obvious that all who are evily inclin'd to Revelation muft plainly fee it; and they accordingly infift upon Mathematical Certainty and Evidence in Religion, and relifh nothing but what hath a *Colour* at leaft of Demonftration: And from thence it is that all our new-fangled *Metaphyfical Morality* is grown into Mode and Fafhion; and that our Modern Writers upon that Subject have unwarily formed their Difcourfes to the prevailing Tafte and Genius of an *Unbelieving* Age.

2. Another thing which appears from the above Oppofition is, that notwithftanding the greateft Evidence we have for natural Religion, it however includes a *Religious Faith*; and that this Faith, as it ought to be, is *Founded* on the utmoft *Moral Certainty*. When from a full Proof and Evidence to their Reafon, Men, have given their Affent to the Exiftence of a Deity; and from thence have inferr'd that he muft have all incomprehenfible Perfection, and infinitely greater than we can imagine; and have accordingly fubftituted the higheft Perfections difcernible in the Creature, and in our human Nature in particular, to ftand for his inconceivable Perfections: Then the hearty Concurrence of the *Will* to that great and fundamental Truth improves and *Completes*

it

it into a *Religious Faith* in God, and in all his Attributes; and *Inclines* the Mind to the Discharge and Performance of all those Duties which are deduced from them by the Light of Nature; so that *without Faith it is impossible to please God* in any Religion. *Faith*, in the strict Propriety of the Word, is as necessary in *Natural* Religion, as in *Reveal'd*; for tho' we have the *Utmost Proof* and *Moral Evidence* for the Existence of a Deity, which is so far *Knowledge* only: Yet still because the *Intrinsic Nature* of God and his *Essential* Attributes are utterly *Incomprehensible* and ineffable, and can be no *Immediate* Objects of our Understanding; Men must *Indirectly*, and by the mediation of their Substitutes, give the *Assent* of the *Intellect* here, as well as the *Consent* of the *Will*, to the truth of things as *Mysterious* as any in all reveal'd Religion; and which they are oblig'd to conceive and apprehend by the same *Analogy* we do all the Mysteries of Christianity.

3. THE last thing I shall observe from the different Nature of *Moral* and *Mathematical* Certainty is, that *Evangelical Faith* (which as we see adds no more to that which is necessary in natural Religion than the believing the *Word* of God, whose Existence and Attributes we were obliged to believe before) is no *Precarious* or *Implicit* Assent of the Mind. The case here is the very same as it is in *Natural* Religion; we have the utmost moral Certainty and Evi-

dence

dence for the Scriptures being the *Word of God*,
or a *Supernatural Revelation* from Heaven; we
neither give our Assent to this great Truth our
selves, nor desire that others should do so, but
upon the utmost moral Certainty and Evidence
Men are capable of receiving for a Truth or
Fact of that Nature. Now whether they *Are*
such or *Not?* is no immediate Point of *Faith*,
but of *Knowledge*; and if Men, sway'd and influenced by Prejudice or Prepossession against
plain and full reasonable Evidence, with-hold
the *Assent* of the *Intellect* here; there can be no
subsequent *Concurrence* of the *Will*, and consequently no *Evangelical Faith*. But if the *Assent* of the *Intellect* is given to that great Truth,
and there is moreover a Concurrence of the
Heart and Will; then Men act just in the
same Manner they did before in natural Religion: They give the Assent of the Mind to
Truths in the *Word* of God, no more *Incomprehensible* nor otherwise *Mysterious* than his Nature and Attributes; to things as *Easily* conceiv'd and expressed by the very same *Analogy*;
things whose real Nature admits of as little *Intrinsick Immediate* Proof or Evidence; and accordingly do afterwards suffer these mysterious
Truths to *Influence* their Lives and Practice;
and that is a complete *Evangelical Faith*.

THESE two things therefore in respect of
Evangelical Faith, are of no small Consequence
to be rightly distinguished in all our Controversies with the Adversaries of Revelation.

1. THE

1. THE firft is, the *Affent* of the *Under-ftanding* to the Truth of any Propofition upon *Sufficient Undoubted Evidence* or a *Moral Certain-ty*; which is thus far merely *Knowledge*, and of a very different and feparate Confideration in itfelf. Here then we are to fix our Foot, and join Iffue with all Ranks of Unbelievers upon the Point of *Knowledge* only; for as in *Natural* Religion the firft and great Queftion is not, Whether we *Believe* the Exiftence of a God? But whether there *Is* a God? So the firft and main Point to be decided with Regard to *Re-velation* is not, Whether we *Believe* the Scrip-tures to be the Word of God? But whether they realy *are* fo? And whether we have fuf-ficient Reafon to *Know* they are fo? Whe-ther we will yield the Affent of the Intellect to that great Point of Knowledge, as to a Truth founded upon the utmoft Moral Proof and E-vidence the *Nature* of the Thing will bear, and that we are now *Capable* of receiving? Nay, fuch Proof and Evidence as would be not only a full Conviction to the Underftanding in any Matters of the fame kind merely *Temporal* and *Human*; but much greater than *They* can ad-mit of. This Point of Knowledge in general is firft to be decided; and when there is an *Af-fent* of the *Underftanding* to it, then the *Con-currence* of the *Will* and its clofing with it, which is *Subfequent* to that Knowledge, com-pletes an *Evangelical Faith*. And the Procedure
is

is thus, *As, when the Existence of a Deity is assented to, in natural Religion, upon full Moral Proof and Evidence, Men Believe in the incomprehensible Nature and Attributes of God: So upon the Assent of the Understanding in general to the Scriptures being a divine Revelation ; the Assent of the Intellect, and Consent of the Will is yielded to all the particular Doctrines contained in them ; tho' some of them relate likewise to things as incomprehensible, as the real intrinsic Nature of God and his Divine Attributes.*

THUS we see that Men must *Know*, before they can rightly *Believe* ; and have a full Conviction of their *Judgment* upon sufficient Evidence, before there is any closing of the *Will* to *Complete* the Nature of Evangelical *Faith* ; which is literaly as the Apostle defines it, *The Evidence of Things not seen*, or the Assent of the Understanding to the truth and Existence of things *Inconceivable*, upon certain and evident Proof of their *Reality* in their *Symbols* and *Representatives*.   This shews the strange Inconsistency of those Men who reject the Faith of Christian Mysteries, under Colour of wanting *Strict Reason* and *Evidence* ; for as it is their present Guilt, so the Ground of their Condemnation hereafter will be their *Want of Knowledge*, when they had all the proper *Means* of attaining it ; and that they did not yield the *Assent* of the *Understanding* upon the same or greater Moral Certainty and Evidence, than would be
a full

a full Conviction to them in Matters merely Human of the fame Sort. That they with-held that Affent either thro' *Paffion* or *Preju-dice*; or for want of *Application* to weigh and confider the Force of that Evidence; and that they infifted upon a *Sort* of Proof and Evidence, which is proper only to a quite different *Kind* of Knowledge, and fuch as would render all *Reli-gious Faith* impracticable.

THE Influence of the *Will* upon the Affent of the Intellect to Truths capable of *Moral E-vidence* only, is fo great, that if Men were once well enough inclin'd to Morality and *Natural* Religion, to wifh the *Gofpel* and all the Doc-trines and *Precepts* in it were true; they would foon difcern the prevailing Strength of that Moral Evidence which *Claims* and *Demands* the Affent of the Underftanding; as Chrift himfelf obferves, *John* vii. 17. ἐάν τις θέλῃ *If any Man is willing*, or *difpofed*, to *Do* the Will of God whatever it appears to be, *He fhall* KNOW *of the Doctrine, whether it be of God? On whether I fpeak of my felf?* But when Men are byaffed and blinded by their Immoralities and Violations of *Natural* Religion; then the plaineft Evidence even of *Senfation* for the Truth of any Doctrine, may be *Evaded*; as the Jews evaded the fenfitive Evidence of *Miracles* for our Saviour's Divine Miffion; nay tho' they called them *Miracles*, yet they attributed the Power by which they were wrought to
Beel-

Beelzebub the Prince of the Devils: And the Romanifts at this Day elude the cleareft Evidence of their *Senfes* in the Point of Transfubftantiation, by refolving an Heap of Contradictions both to Senfe and Reafon, into the Almighty Power of God. The cleareft Evidence and Conviction of *Self-Confcioufnefs* may be ftifled and loft for want of a due Attention and Regard to it; and thus Multitudes have overturned the glaring irrefragable Evidence of their own Minds for a *Freedom of Will*, by Arguments drawn from God's *Prefcience* and *Decrees*; which is oppofing the Evidence of *Reafon*, to that of *Self-Confcioufnefs*; a Knowledge of equal, if not greater Truth and Certainty than that of Reafon, and which ought not therefore to be confronted with it. So again, may the utmoft Degree of *Moral Certainty* always admit of fome *Evafion* or other; as the Jews evaded all the Arguments of Chrift for his Divine Miffion, drawn from *Types* and *Prophecies*; they were realy *Blind* to the Force of them from inveterate Prepoffeffion and Prejudice; and the Perverfenefs of their *Wills* quite obftructed all Affent of the *Intellect* to the Truth of his Doctrine. This is the very Defcription given of them by our Saviour himfelf. *They Seeing, fee not; and Hearing, they hear not, neither do they Underftand:* which was not from any *Natural* Defect in their *Intellectuals*, nor for want of the *Utmoft Moral Evidence*; but as he obferves, *Becaufe their Heart was*

was gross, and *Left they should* UNDERSTAND *with their* HEART.

THUS necessary to the Assent of the Intellect, even where there is the utmost *Moral Certainty* and Evidence, is the Concurrence of the *Heart* and *Will*, and an intire freedom from all Prejudice and Prepossession; and therefore the Guilt and Hypocrisy of the Jews consisted in this, that they were not as ready to give their Assent upon a Moral Certainty and Evidence in Matters of *Religion*, as in things indifferent and *Merely Human*. They could observe that when the *Skie* was *Red* in the *Evening*, it was a *Sign* of *Fair Weather* the Day following; and if *Red* and *Lowring* in the Morning, it was a *Sign* of *Foul Weather* that Day: But they *Could not discern the Signs of the Times*, and of that *Time* in particular wherein there was a Completion of all the antient Prophecies from the Beginning of the World, relating to the personal Appearance of the Messiah; and for this Reason it is that we find Christ upbraiding them not so much for want of *Faith*, as for their stupid and wilful *Ignorance*; calling them *Fools* and *Blind*, as being destitute of that *Knowledge* which was to have been the Foundation of their *Faith* in the promised Messiah.

2. THE other thing necessary to be observed in relation to Evangelical Faith is, that *Consent* of the *Will* and *Concurrence* of the *Heart* which

which is *Subsequent* to the Assent of the Intellect, and founded upon it ; and *is* to be well distinguished from any Influence of the Will which is *Prior* to that Assent. Every Assent of the Mind to the Truth of any Proposition capable of Moral Evidence only, hath been promiscuously and indifferently call'd a *Believing* it, to the great Confusion of our way of Thinking and Speaking. *Every* Assent of the Mind to any Truth in Religion is not *Faith*, tho' all Faith is an Assent of the Mind. This general Word *Belief* must therefore be well distinguished, into that Assent of the Mind which is properly *Knowledge* ; and the *Concurrence* of the *Heart* and *Will* which *Completes* and improves it into a *Religious* Faith, *Consequent* to that Knowledge ⟨and *Founded* upon it. The Assent of the Intellect, or *Judgment* of the Mind, must be *First* fixed or determined, in relation to any Proposition whatsoever in Religion ; the Proposition must be perfectly *Intelligible*, and the Truth of it must appear from a Moral Evidence, sufficient for a *Full* Conviction of the strictest Reason : So that it must be a Point of Knowledge, *Before* that full Consent of the Will and closing of the Heart with that Point of Knowledge, which renders it both *Faith* and *Knowledge* at the same time ; nor can there be an *Immediate* Assent of the Intellect, or Concurrence of the Will to any Proposition that is *Unintelligible* or *Incomprehensible* ; whatsoever is so, cannot be a *Direct* and *Immediate*

mediate

mediate Object either of *Knowledge* or *Faith*. I shall explain this by a few Instances, as particularly in this Proposition.

There is a God. This must be first well *Understood*; for tho' the whole Nature of God, and of all his *Real* intrinsic Attributes is utterly incomprehensible; yet we apprehend them all clearly, and they become very obvious and intelligible in their *Types* or *Analogical* Representations; particularly the Operations and Perfections of an human Mind. The Proposition is then *Proved* from the Light of Nature or Revelation, or from both; and the unprejudiced Mind yields an Assent to it upon the apparent reasonable and *Moral Evidence* there is for it; and this *Assent*, or *Belief* in *General*, as 'tis sometimes named, or *Speculative Faith* (as some call it) is realy so far properly *Knowledge*. But when the Will closes intirely with that Assent, and there is a Concurrence of the *Heart*, as well as of the *Head* to this great Truth; which doth ever more or less influence the Life and Manners of Men, in Proportion to the Attention and Application of their Minds to it; then it becomes a *Religious Faith* founded upon the utmost Moral Proof and Certainty: And as what is *Intelligible* in that Proposition, is the *Immediate* Object both of our *Knowledge* and *Faith*; so the *Remote* and *Mediate* Object of them both, is the *Incomprehensible Nature* and real *Intrinsic Attributes* of the Divinity.

THUS

THUS again, *The Scriptures are the Word of God*, or *A Divine Revelation.* If from the Miracles of our Saviour ; the exact and full Completion of Scripture Prophecies, from the Beginning of the World, centering in him only, and in no other Person whatfoever ; together with that Improvement and Exaltation of Natural Religion and Morality which is apparent thro' the whole Tenor of the Scriptures ; if, I fay, by Arguments drawn from thefe and fuch like Topics Men void of Prejudice yield an Affent to the Truth of this Propofition, it is ftill but *Knowledge* founded upon the utmoft Moral Certainty : And then it becomes properly *Evangelical Faith,* when there is a full Confent of the Will and a Concurrence of the Heart, together with an intire Refolution of yielding an Affent to the Truth of every Propofition contain'd in them ; and when this proceeds on to a ready Obedience, and to an actual Performance of the Precepts of the Gofpel, it may then properly be called a *Practical Faith.*

AGAIN, Chrift *Shall change our vile Body, that it may be like unto his glorious Body.* This Propofition is as *Intelligible* as any other wherein we affert one thing, or one Man to be *Like* another. When from the Proofs of the Scriptures in general being the Word of God, a Perfon unprejudiced yields the Affent of the In-

tellect

tellect to the Truth of this Propofition, he in ftrict Propriety may be faid to *Know* it : But the *Chriftian Faith* founded upon this Inftance of Knowledge, is a clofing of the Heart and Will with what appears to be true from full Proof and Evidence ; the Confequence of which is a lively *Hope* and Expectation of that great Change, tho' we know nothing of the true *Real Nature* and *Manner* of it, and do therefore reverence and regard it as a *Myfterious* incomprehenfible Truth.

Once more, *Chrift ever liveth to make Interceffion for us.* This Propofition is as intelligible as that wherein one *Man* is faid to intercede for another ; and the Truth of it depends upon the fame Moral Proof and Evidence with that foregoing. If a Perfon obftinately with-holds his *Affent* to the Truth of this Propofition it is wilful *Ignorance* properly, and Blindnefs in the midft of the cleareft Means of Knowledge. If he yields the Affent of the Intellect, this may be call'd *Believing* it in the general and confufed Senfe of that Term, as we are faid to *Believe* any thing we *Know* upon Moral Evidence. And then this Knowledge is improved to *Evangelical Faith*, when the full Confent and Concurrence of the Will falls in with it ; which is followed by a *Reliance* upon this Interceffion, tho' the *Nature* and *Manner* of this Divine Performance are fo incomprehenfible, that we can know nothing more of it, than that it cannot be after the fame Manner with any *Human* Interceffion ; or even *Angelic*, if it were poffible for us to have any Notion of fuch Interceffion.

I F it is here objected, that I place the diftinguifhing Character of *Evangelical Faith* in the Act of the Will, *Subfequent* to that Affent of the Intellect which is properly *Knowledge* ; and not in the Affent of the Mind to things *Incomprehenfible*, which feems to be the very thing that makes it *Properly Faith*. I anfwer, that the Affent of the Mind to the *Reality* and *Exiftence* of things *Incomprehenfible*, is not to be *Excluded* from the Nature of Evangelical Faith, for it muft *Mediately* and *Ultimately* refer to what is *Incomprehenfible*. But then this is of an *After* and *Secondary* Confideration ; and the true Nature of a *Religious Faith* is to be clearly ftated and refolved in refpect of what is *Directly* and *Immediately* underftood and comprehended, before any thing which is neither underftood nor comprehended can come into the Account, or be efteemed a neceffary Ingredient of it either in Natural or Reveal'd Religion. To explain this let us inftance in the fundamental Propofition of all Reveal'd Religion ; and the rather becaufe it was delivered by an audible Voice from Heaven.

This

This is my beloved Son.

THAT which makes this a Point of *Know-ledge*, is the *Assent* of the Intellect to the Truth of it, as a Proposition *Intelligible* and perfectly *Understood* as any thing in human Language ; and upon the utmost *Moral Proof* and Evidence of its being spoken from Heaven : This is *Believing* it in the *General* Acceptation of that Term, as you may be said to *Believe* any Proposition even in Civil Matters, which is so proved and understood. That therefore which makes it a *Religious Faith* must be some *Farther* Concurrence of the *Will* than what was necessary to make it *Knowledge* ; and that is a closing of the *Heart* with it as a Proposition in Religion ; and a full Persuasion of the *Mind* that Christ (not in any *Unintelligible* Manner, but) according to what the very Letter and strict Propriety of the Words import, is the *Son* of *God* in as *True* and *Real* a Sence, as one *Man* is the Son of another.

HE who believes thus far, and esteems and reverenceth Christ as such ; without any *Farther* respect to what is *Incomprehensible* in that Proposition, namely the *Supernatural Generation*, and the divine ineffable *Manner* of it ; hath an Orthodox *Evangelical Faith.* What then, you will say, becomes of the so much controverted *Mysteries* of the Gospel, and our *Faith* in them?

They

They are all very secure, and what is *Myste-rious* in the Propositions of the Gospel is all laid up out of our reach, to be the *Direct* and *Im-mediate* Objects of our *Knowledge* when we come to see *Face to Face*; and we are *Now* only to know and believe that they are *Incomprehen-sible.*

BUT you will ask again, What then be-comes of *Divine Analogy*, and of our *Conceptions* of things *Spiritual* by Symbol and Representa-tion; and of what use is this, if the Assent to what is *Incomprehensible* in them, is not the sole *Distinguishing* Mark of Evangelical Faith? I answer, that there was true *Evangelical Faith* in the World long before that *Analogy* was ever thought of; or the true Manner of our con-ceiving things *Divine* and *Spiritual* by Symbol and Representation only, came to be consi-dered and rightly adjusted. Men truly Or-thodox *Believed* as far as they *Understood*; and did not perplex or embarrass either their own Heads or the Christian Faith, with any nice and intricate Notions and Conceptions of what was utterly incomprehensible; it being no matter of *Duty* or *Obligation* in respect either of their *Knowledge* or *Faith*; and it being on the contrary matter of Duty to know and believe what they *Understood*, and not to con-cern themselves with those secret things which belong to God alone. They took every Pro-position in the most plain and *Obvious* Signification

cation of the Words, and yielded the *Affent* of the *Intellect*, and the *Confent* of the *Will* and Concurrence of the Heart to it as *Such*; they believed it as *Far* as it was *Intelligible*, and never did exprefly take what was *Incomprehenfible* into the Account of either their *Knowledge* or *Faith*; and it had been happy for the Chriftian World if it had continued fo to this Day.

BUT fince Infidels and Heretics began, on the quite *Contrary*, in all their Controverfies with the Orthodox, intirely to overlook or lay afide whatever was plain and *Obvious* and *Intelligible* in the Doctrines and Myfteries of the Gofpel; and to raife many Doubts and Difficulties about what is altogether *Unintelligible* or *Incomprehenfible*; fince they now oppofe what we can have no *Direct* Conception or Idea of, to what is plain and obvious and eafily underftood; and charge what is *Intelligible* with Abfurdity and Contradiction, by arguing from an intrinfic *Incomprehenfible Nature*; wherein they cannot judge or difcern what is, or is not *Confiftent* with it. And fince they labour to render the Chriftian Faith, plain and obvious in itfelf, dark and obfcure by judging of the *Antitypes* in all refpects as they do of the *Types*; forming all their Arguments upon this grofs Suppofition, That they muft *Both* be of the fame Nature and Kind in all refpects; and that things *Human* and *Divine* are alike to be

per-

perceived by *Direct* and *Immediate* Conceptions and Ideas. Then, I fay, it became neceſſary to diſtinguiſh rightly, in every Propoſition relating to our Chriſtian Myſteries, what is the *Direct* and *Immediate* Object of our *Knowledge* and *Faith*, which only is Matter of *Duty* and *Obligation*, and binding upon our Conſciences; and what is the *Mediate* only and *Ultimate* Object of them. Then we are compel'd to explain the Nature of that *Divine Analogy* by which we apprehend things otherwiſe incomprehenſible; and to place it in ſuch a full and glaring Light, that there may be a juſt and right Application of it, in all the chief Points of Controverſy with the Adverſaries of Revelation: In order to make it appear that the Aſſent of the Mind may, and muſt be given to the *Reality* and *Exiſtence* of things *Incomprehenſible* and ineffable; and that theſe cannot be *Excluded* from being the *Mediate* and *Ultimate* Objects both of our *Knowledge* and *Faith*.

Now tho' it was neceſſary to diſtinguiſh the *Aſſent* of the *Intellect* to what is perfectly underſtood, upon full Proof and the utmoſt Moral Certainty; the *Influence* of the *Will prior* to the yielding that Aſſent; the *Conſent* of the Will *Subſequent* to that Aſſent, and full *Concurrence* of the Heart to the Truth of the Propoſition aſſented to; and to the *Reality* and *Exiſtence* of what is *Ultimately* ſignified and intended in that Propoſition: Yet I would obſerve

ferve here, that all thefe together are ufualy
and not unaptly call'd by the Name of *Faith*
both in Natural and Reveal'd Religion.

A s *Faith* is founded upon *Knowledge*, fo we
can ftrictly and properly be faid to *Believe* only
what we *Know*; but this Faith at the fame
time neceffarily includes an Affent of the Mind
to the *Reality* and *Exiflence* of things, the true
Nature and Manner of which we can have no
Knowledge of by any *Direct* or *Immediate* Idea
or Conception. For tho' we can neither *Know*
nor *Believe in* God *As* he is *Incomprehenfible*, or
What is incomprehenfible in him; yet we both
know and believe that he *Is*, and that he *Is
Incomprehenfible :* So, tho' we neither *Know* nor
Believe the Myfterious Revelations of the Gofpel *As* they are incomprehenfible, or *What* is
Incomprehenfible in them; yet we both know
and believe them to *Be real, and Incomprehenfible.*

F R O M hence it appears that the Faith of
the Gofpel is no fuch *Implicit* and *Precarious*
Affent (as the Enemies of Revelation reprefent
it) to things altogether *Unintelligible* and *Inconceivable*; fince, as we have feen, nothing that
is *Incomprehenfible* and above Senfe and Reafon
can come at all into any *Queftion* between us :
All this muft be intirely laid afide, in thofe
Contefts and Difputes which have been raifed
concerning the *Evangelical Faith* of any Propofition; we can have no Controverfy but

about

about what is perfectly well *Underſtood*, and *As far* as it is ſo; and concerning that *Moral Certainty* and Evidence upon which Propoſitions as clear as any in human Language are founded. Our Controverſies muſt turn altogether upon the Point of *Knowledge*; and when that is decided, the Appeal muſt be from thence to the *Heart* and *Will*, whether this ought not to cloſe with that Point of Knowledge ſo as to render it Evangelical Faith; for as to what is utterly *Incomprehenſible* in any Propoſition whatſoever, it can be no direct and immediate Object either of *Knowledge*, or of that *Faith* which is built upon it.

III. The third Kind of Knowledge which we have from Deduction of Reaſon, is that of *Opinion*; the ſhorteſt and moſt apt Deſcription of which, that I have met with, is that of *Plato's*, who defines it *A Medium between Knowledge and Ignorance*; it is made up of a Mixture of both, and every *Opinion* is the more or leſs true or falſe, as one or the other of thoſe two Ingredients prevails. So that there can be no *Mere Opinion* of any thing known from external *Senſation*, or *Self-Conſciouſneſs*, or *Demonſtration*, or *Moral Certainty*; or even from *Sufficient Teſtimony* either Human or Divine: Tho' it may be *Founded* upon Topics drawn from any, or all of theſe Kinds of Knowledge, not excluding even *Science*; if they are firſt taken for *Granted*, and each of them eſtabliſhed upon that Certainty

tainty and Evidence which is peculiar to them.
This is a Kind of Knowledge *Inferior* to any
of the aforementioned, and approaches neareſt
to that which is founded on *Moral Evidence*;
but differs from it in this, that whereas in the
utmoſt Moral Certainty the Concluſion admits
but of a bare *Natural Poſſibility* of the things
being otherwiſe than we apprehend it, and leaves
no *Reaſonable* Cauſe of Doubt or Error: Here
the Concluſion ever follows from Premiſes *Indeterminate* and *Uncertain*; and accordingly
leaves room more or leſs for *Doubt*, and for
ſome *Likelihood*, or *Fear*, or *Diſtruſt* of the
things being otherwiſe than we apprehend it;
ſo that in reſpect of all the *Degrees* between the
utmoſt *Moral Certainty* in the *One* Extreme, and
the *Loweſt Probability* in the *Other*; theſe two
Kinds of Knowledge run into each other, and
are not eaſily to be diſtinguiſhed even in Imagination.

Now for the rightly adjuſting thoſe *Extremes*, as well as the ſeveral *Intermediate Degrees* of this *Mix'd* Kind of Knowledge, as we
may now call it; the beſt way I can think of
is, by a Parallel drawn from common Mecha-
niſm. Since all Kinds and Degrees of *Moral
Proof*, and *Probability* are no other than our
conſidering and offering the Reaſons *For* and
Againſt the *Truth* of any Propoſition; you
may imagine your ſelf throwing the Reaſons
and Arguments on both ſides into the *Scales*,
and

and weighing them in a *Balance*. If there is an *Æquilibrium* without any *Inclination* of the Balance to one fide or the other, it is then no Degree of *Knowledge*, nor even of *Doubting*; but downright *Ignorance:* The Reafons on both Sides deftroy each other, fo that the Intellect can form no Judgment, nor can it yield any *Affent*; and if there is any Decifion of the Point in Scrutiny, it muft be from the *Arbitrary* Impofition and precarious Act only of the *Will.* If from any *Natural Weaknefs* or *Defect*, or want of *Improvement* of the Intellect, it cannot find out the *True* Reafons; nor determine upon the intrinfic *Weight* of them, fo that the Judgment *varies*, and that each Scale preponderates *Alternately*; then nothing can be concluded, and it is a ftate of *Hefitation* and Sufpence, of *Doubtfulnefs* and Uncertainty. If one fide of the Queftion preponderates, tho' but a *Little*, and continues in one *Stay*; fo as that the Inclination or Difference is but fcarcely difcernible; it is then only a bare Appearance of Truth, and nothing more than a *Conjecture*. But if the Preponderancy is diftinctly *Plain* and *Vifible*, and yet there is Weight enough of Reafon on the *Contrary* fide of the Queftion, to continue the Scales ftill *Pendent* and in *Motion*; then indeed it is properly *Opinion* and *Probability:* And the matter of Opinion is better or worfe founded, according as it approaches nearer, either to mere *Conjecture* on the one hand; or to *Moral Certainty* on the other.

I
But

But then the *Nature* of it is changed, and it loſes the very *Name* of *Opinion* and *Probability*, and is reſolved into a *Moral Certainty*; when the Reaſons and Arguments are ſo ſtrong and cogent, that the *Scale* weighs to the *Ground*. For then the *Balance* is deſtroyed, and there is no reaſonable Cauſe left for a farther *Oppoſition* or *Scrutiny*; the Propoſition *Claims* the full Aſſent of every unprejudiced Mind, and ought to conclude and *Determine* the Judgment as *Surely*, tho' not as *Neceſſarily* as Demonſtration; the nature of which is to admit of no *Weight* whatſoever to be thrown into the *Oppoſite* Scale.

Now concerning this kind of Knowledge, which is diſtinguiſhed by the name of *Probability* or *Opinion*; whether it is founded *Internaly* upon our own Reaſon, or *Externaly* upon the *Teſtimony* and *Experience* of others, I ſhall obſerve theſe three Things.

1. THAT there are two latent Cauſes of the *Worſt* ſort of *Fraud* and *Deceit* in this Scrutiny for judging and determining upon the Truth of Propoſitions, in Religion eſpecialy, becauſe it is being deceived in Matters of utmoſt Conſequence. The one is in the *Intellect* itſelf, which holds the *Balance*; for if a Man is *Ignorant* and *Weak* in his Judgment, ſo as not to diſcern what Reaſons are proper to be conſider'd, and what are foreign to the Queſtion, he may be groſly
impoſed

impofed upon by *Falfe Weights:* And if his Ignorance proceeds from want of *Induftry* in the *Improvement* of his Underftanding; and of *Application* in the Ufe of thofe Means of Knowledge which are in his Power, his entertaining even *Wrong* Opinions is *Inexcufable.* The other too common Method of deceiving a Man's felf is, when inftead of plain and *Genuine Reafon*, he throws his *Humour*, or *Pride*, or *Paffion*, or *Prejudice*, or *Vanity* into the Scales; fo that thefe, by an invifible Difpofition or Turn of a *Falfe Balance* (which is here no lefs *An Abomination to the Lord*, than in Merchandize) fhall *Outweigh* the plaineft and moft cogent Arguments, which can be offered for the Truth of any Propofition.

2. THAT tho' mere *Probability* or *Opinion* is a kind of Knowledge *Inferior* to that of *Moral Certainty*, yet in Matters of Religion it *Deferves* and even *Requires* the Affent of the *Intellect* and Concurrence of the *Will.* In the common Affairs of *This* World, wherein Men are not fo fubject to Prejudice and Prepoffeffion, the *Higher Probability* always determines the Judgment; fo that in cafes wherein the Difference or Inequality between the two oppofite Sides of the Queftion is not very *Diftinguifhable*, Men ever clofe intirely with the greateft Appearance and Likelihood of Truth, even in Matters of the greateft Confequence; wherein the Health of their *Bodies*, and their whole worldly

worldly *Fortune* is concerned; nay, and when their very *Lives* are at ſtake: And this is ſo remarkably true, that the main Conduct of human Life, thro' the whole Courſe of *Temporal Affairs* is influenced and governed by the *Higheſt Probability*; inſomuch that in many Inſtances it would be eſteemed downright *Folly* and *Madneſs* not to be determined and directed by it.

THIS *Opinion* or *Probability* ought to have its proper *Weight* in matters of *Religion* likewiſe; the beſt Proof that can be thought of, or offered in every Inſtance of any Importance here, *Ought* to determine the Aſſent of the *Intellect*; and this ſhould be follow'd with a Conſent of the *Will*. Religious Matters of *Opinion* only, and founded upon a *Reaſonable Probability* are of no ſmall Conſequence to the promoting Virtue and Holineſs in every Man in *Particular*, and contribute not a little to Peace and Unanimity in the Church in *General*; ſo that tho' the Things themſelves, which are founded on *Probability*, may be in their own Nature *Indifferent*; yet the Determination of the *Judgment* concerning them, as far as Men are able, may become no Matter of *Indifferency*, but of *Duty* and *Obligation*; becauſe all Chriſtians ought, as far as it is practicable, to arrive at a perfect Harmony and Agreement even in religious *Opinions*. *Prove* or try ALL *Things*, ſays the Apoſtle, *hold faſt* or adhere firmly to

4

That

That which is good. We are for Peace fake *Oblig'd* to ufe the beft Means of informing the Judgment in thefe religious Matters even of *Opinion*; which tho' they cannot *Claim* or *Demand* the Affent of the Mind, as in *Moral Certainty*; may yet render the with-holding it, fo as to keep the Mind ever *Fluctuating* and in Sufpence, utterly *Inexcufable*: And this is the Cafe of thofe who, in one Extreme, will give no firm Affent to any thing in Religion, without *Demonftration* and *Mathematical Certainty*; and of thofe, in the other Extreme, who take up their *Opinions* without a juft Regard to any impartial Reafoning of their *Own*, or to the Decifions and Determinations either of the *Church* in general, or of fuch as ought to be prefumed the moft *Wife* and *Knowing* in it; which have been always reckoned the fundamental *Rules* of *Probability*, with regard to religious *Opinions*. The danger of Deceit and Fallacy here is, when Men put any degree of *Mere Probability* upon the Foot of *Moral Certainty* and *Evidence*; or on the *Contrary*, what is moraly *Certain* and *Evident* upon the Foot only of a *Bare Probability*.

3. THE laft thing I fhall obferve is, that no Point of *Mere Opinion* and *Probability*, can be a fufficient Foundation for a religious *Faith*, in the true and *Proper* Acceptation of that Word. *Faith* muft be built upon *Knowledge*; and if that is *Not Clear* and *Certain*, the Affent
of

of the Intellect and Concurrence of the Will muſt
be *Dubious* and *Wavering* ; and of Conſequence
not abſolutely *Obligatory* upon the Conſciences of
Men, as every Article of the *Chriſtian Faith* is.
We may indeed be ſaid to *Believe* things for
which we have *No* moral Certainty ; but then
that *Belief* muſt have the ſame degrees of *Wa-*
vering and *Uncertainty*, with that *Probable Know-*
ledge only upon which it is founded.

Opinion hath been uſed promiſcuouſly, in the
large and *Vulgar* Sence of the Word, to expreſs
indifferently *Any* Judgment of the Mind form'd
either upon *Moral Certainty*, or *Bare Probability*
only ; ſo that nothing is more common than to
ſay, a Man is of ſuch or ſuch *Opinions*, in relation
even to the plain *Fundamentals* of Chriſtianity ;
and the *Equivocation* or *Fallacy* latent in that
Term hath too often given a ſpecious Colour
to the fatal and deadly Errors of ſome Men ;
and hath a tendency to deceive ſuch as are
truly Orthodox into a mild and favourable
Judgment of ſuch Principles as are abſolutely
Heretical : Whereas in the *True* and *Proper* Signification of that Term, it is to be reſtrained to
that Aſſent of the Mind which is founded upon
any Proof or Evidence *Short* of a *Moral Certainty.*
Hence therefore we have this peculiar *Mark*
and *Character* of *Hereſy*, as it is diſtinguiſhed
from all erroneous *Opinions* in the general ; that
it is a Denial of a *Plain* and expreſs *Religious*
Doctrine or Propoſition, in the moſt obvious
and

and intelligible Sence of the Words, which is founded upon a *Moral Certainty* and *Evidence:* And whether fuch a Propofition is denied *Exprefly*, or by *Immediate* neceffary *Confequence*, it makes no *Alteration* in the nature of the thing; there is only this *Circumftantial* Difference, that the one is more *Covert* and clandeftine, the other hath an Air of *Opennefs* and Ingenuity.

FOR inftance, as if a Perfon fhould affert, *That Chrift is not the only begotten Son of God*, in as *True* and *Real a Sence and full Import of thofe Terms*, tho' not in the fame *Literal Propriety* of Them, *as when they are ufed for an human Son*; *but in mere Metaphor only. That the Holy Spirit of God is not God*; *nor ought to be call'd fo. That the Son is not* Originaly *and* Intirely *of the fame real Nature and Effence with his true Father. That the Son and Holy Ghoft are not Divine* Perfons in the plain, and obvious, and moft intelligible Sence of the Term *Divine*; but in fome *Abftract Metaphyfical Acceptation of it, fo unintelligible that it will not admit of any Explanation. That we muft worfhip the Son as an* OMNIPRESENT INVISIBLE *Being*; *and yet muft not pay him* SUPREME *and* ULTIMATE *Worfhip.* And fhould be pofitive that *Chrift is not the true God*; and aggravate this by adding, *That they are worthy of Cenfure who fay he was made out of nothing*; tho' this can mean no more than, *Let Men imagine him to be what elfe they pleafe, yet he is not the true God.* And fhould likewife hold firmly

That

That Christ is not Co-eternal with the Father; and should add, that *They are justly censured who say there was a Time when he was not*; tho' this cannot possibly have any other intelligible Sence or Meaning, but that *Tho' he is not eternal as the Father is, yet they deserve Censure who presume to say he is not Eternal:* Or at best, *Let Men think what they will else of him, yet they must not think him truly Eternal.*

Tho' Men are indispensably bound in *Duty* to agree in all Points of Religion which are *Plain* and perfectly *Intelligible*, and for which there is a *Moral Certainty*, as being the *Essentials* of it; yet they may often be of different *Opinions* in other Points of it which are not so, without any just blame or Censure: For the *Weakness* of human *Understanding* is such; there are such different *Turns* in Mens Minds; they have so many various ways of *Thinking*; and there is such a want of *Education* and *Refinement* in the Generality of Mankind; that after the most *Sincere* and *Diligent* Endeavours they cannot exactly agree in Matters of mere *Probability*. The unavoidable *Necessity* of this variety of Opinions often renders it *Excusable*; and it is attended with this accidental Advantage, that it affords a large Scope for the Exercise of *Humanity*, and *Meekness*, and *Condescention* in Men, and for their *Bearing* with one another. But then it ought well to be consider'd, that tho' this Difference in religious Matters of *Opi-*

T

nion may be very allowable and *Innocent* in itfelf; yet it may become highly *Criminal* when
Men confound things for which there is no
other than a bare *Probability*, with fuch as
have a plain *Undeniable Certainty* and Evidence:
And when with matter of *Opinion* only they
intermix *Pride* and *Vanity*, *Prefumption*, *Pofitivenefs*, or *Prejudice*; *Breach of Communion*,
and Refiftance of *Lawful Authority*, or *Difobedience* to fpiritual *Governors*; who for that very
reafon, becaufe Men cannot be fuppos'd to
agree intirely in religious Matters of mere *Opinion* and *Probability*, and becaufe thefe are not
Fundamental or *Effential* to Religion, have undoubted Power of *Juding* and *Determining* finaly
in *Such* Matters; tho' they have no farther Power in Matters *Effential*, and founded upon plain
Moral Certainty and Evidence than that of *Explanation* and *Illuftration* only.

IV. T H E fourth and laft Head of Knowledge
obtained by *Deduction* of *Reafon* is that which
is derived from the *Experience* and *Information*
of others, and is founded upon *Teftimony*. This
is a kind of Knowledge very different in its
Nature from any of the former, and built on
a very different kind of Evidence; and it hath
been very imperfectly defin'd, *An Affent of the
Mind given to the Truth of any Thing upon the
Teftimony of another*; to which fhould have been
added, *upon a full Conviction of the Reafonable-
nefs of yielding that Affent:* For every Propofition

tion to which we yield an Affent, either *Is* or *Ought* to be a Point of *Knowledge*, before it can regularly be either a *Belief* in general, or a religious *Faith* in particular. The firft Part of that Definition hath blended together thefe feveral things very *Different* in themfelves, and which ought to be well diftinguifhed; namely *Knowledge*; *Belief* in general; a true religious *Faith*; and a blind *Implicit Affent* of the Mind, that is, where there is not firft fuch a *Conviction of Reafon* as is a juft and folid *Ground* for that Affent.

ALL the kinds of Knowledge we have hitherto treated of arofe from *Our felves*, and refulted from the *Immediate* Ufe and Exercife of our own *Natural Faculties*; but this is in a great meafure from *Without* us, and is owing to the *Reafon* and Underftanding of *Others:* Which then becomes truly *Our own*, when we give no hafty and precarious Affent to any Information or Teftimony; but ufe our *Reafon* ftrictly and impartialy in *Searching* and Trying every Inftance of this Knowledge, fo as to *Approve* or *Reject* it as it appears to us to be true or falfe, reafonable or abfurd; or in Proportion to thofe Degrees of *Probability* wherewith it comes recommended.

Now, there muft be fuch a Concurrence of our *Own Reafon* in thefe following Particulars, with regard to every Point of *Information* or *Teftimony*, as fhall render it truly *Knowledge*, as well as *Belief* or *Faith*.

T 2   1. OUR

1. OUR own Reason must be imploy'd in judging of the *Subject Matter* of the Information; and whether the *Words* and *Language* in which the Information is made are perfectly *Intelligible?* If they are not to be *Understood*, the Information is to be rejected, not as *Abfurd* or *Contradictory*; but as being *Sencelefs* and without any *Meaning* at all. No Man can be inform'd of what he is not *Capable* of understanding; and there can be no Information or Revelation to Mankind concerning the *Real Intrinfic* Nature of any thing in itself *Incomprehenfible* to us; the Information must be of something so *Plain* and *Intelligible* that *Reafon* can clearly apprehend it, and judge of it. So that no divine Revelation concerning *God* and his *Attributes*, the *Myferies* of Chriftianity, and all things *Supernatural* and *Spiritual*, reaches any farther than their *Exiftence* only, and that lively *Symbol* and *Analogy* under which they are reprefented to the Mind of Man; which is as *Plain* and obvious, and *Intelligible* as any thing in Nature and common Life.

2. SECONDLY, Reafon must be convinced that the fubject Matter of the Information is *Poffible*, and that it implies no Abfurdity or *Contradiction*. And if the *Information* is concerning any thing *Supernatural* and *Spiritual*, this is a fundamental *Rule* for the Procedure of the Intellect; that it muft deduce no Abfurdity or Contradiction

tradiction but from what is plain and *Intelligible* in every Proposition: And it must conclude that such Absurdities and Contradictions as arise from a *Comparison* between what is plain and *Intelligible*, and that which is *Incomprehensible*, in respect of their real *Intrinsic Natures*, are all groundless and imaginary; as for instance in this Proposition, *Christ is the only begotten Son of God.* Now, that one Person should be the only begotten Son of another, is plain and intelligible; and a Man who believes the Scriptures to be the Word of God, concludes, without any farther Examination of what is *Unintelligible* and *Incomprehensible*, that this is as true and as void of Absurdity and Contradiction in respect of the *Divine* Nature, as it is in common Speech among *Men*; which is the Substance of this Proposition as far as we are obliged to *Understand* and *Believe* it: And he will look upon it as impious *Trifling* with the plain Word of God to raise any Absurdities and Contradictions, from such a *Comparison* between *Human* and *Divine* Generation, as infers that the *Son* cannot be intirely of the *Same Nature* and *Essential Perfections* with the *Father*.

As it is the Office and Privilege of *Reason* to reject every Information, which carries any manifest Absurdity or Contradiction *In itself*; so it must observe narrowly whether it is contradictory to any of the *Preceding* Articles of Knowledge; that of *Sensation* or *Self-Consciousness,*

nefs, or *Demonſtration*, or *Moral Certainty*, or
even to any *Great* Degree of *Probability :* For
tho' theſe may *Combine* together for the Confirmation of the *Same* Truth ; yet ſince they
are all *Natural* means of Knowledge , and
when they are truly genuine can never *Deceive,*
they are every one of them to be duly regarded
in their *Kind,* and are never to be ſet in *Oppo-*
ſition to one another.

3. T H I R D L Y, our *Reaſon* muſt judge and
determine concerning the *Ability* and *Sincerity*
of the *Perſon* from whom the Information
comes. In order to this Judgment, *Informa-*
tion together with the *Teſtimony* or Evidence
upon which it is founded, muſt be divided into
that which is merely *Human,* and that which
is *Divine.* As to *Human* Information, we yield
the Aſſent of the Intellect to it in Proportion
only to what appears agreeable to *Truth* from
our *Own* Faculties of Underſtanding ; and by
the uſe of our *Reaſon* we make what was the
Knowledge of *Others* properly our *Own.* This
is very extenſive, and makes up the greateſt
Part of that Knowledge with which the Mind
of Man is furniſhed ; it takes in all that we
have from the Hiſtory of *Mankind* and of *Na-*
ture ; the Accounts we have of all the Parts of
the World which we have not ſeen ; and in
ſhort all that we have from the Reaſon and
Experience of *Other* Men : And we acquieſce
in all this as ſo much *Real* Knowledge, and not

as

as any *Precarious* implicite *Belief*; but as an Affent of the Mind founded upon fuch human Teftimony, as amounts to a *Moral Certainty*.

As to *Divine* Information or *Revelation*, no Search or Inquiry of this Nature can be made; fince Reafon hath *Already* a full Conviction that it muft exceed all human Certainty; for God can neither be deceived himfelf, nor deceive others. So that in refpect of Divine Revelation in particular, the laft thing our Reafon is to have a full Conviction of is

4. FOURTHLY, that the *Information* or *Revelation* comes from *God*; or that the *Scriptures* wherein thefe Revelations are made are of *Divine Authority*; for a right Apprehenfion of which I fhall obferve thefe two Things.

1. THAT as God hath made *Man* the immediate *Inftrument* of all Thofe Revelations, fo muft *Evangelical Faith* be partly founded upon *Human* Teftimony or Evidence. *Men* were the Authors of all the Books in the Old and New Teftament; and if we confider them abftractedly from any Confideration of their *Divine* Authority, they muft be allow'd of equal Credibility at leaft with all *Other* Antient Writings; that is if we examine them impartialy by the fame Rules of Criticifm, by which we make a Judgment of other Authors.

T 4

If

If we confider the *Characters* of the facred **Pen-Men**; their *Antiquity*, *Style*, and *Manner* of Writing; the *Opportunities* they had of being *Themfelves* well *Informed* of the Truth of what they tranfmitted down to Pofterity; the great Weight and *Importance* of the Subjects they treated of; the Accounts given of them by their *Cotemporaries*, and by thofe who lived in the *Neareft* Ages to them; their intire *Confiftency* with themfelves; together with the perfect *Harmony* there is between all thofe who in feveral *Diftant* Ages have purfued the fame defign: Tho' we fhould fuppofe the Scriptures to be upon the foot of mere *Human* Teftimony and Evidence; yet in thefe, as well as in all *Other* refpects, our *Knowledge* of them, and the *Belief* that is built upon that Knowledge, muft be of equal Truth and *Certainty* with that which is founded upon any *Profane* Hiftory. We may as truly and properly be faid to *Know* all the Facts and Tranfactions related in Scripture, and to be as *Sure* and as well informed of the *Qualifications*, and *Characters*, and *Conduct*, and *Performances* of all the Perfons mentioned in it, and of *Chrift* and his *Apoftles* in particular: And we have the fame *Moral Certainty* even upon the Foot of *Human* Teftimony, that there *Were* fuch Perfons, and that they fpoke and acted fuch things as are related of them; as we have that there were fuch Perfons as *Pilate*, and *Herod*, and *Auguftus*, and *Tiberius Cæfar*; and of all thofe
Actions

Actions and *Exploits* of theirs whereof we have a particular Account in *Profane* History.

Now if to this Testimony merely *Human*, and founded upon the *Credibility* and *Faith* of antient *History* in general, we add that which is *Divine*, and which cannot be *Pretended* for any other Writings in the World; such as the *Miracles* of Christ and his Apostles, to which they always appeal'd for the Truth of their Doctrine and Mission; the concurrent *Completion* of all the *Prophecies* relating to the *Messiah* from the Beginning of the World, in the Person of Christ *Alone*; the Scriptures being the only Book in the World which gives us any Account of the whole Series of God's *Dispensations* towards Mankind, from the first *Creation* for about four thousand Years together; the great *Improvement* of *Natural* Religion, and *Exaltation* of *Morality* so visible thro' the whole Tenor of Scripture. And lastly, the *Providential* Care and Caution so signal and manifest in every Age, for transmitting down Books written at such great distances of time from *One another*, and *All* of them from *Us*; their being at this Day so *Consistent* among themselves, and so void of any *Material* Error, that in the immense Number of *Various Readings*, which have been with great Labour collected, there cannot any one Instance be found of a *Contrariety* or *Opposition* in respect of any *Fundamental* Point of *Faith* or *Practice*. If these

things,

things, I fay, are fuperadded and thoroughly confidered, they give the Scriptures the utmoft *Moral Certainty*, fuch as no merely *Human* Writings can admit of: and are the greateft Proof and Evidence for the Truth of them which we are *Capable* of receiving, without a continued daily *Repetition* of *Miracles* thro' every Generation. It is an Evidence founded upon the *Teftimony* of *God* and *Man*; fuch as *Claims* and *Demands* the Affent of the *Intellect*, and that Concurrence of the *Heart* and *Will* which renders it an *Evangelical Faith* built upon the ftricteft Operation of Reafon, and the utmoft Effort of human Underftanding. So that *Revelation* is a *Solid* Ground of *Perfuafion*; and our *Faith* is founded upon the Teftimony of *God:* But *Reafon* firft provides that the Foundation is *Sure* and rightly laid; that we do not miftake that Teftimony for what is merely *Human*, and build our Faith upon the Sand; and that the fpecious Superftructure be not *Ignorance* or *Superftition*, a blind *Credulity* or *Enthufiafm*.

BUT there is one thing more which clears up this Moral Certainty or Evidence beyond all Evafion; and that is, that the Authors of the Books in Scripture *Profeffed* to have wrote them by an immediate divine Commiffion and *Infpiration*; and moft of them proved the Truth of this by *Miracles*, which were allowed by all to be *Such* at the time they were wrought:
And

And in thofe miraculous Operations they were
fo far from gratifying any *Vanity* or *Intereft* of
their own, that they fuffered the utmoft *Contempt*, and bodily *Pain*, and even *Death* for
the Doctrines they confirmed by them. Now,
had they penned down the Scriptures as dicta-
ted *Verbatim* by an *Audible* articulate *Voice*
from Heaven as loud as Thunder, this would
not have amounted to a greater *Moral Certainty* for the Truth of them, than what we
now have: For the Authors would ftill have
been *Men*; we now muft have rely'd upon the
Teftimony of Men and the fame fecret Providence of God for their being tranfmitted
Pure and uncorrupted down to Pofterity; and
we might as well have been deceived in *This*,
as in the *Profeffion* made by the original Authors, of their having wrote by an immediate
Divine Infpiration.

2. THE other thing well worth Obfervation here is, that as God hath made *Men* the
immediate Inftruments of all his Revelations;
fo in merciful Condefcention to the Weaknefs
of our Underftanding he hath made ufe of
human *Language*, as well as of our *Natural*
and moft *Familiar Conceptions* and Ideas for
the clear and eafy Reprefentation and Difco-
covery of things fupernatural, and otherwife
altogether incomprehenfible. Since Men were
the Inftruments of thefe Revelations, they
could not have been made in the Language of
Angels;

Angels; or in any such *Proper* Terms as would literaly have expreffed the *Real intrinfic* Nature of heavenly Things; there being no *Capacity* in Man for any Ideas or Conceptions of their *Real* Nature, nor any *Words* in human Language to exprefs them. And if we fhould fuppofe that by a *Miraculous* Operation a Man had any fuch *Vifions and Revelations* of their real Nature vouchfafed to him either *In the Body*, or *out of the Body*, they would be *Unfpeakable*, and it would not be poffible for him to utter them; fo that he could not be the Inftrument of *Conveying* them to the reft of Mankind. This made it neceffary to have all the divine Revelations adapted to our natural Way of *Thinking* and *Speaking*; and accordingly the Wifdom of God hath fo ordered it, that we are not obliged to yield either the *Affent* of the *Intellect*, or *Confent* of the *Heart* and *Will*, to any Doctrine which is not as plain or *Intelligible* as any thing in common Life: All therefore *Beyond* this, which is *Unintelligible* or *Incomprehenfible* in any Scripture Propofition, is no *Immediate* and *Proper* Object either of Chriftian *Knowledge* or *Faith*; it belongs to *Another* World; and we are at prefent to know and believe no more of it, than that it is *Incomprehenfible*, and therefore referved intirely for the Beatific Vifion.

THUS we fee no *Affent* of the Mind can be given to any thing *Intirely* unintelligible or incomprecomprehenfible, upon the *Teftimony* either of *God* or *Man*; and if the Divine Revelations had not been very plain and intelligible, they never could have been *Conveyed* down to *Us* by thofe who received them firft; for Men could never have tranfmitted to *Pofterity* what they had no Knowledge of *Themfelves*. So that nothing can be more unreafonable and groundlefs, than the *Objections* of Unbelievers and Freethinkers againft our Chriftian Myfteries, as *Unintelligible* and *Incomprehenfible*; fince they are *Obliged* to know and believe nothing more in them, than what is *Plain* and eafy, and very *Intelligible*. The fame Objections will lie as ftrongly againft all that the *Heathen* Moralifts have wrote concerning *God* and his *Attributes*; nor for the fame Reafon could any *Intelligible* Sence or *Meaning* of their Writings upon thofe Subjects have been ever handed down to us; for nothing can be in its own intrinfic Nature more Myfterious and Incomprehenfible than God and his Attributes; and therefore by that way of arguing Men muft reject all the fundamental Articles of *Natural* Religion.

SINCE it is thus evident that *Evangelical Faith* requires the Affent of the Mind to nothing but what is plain and *Intelligible* in every Propofition, in the moft common and obvious Signification of the Words; let every Man firft have a full Conviction of the Truth of each Propofition in the Gofpel, as far only as it is

Plain

Plain and *Intelligible* ; and then let him firmly *Believe* as far as he *Understands.* Let him believe firmly, and without any bafe *Equivocation* or *Fallacy*, that there is but **One** God, the fole and only invifible Object of *Any* Divine *Worfhip* whatfoever : And *Think* and *Speak* of him, and *Worfhip* him under that plain and perfonal Diftinction of *Father, Son*, and *Holy Spirit*, which moft exprefly runs thro' the whole Style of the New Teftament ; and leave the *Incomprehenfible Unity* and *Diftinction* (as common Sence would direct him) to the great *Author of our Faith* himfelf. Let him believe Chrift to be *The only begotten Son of God*, in the moft *Full* and moft *Obvious* Import of thofe Words ; that is, in as much *Truth* and *Reality* as one *Man* is the *Son* of *Another :* And leave the Divine *Incomprehenfible Generation* to the Veracity of God ; who propofed his Revelations to be *Underftood* and *Believed*, according to the Way of Thinking and Speaking amongft *Men.* Let him believe that Chrift, by his Death, did as *Truly* and *Actualy* make an *Atonement* to God for our Sins; as one *Man* works an Atonement and Reconciliation to *Another* for the Offences of a *Third* Perfon : And leave the *Unintelligible Reality*, and ineffable *Manner* of that Divine Operation for the Subject of eternal Contemplation and Praife in another World. And fo likewife in every *Other* Inftance of what goes under the Name of *Myftery* in the Gofpel : Let him believe the *Blood* of of Christ hath the same intrinsic Virtue and Efficacy, for the *Real* and *Actual* cleansing of the Soul from the Guilt and Pollution of Sin ; that Water hath for the washing any Filth or Dirt off from the Body. That the *Intercession* made in our behalf by Christ is as *Truly*, and *Realy*, and *Actualy* such ; as if it were a strictly *Proper* and *Literal* Intercession. That Men shall undergo a great and glorious *Change* at the Resurrection of the Just; as *Truly* as a Man is here changed from the *Point* of *Death*, to a state of perfect *Health* ; or from the Condition of a *Slave*, to the Glory of a *Kingdom*. Let Men I say *Believe* as far as they thus perfectly and clearly *Understand*, without perplexing and confounding themselves or others with what is *Incomprehensible*, and then they answer all the Ends of an *Evangelical Faith* ; and do fulfil the whole Purpose of God in all his divine Revelations.

IF Men would come about to this *Primitive* Temper and Spirit of *Believing* ; and leave off darkning and disturbing the Faith of Christians, which is plain in itself, by blending what is obvious and *Intelligible* with what is *Unintelligible* and *Incomprehensible :* Then we shall relinquish all *Analogy* ; and there will be no occasion for obviating all their pretended *Absurdities* and *Contradictions*, by shewing how we are under a *Necessity* of apprehending things spiritual and divine in Types only and Symbolical

bolical *Reprefentations*. But fince the profefs'd and open *Arians*, and *Socinians*, and *Deifts*, and *Freethinkers* have utterly declin'd the *Natural* and *Eafy* way of *Believing* ; laying afide all that is obvious and *Intelligible* in the Doctrines of the Gofpel, on account of what is altogether *Unintelligible* and ineffable. And fince our modern *Clandefine Arians* have, from their grofs Ideas of three *Human Perfons*, or rather even three *Bodily Subfances*, argued the *Son* and *Holy Ghoft* to be actualy and intirely *Separate* from the *Father*, as we conceive *Three Men* to be *Separate* from one another ; and confequently *Subordinate* and *Inferior* to him. And fince thefe Enemies of Revelation have gained fo great a Point, as to draw off the Learned and worthy Defenders of Chriftianity from the *Plain* and open *Field* of *Battle*, into *Unknown* Ground full of inextricable *Mazes* and *Windings :* Where they are obliged to *Engage* them by undertaking Solutions of what is never to be folved ; by *Explaining* what is *Inexplicable* ; and by elaborate *Illufrations* of things altogether in the *Dark*. Since, I fay, this is evidently the prefent State and Condition of Chriftianity among us ; the Doctrine of *Divine Analogy* is now become abfolutely neceffary ; and is like to continue fo as long as this Strain of Infidelity fo prevailing in our Age fhall laft ; which it is to be fear'd may, in a greater or lefs Degree, be tranfmitted down to lateft Pofterity.

T H E

THE Reason why I have, in this *Prelimi-nary* Treatise, began with the firſt *Rudiments* of Knowledge; and traced the *Procedure* of the Un-derſtanding thro' every *Step*, from Ideas of *Senſa-tion* up to our Conceptions of things *Supernatu-ral* and *Spiritual*, may not perhaps be ſoon dif-cerned: Yet I doubt not but the *Neceſſity* of it will evidently appear hereafter, when Men come to ſee the great *Uſefulneſs* and Advan-tage of applying this Doctrine to our preſent *Controverſies* with all Sorts of Unbelievers; to-gether with the *Difficulty* of that Application, ſo as to run neither into the ſtrictly *Literal* and *Proper* Acceptation of Scripture Terms, on the one hand; nor into mere *Metaphor* and *Al-luſion* only, on the other.

I HOPE I need not apologize for diſtinguiſh-ing the ſeveral *Kinds* of *Knowledge* with ſome Exactneſs; together with that Kind of *Evi-dence* which is proper to each of them. The Mind of every judicious Reader muſt ſuggeſt to him, what *Light* and *Direction* it adminiſters for the Procedure of the Underſtanding in ge-neral, as well as in Matters of Natural and Reveal'd Religion in particular; and what endleſs *Confuſion* and *Uncertainty* may hereby be prevented in all our Religious *Controverſies* and Diſputes: Eſpecialy if he hath obſerved, how theſe have all ariſen from abſurdly ſup-poſing the ſeveral Heads of Knowledge above-

U   mentioned

mentioned to differ only in *Degree,* and not in *Kind*; from blending and confounding the different Kinds of *Proof* and *Evidence* peculiar to each of them; from Mens insisting upon a Proof and Evidence peculiar to *One* Kind of Knowledge for that of *Another,* which is of a quite different Nature, and will not admit of it; from *Opposing* the different *Kinds* of Knowledge and Evidence to one another, which are each of them perfect in their Kind, and must never be supposed to interfere or clash with one another; and lastly from not distinguishing between a blind *Implicit Assent* of the Mind upon the bare Word or Testimony of another, and that *Faith* which results from a full *Conviction* to *Reason* of the Truth of what is believed.

C H A P.   VII.

Of the farther Improvement of Knowledge by Relations revealed.

WE have now by several Steps brought the Mind of Man to the utmost Bounds of that Knowledge, which it can possibly arrive at by the Strength of its own unassisted Faculties; and where all the declared Enemies of Revelation and Mystery take up their Rest. Whatever Knowledge it obtains beyond that

included

included under the foregoing Heads, is communicated to it from Heaven. Accordingly,

WHEN the Mind comes to learn and consider first, the more *Particular* and *Full* Difcoveries which are made to us of those *Rela-*
tions we had already some Knowledge of by
the Light of *Nature*; and secondly those Relations we bear to God, and he to us, which
are intirely *New* and *Indifcoverable* by Reason;
this Knowledge includes the Substance and
Foundation of all Reveal'd Religion.

1. As to the First, when to that general
Knowledge we have by the Light of Nature of
God as the *Creator* of all things, it is revealed
that he *Spoke* them into Being, and created
them by the *Word*; that he made Man in particular of the *Earth*, to which he added a *Di-*
vine Principle of another Kind, breathed into
it immediately from himfelf; and that the
Living Soul was the refult of that Union of
Matter and Spirit; that he was created in *In-*
nocence, and in the *Likenefs* and *Image* of God;
that *Adam* and *Eve* were the first created Pair,
and that all Mankind defcended from them.

AGAIN, when to the general Relation of
his *Providence* over us, it is more particularly
reveal'd, that he *Upholdeth all things by the*
Word *of his Power*; that *in him we live, move,*
and have our Being; that a *fingle Sparrow doth*

not

not fall to the Ground without him; and *that the very Hairs of our Head are all numbered.* And laftly, when that Relation he bears to us as a *Judge*, is rendered more full and exprefs by thefe farther Particulars; That the *Eyes of the Lord are in every Place beholding the Evil and the Good*; that *God fhall bring every Work into Judgment, with every fecret thing, whether it be good or whether it be evil*; that he hath *Appointed a Day in the which he will judge the World in Righteoufnefs*; that in *Order to this univerfal Judgment there fhall be a Refurrection of the Dead, both of the juft and of the unjuft*; and that thofe who are alive at the laft Day *Shall be changed in a Moment, in the Twinkling of an Eye.*

AGAIN, when it is revealed that there is but *One* God; for tho' the neceffary Exiftence of one *Firft Caufe* of all things, could be inferred by the Light of Nature; yet this was a Degree of Knowledge fo *General* and *Imperfect*, and fo little weighed and confider'd, that Deities were multiplied in the Heathen World according to all the Wants and Neceffities of human Life: Infomuch that Revelation became abfolutely neceffary to fix Mankind in the belief of *One only true God*, and that there is *No other God but one.* Of this one only God feveral Particulars are more exprefly revealed in Scripture; as That he is a *Spirit*; That there is *None good but he*; That he *Only is wife*, and that his Wifdom is infinite; That he is *Almighty*, hath all *Power*, and is the *Only Potentate*, *King of Kings*, and *Lord of Lords*; That he is *Above all*; That he is *Just*, and *Righteous*, and *Merciful*, and *Holy*; That he is *Loving*, and *Gracious*, and *Long-suf-fering*; That he sees the *Secrets of all Hearts*, and will reward every Man *According to his Works*; That he only hath Immortality, and Life *In himself*; That he is the Moft High God and *Lord of Hofts*, *incorruptible*, *invifible*. Thefe and fuch like more *Full* and *Exprefs* Characters we meet with in Scripture of the *One only true God*, and which are applied to him only, and can be attributed to none but him. And thefe, with many fuch other Inftances, are Improvements in that Knowledge we already have by the Light of Nature, of thofe Relations which God and the things of another World bear to us; and have a direct tendency to the Refinement of genuine Morality, and the exaltation of it into Chriftianity.

THESE Expreffions are all plain and intelligible; fo that when we fpeak of the *One* God in this Language of Scripture, we know what we fay; and tho' thefe Points are in fome Meafure agreeable to the Light of *Nature*, yet this *Full* and exprefs and *Clear* Revelation of them is become Matter of *Faith*, in which all Chriftians muft now agree. But as to fuch Words and Expreffions as thefe concerning the only true God; That he is but *One Perfon*,

God

God *Of himself*; *Cause, Principle, Root, Fountain, Original, Archetype*; That he is a *Pure Act, Simple, Uncompounded, Undivided, Self-Existent, Underived, Unoriginated, Independent, Absolutely Supreme*; and Perfect *In himself*; together with the Words *Supremacy, Subordinate, Co-ordinate, Subfistence, Incommunicable*; and above all his *Metaphysical* Substance and Essence; together with a *Metaphysical* and *Potential* Eternity, and such like: They are not the Language of Revelation, especialy when us'd to explain the *Unity* of the Divine Nature; but so many notional *Affected* Terms which some great and learned Men have invented to expres their *Peculiar* Sentiments, and their several ways of Thinking of that *Unity*.

SOME of those Terms are altogether *Unintelligible*, and without any meaning when applied to the Unity of God; several of them are purely *Negative*, and give no positive determinate Notion or Conception at all; and all of them fail in these two material Points. First that none of them have an Authority or Foundation in *Scripture* for any Divine *Analogy*, which will be fully explained hereafter; that tho' the meaning of them may be conceived and understood when they are applied to the one true *God*, in respect of his *Creatures*, and in Comparison with them: Yet when they are spoke of him consider'd *In himself*, and so applied to the *Divine Nature*; not as he is in his *Metaphysical*

phyſical (as ſome Men ſpeak) or imaginary Subſtance and Eſſence, but in his *Phyſical,* that is
in his *True* and *Real* Subſtance and Eſſence ;
their meaning is altogether unintelligible. As
for inſtance, take any of thoſe Words, ſuppoſe
Unoriginated; when this Word is apply'd by
way of Compariſon between God and his Creatures, as between *Him* and the greateſt *Angel*
in Heaven ; it hath a very obvious and determinate Meaning, and we eaſily apprehend how
the Angel is *Originated,* and God *Unoriginated:*
But when the Word is applied to the real Nature of God as he is in himſelf, intirely
Abſtracted from all Reſpect to the Creature ; it
hath no meaning at all. We can form ſome
Notion of what it is for a Being to be *Created*
or not *Created*; but what the Word *Unoriginated* Means when ſpoke of the *True Phyſical*
Nature of God, as when the *Father* is ſaid to
be unoriginated in reſpect of the *Son* and *Holy
Ghoſt,* we are utterly ignorant ; and can fix
no Idea or Conception at all to it.

AGAIN, we know no more of *Pure Act,*
but that they are two Monoſyllables put together without any Signification ; and ſo the
Words *Simple, Uncompounded, Undivided,* when
applied to the Divine Nature without any Compariſon with the Creature, can at the utmoſt
have no other intelligible Meaning but that
he cannot be divided into *More* Gods than *One.*
As to the Words *Cauſe, Principle, Root, Foun-*

tain,

tain, *Original*, *Archtype*, *Prototype*; it is plain
that *God* is all thefe in refpect of his *Creatures*;
and in this Sence they have a very obvious
Meaning, and are very good and pertinent
Terms: But when you intirely lay afide all
refpect to the Creatures, and Comparifon with
them; and apply thofe Terms to the *Father*
only, in refpect of the *Son* and the *Holy Ghoſt*,
as they are *Related* to the Father; the Words
are mere empty Sound without any Signification.

So likewife the Words *Abſolutely Supreme*,
and *Independent*; when they are ſpoke of the
one true God in refpect of the whole Creation,
or any part of it; they are very good Words:
But when you apply them to the Divine Nature, as it is in itſelf; or by way of diftinguifhing the Father from the Son and the Holy
Ghoft, they have no more conceivable or determinate Meaning, than if you repeated their
Syllables backward. As for *The Metaphyfical
Eſſence and Subſtance* of God; *Barbara, Celarent,
Darii* are as good Sence; and it is impoffible
to fix any intelligible Meaning at all to them;
unlefs they mean quite the contrary, his *Phyfical*, that is his real *True Nature* and *Eſſence* as
he is in himfelf, which is utterly incomprehenfible. So that when Men argue thofe Attributes to be *Incommunicable*; if they mean to
any *mere Creature*, the meaning of them is
plain and eafy to be underftood: But when
they

they apply thofe Attributes directly to *God* or the *Father*, without any Comparifon with a *Created* Being, they fpeak of what they have not the leaft Idea or Conception; and they know as little what is *Communicable* or *Incommunicable* in him, in refpect of the *Son* and *Holy Ghoft*; as they do of his real true Phyfical Subftance and Effence.

AND now, can we fufficiently lament and bewail all that irreparable Mifchief, which hath been of late done by the *Rumbling* of thefe and fuch fuch like *Sounding* Words and Phrafes thro' whole Volumes, in that grofs and miftaken Application of them which I have noted? To the diftracting Mens Minds; to the confounding themfelves and thofe Readers who do not fee thro' this *Fallacy*; and to the perplexing and obfcuring the great and fundamental Article of our Chriftian Faith, that of the Holy Trinity; which as it lies before us in *Scripture* and the Language of Revelation is (as far as we are obliged to underftand or believe it) the *Plaineft* Thing in the World. All this pompous Affectation of being wifer and more Knowing in the real *Phyfical* Nature of God and the *Myfteries* of Chriftianity, than the Scriptures can make Men; hath no other main Scope or *Tendency* but to propagate abfurd and inconfiftent Notions, which a plain rational Man would be afham'd of; fuch as thefe following.

THAT

T H A T the Son of God was *Produced* by an *External* Act of the Father's Almighty Power and Will; and yet was not made or *Created.*

T H A T a Person should be by Nature *Truly God*, and yet not the *True God*; and that he should not have one Attribute *Originaly* and properly *His Own*, to render him even *Truly God*.

T H A T there are two Divine Persons who had not any Divine Nature or Essence *Originaly* in them; that one of them *Became* Divine by a *Communication* of Divine Attributes; and the other by *No* Communication at all.

T H A T there are *Three* Degrees of true and genuine *Divinity*, one above another; the lowest of which doth not give the Person who hath it, even the *Name* God. That one of those Divinities is *Subject* to the first; and that the *Third* is *Subject* to *Two* Divinities above him.

T H A T there are three Persons *Truly Divine*; one of them the *True God*, the other *Truly God*, the third *No God* at all.

T H A T there are two Intelligent Agents in the Universe, which originaly were neither essentialy *God*, nor essentialy *Creatures*; who now have fomething of *Both* in them, but are realy and truly *Neither*.

THAT the Work of Creation was effected by a *Delegated* Power only ; that a *Finite* Perfon exercifed *Infinite* Power ; and *That* likewife purely by *Commiffion*.

THAT the Father communicated his own *Effential* Attributes to the Son, without any Communication of his *Real Intrinfick Nature* and Effence : And yet that he communicated to him *True Divinity*, which of all things feems to the Mind of Man utterly *Incommunicable*.

THAT divine *Worfhip*, as well as Divinity itfelf, may and muft be varied in *Degrees*, fo as to be *More* or *Lefs* Divine.

THAT we may and muft pay divine *Worfhip* to *Two* Gods ; and divine *Honour* to a third Perfon who is *No* God, without Idolatry.

THAT there are three different Degrees or Kinds of Creation ; and that there are two intermediate Natures between the *Loweft* of thofe Degrees, and the *Perfon* of the moft high God, in the modern Arian Style.

THAT tho' we fhould grant the Son to be intirely of the fame *Nature* and *Effence* with the Father ; yet he hath not the fame kind of *Exiftence*,

iftence, nor *Independency*, nor *Supremacy*, nor *Dominion* or *Authority*; tho' thefe are *Neceffarily inherent* in that Nature, and *Infeparable* from it even by the moft exquifite Abftraction of the Mind.

THAT tho' the *Pre-exiftent* Nature of Chrift be truly Divine, yet it could not be in Heaven and Earth at the fame time; altho' no Being can be truly Divine without *Ubiquity* and Omniprefence: Nor otherwife be *Supreme* at all over all created Beings; as Chrift is allow'd to be by thofe who make the former Affertion.

THAT the *Pre-exiftent* divine Nature of Chrift was in as much Truth and Reality *Exalted* to his mediatorial Kingdom and Glory, as his *Human* Nature, and *Together* with it at the fame time; tho' it is downright Contradiction that a Nature *Truly Divine* fhould admit of any *Exaltation*; becaufe it implies the being exalted above Divinity.

THAT tho' the Son be a *Divine, Intelligent, Free* Agent, yet the Father alone is the *Sole Principle* and *Author* of whatever is done by the Son; and confequently that the *Son* did not properly redeem us, but the *Father* only.

THAT a *True Son* may *Not* be originaly of the *Same Nature* and Effence with his own *True Father*, by whom he was actualy begotten.
THAT

THAT by the Name *God*, we muſt mean the *Perſon* of God in the *Literal* and common Meaning affixed to that Term ; tho' it cannot be attributed to Father, Son, or Holy Ghoſt in a literal or proper Acceptation, any more than the Word *Man*.

THAT by the Term *Trinity* we muſt, in Propriety of Speech, mean a Trinity of *Two Gods*, and *One Divine Perſon* who is *No God*; tho' that Term was ever uſed in the Church to expreſs ſuch a real and incomprehenſible *Unity* of Nature, as well as a *Diſtinction* of Divine Perſons, that it is abſurd and prophane to call *Michael*, *Gabriel*, and *Raphael* a *Trinity of Angels*; or *Peter*, and *James*, and *John* a *Trinity of Men*.

THESE Poſitions, and many ſuch like, are either in *Expreſs* Words, or by plain Implication and immediate neceſſary *Conſequence*, contain'd in ſome of our Modern Syſtems of Religion: And in particular, they are but a light Taſte of the Poiſon ſtill latent in the late famous *Fifty five Propoſitions:* Which are a Body of *Clandeſtine* Arianiſm; and the moſt artful Diſguiſe and ſubtle Refinement of this Hereſy, that ever appear'd ſince the thirty ſix Hypothetical Propoſitions of *Aetius*, down to this Day; or perhaps ever will be publiſhed to the end of the World. Theſe Poſitions are mentioned

tioned here, only as they are a bold and arbitrary Impofition upon the common *Sence* and *Reafon* of Mankind; and not as they are a total Subverfion of the whole *Faith* of *Chriftians.*

C H A P. VIII.

Of Revealed Relations intirely new.

AS the Relation we bear to this firft Caufe of all *Created* Beings, becomes more *Strict* by intirely removing all falfe Deities, and the fully eftablifhing a belief of *One* God only; fo it is rendered *Nearer* yet, and more dear and engaging, by that Diftinction in the Divine Nature fo fully and exprefly revealed to us under the Names and different Characters of *Father*, *Son*, and *Spirit*; and by the feveral unfpeakable Bleffings derived upon Mankind from them, by their feveral Operations and Offices.

THIS is a Diftinction which could not have been the Invention of Man, becaufe it is altogether incomprehenfible; and accordingly could never have entered into the Head or Heart of Man to conceive, if it had not been revealed to us. Nor were we capable of *Any* Notion or Conception of that Diftinction, if it had not been difcovered to us under the Semblance and *Analogy* of fuch Relations as are *Familiar* among Men; as that of a *Father*, and a *Son*, and the
Spirit

Spirit of a Man that is in him. If we admit the Diftinction at all, we muft hold it not to be fuch only as, in our way of conceiving God, we make between three *Attributes*; as between his *Power*, and *Wifdom*, and *Goodnefs*; but to have fuch a real Foundation in the divine *Nature* itfelf, that we can think and fpeak of it no otherwife than as *Perfonal*. For the Father, Son, and Holy Ghoft are, in refpect of *one another*, diftinguifhed thro' the whole Language of Revelation, after the fame manner, and in the fame Style in which we fpeak of three *Men* or three *Angels*: And in refpect of *Mankind*, they are ever exprefly diftinguifhed by fuch different Operations and Offices, as we diftinguifh human Perfons among us. But the Divine *Attributes* are never fo diftinguifhed in the Style and Language of Revelation, either in refpect of one another; or in refpect of Man: So that whatever is denoted by that Diftinction of Father, Son, and Spirit, it is plain we muft either flatly reject the Scripture; or elfe for ever think and fpeak of thofe three, after the fame manner and in the fame Style we do of three *Human* Perfons.

THAT Chrift the fecond Perfon had a *Being* before he was born of the Virgin *Mary*, is fo evident from Revelation, that we can make no Sence or Coherence of Scripture; nor find any Confiftency in the whole Gofpel Difpenfation without allowing it. The flatly denying

nying of this by the *Socinians*, and evading it by
that hardy and shameless Invention of his afcending into Heaven and returning to Earth
again before his Death, on which their whole
Religion and intire Scheme of Divinity is built,
will (as a great Man said of Transubstantiation
in respect of Popery) prove a *Milstone* about the
Neck of their whole Hypothesis, which must
Sink it at length.

THAT we can form no other true Notion
of Christ from Revelation but that he is God
Equal with the Father, is plain; if it be consider'd that he is every where represented unto
us under the Semblance or Analogy of a *Son*,
A beloved Son, and the *Only Begotten* Son of
God. Which Words are apply'd to Christ,
not only as he was *Miraculously* born of the Virgin *Mary*; but in regard to his *Pre-exisent*
State; and in respect of the incomprehensible
Communication of the *Divine Essence* to him;
as, instead of many Arguments, appears irre-
fragably from *Coloss.* i. 13, 15. where he is called the *Son of his Father's love*, the *Image of the
invisible God, and the first-born of every Creature*;
that is born *Before* the *Creation* of any thing
in Heaven or Earth. For the true rendering
of the Words Πρωτότοκος πάσης κτίσεως is, *Born
before all Creation*, the Genitive Case being governed of Πρῶτος in Composition, instead of
Πρότερος (as will fully appear hereafter) And
the Import of these Words is explained by those
paralel

parallel Words in Verſe 17, Καὶ αὐτός ἐστι πρὸ πάντων, *And he is before all things.* In which likewiſe we ſhould obſerve that it is ſaid, he *Is,* not he *Was* before all things; to denote his Eternity: And withal that Πρωτότοκος here in the 15th Verſe, is apply'd to the eternal Generation of the *Divine* Nature, in plain Diſtinction from Πρωτότοκος in the 18th Verſe, where it is apply'd to the *Human* Nature's riſing from the dead, and being the *Firſt Fruits of the Reſurrection.* From whence it appears that the Communication of the Divine Eſſence to the *Pre-exiſtent* Nature of Chriſt was not made *After* he came into Being; ſo as from not being *Originaly* Divine, to become ſuch afterwards: But that the Communication was made *Together with* his Derivation from the Father; as a Son in the way of Nature hath all the Eſſence and Attributes of Humanity communicated to him from the Inſtant he can be call'd a *Son.*

Now theſe Words and Expreſſions of *Son,* and *Born,* and *Image* as a Man is the Image of his Father who begat him; as alſo the Word *Begotten,* being applied to Chriſt in reſpect of his *Pre-exiſtent* State, *Neceſſarily* leads us into a Conception of his Equality with the Father in all eſſential Perfections. For that thoſe Words are not to be underſtood in their ſtrictly *Proper* and *Literal* Senſe muſt be allowed; it were the height of Impiety to imagine it; nor are they

X 　　　　 **a mere**

a mere *Figure* and nothing more, without any farther real *Correspondent* Import or Signification: But they are to be understood *Analogicaly*; That as a Person among Men is the *Son* of his Father by *Natural* Generation; so Christ is the *Son* of God (not by any transcendent Act of *Creation*, or by *Adoption*, in each of which there may be mere *Metaphor* but no *Analogy*; but) by a *Supernatural* Generation, or ineffable Derivation of him from the very *Substance* and Essence of the Father.

THERE can be no other Scope or Purpose, in revealing all things relating to Christ under the Characters and Semblances of a *Son*, an *Only* Son, and *Begotten* of the Father, and *Born* before the Creation of any thing, but to imprint in us this Conception of him; that he hath all the natural and *Essential* Perfections of the Father, who begat him; and that as an *Human* Son possesses the complete *Intire* human Nature, so did Christ receive the intire Divine Nature. It can import nothing short of such a complete *Identity* of *Essence*; and we could neither think nor speak of him with any Truth as the *Only Begotten* Son of God, if he wanted any essential Perfection of the Divinity. So that they who oppose the Son's partaking of the divine Nature with the Father, of whom he was begotten, and his *Equality* with him; must find out some other Analogy for representing the Person of the Son,

2   than

than what the Wifdom of God hath made
choice of: Unlefs they will allow him to be a
Son by *Nature*, and *Begotten* of God; and then
fay that this leads us into a Notion that he is
intirely *Different* from the Father who begat
him; and fure nothing is fo monftrous and contradictory to our common Sentiments and manner of fpeaking, than that the Divine Nature
fhould thus *Beget* a mere *Creature* or *Man*.
That the Son was thus fupernaturaly *Derived*
from the Father, doth not in the leaft hinder
the neceffary Conception we have of his *Equality* with him, in all the *Effential* Perfections of
the Divinity; for it is no more than we fee
every Day among *Men*; the Son is derived
from his Father and begotten by him, and yet
is as truly Man; and equal to his Father in all
the Effentials of human Nature.

THAT we muft underftand thofe Terms
Son, *Begotten*, *Born* in this very Acceptation is
evident; becaufe the Mind of Man cannot poffibly without Force affix any other real Idea
or Conception to them. They cannot, as I
obferved before, be underftood in a ftrictly *Proper* and *Literal* Senfe, as they are firft apply'd
to human Nature; for this is altogether unworthy of God. Nor can they be taken in a
purely *Metaphorical* Acceptation; for that is
turning them into mere *Allufion* and *Figure*,
without any real or folid *Correfpondent* Import
in refpect of the *Father* or the *Son*; and is an

Opinion full of Imputation on the *Goodnefs* and *Veracity* of God, and the *Juftnefs* of thofe Terms he makes ufe of in this Revelation; which neceffarily convey a Meaning totaly different from that of other Terms us'd to exprefs *Creation*, or any *Other* Operation of the Father. So that there is no other reafonable Way left of underftanding thofe Scripture Terms, but by *Analogy* with what they fignify in common Speech among Men: That is, with the Derivation of a Son from his Father in the way of *Nature*; fo as by means of that Derivation, originaly to partake of all the *Effential* Attributes of a *Man*, and to be upon an intire *Equality* with his Father in all the *Perfections* of human Nature. This is the only Method remaining to the Intellect, of forming a Judgment upon the Sence and Acceptation of thofe Terms; it muft either underftand them thus, or affix no *Correfpondent* determin'd Meaning at all to them: And it is plain we reduce the Faith of Chriftians to *Nothing*, unlefs we conceive the Divine *Generation* of the Son to differ as *Effentialy* from *Making* or *Creation*; as a Man's *Begetting* a Son, differs from his *Making* a Statue or *Building* an *Houfe*.

THAT the *Holy Spirit* which we find in Scripture diftinguifhed from the Father and the Son, is a *Diftinct* and different Perfon from them both, is plain from the Commiffion given the Apoftles which runs in the Name of
2   the

the *Father*, and of the *Son*, and of the *Holy Ghost*; and from that solemn Form of Blessing, which is pronounced in the Name of *Christ*, and of *God*, and of the *Holy Ghost*. For if the Spirit be not a *Distinct* Person, as well as the Father and the Son; it must be own'd, that these Forms sufficiently tend to puzzle and confound Mankind; by leading them necessarily into the Opinion of a *Personal* Distinction where there is realy *None:* And then the Sence would be thus, Go teach and baptize in the Name of the *Father* and of the *Son* who are *Distinct* Persons, and of the *Holy Ghost* who is *No* distinct Person; and it will amount to this, Baptize in the Name of the *Father*, and of the *Son*, and of the *Father* again. Therefore to argue the third Person mentioned to be a mere *Name*, and nothing more; and to import only the *Power* or Energy of the *Father*, is not only charging God with laying a Snare for deceiving us; but it is perverting the received Use of Words and Language; and abusing the common Sence and Understanding of Men: Who are naturaly led into the Interpretation of this *Commission*, and of that Form of *Blessing*, by a Comparison and Analogy with Commissions from Princes for lifting Men into their Service, or for conferring their Grace and Favours upon them. If one of their Commissions ran in the Names of *Three Men* jointly and severaly, it would be playing upon our Reason and even ridiculous to argue, that the *Third* Name was

only

only a Word for the *Power* and Authority of the *Prince*; fo that if we will make even common Sence of that divine Commiffion and Form of Blefling, we muft underftand the Holy Ghoft to be a fpiritual intelligent Being, *Perfonaly* diftinct from the Father and the Son.

THAT this Spirit is *God* or partaker of the Divine *Nature*, is evident from Revelation; becaufe he is every where diftinguifhed by the peculiar Character of *Holy*. *Abfolute* confummate *Holinefs* is the peculiar infeparable Attribute of the *Self-Exiftent*, *Unoriginated*, *Independent*, abfolutely *Supreme* God. Of him it is faid, *Thou only art Holy*; and upon the High Prieft's Mitre was written *Holinefs to Jehovah*, that is to him *Only*. Now the Spirit being every where called Holy, as his peculiar diftinguifhing Character; and accordingly the Words not capable of being rendered *An* Holy Spirit, but *The* Holy Spirit, by way of Excellency and Diftinction from all *Created* Spirits (the greateft of which cannot without Blafpheming be called *The* Holy Spirit abfolutely) that Epithet muft mean an *Intrinfic original* and *Effential* Holinefs in him; and not barely the Spirit which fanctifies or *Makes Holy*; efpecialy fince even *This* could not be fuppofed of him, unlefs he had effential Holinefs in himfelf. This way of Thinking of the Spirit is unavoidable, if we obferve that Holinefs is his conftant diftinguifhingCharacter, not only where

he

he is mentioned in the Relation he hath to *Us*;
but that he is called Holy even where he is
named together with, and in respect to the *Father* and to the *Son*: As *In the Name of the Father, and of the Son, and of the Holy Ghost*. And
in the Form of *Blessing*; and where it is said,
*The Holy Ghost, whom the Father will send, in my
Name*; and in many other Places: So that he is
characterized as Holy, not only in respect of *Us*
who are sanctified by him; but in respect of
the *Father* and the *Son*; insomuch that he *Alone*
is stiled Holy wherever the three Persons are
expresly named together in Scripture.

THE Word *Holy* in those Places cannot be
added in *Opposition* to the Father and the Son;
nor as *Exclusive* of the Father and the Son;
because *They* are both absolutely *Holy* as well
as the Spirit; nor is it the *Less* but the *Greater*
Holiness for his being expresly mentioned in
Conjunction with them: So that the Words of
those Places naturaly lead us into an Opinion
that *His* must be the same Holiness with that of
the Father and of the Son, who are both called
The Most Holy; that is, the very intrinsic *Essential* Holiness of Jehovah the most high supreme God. To which if we add, that he is called
*The Spirit of Holiness, the Spirit of Glory, the
eternal Spirit*, and very often *The Spirit of God*;
and particularly at the Baptism of Christ, where
he was *Personaly* distinguished from the Father,
even in a *Visible* Appearance; we must have

X 4   our

our Reason amused by Subtilty and Criticism, and be quite turned out of the plain and common Way of Thinking; before we can understand the Revelations made of the Holy Ghost in any other Sence, than as of God *Equal* with the Father.

BUT that which puts this Matter out of all doubt is, that the Term *Spirit* is taken originaly for the *Breath* of Man; from thence it came afterwards to be used for the *Immaterial Principle* of our Composition, which in common Speech is call'd the *Soul:* And from thence again it came to be transfer'd to the *Divine Nature*; and accordingly hath been apply'd by the Wisdom of God in Scripture, to express the third Divine Person, or *Holy Spirit* of God. Hence it is plain, that we must not understand that Term *Literaly* and in its strict Propriety, as it is used to express an human Spirit; let this be far from us: Nor can it mean a purely Figurative and *Metaphorical* Spirit only; for that is no Spirit at all. Nor can it be a mere Figure for God the *Father*; for that would be a *Delusive Tautology* running thro' the whole Style and Language of Revelation, sufficient to confound the Reason and Understanding of Men; who are under a Necessity from thence to suppose them *Personaly Distinct*; and especialy where they are named *Together* as expresly distinguished from each other. So that there is no way left to the Mind of Man to affix any *Just*, *Real*,

and

and *Solid* Meaning to that Scripture Term, but by *Analogy* with the *Spirit* of *Man* that is in him; which is an *Essential* Part of his Composition, and yet in Truth and Reality capable of being actualy *Distinguished* and separately considered from the other Part of the Compound.

THIS personal Distinction hath very aptly in the Church been termed the *Trinity*; as the necessary conceiving of it to be in one and the same Divine Nature, is called the *Unity*: And tho' neither of these Terms are found in Scripture applied to the Divine Nature; yet all the Scoffs and Sarcasms by which Men ridicule and expose them, are no other than Blaspheming that *Distinction*, and that Sameness and *Identity* of the Divine Nature, whereof the Revelations of God are full and expressive; and exploding the whole *Christian Faith*, which is founded upon the *Reality* of them; and which must all fall to the Ground upon the denying or rejecting the true Meaning of either.

NOW since both Reason and Revelation shew us there can be but *One* God, we can own and worship but one; that one God alone who *Only hath Immortality, and Life in himself*: who is the *Most High, above all, Incorruptible, Invisible*; or to speak in Words of *Human* Invention, who is *Unoriginated, Independent, Absolutely Supreme.* And since the Books of Scripture

ture

ture are full of a *Perfonal* Diftinction in the Divine Nature, beyond our Difcovery any where but in them ; and fince we find that *One* God fet forth to us under three diftinct and different *Relations*, which the three Perfons bear both to *One another*, and to *Us* ; and accordingly diftinguifhed by different perfonal *Names*, and *Characters*, and *Operations*, and *Offices* ; therefore we worfhip that one God with this Diftinction of his *Own* making, and not of *Ours.*

As we cannot conceive any *Intermediate* Being between that abfolutely *Supreme God*, and a mere *Creature* ; fo neither is there, nor can there be any Medium between *Worfhip* abfolutely *Divine*, and *Civil Worfhip*, or rather *Honour* to be paid to a Creature as fuch. And therefore if the Son and Holy Ghoft are to be properly and realy worfhiped at all, as all Chriftians allow ; the *Same* Worfhip muft be paid *Them* which we pay the moft High or abfolutely *Supreme God* ; that Worfhip which confifts in addreffing our felves in any Religious Act of the Mind, or Pofture of the Body, to an *Invifible* Being : Which is that very *Supreme* and *Ultimate* Worfhip due to the Supreme, the abfolutely Supreme Deity alone ; and therefore can admit of no *Degrees*, fo as to be paid to any other *Inferior invifible* Being whatfoever ; That Worfhip which is *Truly* Divine, which is *Abfolutely* fo, and which without *Idolatry* cannot be paid

to

to any Creature whatſoever. All our *Prayers* and *Praiſes* muſt be firſt and laſt, *Primarily* and *Ultimately* directed to the Honour and Glory of that *One* abſolutely *Supreme* God ; and no degree of Divine Worſhip, if it *Could* admit of ſuch, ought to be directed to the Honour or Glory of any other inviſible Being whatſoever, but of him alone. The Holy *Scriptures* leave no room for us to imagine any ſuch degrees in Divine Worſhip; or for any *Medium* between that Worſhip which is abſolutely *Divine*, and to be paid to the abſolutely ſupreme God ; and that which is a purely *Civil* Reſpect or Honour, and to be paid to a mere Creature.

It is ſaid, *Thou ſhalt worſhip the Lord thy God, and him only ſhalt thou ſerve* ; the one only independent *Abſolutely ſupreme* God ; ſo that all Divine Worſhip is, by that Precept, abſolutely *Excluded* from the *Son* and *Holy Ghoſt*, and they muſt have no other Kind of Honour than we might pay an inviſible Angel or departed Saint, unleſs they are incomprehenſibly *One* in *Nature* and all *Perfections* with that abſolutely ſupreme inviſible God. Again, *The Lord our God is one Lord*, whom we are to *Love* with *All* our Heart, with *All* our Soul, with *All* our Mind, and with *All* our Strength ; and if ſo, there is no room left for the Divine *Love* of *Son* or *Holy Ghoſt*, unleſs we ſuppoſe them that *One* Lord our *God*; who is repreſented as a *Jealous* God, and will not in the
leaſt

leaſt ſhare with any other in Divine Worſhip, which is altogether to be paid to him alone : And if the Son and Holy Ghoſt are not ſome way or other *Truly* that *One God* and *Lord*, it would be as far from Idolatry to addreſs our Prayers and Praiſes to an *Angel*, as to *Them* ; ſo that thoſe Prayers and Praiſes be *Primarily* and *Ultimately* directed ſtill to that *One* **God.**

ACCORDING to this plain and natural Way of Thinking, as we are firſt jointly and ſacramentaly Baptized, by one and the ſame ſolemn Act of Worſhip, *In the Name of the Father, and of the Son, and of the Holy Ghoſt* ; ſo we ever after unite them in our Worſhip, and adore them without any *Degrees* or *Inequality* in that Worſhip ; which being truly Divine can admit of no Degrees or Inequality. Whereas they who argue for an *Inequality* in the Divine *Perſons* ; and for an *Inferiority* of *Nature,* and a *Subjection* in the Son and Holy Ghoſt to the Father ; neceſſarily involve themſelves, and all who adhere to their Principles, in endleſs Uncertainty and Confuſion. Becauſe they can never fix and ſettle the different *Kinds* and *Degrees* of that *Lower Divine Worſhip* (a Contradiction in the very Terms) which is to be paid to the Son and to the Holy Ghoſt ; nor diſtinguiſh it with ſuch Exactneſs and Nicety, that it ſhall neither be the Worſhip due to the *Unoriginated* abſolutely *Supreme God* ; nor that mere Honour and Reſpect only which

is

is to be paid to *Creatures*, and varied according to their several *Ranks* and Dignities.

But to make it yet more clear, that the Mind of Man cannot without Abfurdity have any other Notion or Conception of the Son and Holy Ghoft, than as their being incomprehenfibly *One* abfolutely *Supreme Deity* with the Father, without a *Figure*; and *One* joint and ultimate *Object* of all Chriftian *Worfhip*; let us collect the two feemingly inconfiftent Doctrines into oppofite Propofitions thus.

There is no other God but one.	*Let all the Angels of God worfhip him.*
Thou fhalt worfhip the Lord thy God, and him only fhalt thou ferve.	*Go —— baptize all Nations in the Name of the Father, and of the Son, and of the Holy Ghoft.*
ON this Side the Precepts are exprefs and pofitive for the believing in *One* God alone; and for paying Divine Worfhip to him *Only.* They are full and peremptory againft addreffing our felves religioufly in	THE Precepts on this Side in Scripture, are no lefs plain and pofitive and peremptory; that the whole intelligent Creation is to pay Divine Worfhip to the *Son*; and Mankind in particular, by exprefs Precept and Exam-

Body or Mind to any other invisible Deity, than to that one only and absolutely *Supreme* Deity; who is a jealous God, and will not suffer any Kind or Degree of Divine Honour or Worship, to be directed to any other Deity whatsoever, *Equal* or *Inferior* to him. The Mind of Man can understand these Precepts no otherwise; nor can it frame any other Notion of *Idolatry*, than the addressing our selves either in Body or Mind, by way of Religious Worship, to any other Being, especialy *Invisible*, than to the Most High and absolutely Supreme Deity alone.

Example. The Son is called *God* absolutely; and the constant Style for the Holy Ghost is the *Spirit of God* himself, and not *One of God's Spirits.*

THE Precept is express for performing one of our most *Solemn Sacramental* Acts of Divine Worship *Jointly* to the Father, Son and Holy Ghost. As we are first initiated into the Christian Religion by one Act of Worship paid to them jointly; so are we ever after blessed jointly in the Name of all the Three: And all this without the least direct or indirect Mention or Intimation of any *Inequality*; or of any Difference of *Nature* or *Degree*; or of any *Distinction* of Worship.

AND

AND what is yet more fully decisive to the plaineſt Reaſon is, that thro' the whole Tenor of Revelation ſuch *Eſſentialy Divine* Attributes are given to the Son and Holy Ghoſt; as cannot, without *Blaſpheming*, be ſpoke of any Being *Inferior* to the Moſt High Supreme Deity.

Now both theſe Precepts here oppos'd, are expreſs Scripture; they are both from God, and both true; both are therefore equaly the Objects of our Knowledge and Faith; and both of them to be obſerved and obeyed. Since it is evident that there is no Contradiction in *Terms* here, and no more can be pretended than an *Appearing* Oppoſition and Inconſiſtency; and that too in Relation to an Unity and Diſtinction, for the direct Apprehenſion of which there is no Capacity in the Mind of Man; therefore the Wiſdom of God hath left it to us, to believe them *Both* true, and to reconcile them according to the beſt of our Underſtanding. Not by taking upon us to ſhew *How* the Divine Nature is *One*, and how it is *Three*; by labouring after abſtracted *Metaphyſical* Solutions

lutions of the *Real true* Nature and *Manner* of that Unity, or Diſtinction; or by any auk-ward and unſeemly *Illuſtrations* of them, and mean unworthy Compariſons of our *Own* with any Unity or Diſtinction whereof we can poſ-ſibly have a *Proper Direct* Notion or Idea. But by ſolving the ſeeming Oppoſition in a way moſt eaſy and obvious to the plaineſt Under-ſtanding; that is, by concluding, that ſince there is but *One God* who alone is to be *Wor-ſhiped* and ſerved; and ſince the Son and Holy Spirit are each of them *Called* God; and are expreſly commanded to be worſhiped likewiſe with *Sacramental,* and conſequently with *Su-preme* and *Ultimate* Worſhip: Therefore they muſt certainly be incomprehenſibly *One* with the Moſt High God in *Reality,* and not in *Fi-gure* alone; and for that Reaſon only are de-clar'd to be, together with the Father, the *Joint* and *Supreme* Object of all truly divine and ultimate Worſhip.

THUS all Abſurdity and Contradiction, which can poſſibly be urged againſt the Doctrine of the *Three* Divine Perſons, and *One* only Moſt High *Supreme* Deity, are reſolved into this; that we know not *How* to reconcile this to the intrinſic *Nature* and *Eſſence* of God; which we freely acknowledge, as we do every thing in the Nature of God to be *Inconceiv-able* and ineffable. The Mind of Man can *Reſt* in this; and acquieſce intirely in believ-

ing

ing the Diftinction between Father, Son, and
Holy Ghoft to be as *Real* and *True* as if it
were *Literaly* Perfonal ; and their Unity to be
fo *Strict* that it renders them *One Joint* and *Supreme Object* of all truly Divine and Chriftian
Worfhip : Thus we receive and embrace the
glorious Revelation as we find it in the Scriptures ; and leave the real *Incomprehenfible*
Ground and *Foundation* of it in the Nature of
God, to his own Veracity ; with this full Perfuafion, that he would never lead us by any
invincible Temptation into grofs and inevitable *Idolatry*.

ALL this is obvious and eafy, falling in
with common Sence and Reafon ; and hath a
Plainefs worthy of God, as it is a Doctrine
calculated for the *Knowledge* and *Faith* of all
Mankind both learned and unlearned : But according to the *Modern* Scheme of Religion in
the aforemention'd fifty five Propofitions, the
Cafe will ftand thus.

There is no other God but one.	THERE are *More* Gods than *One*.
Thou fhalt worfhip the Lord thy God, and him only fhalt thou ferve.	THOU fhalt *Wor-fhip* and ferve *Another* God, *Befides* the Lord thy God. And thou fhalt pay Divine *Ho-nour* to a third Divine

Perfon, who is not even to be *Called* God.

On this Side, in Purfuance of that Scheme, you muft underftand thefe Precepts thus. There is no other but one *Perfon* of God. Thou fhalt *Worfhip* that one Perfon of God, and that one Perfon *Only* fhalt thou ferve.

Here you muft believe *Another* feparate *Perfon* of a God. You muft ferve and *Worfhip* that diftinct and feparate Perfon. And you muft *Honour* a third feparate Perfon, not exprefly own'd for either *God* or a *Creature*.

Here there is no *Seeming* Oppofition only and Inconfiftency, but downright *Flat* Contradiction in exprefs *Terms*; rendred ftill more flagrant, by fuppofing the Moft High God or Supreme Deity to be but *One Perfon*.

The Method that Author prefcribes to Mankind for evading this monftrous Contradiction is, an Advice to add *Caufe, Origin, Author, Principle, Monarchy, Self-Exiftence, Independency, Abfolute Supremacy* to the Perfon on *One* Side: And to the Perfons on the other; *Effect* or Efficiency, *Separate Exiftence, Inferiority, Dependency,* and *Subjection.* Now if you ufe thefe Terms of human Language either in their firft *Propriety* and ftrictly *Literal* Acceptation (as he all along doth) or even *Analogically,*

logically, but to no other Purpose than that Author uses them, namely to distinguish the Divine Persons from *Each other*, and not from the *Creatures* only; both the Terms themselves, and all the Consequences deduced from them, are so far from helping Christians to any way of Reconciling the palpable Contradiction either to their Understanding or Consciences; that they serve only to establish and confirm it, and if possible to render it more glaring and insuperable than it first appeared in the contradictory Propositions themselves.

THE Use and Application of all those *Unscriptural* Terms is to argue the Persons on both Sides to be not only *Distinct*, but intirely disjoin'd and *Separate* from each other, as human Persons are; nay more, to be of a quite *Different Nature* and Degree: So that the whole Scope and Tendency of the fifty five Propositions must center at last in the utter Exclusion of the *Son* and *Holy Ghost* from all *Divine Worship* and Honour; the Understanding is here quite baffled and *Confounded*; and no evasive Subtilty can ever reconcile this Contradiction to the Mind of Man; you shall *Worship* and serve the *Person* of the *Most High God alone*; and yet you shall *Worship two other Persons besides him*.

To do the Author justice, he doth not *Attempt* any Reconciliation of it; he contends

only

only for the *Difunion* and *Separation* of the **Divine** Perſons thro' all his Propoſitions; and intirely deſtroys all *Real* Unity, allowing only that of the *Perſon* of God *In himſelf*; a *Figurative* Unity of *Power* with the *Son*; and no Unity *At all* with the *Holy Ghoſt*. The Foundation of the whole is laid in this Criticiſm; *Perſon* or *Intelligent Agent* is always in Latin and Greek expreſſed by the *Maſculine Adjective*; therefore when God is in Scripture ſaid to be Εῖς, it means, not only that he is one *God*, but likewiſe that he is one *Perſon:* From whence the Concluſion is, that he cannot be diſtinguiſhed into *Three Perſons*; ſo that the Son and Holy Ghoſt cannot be, even in any *Incomprehenſible Real* Manner, *One* and the ſame Supreme Deity with the *Father*. But the Argument rightly formed ſhould ſtand thus.

I f the Word Εῖς is always uſed to ſignify one individual *Man*; then it muſt likewiſe ſignify one *God*, when apply'd to the Divine Nature.

B u t the Word Εῖς is always uſed to ſignify one individual Man. *Ergo,*

T h i s is a fair way of Arguing, and the Conſequence intirely true; for this is the very Purport of the Maſculine Adjective, and of Εῖς in particular, when it is apply'd to expreſs the *Unity* of God in Scripture. But this will

not

not ferve the Author's turn; his Confequence is, Therefore Εἷς muft fignify one *Perfon* of God; it muft exprefs juft fuch another *Numerical* individual Unity, as we conceive in one fingle *Man*; but not as he is made up of *Spirit* and *Soul* and *Body*, which is a faint and diftant Emblem of the *Trinity*; and therefore fuch an *Unity* is no way agreeable to this Author's grand Principle: Who every where argues the Father to be a feparate *Subftance* from the Son and Holy Ghoft; which directly leads Men into a Notion, that we muft conceive the Unity of the Father by that of one human Syftem of Matter. According to him, at beft you muft imagine *God* to be *One*, as a *Man* is *One*; which cannot be, unlefs you conceive him to be fuch another *Perfon* or intelligent Agent, as one of us.

IF to obviate this grofs Notion, we obferve that the Terms *Perfon* and *Intelligent Agent* cannot be fuppofed applicable to the Divine Nature in that *Literal* and ftrict Propriety, but in a *Divine* Sence and by *Analogy* only; then by *Clofing* with the Analogy, that Author's Argument will be carried to the utmoft thus.

As the mafculine Adjective Εἷς in its firft and *Literal* Propriety fignifies *One human Perfon*; fo when it is transferred to God (even *Analogicaly*) it muft fignify *One Divine Perfon only*, *Whatever* that incomprehenfible Perfon

is

is in his real Nature. Now if you do but word this likewise right, you will extricate it intirely from the Fallacy; and the Consequence will be very good and clear.

As the masculine Adjective Εἷς in its first and *Literal* Propriety signifies the Unity of one individual *Man*; so when it is transferred to God, it must signify the Unity of one absolutely supreme *Deity*; of whatever *Kind* that incomprehensible Unity is. Thus by the *Natural* Unity of one individual Man, of which we have some Idea or Conception; we conceive as well as we can the Unity of one God, which is altogether *Supernatural* and *Otherwise* inconceivable.

So that to the Argument as it stands in full Force, I answer. That the Word Εἷς according to that Author signifies both the Number *One*, and *Person*; both which being jumbled together into one Word in the Greek, are plainly distinguished in the English, which hath a different Word for each of those Conceptions, and so lays open the Fallacy. For the Word Εἷς when transferred to God, realy denotes the *Number* or *Unity* only; and not the *Personality*.

But granting, what is grosly absurd, that it denoted the *Person* of God; yet the most which can be made of it is, that it then denotes
a Person

a Perfon *Incomprehenfibly One* ; a Perfon whofe *Unity* is as incomprehenfible as his *Effence*, or as any of his *Other* Attributes, and of the manner of which we can have no proper Idea or Conception; tho' thus much we are fure of, that it cannot be the fame with that of one individual *Man.* Wherefore the Word *Perfon* adds nothing to our Knowledge of that Divine Unity ; and confequently all the Inferences drawn from that Term are utterly vain and groundlefs: And nothing will ferve the Ends of this Author, but proving that both the Terms, *One* and *Perfon*, when transferred to God muft be taken as *Literaly*, and in the fame meaning, and with the fame *Conception* or Idea as when they are applied to the Perfon of a *Man.*

Tho' the Application of the Word Εἷς to God as it denotes his incomprehenfible *Unity* only, is clear and eafy ; agreeable to the common Sence of Mankind ; and anfwers all the theEnds of Chriftian Faith : Yet it will not ferve the Ends of that Author, unlefs you add the very Conception of *Human Unity* to that Term, and call it *Perfon* or *Intelligent Agent* ; and then transfer it to the Divine Nature ; which you muft fuppofe to have literaly the very fame individual *Numerical* Unity that you conceive in *One Human Perfon.* Then he hurries you away, with that grofs Notion in your Head, thro' a Labyrinth of abftracted metaphyfical Herefies ; out of which you can never fully extricate your

Y 4　　　　　　felt

felf by any other *Clue*, than that which leads
you directly back again; to the plain and open
manner of conceiving both the *Unity* of the
Divine *Nature*, and the *Diſtinction* of the Divine *Perſons*, by Semblance and *Analogy* only
with that Unity and Diſtinction familiar to us
in the Individuals of our own Species.

W E freely grant that God, thro' the whole
Scripture, is ſpoke of in the very ſame Style
and Language wherein we always ſpeak of one
human Perſon; as in the ſingular Perſons of
Verbs, and in maſculine *Adjectives*, whereof Εἷς
is but one inſtance of a thouſand: And the
Father, Son, and Holy Ghoſt are likewiſe
every where ſpoke of in the ſame Style and
Language by which we diſtinguiſh three human perſons; and yet this doth not argue that
God is *Literaly one Perſon*, any more than it
concludes all the Perſons to be *Three* ſtrictly
proper and *Literal* Perſons.   The Term *Per-*
ſon is not a ſcriptural one, either for *God*, or
for the three Divine Perſons; ſo that in truth
no Inferences ought to be made from it concerning either the *Real Unity* of God as he is in
his own Nature, or the real true *Diſtinction* of
the Divine Perſons. Whence it will be evident to
every plain Underſtanding, that not only Εἷς,
but any other maſculine *Adjectives* and *Per-*
ſons of *Verbs* may, nay *Muſt* neceſſarily be
uſed indifferently when we ſpeak of *God*;   or
of *Father*, *Son*, or *Holy Ghoſt*:   And that to

make

make any Inferences from thence concerning the *Real Nature*, or *Degree*, or *Manner*, or *Strictness* of that Divine Unity ; or concerning the *Greatness* of the Distinction, is no other than shameful trifling with the sacred Oracles, and with the Faith and Consciences of Men.

As trifling and even profane as that manner of Proceeding now appears to be ; and the very same as if the Author had inferr'd from the Term Ἐις, that the absolutely supreme Deity must be of the *Masculine Gender* ; yet it is the single *Point* upon which the whole Scheme of Religion contain'd in his fifty five Propositions is erected. Wherein a Multitude of unorthodox Notions, Absurdities, and Contradictions are with singular Dexterity and Slight piled up together upon it, as it were into a bulky *Cone* inverted : Which for a time served for a pleasing Amusement to *Deists*, and *Freethinkers*, and *Unbelievers* of all Ranks and Degrees ; till the mock Foundation being touch'd, it tumbles all at once into Dirt, and Stench, and Rubbish.

CHAP.

C H A P. IX.

Of the Improvement of Morality by Revelation.

FROM what hath been said concerning those several *Nearer Relations* we bear to the *First Cause* of all Things, intirely *New* and undifcoverable by Reason, and which we could have only from Revelation; we may plainly and diftinctly difcern wherein confifts the Enlargement, and Exaltation, and Improvement of *Morality* by the Gofpel Difpenfation. The Revelation of that perfonal Difference and Diftinction in the Deity, opens to our Underftanding a large Field of divine Knowledge; the Knowledge of many Bleffings, and Advantages, and Privileges of Mankind relating more immediately to another World, which were intirely unknown by the Light of Nature; and clears up many Particulars, of which mere Reafon gave Men but a very dubious and uncertain View.

1. As to the Perfon of the *Father*, the very particular *Manner* of God's being a Father to us is fully and clearly defcribed; as that he made the Body of Man of the *Duft* of the Ground; *Breathed* into it a *Spiritual* Principle immediately from himfelf; and that from the *Union* of both thefe Man became a *Living Soul*.

That

That our firſt Parents were created in perfect Innocence; in the *Image* and Likeneſs of *God*; to which is added the true Cauſe and exact Manner of the miſerable Corruption and Degeneracy of human Nature; which all Mankind were conſcious of and ſadly lamented, but none could account for. That we were to be reſtored to the Favour of God by the *Seed of the Woman*; which Prophecy was, in ſucceeding Ages, gradualy diſcovered to be ſpoken of a divine Perſon coming into the World, and taking *Our Nature* upon him: And the Subſtance and Import of it in due time appeared to be this, *That God ſo loved the world that he gave his only begotten Son, that whoſoever believeth in him ſhould not periſh, but have everlaſting life.* And that which renders this Relation yet nearer and more intimate and engaging is, that we have *Received the Adoption of Sons*; of which the Apoſtle ſpeaks with this Solemnity, *Behold what manner of love the Father hath beſtowed upon us, that we ſhould be called the Sons of God; having received the Spirit of Adoption,* that ineſtimable Privilege of crying *Abba Father*; and of addreſſing our ſelves to him as to our Father, with the Affection of legitimate Children, in full Truſt and Aſſurance That *The Father himſelf loveth us*; That *He hath prepared a Kingdom for us before the Foundation of the World*; and that he ſends the *Comforter*, that *Promiſe of the Father* to guide, and ſtrengthen, and ſup-

support us under all the Infirmities of Nature.

2. In the Person of *Chrift*, we have it revealed, that he is the *Only Begotten Son of God*. That is, if we will underftand the Words in any *Real* Sence or Meaning they will bear, The only Son of his own *Nature* and *Effence*; the intire Perfection and Tranfcript of *Himfelf*, that is of his *Divinity*; fo as to come up to the *Brightnefs* of his Father's *Glory*, of his *Divine* Glory; and the exprefs *Image* of his Perfon, that is of his *Divine* Perfon: The Words *Son*, and *Begotten*, and *Brightnefs*, and *Image* being fpoken by way of *Analogy* with human Generation (in which the Son is the Brightnefs and Image of his Father, by receiving the whole intire human Nature) muft import all this, or elfe have no fix'd Application or determinate Meaning at all.

CONCERNING this one only begotten Son we learn, that having it in his *Own Power* and Election to take upon him either the Nature of Angels, or of Men, he took on him the *Seed of Abraham*; and came into the World to be a *Sacrifice* for our Sin; to give his Life a *Ranfom*, and his Blood a *Price* and *Purchafe* of Redemption for us; to redeem us to God by his Blood, fince without *Blood*, and without *His* Blood there was no *Remiffion of Sins*. That he came to teach us the Will of God; to fet us an *Example* of Virtue and Holinefs in the greateft cſt Height and Perfection of them; and to work eternal Salvation for us by his *Mediation* and Interceſſion. We learn farther that as he being the only begotten Son of God, became *Heir* of all Things; ſo we by virtue of the Relation we bear to him are made *Heirs* of God, and *Joint Heirs* with him; inſomuch that he ſtyles us *Friends* and *Brethren*; and declares us *One* with him, as he is with the Father. That thro' Means of this inconceivable *Union* we have with him, we ſhall be *Raiſed* at the laſt Day by the Power and Efficacy of his Reſurrection. That when he ſhall appear to Judgment we ſhall be *Like* him; and that our *Bodies* ſhall be faſhioned like unto his *Glorious Body*; that the Good ſhall be caught up into the *Air to meet the Lord*, and ſhall go in with him to *Poſſeſs the Kingdom.*

3. ANOTHER great Improvement of our Knowledge are the Revelations made to us concerning the *Holy Ghoſt.* Who being every where ſpoke of in Scripture as of a *Diſtinct* Perſon; and no where repreſented as a *Creature*, we muſt, in our plain and obvious way of Thinking, neceſſarily conceive him as a Perſon *Truly* and *Eſſentialy* divine: Eſpecialy ſince any Medium between a Perſon truly *Divine*, and a made or *Created* Perſon, is directly contrary to plain Reaſon and our natural Sentiments, to which all Revelation is adapted. The particulars revealed concerning him as ſuch a divine Perſon, do greatly improve the Relation

we

we bear to *God*; namely the miraculous Conception of our Saviour Christ by the Power of of the *Holy Ghost*, or of the *Most High*, or of *God*, all which he is called in one Verse of Scripture, *Luke* i. 35. That he inspired the Apostles with the Gift of *Tongues and Miracles*, for the Proof and Propagation of the *Gospel*; That he brought all Things to their *Remembrance*; That he gives us *Wisdom*, and *Knowledge*, and leads us into all *Truth*; That we are the *Temples of the Holy Ghost*, and that he *Dwells* in us; That by him the *Love of God is shed abroad in our Hearts*; That he helps our *Infirmities*; enables us to *Mortify the Deeds of the Body*; and that he fills us with *Righteousness*, and *Peace*, and *Joy*.

Now all these things are the *Riches* both of the Wisdom and Knowledge of God; and tho' the depth of them be unfathomable, yet their being thus far opened to our View doth give us great Conceptions of the *Dignity* of human Nature; the Renovation of which by Pardon of Sin, the washing us from Guilt, and the Sanctification of the whole Man in Body and Soul, is as great, if not a more amazing Instance of the Power, and Wisdom, and Goodness of God, than our first Creation out of nothing. All this, (notwithstanding its being thought by some to be fruitless *Speculation*, and to have little or no Influence on the *Practical* Part of Life) not only greatly enlarges our Intellect,

2

tellect, and gives an immense Scope to human Understanding: But hath a direct and immediate *Tendency* to engage us powerfully in the highest Acts of Duty to God, our Neighbour, and our selves; to the Exaltation of Morality; to the increase of all Virtue and Holiness; and to the Restoration and Healing a corrupt Nature, in such a degree as we were utterly incapable of without these Revelations.

1. **FOR** first, we are by this means led into the Knowledge and Practice of some Virtues intirely *New* and unknown before; such as *Evangelical Faith*. Without Revelation there could be no such thing; for that Faith is an Assent to a reveal'd and express Proposition upon the Testimony of God; and till something was so revealed by him there could be no Assent given by us to any such Proposition; we could not believe his express Word before he spoke to us by the Prophets, and his Son. And now that all these things concerning himself and us are delivered to Mankind, Men still have it in their own natural Election whether they will either *Confider* them, or give any *Affent* to them; but we are told he that *Believeth* them shall be *Saved*, and he that believeth *Not* shall be *Damned*. And concerning those who have been once *Enlightened* with this Knowledge, who have *Tafted* the good *Word* of God, and been Partakers of these Revelations of the Holy Ghost; if they shall fall away from it, we are
told

told it is impoſſible to *Renew* them again to *Repentance* by any other Means or Method in Nature or Grace. So again *Hope* for Mercy and *Remiſſion of Sins*; for the *Reſurrection* of the Body in the Likeneſs of *Chriſt*; and for a glorious Immortality in the *Preſence* of God for Soul and Body united, is a Grace purely evangelical and new under the Goſpel. The *Love* of God likewiſe as of a Father by *Adoption*, is new under the Goſpel; that is the grateful Affection we ought to have for him on account of thoſe ſeveral *Reveal'd* Relations we bear to him; and of thoſe manifold *Bleſſings* derived upon us under that Diſtinction of the Perſons in the divine Nature. And ſo is the Loving our Neighbour *As our ſelves*, and the *Love* of our Fellow Chriſtians as our *Brethren* in *Adoption*, and joint *Heirs* with Chriſt, a *New Commandment*, as it is called in Scripture.

2. ALL that were merely *Moral* Virtues before, are by thoſe Revelations heightened and exalted into evangelical *Graces*. And this is done by transferring the Merit of all Inſtances of Virtue and Goodneſs, from the *Outward* Actions and Deportment only; to the *Inward* Diſpoſition of the Mind and Conſcience form'd and regulated by an evangelical Faith.

NEITHER Jew nor Heathen had any true and proper Notion of *Internal* Holineſs.

A2

As for the Heathen particularly, their moft
elevated Moralifts efteemed the inward virtuous Temper of the Mind, in Proportion only
either to the *Influence* it had on Mens *Outward*
Actions; or its Tendency to the Eafe, and Complacence, and Happinefs of Mankind in *This*
Life: And not as having any *Intrinfick Excel-*
lency in *Itfelf*; nor as it is a Recovery of the
Divine Image and Similitude to which we were
originaly formed; not as univerfal Holinefs is
an indifpenfable Qualification for the beatifick
Vifion or *Seeing of God*; nor as everlafting
Happinefs in *Another* World, is the *Natural* neceffary Confequence of an inward Frame and
Difpofition of Soul altogether regenerate and
fanctified. And as to the future *Rewards* themfelves, they never entertained a Thought of
their being confequent to inward Virtue and
Holinefs, any further than it was reduced into
outward Practice and Behaviour.

As to the Jews, the whole Style of their
moral Law ran intirely upon the Outward Act.
Nay, they interpreted even the Tenth Commandment after fuch a Manner as to conclude,
that if this external Obedience was paid, the
Law was fully and completely anfwer'd: So
that how violent foever the habitual Inclinations of the Soul were to Covetoufnefs or Luft,
or Injuftice, to Cruelty, Malice, or Revenge;
if they did but effectualy reftrain thefe Tendencies from breaking out into an open Vio-

Z   lation

lation of the Law, they deem'd themfelves
perfectly innocent; and acquiefc'd as Perfons
who had fulfill'd all Righteoufnefs. In fhort
they never imagin'd there was any Punifhment
for evil *Habits* or mere *Intentions* of the Mind,
either here or hereafter. The Jewifh Doctors
are full and exprefs in this Point; and the Inference they make from that Text in *Pfal.* lxvi.
*If I regard Iniquity in my Heart, the Lord will
not hear me,* is this; that God does not in the
leaft regard the Wickednefs of our Thoughts.
Nay their celebrated *Kimchi* fays upon this
Text, *Altho' I fhould defign Iniquity in my heart,
and were juft ready to execute it——— Yet God will
not hear it; for God never efteems an evil Defign
for the Deed.* This was the very Hypocrify of
the Pharifees, who valued no Inftance of Religious Duty, but as it was *Seen of Men*; nor
have the Jews at this Day any Opinion of the
Neceffity of *Internal* Holinefs.

BUT now we learn from the Gofpel, that
the true and real *Excellency* and Perfection of all
moral Religion is *Within* us, and feated in the
Heart; and accordingly the whole Subftance of
it is made to confift not only in the outward
Deportment and external Difcharge of all Duties; but chiefly in the inward Rectitude and
Sanctification of the *Mind* and *Confcience.* This
is the main Scope and Tendency of our Saviour's whole Sermon on the Mount, as is obvious to any one who will look over thofe Particulars

ticulars there mentioned and infifted on: And the true Meaning and Application of that faying, *Be ye perfect as your Father in Heaven is perfect*, is that we fhould imitate the Divine Perfections in the *Internal* Holinefs and Sanctification of our Nature; in bringing our felves to an *Habitual* State, and Temper, and Inclination of the whole Heart and Mind to all Virtue and Goodnefs; which is not only the curbing and *Reftraining*, but the *Renewing* and *Healing* a corrupt Nature. We are to be *Holy* as *He is Holy*; that is in the *Internal* Frame of our Mind, in the Sanctification of our whole Nature; not only in the external Obfervance of thofe Laws which are made for this World alone: But in ordering and compofing our Souls according to fuch Rules and Meafures of Purity and Holinefs as are for Eternity, and of everlafting Force and Obligation; which truly perfect our Nature, and give us a near Refemblance of the Divinity.

THIS is the Import of thefe new Phrafes in the Style of the Gofpel, That of *Regeneration* and being *Born again*, apply'd to the whole Man; becaufe of the intire Change of the Bent and Tendency of all his Paffions, and Affections, and Defires, from what they were by corrupt Nature; even to the reftraining and mortifying of all his bodily Appetites, and bringing them under the Conduct and Direction of Reafon and Religion. That of the *New*

Man,

Man, and the *Inward Man*; becaufe the change of all a Man's Inclinations and Affections from Vice to Virtue makes him more truly *Another* Man, than any Alteration in his *Body* could do. That of being *Renewed in the Spirit of our Minds*, which plainly alludes to that Diftinction of the Apoftles of *Spirit, and Soul, and Body*; and fignifies the freeing and difengaging our purely fpiritual and immortal Part, to the utmoft of our Power, from thofe irregular Paffions and Appetites of the inferior Soul, in which it is involved by its Union with the Body.

THIS is the great Glory of the Gofpel pro- phefy'd of fo long before and thus defcribed, *I will put my Law in their inward Parts, and write it in their Hearts*, which before confifted in external Ordinances, calculated only for out- ward Performances; and provided no exprefs *Punifhment* or *Reward* for the fecret Frame and Difpofition of the *Soul*. But now the full *Purpofe* of the Mind to commit a Sin is, in the fight of God, as high a degree of Guilt as the *Actual* Commiffion of it; and we learn that *Evil Thoughts, Murders, Adulteries, Fornications, Thefts, Falfe Witnefs, Blafphemies* defile a Man in Proportion to the Corruption of the Heart from whence they come forth. And fo on the other hand, if there be a fincere *Refolution* and *Intention* in the Mind for the Practice of Virtue and *Goodnefs* in any Inftance, it is as valuable in the Sight of God as if there were frequent Oppor-

Opportunities of exerting it in outward *Actions:* These are no otherwise esteemed by him than as they are sure and full Indications of the inward Temper and habitual Disposition of the Mind, which alone is of the very *Essence* of Virtue and Holiness; whereas its displaying itself in outward Performances is often but *Accidental* to it.

THUS we see what an unspeakable Treasure of Knowledge the Gospel is, which till Christ came lay buried under the *Ruins* of human Nature; and what a Turn was thereby given, all at once, to the whole Religion of the World. By this we see how it is that our Saviour came not to *Destroy* one Jot or Tittle of the Law of Nature, but to *Fulfil* it; by enlarging our narrow Conceptions concerning it, and removing our Thoughts from those outward Performances, which consider'd by themselves, are in truth but as the *Carcase* of Virtue and Goodness, to that wherein the true *Life* and *Spirit* of it consists; to that regular and harmonious Frame and Disposition of the Mind and Conscience, where it was at first; and should have continued, were it not for the miserable Corruption and Degeneracy of Man. So that *Evangelical* Holiness is *Morality* refined and exalted; genuine Morality is of the very Essence of Christianity, and nothing ceases to be such by the Gospel which was truly so before. The Law of *Nature,* the *Moral* Law of the

Jews,

Jews, and the *Gospel* are all one and the same eternal immutable Law of God; divulged after a different Manner, in different Degrees, and at different Times as Mankind could bear it; and the Purity and Perfection of the Gospel is that very State of Innocence in which our first Parents were created, and which they were originaly formed to, when they came out of the Hand of God. Thus the Gospel differs from the Law of Nature since the Fall, as a *Man* at his *Full Stature* differs from himself when he was a *Child*: The Gospel continues all the *Lineaments* and *Proportions*, and only gives the Law of Nature a greater *Increase* of all its Parts; so that if you cut off any one Instance of genuine Morality, you so far render Christianity maimed and deformed.

As therefore the main Scope of the Gospel is the whole change of the Man into an internal habitual Holiness; so also it introduceth a way of *Worship* intirely new, and calculated for the Increase and Improvement of that inward Sanctification of Mind, which shall ever dispose us to the Performance of all Instances of Virtue and Goodness outwardly, when Opportunity offers. Before, there were few or no express Directions for any but *External* Ordinances and visible *Ceremonies* of Worship; which being once performed, the whole Law of God was thought fulfilled in this Point; and the Consciences of Men were supposed to

be

be cleared and difcharged from all Penalty, whatever Temper and Difpofition of the Mind they were performed with.

But, fays the Gofpel, *the Hour cometh*, and now is, *that the true Worfhipers fhall worfhip the Father in Spirit and in Truth*; in the *Inward* Difpofition of the *Soul* to all Virtue and Holinefs; and in the lifting up a *Pure Mind* in devout addreffes immediately to God alone. This is worfhiping God *In the Spirit*, and having *No confidence in the Flefh*, that is in any outward Ordinances only. Worfhiping him *In Truth* is, not only ferving him in the *Subftance* of all that was *Shadowed* in *Types* and Ceremonies; but in the Purity and Holinefs of the Mind and Confcience. This is worfhiping in Truth and Sincerity; and this is oppos'd alfo to that outward difcharge even of Moral Duties which proceeds only from *Fear*, or any undue Motive; but is ftill againft the habitual Bent and Inclination of the Soul, and is therefore fo far infincere and hypocritical. This is that inward Law *Written* not with *Ink*, but with the *Spirit of the living God*; not in Tables of *Stone*, as the Moral Law was, *But in flefhly Tables of the Heart*; our *Sufficiency* for which is *Of God*, and from the inward Affiftanceof his Holy Spirit.

THUS it is that *Grace and Truth came by Jefus Chrift*; that true Worfhip of God which alone can intitle us to his Grace and Favour.

Thus

Thus it is that inftead of a multiplicity of *Sacrifices* and legal *Cleanfings*, we are to cleanfe our felves *From all Filthinefs of Flefh and Spirit, perfecting Holinefs in the Fear of God:* And hence it is that we have but two Sacraments, one of them expreffive of our *Dying* to all *Sin* in the inward Man, and *Rifing* again to internal *Holinefs*; the other Reprefentative of *Wafhing* away the *Guilt* and Pollution of the Soul by the Blood of Chrift, and of giving it inward Strength and fpiritual Nourifhment. Nor is the Difcharge even of thefe any farther acceptable to God, than as they have the Concurrence of the inward Devotion of the Heart; as they are performed with a filial Reverence and Love, and by Perfons endued with a real Sanctification of the Mind and Confcience,

To which I fhall add, that whereas before the Revelation of the Gofpel Men hoped to be accepted, to reconcile themfelves to God, and compenfate for many other wilful Failings by fome *Particular* fhining Virtues; now we learn, *That whofoever fhall keep the whole Law, and yet offend in one Point, he is guilty of all*; which was never fuppofed before that Affertion: Nothing will fuffice now except the becoming intirely *A new Creature*, as far as our fincere and hearty Endeavours can carry us in the univerfal Change of the whole State, and Temper, and Difpofition of the Soul.

3. As the Religion and Worſhip of Men, before Chriſt, was all external; ſo there was no *Expreſs Reward* promiſed, or *Puniſhment* threatned but what related to *This* World: But now that the whole Subſtance of them is become internal, the Rewards and Puniſhments are ſuch as relate chiefly to another Life. Firſt,

As to the *Rewards*, theſe ſeveral Particulars are new by the Revelation of the Goſpel.

1. WHEREAS it never entered into the Mind of Man to imagine or expect in another World any other than *Senſual* Pleaſures for the Body, and delightful *Contemplation* for the Mind; now we learn the Joys of Heaven to be of ſuch a Nature that they cannot enter into the Heart of Man, and that we cannot now have the leaſt direct Conception or Idea of their *Real Nature.* And therefore they are reveal'd to us under the Ideas or Conceptions of *Light*, a *Kingdom*, a *Crown* of Life and of Righteouſneſs; an eternal *Weight* of *Glory*, by way of Alluſion to the Weight of Gold and Jewels in a Temporal Crown; and an *Inheritance incorruptible and undefiled, reſerved in the Heavens.* Tho' theſe are no more than ſymbolical Repreſentations of the Joys of Heaven in a future State, yet they are ſo refined and exalted that they tranſcend the utmoſt Stretch of mere

human

human Invention; and nothing but Revelation could raife our Knowledge and Contemplation of them fo high. Nor are thofe Joys the lefs *Real*, becaufe we have no fuch *Direct* and immediate Conceptions of them, as we have of the Pleafures of Senfe; but on the contrary they are in Truth a much more *Powerful* Motive to all Virtue and Holinefs, than if we efteemed the Nature of them fuch, as could in any degree be now directly and immediately conceived or apprehended by us.

2. THE *Refurrection* of the *Same* Body is a Revelation intirely new, of which we are affured by the Rifing again of Chrift's Body which was individualy the fame; and who was *The firft Fruits of the Refurrection.* Indeed to own the *Refurrection*, and yet to deny it to be of the *Same* body, is no other than faying the Body *Shall*, and fhall *Not* rife again; for the Word *Refurrection* can have no other meaning but the rifing again of the fame Body. That this Body will be *Changed* (which muft be a Change of the *Same*, or the Propofition will have no Truth in it) is likewife intirely new; that this Change fhall be effected *In a Moment, in the Twinkling of an Eye*; that the *Dead in Chrift fhall rife firft*; that their Change fhall be into the *Likenefs of Chrift's glorious Body:* And that the Comprehenfion of this Likenefs is out of the Reach of all our Capacities and utterly *Inconceivable*; is that which heightens the *Value*
and

and Dignity of the Reward, and elevates our *Hope* beyond all that could have been suggested by the mere Reason and Understanding of Man.

3. ANOTHER Instance of Revelation intirely new with respect to those Rewards in another World is, that of *Living for ever in the more immediate Presence of God,* who is the Fountain of all Happiness. We are now informed that Christ is gone *To prepare a Place for us,* where we shall see God as he is, *Face to Face, in whose Presence is the Fulness of Joy*; that we shall be where he is to *Behold his Glory,* and that *The Righteous shall shine forth as the Sun in the Kingdom of their Father.* This is a Strain no Imagination merely Human could reach or aspire to; and the Happiness and Bliss brought down to the Level of our Understanding by those *Resemblances* is so immense and ineffable, that the *True Nature* of it can never be known till it is enjoyed: But it will surely be worthy the infinite Perfection of the Divine Nature; and of the Nature of Man when he is transformed into the Likeness of Christ. All things ever thought of or spoken concerning the Happiness of Men in another Life, before this Revelation, must appear jejune and insipid if compared with it; and were such feeble Motives to Virtue and Holiness, and to the surmounting Temptations, as are not worth the naming in Comparison with it: Especialy if to all this we add, that

what-

whatever Knowledge the greateſt Men among the Heathen had of the Rewards of a future State, it was the Reſult only of their own Rea-ſonings and Argument, and proved at beſt no more than probable *Conjecture*, and ſurmiſes of their own Mind ; but now we have the plain, and *Expreſs*, and repeated Promiſe and Word of *God* for them.

2. As to the *Puniſhments*, theſe likewiſe are by the Goſpel all adapted chiefly to *Inward* De-filement and Tranſgreſſion, and transferred from this, to another World; inſomuch that all the Breaches of the Divine Laws are not cogniza-ble till after our Departure out of this Life, and no Sentence of Condemnation for them is to be pronounced before the Day of Judgment; and in the ordinary Diſpenſation of the Goſpel, there is not the leaſt poſitive *Temporal* Puniſh-ment for the greateſt Sin. Becauſe, of the Tranſgreſſions of this Law none can be judge but he who is the Searcher of Hearts; who diſcerns from what inward Principle all out-ward Commiſſions of Sin do flow, and from whence they receive a greater or leſs *Degree* of Guilt: So that even Murders, Adulteries, For-nications, and all other outward Tranſgreſſions defile the Man as they come *From within*, and are puniſhable in Proportion to the Corruption of the *Heart* out of which they proceed. Of theſe Puniſhments we learn from Revelation only,

I. **That**

1. THAT they are both for *Soul* and *Body*, which are diftinguifhed in Scripture by the *Worm* that dieth not, and the *Fire* which fhall never be quenched; and accordingly we are bid to fear him who is able *To deftroy* both Body and Soul in Hell. Upon which I fhall only make this Remark, that whereas we find by Experience in this Life, that Body and Mind are not capable of fuffering the Extremity of Pain and Anguifh at the fame time; infomuch that the greateft Anxiety and moft fierce dif-tracting Anguifh in the *Mind*, is loft and di-verted by acute and pungent Pain in the *Body:* Yet we now learn that in Hell the Wicked will be fubject to extreme and exquifite Torments of both together.

2. THAT they will confift in *Everlafting Deftruction from the Prefence of the Lord, and from the Glory of his Power.* That the chief Caufe of all Mifery in another Life, will be an eternal Exclufion from the beatific Vifion of God, was never thought of by the Wifeft of the Heathen Philofophers; who placed all Happinefs within *Themfelves*, and generaly held *Virtue* to be its *Own* Reward. This exclufion feems to be the only Punifhment to which we can now conceive a *Pure Spirit* liable; and ac-cordingly, as all intelligent Beings are at a *Lefs*, or *Greater* Diftance from this *Fountain* of all Happinefs, fo they muft neceffarily be more or lefs Miferable or Happy. 3. THAT

3. THAT one Part of those Punishments will be by *Fire*, than which we have not any Revelation more express and positive. They are described by the being *Cast alive into a Lake of Fire burning with Brimstone*, by the *Fire that is not quenched*; by a *Furnace of Fire*, where there is *Wailing and Gnashing of Teeth*; by *Everlasting Burnings*; and *Everlasting Fire prepared for the Devil and his Angels*. If *Burning* be a Word merely *Metaphorical*, as it seems to be in respect of *Pure Spirits*, then it is a Word and Idea substituted instead of a Punishment so great that it cannot be otherwise described to us; because we are no otherwise able to conceive it, than under a Semblance of the most exquisite Torture we are subject to in this Life. But if the Word is to be taken in its strictly *Proper* and *Literal* Sence, as it seems to be with respect to the *Body*; for tho' it is an instance of great *Goodness* in God that the *Joys* of Heaven are represented to us under the figurative Images of *Light*, and *Glory*, and a *Kingdom*, and that the Substance and Reality shall exceed the utmost of all our Conceptions; yet it seems to be an Argument of the Strictness of his *Justice*, that the *Punishments* in another Life should be more *Literaly* the same they are threatned and foretold. If it be thus I say, then that is a very needless Question, *How material Fire can affect an human Soul?* Since we are told there is a *Worm which never dies,*

dies, as well as a *Fire which is not quenched*; and when we find by Experience how much the *Mind* regrets and bemoans every Pain in the *Body* here; and how infupportably miferable the whole Man is render'd by the Share it bears in the exquifite Torture of any one of our bodily Members.

4. T H E *Eternity* of thefe Punifhments is revealed as plainly as Words can exprefs it; and the Difficulty in that Queftion, *What Proportion endlefs Torments can bear to momentary Sins?* is quite removed, by confidering that the Punifhments denounced and threatned are not in themfelves Sanctions intirely *Arbitrary*, as it is in Punifhments annex'd to *Human* Laws: But they are withal fo many previous *Warnings* or *Declarations* of the *Inevitable* Confequence and *Natural* Tendency of Sin in itfelf to render us miferable in another World. So that a hardned and unrepenting Sinner cannot be otherwife than miferable in another Life by a Neceffity of *Nature*; and therefore not capable of Mercy; fince there never can be any Alteration of his State and Condition, without fuch a Change of the whole Man, as would put the natural and fettled Order of the Creation out of courfe.

5. T o all this we may add, that in refpect to thofe Rewards and Punifhments we have thefe farther Revelations. That the very particulars

I

ticular *Day* is appointed by God in which *He will judge the World in Righteousness, by that Man whom he hath ordained*; that he hath *Committed all Judgment to the Son*; and that all Mankind must come upon their Tryal at *Once.* The glorious *Pomp* and Majesty of his Appearance, the awful Solemnity of the whole Procedure; nay the very Words of the *Sentence* are described; and it is foretold that in this *Day of God, the Heavens being on Fire shall be dissolved, and the Elements shall melt with fervent Heat.* These are *The Terrors of the Lord* which are sufficient to overwhelm the Mind; and such Motives to all holy Conversation as nothing but Infidelity or want of Consideration can render ineffectual. Concerning which I shall farther observe, that all the *Doubtful* Opinions, and uncertain Reasonings; all the Imaginations and boding Surmises of Men before are now by the Gospel, cleared up into a *Full, Distinct* Knowledge and Certainty : And how far soever the Understandings of Men proceeded in the Nature of these Punishments before, yet they are all now become *Express Positive* Sanctions of the Laws of the Gospel ; as it regulates not only our outward Deportment, but also the inward Frame and Disposition of our Souls.

CHAP.

C H A P. X.

Of Spirit, and Soul, and Body; and the great Usefulness of this Distinction in Religion.

NOw in order to promote and carry on this inward Holiness of the Mind, that Opinion of Man's being τριμερὴς ὑπόστασις *A Person composed of three distinct constituent Parts*, not altogether unknown before to some heathen Philosophers, is now cleared up and expresly established by the Apostle in 1 *Thess.* v. 23. which according to the Original is thus, *And the very God of Peace sanctify you* ὁλοτελεῖς *intirely in every Part: And may* ὁλόκληρον ὑμῶν *the whole of you*; τὸ πνεῦμα *the Spirit*, and ψυχὴ *the Soul*, and τὸ σῶμα *the Body, be preserved blameless unto the coming of our Lord Jesus Christ.* Which Text is a plain Comment upon *Genesis* ii. 7. and an Explanation of those Words concerning our Creation, which expresly distinguish between *The Dust of the Ground*, which is the *Body*; that Principle which was *breathed* immediately from God, which is the *Immaterial* Part of us; and that *Living Soul* which resulted from the *Union* of Body and Spirit: And these are in that Text of the Apostle's named according to their Order and Dignity, *Spirit*, and *Soul*, and *Body.* Accordingly

I. IT is of the purely fpiritual Part of our Frame that thefe Texts are fpoke, *The Word of God—— is fharper than a two edged Sword, piercing even to the dividing afunder of Soul and Spirit*; of the *Inferior* Soul, the Seat of all our irregular Paffions and Affections, and the purely *Spiritual* and immaterial Part of us: Teaching us to diftinguifh them fo exactly as to difcern all the *Thoughts and Intents of the Heart*; all their fecret and *Contrary* moral *Tendencies* and Inclinations; all the Struggles and Contentions between thofe two Principles within us; and to make a right Judgment of them, as they tend either to the Healing and Prefervation, or the Corruption and Ruin of our whole Nature. *Be ye renewed in the Spirit of your Mind*; how? By putting on the *New Man*, in which that purely fpiritual Part of us hath a great degree of the fame Dominion and Sway over the inferior Soul, which it had when it was firft *Created in Righteoufnefs* after the Image and Likenefs *Of God*. Again, *The Spirit itfelf beareth witnefs with our Spirit that we are the Children of God*; that is the miraculous Operation of the Holy Spirit immediately upon the purely fpiritual and rational part of us, and fo endowing us with Knowledge and the Gift of Tongues, is an undoubted full Conviction of our Adoption. Again, *The Grace of our Lord Jefus Chrift be with your fpirit*; becaufe the fecret Influences of the *Holy Spirit* in

the

the work of Grace, are directly and immediately upon *Our* Spirit; by a Communication of Strength and Assistance, in order to disentangle it from the Allurements of the inferior Soul and sensitive Appetite. To which we may subjoin the last dying Words of our Saviour, *Father, into thy hands I commend my spirit. The God of the spirits of all flesh.* And, *The Father of spirits.*

To the preceding Passages I shall add two Places more, wherein the *Spirit* is plainly taken in *Distinction* from the other constituent Parts of our Frame, and in direct Opposition to the *Body*.

Eccles. xii. 7. *And the Dust shall return unto the Earth as it was; and the Spirit shall return to God who gave it.* The Word *Return* here and the Repetition of it to both sides of the Opposition, renders it very expressive and emphatical; for this shews that the Spirit is in its *Own Nature* disposed to *Ascend* upward (whenever disengaged from the Body) without the Interposition of any immediate particular Act of almighty Power: And that the Body, which is surely *All* of it denoted by *Dust* (otherwise the Opposition would be imperfect and mislead us) hath an *Innate* Gravity or *Natural* Tendency *Downward* to its congenial Earth. Now if the Body is such in the *Whole*, every *Particle* of it must have the same natural Tendency;

and

and if the *Spirit* were Duſt or *Matter*, or any
Part of it ſuch, *All* that is material in our
Compoſition would neceſſarily deſcend toge-
ther; and nothing of it could be ſaid with any
Truth to leave the Body and aſcend upward.

WHAT makes this yet plainer is, that the
Word which is tranſlated *Gave it*, is here oppoſed to the Word כַּשֶׁהָיָה which imports, *According to what it was before*. It is ſure God
gave *Both*; but this ſhews that the Spirit was
given in a Sence totaly *Different* from that
wherein the Duſt was given; that is, as it is
here ſaid, *Immediately* from himſelf: And it is
as ſure, that *All* the Duſt was given in one and
the ſame Sence; and the *Intire* Spirit in a
quite different Sence; whereas if the Spirit or
any part of it were material, it could not be
ſaid by way of Oppoſition that it *Returned* to
God who gave it.

IF כַּשֶׁהָיָה means *According to what it was*
juſt before its Separation from the Spirit; then
it muſt have been a quite *Different* Subſtance
from it; for otherwiſe there could have been
no other Separation but of *Duſt* from *Duſt*,
or of one Part of Matter from another;
which is contrary to the expreſs Oppoſition in
the Text; to which upon that Suppoſition it
will be impoſſible to affix any determinate
Sence or Meaning. But if that Word means,
According to what it was before, when firſt ta-

ken

ken out of the Earth, then it is plain that one part of our Frame was taken from the Earth, or Duſt, or *Matter*, and that the other was not; that is, one Part of us is *Material*, the other *Immaterial*, given by God; or in other Words, a *Subſtance* or Being *Superadded* to the Duſt or earthy Part of us.

Eccleſ. iii. 21. *Who knoweth the Spirit of a Man that goeth upward, and the Spirit of a Beaſt that goeth downward to the earth?* The Inference made by too many from this Text is, that the *Same* Word רוּחַ being uſed here to expreſs the *Spirit* both of *Man* and *Beaſt*, they muſt *Both* be material, or both immaterial. But tho' the *Word* is the ſame, yet that it ſignifies *Two* things here not only of a *Different*, but even of a quite *Contrary* Nature, is moſt evident from the Context; and from the Words of the Original.

THE Context is thus; One Inſtance among many of the Vanities in human Life given by *Solomon* is, that Men are ſubject to *Death* as well as Beaſts; *All go to one Place, all are of the Duſt, and all turn to Duſt again.* So that in this reſpect Man is truly upon the ſame level with the Beaſts; and therefore to the generality of Mankind he is in *Appearance* upon the ſame Level as to his *Spirit*, as well as his *Body* which moulders into Duſt. Then immediately follows, For *Who knoweth* or conſiders; or according to the Hebrew Idiom, *How few are*

there

there who confider or diftinguifh between the *Spirit of a Man that goeth upward, and the Spirit of a Beaft that goeth downward to the earth?*

THE *Oppofition* in the *Original* is abundantly more full and emphatical, which rendered more literaly is thus. *Who knoweth the Spirit of the Sons of Men*, that is of Mankind; *which afcendeth itfelf*, or of itfelf, *up on high*; *and the Spirit of a Beaft, which defcendeth, itfelf, down below to the earth?* That this is the true rendering is evident; and not *Who knoweth whether the Spirit of a Man goeth upward?* &c. for, as fome learned Men have juftly obferved, ה in the two Participles הָעֹלָה and הַיֹּרֶדֶת is not *Interrogative*, but *Emphatical*. To which I fhall add that there is no fmall Emphafis even in the ל prefix'd in the Words לְמַעְלָה and לְמַטָּה; And that the greateft Emphafis of all is in the Word הִיא *Itfelf* immediately following the two Participles, which evidently confirms the ה prefixed to them both to be *Emphatical*. The Sence would not only have been perfect without any of thefe Emphafes; but they would all furely have been omitted, if no more was defigned to be fpoken but barely that the Spirit of one goes *Upward*, and the Spirit of the other *Downward*. From hence therefore thefe three things are plain.

1. THAT the Spirit of Man, and the Spirit

Spirit of Brutes go two *Contrary* ways at their Diſſolution. The Mind of Man cannot ſurmiſe otherwiſe, than that whatever is *Material* in him muſt naturaly go one and the ſame way, all together ; and that whatever is ſeparated from it, ſo as to go a *Contrary* way, muſt be a Subſtance of a quite *Different* Nature, or elſe it could never admit of ſuch a *Separation*; ſince it was before *Equaly Eſſential* to the Man as the Duſt or other earthy Part of his Compoſition.

2. **THAT** whereas the Spirit and Body of a Man go two quite *Contrary* ways upon their Separation, the Spirit and Body of a Brute are never *Separated* but periſh *Together* at once. The Spirit of a Brute hath the ſame natural Tendency downward with the Body ; it hath the *Gravity* of a material Subſtance, and cannot therefore have any other Being or Exiſtence, than in the exquiſite Frame and Contexture of thoſe Particles of Matter which go to the Conſtitution of the Animal : And nothing is more ſure, than that if there was any thing in the Spirit of a *Man* common with that of *Brutes*, it would *Deſcend* downward with the Body as theirs does.

3. **THAT** the Spirit of Man goes upward, and that of a Beaſt downward, by an *Innate Natural* Propenſion. This is plain from the Original, which expreſſeth the Oppoſition thus ;

the

the *Spirit which is Afcending*, and *The Spirit which is Defcending*, that is, in their own *Intrinfic Nature*; otherwife thofe Participles would be here a mere Impropriety of Speech. But even in the *Common* rendering, one is faid to go *Upward*, that is to God; the other to go *Downward*, that is from God. And fo in *Ecclef.* xii. 7. it is faid the Spirit *Returns*, as we are faid to move *Of our felves*; or as the Body itfelf when it is fpiritualized will move to meet the Lord in the Air. If it is objected that *Fire* is material, and yet goes upward; I anfwer, that fuppofing this to be true (which it is not, fince the Particles of Fire move upward only in *Appearance* and for a while, but do realy *Defcend* again by their *Gravity* to the Earth) yet it would be nothing to the Purpofe; for if the Spirit of a Beaft were a fpark of fuch Fire, and went upward likewife, there could be no *Truth* or *Oppofition* in the Text upon that Suppofition. Here it is faid the *Spirit* of Man only goes upward, and both *Body* and *Spirit* of a Beaft go downward together; this fhews that the Oppofition in the Text refpects the very *Subftance* and whole *Effence* of the things oppofed, and not any more *Refin'd*, or more *Grofs Parts* only of either the one or the other.

To fuch as do not difcern the Emphatical Oppofition in the *Original*, nor the Force of thefe Confequences drawn from thence; it will

be

be fufficient to obferve, that רוּחַ or *Spirit* cannot denote the *Same* thing when apply'd to *Man* and *Beaft* in the Text. Becaufe the Term רוּחַ originaly fignifies *Wind* or *Breath*; and from thence it came to fignify the *Animal Life* both in Man and Beaft: So ψυχὴ or *Anima*, or *Soul* is indifferently ufed for the Animal Life in both. From thence again it was ufed to fignify *The Spirit of a Man that is in him*, or the immaterial part of our Frame; of which we have no direct and immediate Idea, and therefore have no Term more ftrictly literal and proper for expreffing the immateriality of it: So that by a mere *Neceffity* it is in common apply'd to Man and Beaft. Laftly, from fignifying the Spirit of Man, that Term was transfer'd to the Divine Nature; and ever ufed, thro' the Scriptures of the old Teftament, to exprefs the incomprehenfible *Spirit of God:* And *That* by a more abfolute Neceffity than in the foregoing Cafe; becaufe we can have neither a proper Idea or Term, to reprefent and exprefs truly what is altogether inconceivable and ineffable as it is in itfelf. Now tho' רוּחַ is ever ufed to fignify the Spirit of *Man*, as well as the Spirit of *God*; yet no body can juftly argue from thence that thefe two muft both be the *Same in Kind*. Why then will fome Men argue that the Spirit of *Man* and *Beaft* muft needs be of the *Same Kind*, merely becaufe the *Same Word* is ufed for *Both*; when there is no other Reafon for this, but the want of *Immediate* Conceptions

Conceptions and *Proper* Terms whereby to diftinguifh their *Different Natures.*

THESE two Texts of *Ecclefiaftes* are a plain and exprefs Revelation of the *Immateriality* of the Human Soul; and of the *Materiality* of that in Brutes. Of the *Separate Exiftence* of the human Soul after Death. Nay and of the *Eternity* of its Exiftence likewife, by plain Implication; for if it were ever to be diffolved and perifh, nothing is more reafonable than to conclude, that this would moft naturaly happen at the time of its *Separation* from the Body, to the Diffolution of which it is here oppofed: And if it fubfifts to the Day of Judgment, and fo carries its Exiftence into Eternity, we cannot imagine how it fhould *naturaly* ever have an End.

BUT the too common Objection here is, that all this doth not amount to a *Demonftration* for the Immateriality of the Soul of Man. I grant it does not; but it is a moft exprefs and emphatical *Revelation* of it, in Oppofition to the Soul of Brutes, which is as exprefly declared *Material:* It contains as much plain and genuine Truth as could poffibly be expreffed in fo few Words; and is likewife founded on the higheft *Moral Certainty*; and you have no more for the Truth of any Point either of natural or revealed Religion. Tho' it is fuch Evidence as doth not *Compel* the Affent; yet it is

fufficient

fufficient to render the with-holding of it *Inexcufable* to God and our own Confciences.

AFTER all I muft obferve, that tho' the Letter הּ fhould be taken *Interrogatively*, it alters not the main Scope and Import of the Text; tho' the Expreffion were lefs *Emphatical*, yet the Doctrine is equaly *True*, as well as the Confequences drawn from the Text. For *Who knows* or confiders *The Spirit of the Sons of Men*, whether *Afcending itfelf up on high; and the Spirit of a Beaft*, whether *Defcending itfelf down below to the Earth*; imports the very fame with, *Who knows or confiders the Spirit of a Man afcending itfelf*, &c. And if it were not fo in *Fact*, that one did actualy *Afcend*, and the other *Defcend*, it would never have been made a *Queftion* by the Wifdom of God, and *Solomon* whether it were fo or not? Becaufe this would be no other than making Men furmife that to be true, which is abfolutely falfe. Only I muft take Notice, that the literal Tranflation of the Original upon this *Laft* Suppofition, is abrupt and imperfect; and I appeal to any Perfon skill'd in the Hebrew, whether taking the הּ *Interrogatively* he is able to perfect and complete the Sence of that Text?

I SHALL only add, that no Thought can be more natural and obvious to our Mind, than that fince the Spirit of Brutes goes *Downward* to the Earth, they can have no Degree of *Reafon;*

fon; and that if they had any Degree of Reafon, they would have a proportionable Degree of the Knowledge of *Moral Good* and *Evil*, and of *Freedom of Will*; they would have fomething of a *Natural Religion*, and be liable to a proportionable Meafure of *Reward* and *Punifbment* here, or in another Life: In order to which,*Their* Spirit, as well as that which is *Human*, muft have *Survived* their Bodies; and have afcended *Upwards* likewife for *Judgment*, and a Sentence of Abfolution or Condemnation.

I t having fo plainly appeared that the pure Spirit is a *Diſtinct* conftituent Part of our Frame, I fhall now proceed to a *Farther* Confideration of that Diftinction of *Spirit*, and *Soul*, and *Body*; and of the great *Advantage* and Ufefulnefs of this important Point of Revelation. This *Spirit of a Man which is in him* knoweth the things of a Man, and is compared with the *Spirit of God* which knoweth the things of God; and of which St. *Paul* fpeaks when he fays *Rom.* i. 9. *God is my witnefs whom I ferve in my Spirit*, that is in the inflexible bent of his *Will*, and firm Purpofe and Steadinefs of his *Purely Spiritual* Part: So ftrengthned and confirmed as never to be led away, with the moft violent Inticements of the animal Soul in Combination with the Body, into any deliberate Tranfgreffion; tho' the Frailties and *Infirmities* of Nature arifing from their reftlefs continual *Struggle* againft the Spirit, can never

be

be totaly overcome in this Life. So that here in the Beginning of this Epiftle, he lays a Foundation for a clear and eafy Expofition of thofe Paffages in the 7 and 8 Chapters, which have been fo much miftaken, and fataly mif-apply'd to the quieting People's Confciences under wilful and deliberate Sins. For there the Oppofition is all along between the *Flefh* and *Carnal Mind* (as he calls the *Animal* Soul) on the one hand; and the *Spirit* on the other; which by the *Antithefis* plainly appears to be a conftituent Part of the Man, as well as the flefh and carnal Mind: And in this Sence *Living after the Spirit*, is oppofed to living *After the Flefh*; as the being *Spiritualy minded*, is op-pofed to being *Carnaly minded.*

Now, there the Apoftle inftances in his own Perfon, and fpeaks of the pure Spirit or Mind as of the Man *Himfelf*, that being the moft excellent and fuperior Part; in oppofi-tion to the Flefh, which includes the *Animal Soul* or *Carnal Mind*, with all its corrupt Ten-dencies and Inclinations. He ferv'd God in his *Spirit*; with the *Mind he ferv'd the Law of God*, and *Delighted* in it in the *Inward Man*; but found a Law in his *Members* warring againft the Law of his *Mind*; and from thence he proves his Affertion, *That the Law and the Commandment is Holy, and Juft, and Good*; becaufe it is fo apparently agreeable to the genuine Sentiments of the *Pure Spirit* within us, and

accord-

accordingly fo readily approved of and affented
to by unprejudiced Reafon. And that this
Law is no otherwife the *Caufe* and Occafion of
Sin and *Death* to us, than as it is directly *Contrary* to the Law we find in our *Members* ;
and as it is enacted againft all thofe Inclinations
and Tendencies of the flefh and carnal Mind
which we *Our felves* (that is, the *Spiritual* and
purely intellectual Part of us) judge and pro-
nounce to be finful and wicked.

I KNOW the *Spirit* here, and in other parallel Places, is ufualy expounded of the Motions of the *Holy Spirit* within us; which is
fo far true, but is not *All* the Truth; for it
fignifies the πνεῦμα or Spirit of a Man excited
and affifted by the Spirit of God : Which Acceptation of it is unavoidable in fome Places;
and renders others eafy and intelligible ; and
without including this *Spirit of a Man*, it will
be very difficult to find out the Scope and Coherence of thofe Paffages where it is mentioned.
Befides that the Sence and Context of thofe
Places require this, it is *Natural* to underftand
it of *Both* ; becaufe inward Grace, or the Influences of the Holy Spirit, are immediately
applied to the fpiritual immaterial Part of us,
to prepare and ftrengthen it for a Combat
with the Flefh and inferior Soul ; and enable
it to recover that original Purity and Holinefs which is innate to it, and in which it was
firft created.

THIS

THIS is that Part of our Frame which is *Immaterial*, and confequently hath Immortality in its Natural *Frame* and *Effence* ; whereas the *Inferior Soul*, which owes its Being to the Union of the Body and Spirit, is diffipated and diffolved upon their being feparated again from one another. In this Spirit confifts the *Dignity* of our Nature ; it is that by which we are, not only little lower than Angels ; but whereby we have a remote Refemblance of the Divinity, and bear the Image and Likenefs of him from whom it was originaly breathed into Man. It is, confidered *Abftractedly* and in *Itfelf*, pure, unpolluted, and uncorrupt ; its firft and *Innate* Tendencies are all to good ; all its native Defires and Inclinations are to Virtue ; and it is originaly fo framed for the *Beauty of Holinefs*, as to be ever carried towards it by an inceffant ftrong Propenfion. It is the chief Seat of the *Intellect* and *Will* ; and would *In itfelf* have an inflexible Inclination to *Truth* and *Goodnefs*, and an undifturbed Complacence in a freedom from all Vice and Error. And were it to refide *In* the Body only as in a *Seat* or *Throne*, fo as to be difengaged and act *Of itfelf*, without the neceffary Conjunction and Co-operation of the fenfitive Soul, by which fome hold it to be united to the Body ; then to ufe the Similitude of a Philofopher, It would, *Like the Top of Olympus, enjoy an uninterrupted Serenity ; and from thence look down upon all the Com-*

motions

motions and Perturbations in the irrational Soul,
as on so many Clouds, and Storms, and Thunders in
an inferior Region under its Feet.

I F it be objected here, that suppofing what
I have faid of the Spirit to be true, and that
it is in its own *Nature* a *Pure* and uncorrupt
Principle; then it can have no fhare in the
Guilt of Sin, nor be liable to any Moral Corruption but by *Force,* and contrary to its native Inclinations; and confequently ought not
to be punifhed merely for being in bad Com-
pany, to which it was *Neceffarily* confined. I
anfwer that the Objection proceeds upon a miftake, in fuppofing that becaufe the Spirit is
thus pure and uncorrupt, confider'd feparately
and in its *Own Nature*; therefore it continues
to *Preferve* itfelf unpolluted in the midft of
Heaps of Filth and Corruption that lie all about
it during its *Union* with the Body; *In* which
the Objection fuppofes it to refide as in a
Prifon.

W H E R E A S it is now fo effentialy united
to the Body, that during the Union neither of
them can act alone; it is the *Compound Nature*
that acts; the pure Spirit cannot exercife the
moft abftracted Act of *Volition* or *Thought* any
otherwife than in Concurrence with Matter;
It exercifes all its Operations as a *Part* only of
the whole Perfon, and not as a *Separate* and
Independent Spectator. From this ftrict Union
it

it is, that the Spirit of Man became at firſt *Liable* to be drawn into any Moral Corruption at all, at the Fall; and that ever ſince, it is **vaſtly** more liable to be *Seduced*, tho' not *Forced* into a Compliance with the Sollicitations of corrupt Paſſion and Appetite, and all the ſinful Tendencies which infected our inferior Soul and Body from eating the forbidden Fruit. For our unruly Paſſions and Appetites then gained ſuch an *Addition* of Strength, as *Proportionably* abated the native Power and Influence of the pure Spirit, and conſequently rendered it more liable to an Abuſe of its Liberty.

But you will ſay the Objection is not quite removed; for where is the *Juſtice* of adding a Principle pure in itſelf, to another which is impure, in Conjunction with which it muſt neceſſarily be corrupted? If it muſt *Neceſſarily* be corrupted, the Objection would hold; but on the contrary, it is ſtill indued with *Freedom of Choice*, which it can and ought to exert effectualy in its Union with the Body. During which Union, notwithſtanding the Diſadvantages it is under from the Strength of Paſſion and Appetite, it ſtill remains the *Directing* Principle, and ſhould always aſſert its right; conſtantly and vigorouſly ſupport its *Native* Title to Dominion; and not permit the Fleſh or inferior Soul by any Importunity to prevail for its Compliance with their unreaſonable Demands;

or

or ever to become the concurring Inftrument of their finful Lufts and Paffions.

WHAT I affert is no more than that the Spirit is *Originaly* and in its own Nature, feparately confider'd, pure and uncorrupt; as the whole *Compound Nature* was at firft. But ftill it may become Partner in all the Guilt, Partaker of all the Defilements of the Flefh and inferior Soul, and Sharer in their Pollution by its own Default or free *Confent*, tho' not by *Force*. And for want of exerting its proper Authority, it becomes itfelf actualy defiled, and together with them juftly liable to Condemnation and Punifhment: According as it proves fupine and unactive; as it yields to Temptation; and fuffers itfelf to be led away Captive by thofe Paffions and Appetites, which cannot move one Step further into *Act*, than they have its full Confent and Permiffion. And what renders it truly *Criminal* in fuch finful Compliances is, a Confcioufnefs of their being all directly contrary to its own pure native Sentiments and Tendencies; and that it could have acted otherwife. So that its Moral Imperfections are no way neceffary; but ftrictly imputable to it by its own failure, and abufe of its innate Liberty of Choice.

Now in order to prevent farther Miftake and Objection here; it muft be confidered, that tho' all the Operations of *Man* are realy and

truly

truly *Joint* Acts of the three Parts of the Compound in essential Union : yet each Operation, considered *Singly* and by itself, may proceed in a *Greater Degree* from any *One* Part, than from the rest. Tho' all our Operations proceed from the whole *Compound Nature*, yet they do not *Equaly* proceed from *Each Part* of it. For instance, *Thinking* and *Willing* are Acts of all the Parts in essential Union, or Acts of the compound Nature ; and yet they are principaly and *Chiefly* the Operations of the pure *Spirit*; in a lesser Degree the Operations of the *Animal Soul*; and least of all of the *Body*. So in the Reverse, the *Appetites* in Man are Operations of the compound Nature, but much more Acts of the *Animal Soul* and *Body* than of the *Spirit* : And yet were they not in some degree Acts of that Spirit, which *Informs* the whole, they could be no way *Governed* or regulated by it ; nor could any Appetite become *Sinful* in us any more than in Brutes. So again, every human *Passion*, as *Anger* for instance, is the Act or Motion of the compound Nature, but chiefly and in a greater Measure of the *Inferior Soul:* And as all the Passions are of a *Middle* Nature, they are jointly, tho' in a less degree, the Operations of Body and Spirit likewise.

FOR this Reason only it is, that such of our Operations are called *Bodily* by way of Distinction, in which the Body bears the

Greatest

Greatest Share; thofe are called *Animal* which proceed moft from the *Inferior Soul*; and thofe *Spiritual* which proceed principaly from the *Spirit :* And not becaufe, according to a vulgar Error, they proceed intirely and *Totaly* from any *One* of the Parts *Separately*; nothing being plainer than that while all the Parts of the Compound continue *Effentialy* united, our Operations muft proceed jointly from them all; unlefs we could fuppofe them capable of being *Effentialy United*, and yet *To act feparately* at the fame time. And hence it comes, that tho' the Spirit does not Act *In* the Body, as an *Independent* Principle; yet there may be a natural Oppofition and Struggle between thofe Motions and Tendencies which proceed *Chiefly* from the *Body* or *Inferior Soul*, and thofe which proceed *Principaly* from the Spirit. But then as the Spirit is made the *Governing* Principle of the Compound, and is accordingly indued with *Reafon* and *Liberty of Choice*; fo it may permit any *One* of the Tendencies, more *Peculiar* to each particular *Part*, to become fo ftrong as to fway and carry with it all the reft, even to the Prefervation or Deftruction of the whole compound Nature. Whereas its proper Office is, fo to adjuft all the *Particular* Tendencies and Operations, as to make them combine together in a beautiful Union towards obtaining the moft commendable common End; and not to fuffer any *One* to prevent or obftruct the moft *Rational*, and what fhould

always

always be the moſt *Prevailing* Inclination, from being gratified. Thus ought our *Little* World to be govern'd after the Model of the great *Syſtem* about us; where the heavenly Bodies, notwithſtanding very *Different* and *Oppoſite* Tendencies, are made to conſpire harmoniouſly towards the glorious End of the *Whole*:

N o w the *Underſtanding* and *Will* being *Principaly* the Operations of this pure Spirit, tho' they are neceſſarily tranſacted in Concurrence with material Organs; we may obſerve from what paſſeth within us, that they remain the ſame, and unaltered in *Approbation* and *Deſire*, even when they are moſt violently oppoſed and contradicted by the Inclinations and Appetites of the animal Soul ; nay even when the Spirit is prevailed on to *Comply* with them. So that we ſhall in *Spirit* approve and *Deſire* or *Will*, that very inſtance of Virtue and Goodneſs, which upon the vehement Reluctance of the Fleſh and inferior Soul we chooſe to decline : And we ſhall *Condemn* that very Vice or Wickedneſs which we *Chooſe* to commit, and to which we bear in *Spirit* the greateſt Hatred and Averſation; or in the Apoſtle's Phraſe, *That which I do, I allow not ; for what I would, that do I not ; but what I hate, that do I.* The pure *Intellect* and *Will* are rarely or never ſo brought over to the Enemies Side, as to fall in with them intirely, or to abet and maintain their Cauſe with *Pleaſure* and *Approbation* ;

B b 3   tho'

tho' they may be carried into Captivity by our own Default; and into such a State of Bondage and Subjection as to be past all Hope or Prospect of any Releafe. But still in the midst of *Chains* and Fetters, the Spirit, like a royal Captive awful even in Distress, will affert its native right of Dominion, and upbraid its Betrayer with unjust and treacherous Ufurpation. From thence come *Remorfe* of Confcience, and boding *Expectation* of inconceivable Mifery in a future State, occafioned by going out of the World with our whole Frame voluntarily *Inverted*; and by the *Pure Spirit's* being probably configned over by Death to the endless Tyranny of the *Inferior Soul*, upon the Re-union of Body and Spirit at the Refurrection.

II. THE Word ufed in Scripture to denote the fecond Principle in Man is Ψυχὴ ·which hath various Acceptations. In 1 *Pet.* ii. 11. it is taken for πνεῦμα or the pure Spirit of Man, *Beware of flefhly Lufts which war againft the Soul*; and thus it is to be interpreted whereever it is apply'd to a pure Spirit in a State of *Separation*. Sometimes it is taken for both thefe, *Spirit* and *Soul* together, as *Thou Fool, this Night fhall thy Soul be required of thee*; as likewife in all Places where mention is made of *Saving the Soul*, or of loving God with *All the Soul*. Very often it is taken for the whole Man, let *Every Soul be fubject to the higher Powers*.

Powers. And laftly, it is ever included in the Word *Flefh* when it is fet in Oppofition to πνεῦμα or the pure Spirit; as where it is faid, *The Spirit indeed is willing, but the Flefh is weak. The Flefh lufteth againft the Spirit, and the Spirit againft the Flefh. I know that in me,* that is *in my Flefh, dwelleth no good thing.*

THIS Part of us is *Mortal,* fubject both to *Moral* and *Natural* Corruption; and as it owes its Being to the Conjunction of the pure Spirit with the Body; fo it ceafeth and is diffolved again immediately upon their Separation: This is the Seat of all our irregular *Inclinations* and *Defires*; and as it is *Nearer* ally'd to the *Body* than the Spirit, fo it is greatly taken up in the Confervation of its being, and providing for the full Gratification of all its Appetites. For which Reafon it is by the Heathen Philofophers branded with fuch Names of Contempt as thefe; the *Horfe,* becaufe it is headftrong and runs away with the *Man,* or rather with the *Spirit* which ought to have the governing of the Reins. The *Beaft* in us, becaufe the animal or fenfitive Soul is fuppofed common to us with Brutes. The *Woman* or *Child* in us, becaufe the Paffions and Affections of Women and Children are commonly ftronger, and their Reafon weaker than in Men. So that, as I have met it well obferved, *Man is an amphibious Creature, of a middle Order and Nature between Angels and Brutes: With thefe he partakes*

takes of a corporeal Soul, vital Blood, and a Mass of animal Spirits; with the former he partakes of an intelligent, immaterial, immortal Spirit.

Now whether we suppose this inferior Soul an *Original, Distinct, Constituent* Part of our Frame, answerable to the same in Brutes; or some third Principle necessarily arising from the essential *Union* of an immaterial Substance with Matter; yet if considered abstractedly from that pure Spirit, it is best conceived and spoke of in this *Abstracted* Sence, by the Soul of a Brute; which of itself could give no more than *Life*, and *Motion*, and bodily *Appetites*; and perhaps some superior Degree of natural *Instinct*, as is most observed in those Beasts which approach nearest to human Shape: And were the Body of a Man to grow up with that *Alone*, without the addition of an *Immaterial* Substance, he would be no more than a Beast in human Shape. When the pure Spirit was breathed into the Body, Man became a *Reasonable*, as well as a *Living* Soul; and thence, what would otherwise have risen no higher than *Bodily Appetite*, *Sense*, and *Instinct*; is improved, not only into *Understanding* and *Will*, but into all the *Passions* and *Affections* of a reasonable human Nature.

THESE Affections were all regular in our first Creation; but by the Fall our bodily Appetites

petites got the upper hand of our Reason, and
became so headstrong and violent as to draw
off all the *Passions* and *Affections* of the Mind
from *God*, and Goodness, and the things of another Life; and ingage them too much on the
present Objects of *Sense*, which were adapted
to the more immediate Pleasure and Gratification of those Appetites common to us with
Brutes. These in a State of corrupt Nature
being craving and impetuous, do with Clamour
and Fury in a tumultuous manner, hurry
away all those *Affections* of the Mind; in Contradiction to the still Voice, and calm tho'
constant Advice and Tendency of the pure
Understanding and Will; and bring them over
to the Flesh. Thus it is that these Affections,
from being the Instruments of all Virtue and
Holiness; become corrupt and degenerate, and
are subservient to all manner of Vice and
Wickedness: And thus at last is the pure Spirit itself importun'd into a *Consent* to their
sinful Motions, tho' not to an intire *Approbation*
of them.

AND now we see what a spacious Scene of
Knowledge the clearing up this Distinction of
Spirit, and *Soul*, and *Body* in Man, hath opened
to the Mind with respect to the whole System
of *Moral* and *Practical* Religion; by pointing
out to us wherein our *Strength* lies, and where
our *Weakness*; and discovering to us the true
Seat of all our *Corruption*, and the means and
method of our *Cure*.   OUR

OUR *Strength* lies in the *Immaterial* part of us affisted by the *Grace* of God, which is the fecret and ineffable Communication of the holy Spirit to the Spirit of a Man which is in him; to enable it to refift and overcome all the Allurements and Temptations of the fenfitive Soul; and recover its native right of Dominion over all the Faculties of the inferior Man. This purely fpiritual Part of us may be enticed and *Allured*, but never overcome by *Force*; for it is a noble Principle, whofe Ruin muft proceed from itfelf; it can lie under no Compulfion or *Abfolute Conftraint* from any thing without it, but from that only which is Almighty. As there is nothing more *Feeble* than the Mind of Man, when it refigns itfelf up to irregular Paffion and Appetite; fo there is nothing in Nature fo *Strong* and invincible, whenever it is truly and fteadily refolved to be fo: When by divine Affiftance it exerts itfelf to the utmoft, the World and the Flefh are not able to Cope with it, nor the Devil to ftand before it.

IN a mere ftate of corrupt Nature indeed, this Godlike Part of us is without a fufficient Power of *Direction* and Government; it is fo overcome and obftructed, that of itfelf it is utterly unable to reftrain any one irregular Inclination or Appetite in the fenfitive Soul, or Body: To which tho' it be effentialy *United*, yet it cannot

not diffuse its own native Inclinations and Defires thro' the unwieldy Mass; which sets up
a great Variety of Lusts and Appetites of its
own in direct Opposition to it; so that it cannot
when *Unassisted*, commendably and effectualy
exert itself to the Performance of any Virtue
or Goodness in Thought, Word, or Deed.
This made the secret Influence of the *Spirit of
God* upon our Spirit necessary for us; that the
same Breath of God which first gave it *Being*,
might supply it with new *Life* and *Vigour :*
Stirring up its original Inclinations and Tendencies; awakening and reviving those native
Desires of Virtue and Holiness, which lay dor-
mant and unactive under the Ruins of human
Nature; and this is the Beginning of a Christian Life. When by God's *Preventing* Grace
the Spirit is rouzed out of its Lethargy, then
comes on the Struggle; the Principles of *Reason*
and *Grace*, against the corrupt *Appetites* and
Propensions of Nature. If it cherishes and
encourages these *First* Motions of the Holy
Spirit, and holds out resolutely and with firm
Perseverance, it gains Ground every Day; and
goes on gradualy from Strength to Strength :
Till at last, like a glorious Monarch restored
and confirmed, it rules the rebel Affections and
Passions of the sensitive Soul, and the Appetites of the Body, with a Rod of Iron, and
sways them all with its Nod. It may then
approve or reject; suppress or excite; check or
encourage all our Inclinations at will; it may
Still

Still the raging and swelling of our Passions, and say to each of them, *Hitherto shalt thou come and no further* ; and in short nothing shall be transacted in the little World without its Permission or Command.

OUR *Weakness* lies in the *Sensitive Soul*, the immediate Seat of all our *Passions* and *Affections* ; which being as it were in the *Middle* between the *Pure Spirit* and the *Body*, is solicited on both sides, and must incline to one or the other : If it join with the *Spirit*, it will itself become spiritualized in all its Tendencies; but as it more or less inclines to the *Flesh*, so far it becomes carnal and degenerate. Now because all the Motions and Affections of this inferior Soul are more immediately conversant with the Objects of our bodily Appetites ; and more strongly importuned by their constant and intimate *Presence* ; they are in their own Nature apt to close with these, and *Dwell* upon them : And it is not without great Difficulty and Resolution that they can be weaned and drawn off from them ; so as to be chiefly imployed upon the invisible Things of another World, and such Things here as have a more immediate Relation to them. For this Reason both the *Inferior Soul* and *Body* go under the Denomination of *Flesh* ; and accordingly of this it is said, that the *Flesh lusteth against the spirit, and the spirit against the flesh ; and these are contrary the one to the other.*

THESE

THESE are the two Enemies which muſt engage; *Implacable* irreconcilable *Enemies*, ever ſince the Fall; and the ſhort fierce Combat is for Eternity. The ſecret Influences of the *Holy Spirit* of God come into the Aſſiſtance of the purely *Spiritual* Part of us; the Devil on the other ſide is a conſtant Auxiliary to the *Fleſh*; the ſtruggle is for no leſs than Life or Death everlaſting; and the one or the other muſt obtain a complete Victory.

BOOK

BOOK III.

A SUMMARY

of

The NATURAL ORDER,

and

WHOLE PROCEDURE

of

The INTELLECT.

CHAP. I.
The Mind at First a Tabula Rasa.

THAT Maxim of the Logicians is to be taken for a sure and fundamental Truth, *Nibil eft in Intellectu quod non fuit prius in fensu*; the true Meaning of which is, that the Ideas of *Senfe* are the *First Foundation* on which we raife our whole Superftructure of Knowledge; and that all the Difcoveries we can make in things *Temporal* and *Spiritual*, together with the moft *Refined* and *Abstracted* Notions of them in the Mind of Man, take their Rife originaly from *Senfation*.

AT our Birth the Imagination is intirely a *Tabula Rasa* or perfect *Blank*, without any Materials either for a *Simple View* or any *Other O-*
peration

peration of the Intellect. We are not furnished with any *Innate* Ideas of things material or immaterial ; nor are we endued with a Faculty or Difpofition of forming *Purely Intellectual* Ideas or Conceptions independent of all Senfation: Much lefs has the human Soul a Power of raifing up to itfelf Ideas out of *Nothing*, which is a kind of *Creation*; or of attaining any *Firft Principles* exclufive of all *Illation* or confequential Deduction from Ideas of *Material* Objects ; without which the Mind of Man, during its Union with the Body, could never have arrived even to a Confcioufnefs of its own *Operations* or *Exiftence*.

D A I L Y Experience fhews us that as far as Perfons are from their firft Infancy deprived of any of their *Senfes*, they are fo far imperfect in their *Intellectuals*. What a vaft degree of Knowledge do we find cut off together with that one Senfe of *Hearing*? Take away the *Sight* likewife, and then confider how limited and confin'd the Operations of the Intellect muft be ? If after this you remove from a Man all *Tafte* and *Smelling*, and if he hath no Ideas left for the Mind to work upon but thofe of his *Feeling*; how far would he differ from the fenfitive *Plant*? The Mind in fuch cafe would not be able to infer the bare Exiftence of any thing external to it but what was *Felt*; and if it were poffible for the Man to have *Animal Life* without

Feeling,

Feeling, he would be as utterly void of *Know-*
ledge as one in a Swoon or Apoplectick Fit.

Now this is so far from being a just reason to think the Soul of Man *Material*, that it
is an Argument of the quite *Contrary*. For let
us restore that Man to all his Senses again, in
the greatest degree of Acuteness he is capable
of, insomuch that he shall have his Imagination furnished with the Ideas of all *Sensible Ob-*
jects; yet you have not restored him to any use
of his *Reason* and *Understanding*; not even to that
of a *Simple View* or Apprehension of those
Ideas. With respect to the simple Perception of
Mere-Sense he is still upon the same Level
with *Brutes*; he is altogether *Passive*; he retains
all the Signatures and Impressions of outward
Objects, but in the very Order only in which
they are stamped; without *Transposing* or *Al-*
tering, *Dividing* or *Compounding*, or even *Com-*
paring them one with another: And they would
always continue so in the Imagination, if there
were not a Principle *Above* Matter, first to
contemplate or view them; and then to work
up those rude and gross Materials into a great
Variety of curious Arts and Sciences.

CHAP.

C H A P. II.

Ideas of Senfation.

THE *Firft* ftep therefore made towards Knowledge is *Antecedent* to any Operation of the *Pure Mind*, and without any Concurrence of the Intellect; and that is, the Attainment of *Ideas*, or fome Likenefs and Reprefentation of external Objects which may remain in their Abfence; and (fince all Senfation is of *Particulars* only, and *Succeffively* of one Object after another) which may bring them all together, as it were into one Place, for the more convenient View and Obfervation of the Mind. Whether this is perform'd by any actual Impreffion of the *Object* upon the Organ of Senfation; or by fome Operation of the *Senfe* upon the Object? And whether the Idea is always an Emblem of the *Real True* Nature of the Object; or of its external *Appearance* alone; or only *Occafion'd* by it? are Queftions perhaps never to be *Thoroughly* decided; and therefore we leave them to be for ever debated by the Curious. Thefe feveral Remarks following, which are within the Compafs of our Knowledge, are more material to be obferved.

1. THAT thefe Ideas of Senfation are all *Simple* Perceptions, and of Particulars only; which

is evident enough with respect to *Four* of our Senses; and will appear to be so likewise of the *Sight*, if it is confidered that tho' the Eye can take in a *Confused* Profpect of a great Variety of Objects at *Once*, yet it can take a *Diftinct* View of them no otherwise than *Succeffively* one after another: And tho' the fame external Object may make Impreffions upon *More* of our Senfes than one at the fame time, yet *Each* of those Impreffions are of a *Different* kind, and each a *Simple* Idea in itfelf; tho' the Mind may afterwards put them together to make up one *Compound* Idea of that Object.

2. THAT this fimple *Perception* of Objects by their *Ideas*, which is common to us with Brutes, is to be well diftinguifhed from the fimple *Apprehenfion* of those *Ideas* by the Intellect after they are lodged in the Imagination; which is an Operation never to be performed by mere Matter, without the Concurrence of an immaterial Principle.

3. THAT these fimple Ideas of Senfation only are, in the ftrict and truly proper Sence of the Word, to be called *Ideas*; and that tho' this Term may improperly be extended to fignify any of *These* confider'd in Conjunction with the *Operations* of the Mind upon them, yet it then ferves only to darken the Subject and confound the Underftanding.

THAT

4. THAT these are the *Materials* and Ground-work of all our Knowledge. And if any one hath a Doubt whether they are so, let him in-stance in some one *Simple original Idea*, which we are not beholden to the Senses for; one that the Intellect can call altogether its own; and which it acquired intirely *Independent* of them. The very Idea of *Existence*, which is the most direct and immediate one we have with respect to *Immaterial* Beings, is from the Senses; in the Knowledge of which the Intellect proceeds thus: As from the Existence of one thing *Material* actualy perceived, I infer the possible and even probable Existence of other things Material which were never the Objects of any of my Senses; so from the known Ex-istence of things Material I draw this Conse-quence, That other things may and must exist which are *Not Matter*. Were it not for our *Actual* sensible Perception of *Bodily* Substance, we should not know what it was to have a *Be-ing*, nor could we be conscious of even our *Own Existence*.

So likewise all the Idea or Notion we have of *Power*, is from the Operations we observe in things purely Material one upon another; or from the Operation of the *Mind* upon its *Ideas*, and its voluntary moving of the *Body*: And therefore because we can have no *Proper* No-tion or *Direct* Idea of the Power of *Creation*,

or

or of producing a Thing into Being no Part of which existed before; we *Endeavour* to conceive it after the best manner we can, by the Power of a *Man* in making something out of *Pre-exiſtent* Materials. Thus we form a Conception even of *Eternity* itſelf from *Time*, which is meaſured by the Motion of the Heavenly Bodies; and from the Duration of things material. So likewiſe by enlarging the Idea we have of *Space* and *Extenſion*, the Mind forms to itſelf the beſt poſitive Conception of *Infinity* it is capable of; and all the Notion of it we have beyond this, is only a *Negation* of any Stop or Boundary. Nay when we attempt to form any *Simple* Idea of God himſelf, it is by no other than that of *Light*, or the Glory of the *Sun*. For this Reaſon we naturaly fall into that way of ſpeaking of things immaterial, and whereof we can have no direct Perception or proper Idea, in the very ſame Style and Language we ſpeak of *Ourſelves* and other things of this World; or elſe expreſs them in Terms purely *Negative*, ſuch as *Infinite, Immaterial, Immortal, Incomprehenſible*, and ſuch like.

FOR the ſame Reaſon it is, as I have met it well obſerved, that we expreſs the pureſt Operations of the *Intellect* by Terms borrowed from Senſation, *Animi ipſius Functiones vocibus quæ a rebus corporeis ſunt tranſlatæ deſignamus; quod nimirum res apprehendat, quod diſcurrat*, &c. As we ſay in Engliſh, that the Mind *Apprehends*

bends or *Takes* a thing, that it *Runs* over it,
and fuch like: Becaufe we have no *Ideas* of
thofe Operations; and therefore when we form
the moft *Abftracted Conceptions* we can of them,
it is not to be done exclufively of thofe *Objects*
which are *Thought of* or *Willed*; in the moft refined Compofition of which Objects, there will
always be found a *Mixture* of fenfitive Ideas
or a *Dependence* upon them. And thus likewife all the Conceptions we have of the particular *Affections* and *Paffions* of the Soul of
Man, are in fome Meafure made up out of Ideas
of *Senfation*. We cannot form any Notions
of them exclufive of the *Objects* which occafion
them, and of their different *Manner* of affecting the *Body*, by which they become *Vifible* in the
Lineaments of the Face, or the outward Deportment of the Perfon: And by joining fuch
Ideas to a *Confcioufnefs* of *Pleafure* and *Pain* in
the Mind, we form a *Complex Notion* of each
Paffion. Thus we partly conceive *Joy* and
Gladnefs by the fparkling of the Eyes and di-
lating of the Countenance; *Sorrow* by a down
Look and a Contraction of all our Features;
and *Anger* by the Diftortion of them. There
is a peculiar Look of *Envy*, another of *Shame*,
and another of *Defpair*. Let any Man try to
form an *Idea* or *Conception* of any particular
Paffion abftractedly from all *External Things*
which are its Objects, and from all Effects of
it on the *Body*; and he will foon perceive what
a Dependence it has on Ideas of *Senfe*, and what

a Portion

a Portion of them muſt be taken into the Account. In ſhort whilſt the Spirit is in Conjunction with the Body, if you remove from it all Ideas of Senſation, the whole Superſtructure of Knowledge Human and Divine falls to the Ground; the Intellect could then have no *Thought*, having nothing left to think of: Nay tho' at the ſame time we ſhould ſuppoſe the Exiſtence of Myriads of *Immaterial* Beings; ſince nothing is plainer, than that it could have no direct and proper Idea of them.

WHEN theſe Impreſſions which we are by God and Nature diſpoſed to receive from outward Objects, are imperceptibly conveyed thro' the Organs of Senſation inwardly to the *Imagination*; to be there repoſited and ſtored up as the Groundwork and groſs unwrought Materials of all Knowledge, whether of things Material or Immaterial; then it is that they obtain the Name of *Ideas:* Which are ever more clear, and diſtinct, and permanent according to the preſent Diſpoſition of the *Organ* of Senſation; the juſt Diſtance of the *Object*; the *Strength* of the Impreſſion made upon theSenſe; the frequent *Repetition* of that Impreſſion; and the Diſpoſition of the *Medium.* It is called the Imagination from the *Images* of external Objects lodged in it, in the ſame confuſed and diſorderly manner they are tranſmitted from the Senſes; and *Senſus Communis,* becauſe it is the inward common Receptacle of all the outward

Impreſſions

Impreffions made upon them. This is a Faculty in Man, as well as Brutes, purely *Paffive*; and differs from *Memory* in that it is, more diftinctly fpeaking, the *Storehoufe* or *Repofitory*; but Memory regards rather the *Furniture* or vaft Variety of Ideas themfelves, lodged there for the ufe of the pure Intellect; and is not a *Diftinct* Faculty from the *Intellect*, as the Imagination realy is; but an Ability in it to *Revive* again and bring into View any Ideas or Notions wherewith the Imagination has been once impregnated, without the repeated *Prefence* of the Objects or Occafions which firft excited them. When we fay a Man hath a lively or working *Imagination*, it is but a miftaken and vulgar way of expreffing the more dextrous and fprightly Operations of the *Intellect* upon the Ideas *That* is ftored with: And confifts particularly in a quick and ready *Comparifon* of them with one another; and placing them together in fuch a Light, as that they fhall mutualy reflect a Beauty and Luftre from one to the other, and by that means produce a Surprife and Pleafure in the Mind.

THO' all hitherto is not properly *Knowledge*, but only what is common to us with Brutes; yet it is an immenfe Fund of Materials laid in for the Imployment of the Mind. The Ideas which the Imagination is capable of containing are not within the Power of Number; efpecialy fince the great increafe of

them

them by Telescopes and magnifying Glasses: It is a Faculty wide and extensive as that System including the fix'd Stars; and is of Capacity enough to take in Ideas from all the Objects of the whole visible Creation.

CHAP. III.

The simple Apprehension of the Intellect, or its View of those Ideas.

THE next Advance in the Order of Nature is to what is truly and properly *Knowledge*; and that is a bare *Contemplation* or *Simple View* by the pure Intellect of those Ideas lodged in the Storehouse of the Imagination; in the very same Order and Condition they were transmitted from the Senses: Without any Transposition or Disturbance of their Situation, and without any *Comparison, Composition* or *Division, Enlargement* or *Diminution*; without any Change or Alteration of them whatsoever; and without any *Judgment*, or *Remark*, or *Observation*, which may be formed into an affirmative or negative Proposition. By the *Pure Intellect* I do not mean the *Pure Spirit* or immaterial Principle in our Composition, in *Distinction* from all that is *Material* in us: But the Spirit in essential *Union* with the Body; and particularly with those animal Spirits, and imperceptible exquisite Fibres of the Brain, which are the

more

more immediate Inftruments of Reafon and Underftanding.

THIS firft Operation of the Intellect is by the Logicians very aptly call'd *Apprehenfio Simplex*. But then it hath been confounded with Senfation or the fimple Perception of the Senfes, to which it is fubfequent ; whereas *This* pre-fuppofes all *Simple Ideas* of Senfation *Already* formed and lodged in the Imagination, and actualy prepared for the Operations of the *Intellect :* I do not fay of the *Mind*, becaufe this is a more complex Term, and includes not only the *Intellect*, but the *Will*; together with the *Memory*, and all the *Paffions* and *Affections* of that inferior Soul which refults from the Union of the pure Spirit with the Body. This is the only *Intuitive* Knowledge we have, properly fpeaking; and is the firft Degree of Knowledge, as it is rightly diftinguifhed from that fimple Perception of outward Objects which is common to us with Brutes: And it is a peculiar Privilege of Man to be capable of this Contemplation or View of his own Ideas, by having an *Immaterial* Principle in his Compofition.

THAT *Brutes* cannot have even this *Simple View* or Contemplation of their own Ideas, not having an immaterial Principle in their Nature, is evident ; for all external fenfible *Objects*, and the *Organs* of Senfation which are
difpofed

diſpoſed to receive their Signatures or Impreſſions; and the *Imagination* likewiſe in Brutes
which receives and retains thoſe Impreſſions,
are all purely *Material:* So that what a *Figure* in
the Wax is, to the *Seal*; that an *Idea* is, in
reſpect of the Object of which it is a *Similitude*
and Repreſentation.   It is no more than the
Impreſſion of one thing material upon another;
and let this be ever ſo *Strong*, or ever ſo often
Repeated; and let the Number of Ideas be ever
ſo *Many*, ſtill the Imagination is in this caſe
but purely *Paſſive:* And therefore theſe Ideas
cannot exert any Operation upon *Each other*;
nor can any *One* of them take a View of the
Reſt, or exerciſe any Power whatſoever beyond
that of a material Impulſe.

THE ſimple Perception of Brutes is properly ſpeaking a Perception of the *Object* by
the Idea; and not of the *Idea* itſelf, or any
View or Contemplation of it in *Diſtinction*
from the Object. Which ſimple Perception of
Senſe they have, from their all-wiſe Creator,
often to a greater Perfection than Man; becauſe
the Ideas of *Senſe* in the Imagination of Brutes
are the whole *Sum* and Subſtance of their *Knowledge* (to ſpeak by way of Analogy) which in
Man are but a *Foundation* for it, and *Materials*
only for a great and glorious Superſtructure:
And becauſe theſe are their ſole *Principle* of
Action; inſomuch that they are wholy and
Paſſively conducted in all their Purſuits by the
Force

Force and Impulse of those Ideas of *Sensation* alone (which is *Natural Instinct*) and not by any separate *View* or Contemplation of them; which is the Beginning of Reason or Knowledge.

BRUTES are under a natural *Necessity* of always following the Force and Impulse of those sensible Impressions, which alone set them a going; they continue to operate as long as there are any Remains of that Impulse, and in Proportion to the Strength or Weakness of it: And are ever disposed to take a different Turn and Propension from every Renewal or *Change* of those sensible Impressions; which they can never *Revive* or renew when impair'd, by any Power in *Themselves*, without the repeated *Presence* of the Objects. It may give us a tolerable Image of their Proceeding in all their Operations, as they are prompted and urged on by Impressions of outward Objects upon their Senses; to observe how one *Globe* or *Ball* striking upon another, gives a very *Different* Determination to its Motion according to the *Force* which is communicated, and the *Point* which it happens to touch upon: That which receives the Stroke hath no Power *Within* it either to divert its Course, or to abate or stop the Motion, which is necessarily continued whilst there are any Remains of the first Impression; but fails gradualy, and wears away till it ends in *Rest*; and so it continues till the same Stroke

is

is *Repeated*, or that it happen to receive fome *New* and different Determination of its Motion.

How great the Number of our *Simple Ideas* is, will not eafily be conceived, otherwife than by confidering that our Imagination, from being at firft a perfect Blank, doth in our Infancy receive fome *Obfcure* and *Confufed* Delineations of external Objects of Senfation ; together with a *Dead* and *Lifelefs* Colouring only : All which are cleared up gradualy by frequent Impreffions, as with the repeated touches of a *Pencil*, and grow every Day more Confpicuous and *Diftinct* ; till at length they become a delightful Reprefentation and *Lively* Picture of all Nature.

This comprehenfive *Intellectual View* of univerfal Nature in *Miniature*, muft give no fmall Pleafure to the Mind of Man ; when it thus fees the vaft extent of human Underftanding, and that it hath no Limits on this Side the fix'd Stars. It muft be tranfported to find it can look *Inward* for a Profpect of all things *Without* it, as far as the Eye, the moft extenfive Organ of Senfation can reach, or Optic Glaffes can carry it : And in fhort that the Man can behold a *Little World* within his own Brain, in its *Ideas* ; which are all his own proper Goods, and which he is intire Mafter of, fo as to manage and difpofe them at his arbitrary Will

and

and Pleasure. Whereas *Brutes* carry their *Ideas* about with them, as *Passively* as they do their *Burdens*; at least for no other Purpose properly of their own, except for a *Necessary* Direction and Guidance in all their Motions.

HOWEVER, these original *Simple Ideas* are still in Reality but a numberless Variety of choice and excellent *Materials* of all Kinds for the Intellect to work upon; and for the Exercise of all its Operations in respect of Human and Divine, Speculative and Practical Knowledge. These are the only Foundation of it all, laid by God and Nature; but the *Workmanship* out of them is various, according to the different Temper, and Disposition, and Application of Men's Minds: And the Superstructure raised upon this Foundation is either *Gold, Silver,* and *Precious Stones* which will abide the Trial; or on the contrary *Wood, Hay,* and *Stubble* which are fit only to be burnt.

BUT to be a little more Particular. The generality of Men are so indolently *Incurious* and unobserving, as to make little farther Improvement of Knowledge from these simple Ideas, than what they are daily prompted to by their *Appetites* and *Passions*; and so of course make the nearest Approaches to those irrational *Animals*, which are altogether under the Power and Conduct of *Sensible* Impressions.

OTHERS

O T H E R S there are who may be said only to *Play* with these Ideas, as Children do with their *Trifles*. Who by arriving, with long Practice, to a great Dexterity in *Rattling* them one against another by *Strained* and unnatural *Comparisons*, which are mostly expressed in a Style *Inverted* and perplex'd, together with a *Gingle* of Words; do tickle the Ears of the *Superficial* and *Lazy*. Thus under the plausible Titles of *Wit*, and *Fancy*, and *Humour*, they *Strike* out of their Ideas a false and flashy *Light*, to *Amuse* and surprise; but not *Instruct* or improve the Understanding. The Performances of this sort either in Writing or Conversation, for the most part please by their *Odness* only; by their Author's straying not only out of the *Common*, but out of the *Natural* and *Useful* way of Thinking: They are calculated chiefly for the use of such as consult nothing but Ease and Pleasure of Body and Mind; and who have not Capacity or Resolution for the Attainment of any Knowledge that is *Solid* and *Useful*; they serve only for filling up that Time which is not employ'd in other Diversions; and then grow flat and insipid, when they have for *Once* gratified an Itch of the Mind. As the former supine *Carelesness* of the Vulgar is properly to be ranged under the Denomination of *Folly*; so this is no other than a sort of voluntary *Frenzy*, as the Men of this Strain themselves are pleas'd to describe it; *Great Wits to Madness sure are near ally'd.*   A

A VERY different or rather oppofite fort of Men there is, who having a *Solid* natural Genius, cultivated by a fober and happy Education, do work up thofe fimple and grofs Materials into *Lafting* and *Stately* Superftructures, for the real Ufe and Ornament of Human Life. This is performed by a nice and curious Obfervation of all their mutual *Relations* and *Connections*; by finding out the real *Likeneffes* of thofe that are different, and the real *Differences* of thofe that are like; by *Sorting* and ranging them all into proper Claffes, under peculiar and diftinct Heads and Denominations; by refolving them into a Series of *Caufes* and *Effects*; and by purfuing them thro' many *Confequences* and Deductions, till they are at laft form'd into regular *Schemes* of Arts and Sciences, and into rational *Syftems* of natural Religion and Morality.

AND here I muft obferve, that Men of the moft *Solid Judgment* never decline what is *Truly* Wit, but cultivate and intermix it in their moft ferious Performances. I mean that kind of Wit which animates the Works of the celebrated ancient Authors, like the agreeable *Life* and *Spirit* proper to fine *Gentlemen*; without any mixture of the *Antick* Quicknefs and *Preternatural* Agility of *Dancers*, and *Buffoons*, and *Pofture-men*; not to fay even of *Apes*, and *Reptiles*. It is this which makes them outlive

4   all

all their Defcendents; which renders them very
hardly imitable, and the *Standards* of good
Sence and Expreffion thro' all Ages and Lan-
guages; becaufe they never lofe fight of *Nature*,
but ever keep clofe to her in all her Windings
and Labyrinths.   This is a Felicity and Ex-
cellence fo peculiar to them, and fome few o-
thers, that it is as difficult in the *Defcription* as
in the *Imitation*; but thus much we may venture to fay, that their Wit is ever *Free*, and
Eafy, and fuch as flows of itfelf.   It is truly an
Imitation of Nature, and not a miferable wrefting and *Diflortion* of it; by either reprefenting
her *Swoln* and *Bloated*, and *Larger* than the Life,
which is *Monftrous*: Or *Lefs* than her own juft
Size and Stature; cramping and diminifhing
her Features in low and *Homely* Comparifons;
which is to make her appear *Dwarfifh* and de-
fpicable.   Wit is ever truly valuable whilft it
is an *Handmaid* to Reafon; and not a proud, and
freakifh, and domineering *Miftrefs*.   When it
ferves to all the Purpofes of *Brightening* and
Polifhing, without *Defacing* our Images; and of
giving *Light*, and *Illuftration*, and even *Splendor*
to things in themfelves *Dark*, and *Obfcure*, and
Difficult to be apprehended; inftead of *Glaring*,
and fo *Dazling* the Eye of the Mind, that it
cannot have a *Diftinct ufeful* Perception even of
the plaineft Object.   In fhort, when it is fuch
a Defcription and Picture of Nature, as keeps
ftrictly to all her juft *Proportions* and *Lineaments*;
in which fhe may be feen and admired by the

Beholders in her own *Genuine Simplicity* and *Native Modefty*: And which doth not deck her out in a *Tinfel* and *Gawdy* Drefs; or expofe her to publick View in *Loofe* and *Wanton* Apparel.

THIS great and commendable Progrefs, in raifing fuch lofty Superftructures out of Materials fo mean in Appearance, is often attended with no fmall *Danger* and Hazard; as the fad Experience of too many hath fhewn us. For when they have carried them on to the greateft Height of Knowledge attainable in things merely *Natural* and human; and do find that from thence they cannot look *Strait* into Heaven, or have fuch a Profpect of things *Spiritual* and *Immaterial* as they have of the Objects of *Senfe*; and that their Minds cannot be furnifhed with fuch *Clear* and *Diftinct* Ideas of them, as are alfo *Direct* and *Immediate:* Then they intirely acquiefce and feek no farther; fetting up here their *Marks* of the utmoft Boundaries to human Underftanding, engraven and diftinguifhed with this celebrated Motto, *Quæ fupra nos, nihil ad nos.* From thefe imaginary Altitudes of theirs they look down, with a contemptuous Air, upon all the Advocates of *Revelation* and *Myftery*; perpetualy calling upon them for *Ideas*, nay even *Simple Original* Ideas of things altogether imperceptible and inconceivable by any *Proper* and *Direct* Ideas; and ever upbraiding them with their having *Faith*

D d   with-

without *Reason*; with *Believing* without *Know-ledge*; and with having *Knowledge* without *Ideas*.

THUS these Men continue to live and die in a polite and learned Infidelity, for want of this plain and obvious Confideration; that upon their grand Principle of allowing no *Know-ledge* farther than they have *Direct* and *Proper Ideas*, there could be no fuch thing even as *Natural* Religion: Nay they muft not acknow-ledge the Exiftence of an *Angel* or Spirit; or of *God* himfelf, fince it is plain that they can have no *Direct* Perception or *Proper* Idea of him; and that for want of any fuch Idea, we are obliged to form to our felves a very *Com-plex* and *Analogous Notion* or *Conception* of him, out of the beft Ideas the Mind is fupplied with from the vifible Creation, confider'd together with its own Operations upon thofe Ideas. And this Notion or *Conception* of him (for it is no *Idea*) is fo very *Complicated*, that perhaps it is not exactly the fame in any two Men what-foever: Yet however *Complex* it is, and col-lected from all the Excellencies we can difco-ver in the vifible Creation (but more efpeci-aly from the greateft Perfections obfervable in Man) and however *Analogous* only; yet it is a *Solid Ground* and Foundation for all the Pre-cepts of natural Religion, and the practical Duties of Morality.

CHAP.

CHAP. IV.

Compound Ideas of Senſation.

FROM this ſimple Apprehenſion or *Intuitive Contemplation* of Ideas in the Imagination, the Intellect proceeds not only to make its own manifold *Remarks* and *Obſervations* upon them, in the ſame Situation and Condition they appear there: But intirely to *Invert* their whole Order and Diſpoſition at Will; and to fit and prepare them by numberleſs Changes or Alterations in whole or in part, for any Uſe or Purpoſes of its own. For tho' the pure Intellect cannot *Add* one *Simple* original Idea to the Number already in the Imagination, yet it hath an arbitrary and deſpotick Power over all that it finds there; and exerts itſelf to the utmoſt in a great Variety of *Operations* upon them. It *Enlarges* or *Diminiſheth* them at Pleaſure in any Proportion; as for inſtance, the Idea of a *Mite* may be increaſed to the bigneſs of an *Elephant*, and that of the *Sun* may dwindle into the Size of a *Spark* of Fire. It *Compounds* or *Divides* them; as the Idea of a *Man* and *Horſe* may be put together into one; and when the Compoſitions are thus *Againſt* Nature, they are ſtiled *Chimeras:* So again the Idea of a Man's Body may be divided into its integral Parts, or bodily Members. It *Unites* or *Separates* them;

as it can bring a multitude of particular Ideas of *Man* together to make up the compound Idea of an *Army*; fo it can *Separately* confider things *Infeparable* in *Nature*, as the *Pure Intellect* from the *Will* and *Affections*, for the more *Diftinct* View and Reafoning of the Mind, and this is truly *Abftraction*. It *Improves* or *Debafes* any of its Ideas; as the Idea of Light may be carried on beyond that of the brighteft Sun Beams, which Men do when they attempt to form any *Simple* Idea of God's *Glory*; fo again a *Shadow* may be aggravated till it ends in thick and palpable *Darknefs*. It *Compares* them infinitely to find out their *Relations*, and *Similitudes*, and *Oppofitions*; and then by forting, and tranfpofing, and bringing them together, it forms to itfelf an endlefs Variety of *Compound Ideas*. It places one Idea to *Stand* for many or all others of the fame kind, and thus renders it *Univerfal* in its Signification. It fubftitutes the Idea or Conception of one thing for another whereof it has even an *Imaginary* Refemblance, as in *Metaphor*; or of which it has a *Real* and *Known* Similitude, which is *Human* Analogy. And laftly it fubftitutes our Conceptions of Things human and *Directly* known, for the Reprefentation of *Immaterial* Objects whereof we have no *Direct* Idea or Conception; and this, not on account of any *Known*, but an *Unknown* tho' *Real* Similitude, or Proportion, or Correfpondency which is *Divine* Analogy.

Here

HERE again is a *New* Enlargement of the Mind of Man, and an Advance towards Knowledge which *Brutes* are not capable of: For as they have not even that simple Apprehension of the *Intellect*, which is distinct from the Perception of *Sense*; so are they much less capable of any of these Operations that are all *Subsequent* to this simple Apprehension. They have not the least Power over their Ideas, either to *Enlarge* or *Diminish* them; to *Compound* or *Divide* them; to *Unite* or *Separate* them; to *Improve* or *Debase* them; but above all to *Compare* them with one another, to *Substitute* Ideas or Notions for the Representation of others, on account of any *Real* or *Imaginary*, *Known* or *Unknown* Proportion or Similitude. In short Brutes can neither *Transpose* nor *Alter* any one Idea in their Imagination; but are on the contrary altogether under the Power of their Ideas or sensible Impressions, as to their whole Direction and Conduct.

How great a Privilege of a rational and human Mind this is, and what a vast *Scope* it gives to the Understanding, will immediately appear when it is considered; that the very same Power the Intellect hath over its *Simple* Ideas, it hath also over all its own various *Alterations* of them, and endless *Compositions* out of them. The very *Same* Operations of the Intellect are renewed and exerted to the

utmost

utmoft *Over again* upon thefe likewife; fo as
to tranfpofe, and alter, and combine them
with the fame defpotick Power: And as thofe
Operations are all thus repeated upon this *New*
Sett of compounded Ideas; fo it may proceed
to operate after the fame Manner upon thofe
that are *Doubly* compounded, as we may fay;
and fo on according to the working or dexterity of the Mind. If our ftore of *Simple* Ideas
only are *Innumerable*, as we have feen they are;
furely the *Alterations* and *Combinations* of them
by the Intellect, together with its own *Obfer-*
vations upon their feveral *Qualities* and *Rela-*
tions muft be more fo: And if the Intellect can
exercife the fame Operations over again upon
its own *Further* voluntary Compofitions out of
them; then our *Compounded* Ideas can hardly
come within the Power of Arithmetick to
number. As I have met it expreffed with Hy-
perbole enough, *The Truths and Refolutions of*
the Intellect from thence, muft be prodigioufly more
than have yet been difcover'd by the Sons of Men:
And perhaps they contain more than would ever
be difcovered, were the prefent Frame of things
to continue as it is for Millions of fucceeding
Ages. And again, *If a few Letters are capable*
of infinite Combinations and Alterations, what
endlefs Variety muft the Combinations and Altera-
tions of the Ideas we are furnifhed with from all
the Objects of the vifible Creation, afford?

IT is of no fmall Confequence to our Progrefs

grefs in Knowledge to obferve here, that the Term *Idea* is attributed to thofe Alterations and Combinations of the Intellect in a *Lefs proper* Senfe; and not in the fame *Strict* Propriety in which it is attributed to the *Simple* and *Original* Perceptions of the Senfes, when conveyed to the Imagination. However as thefe are the *Primary*, fo the other are a *Secondary* Sett of Ideas: But then we muft intirely drop the Term here, and carry it with us no farther; for all *Beyond* thefe are either *Notion*, or *Conception*, or *Apprehenfion*; or what you may more properly call by any other Denomination, than that of *Idea*.

THE want of diftinguifhing rightly between the *Simple Perceptions of Senfe*, and the *Simple Apprehenfion* of the *Intellect*; between the *Primary* and *Simple* Ideas of *Senfation* which are *Independent* of the pure Intellect, and thofe *Secondary* compound Ideas which are its *Creatures*; between all thofe, and the *Complex Notions* and Conceptions of the Mind: But above all, the want of diftinguifhing between the Conceptions of things human, when they are *Direct* and *Immediate*; and when they are transferr'd to things fpiritual and immaterial by *Semblance* only and *Analogy*. For want, I fay, of obferving thefe fundamental Diftinctions thro' our modern Syftems of Logic and Metaphyfics; their Authors, inftead of *Helping* the Underftanding and enabling it to clear up things obfcure and difficult;

have

have on the contrary rendered the plaineſt Truths *Myſterious* and *Unintelligible:* To ſuch I mean who will ſtrictly keep within their Method and Rules of reſolving even all that Knowledge which conſiſts in *Complex Notions* and *Conceptions*, indifferently and promiſcuouſly into *Ideas* of *Senſation* and *Reflection*, as equaly *Simple* and *Original*.

TAKE an Inſtance of this truth in one Point of Knowledge; *God is to be worſhipped by Man*. In this Propoſition there are three *Complex Notions* or Conceptions expreſs'd; that of *God*, which is a Conception or Notion not only very *Complex*, but made up of the utmoſt Perfections of our own Nature *Analogicaly* attributed to an infinite Being who is *Incomprehenſible*, that is, of whom we have no *Proper* or *Direct Idea*; and this is a Conception the plaineſt Man is capable of forming to himſelf, according to the Meaſure of his Underſtanding. Divine *Worſhip* is a complex Notion, formed by putting together the outward *Poſture* of the *Body*, the *Intention* of the *Mind*, all thoſe *Paſſions* and *Affections* which are the Ingredients of Devotion in the *Soul*; together with the *Inviſible Object* to which all theſe are directed. *Man* is likewiſe a very complex Notion or Conception, including the outward *Figure* of the *Body*, the immaterial *Spirit* with the pure *Intellect* and *Will*, and all the *Paſſions* and *Affections* of the inferior Soul; and every one puts as many of theſe

thefe together as he can to make up his Notion of a Man. Thus that Propofition is *Plain*
and *Intelligible* to every Capacity; and if this
Point of Knowledge fhould come to be *Refol-*
ved Analyticaly, it would be found to have taken its firft *Rife* from our fimple original Ideas of
Senfation, particularly that of an human Body:
From whence the Intellect, proceeding gradualy thro' all its own Obfervations and Deductions, came at length to form that Propofition
which is of fo much Confequence in Religion.
So that it evidently appears this Affertion may
very well be granted to our Freethinkers as
true, *That we can have no Knowledge without*
Ideas, nay even without Ideas of *Senfation*; and
yet be very falfe in *Their* Sence of it, which
is *That we can have no Knowledge of things*,
whereof we have no Ideas.

BUT according to the modern Affectation of
refolving all our Knowledge into *Ideas*, nay
Original Simple Ideas, tho' *Not* of *Senfation*; fee
what a long *Chain* of Ideas muft be *Drawn* out
before you can arrive at a true Knowledge of
this Propofition. You muft have an Idea of
God, of whom you can have no Idea; and of
all his *Attributes*, every one of which are *In-*
comprehenfible. You muft have an Idea of
Worfhip, whereof you can have no Idea farther
than of the bodily *Pofture*, or of the *Elements*
and outward *Materials* ufed in Worfhip; all
the other main Ingredients of Divine Worfhip
added

added to thefe make up a *Complex Notion*, not an *Idea* of it. Nay you muft have diftinct and feparate *Ideas* of all the *Operations* of the Intellect; and of all thofe *Paffions* and *Affections* which are the Ingredients of Devotion in the Mind, by *Reflection:* And by joining all thofe Ideas of *Reflection*, to the Ideas of *Senfation* which you have from the bodily Pofture and outward Materials, you make up, in their way, a very *Clear* and *Diftinct Idea* of Divine Worfhip. You muft have the Idea of an human and *Rational Creature* or intelligent Agent, of whom you can have no other Idea but that of his outward *Bodily Figure* and *Motion.* Nay before you can lay down that Propofition for a fundamental Principle of Religion, you muft have an Idea of *Thinking*, of *Reafoning*, and Deduction; the Idea of a *Law* ; the Idea of *Sanction* ; the Idea of *Obedience* and of *Tranfgreffion* ; the Idea of *Pleafure* and *Reward* ; the Idea of *Punifhment* and *Pain* ; the Idea of *Power* to give Reward, and to inflict Punifhment ; and all thefe muft be *Simple Original* Ideas either of *Senfation* or *Reflection.* And thus if you go about to refolve any other Inftance of plain and obvious Knowledge into its firft *Originals* according to this *New* Method, it will be intirely loft in a confufed *Jumble* and *Rout* of *Ideas.*

THUS far are our tedious modern Syftems, which run altogether upon the Doctrine of *Ideas,*

Ideas, from contributing any *Real* Help and Improvement to the Underſtanding; inſomuch that when you have read them over with the greateſt Attention, your Head only *Chimes* and *Tingles* with a continued inceſſant Repetition of the Word *Idea:* And you are ſo far from any true *Advancement* of Knowledge, that you have been ſo long wandering out of your way; and can make no Progreſs till you come into the plain and open Road again. But what is yet worſe, you are, by that confuſed and indiſtinɛt Method of proceeding, inſenſibly drawn into an Opinion, *That you can have no Knowledge of any thing but what you have a direɛt and immediate Idea of*; which is a Propoſition fataly falſe, and the great fundamental Principle of all thoſe, who ſet up for *Reaſon* and *Evidence* in Oppoſition to *Revelation* and *Myſtery.*

C H A P. V.

The Intelleɛt's Conſciouſneſs of its own Operations. Its complex Notions and Conceptions.

WHEN the Imagination is ſtored with ſuch an immenſe Fund of *Simple* Ideas, and with its own manifold *Compoſitions* out of them; the Intelleɛt naturaly proceeds to a Conſideration of thoſe ſeveral *Operations* of its own which it exerts and exerciſes upon them; but not to a View of any *Ideas* we have of them either

either *Direct*, or by *Reflection* : Andtherefore **I** would choose to say, it begins to mark and observe its own Operations from an inward and immediate *Conscioufnefs* it hath of them ; and not by the *Mediation* of any *Ideas*.

AN *Idea of Reflection* is an empty Sound, without any intelligible and determinate Meaning. It hath been used in Oppofition to our *Direct* Perception of fenfible Objects, from whence we have Ideas of Senfation ; and the Mind is prepofteroufly fuppofed to come by Ideas of its own Operations, from a *Reflex* Act or looking back upon itfelf. But as the *Eye* is incapable of furveying its *Internal* Frame by any *Direct* or *Reflex* Act ; fo is the *Mind* utterly unable to know its own Operations by any *Direct* or *Reflex Ideas :* Or to have any other *Knowledge* of them than an immediate *Self-Confcioufnefs*, obtained while it is employed on the Ideas of *External Objects*. It is by thofe Operations upon fuch Ideas, that the Intellect comes to the Knowledge even of a *Power* within itfelf of exerting fuch a Variety of Operations. It would not perceive that it had even an *Exiftence*, or a Faculty of *Thinking* or *Willing*, were it not for fome *Idea* or *Notion* of the *Object* which it actualy thinks upon, or defires and choofes. The Intellect firft operates either upon fome original Ideas of *Senfation* ; or upon fome Compofitions and *Combinations* made out of them ; or upon fome *Complex*

plex *Notions* and Conceptions of its own forming (which three take in all the Objects of
human Underftanding) and then it obferves as
exactly as it can the *Nature* and *Manner* of
thofe Operations; and fo forms to itfelf the
beft *Complex Conceptions* of them it is able.

THAT there can be no fuch thing as *Ideas*
of the Operations of the Mind by *Reflection*,
is moft evident; for granting (what we have
feen is evidently falfe) that the Mind could
take a View of its Operations by *Turning in*
upon itfelf, then there would be no want of
Ideas to difcern them by. An Idea is fome
Reprefentation of an *External Object* in the
Mind; it ftands *For* the Object, and fupplies
its abfence; and there would be no *Need* of
any Reprefentation, if the Object itfelf were
there: But the Operations of the Mind are all
Within it felf; and in order to prove Ideas of
Reflection, you muft fuppofe either that thefe
Operations are their *Own* Ideas; or that the
Objects themfelves are overlooked, and their
Ideas only made the Objects of the Intellect.

To fay that the Operations *Themfelves*, and
the *Ideas* of thofe Operations are in the Mind
Together at the fame time, is moft abfurd;
as being *Superfluous*, and altogether without
any Neceffity in Nature, which doth nothing
in vain. Upon this Suppofition it would be
utterly impoffible for the moft acute Logician

to determine which of the two were the *Object* of our *Understanding*; and the best Resolution of the Case would be, that either one or the other may be so *Indifferently*; for that it would be impossible to distinguish between them. But if any one yet thinks that he hath a *Simple*, *Original*, and purely *Intellectual Idea* of any Operation of the Intellect, or of the *Will*, or of any *Passion* or *Affection* of the Mind; let him shut his Eyes, and abstract intirely from the Idea of the *Object* known or desired, or upon which the Passion is bent; from all *Commotions* in the *Body*; and from all the *Effects* and Consequences of the Passion which are *External* to the Mind, and then he will find nothing left to be equaly the *Original* Foundation of his Knowledge with Ideas of *Sensation*; as some would have Ideas of *Reflection* to be.

HAVING as I hope intirely removed that stumbling Block out of the way, upon which those who have had the misfortune to fall, have *Halted* ever after; and having left the Term *Idea* behind us, we may now go on to observe how the Mind proceeds to raise up to itself, out of those Ideas of *Sensation* consider'd together with its own *Operations* upon them, an endless Variety of *Complex Notions* or *Conceptions* of all those things, for which it can have no *Ideas* simple or compounded. How we come to have no other than complex Notions or Conceptions of *God*, and of *Man* as a rational Animal,

mal, of the *Mind*, and of Divine *Worſhip* we have already ſeen. We have no other of the *Intellect*, and of all its *Operations*, or of any *Paſſion* or Affection of the Soul, or of things *Immaterial* and ſpiritual; or in ſhort of *Any* thing, excepting only of *Senſible* Material Objects. The *Notion* we have even of the Intellect is, that it is made up of *Spirit* and *Matter* acting in eſſential Union; and exerting itſelf in all thoſe Operations we obſerve it exerciſe upon external Objects or their Ideas. Thus likewiſe it is in all our *Conceptions* of the Paſſions and Affections, as we obſerv'd before: And ſo we form a *Complex Conception* of an *Angel*, by ſubſtituting all the Operations of an human Mind to *Stand* for its Perfections; which we conclude muſt ſubſiſt in a Subſtance or Being whereof we can have *No Idea*, unleſs that which we attempt to form from the moſt refined and ſpirituous Parts of *Matter*.

THE complex Notions or Conceptions of the Operations of the Mind are wrought up ſo gradualy, and obtain'd ſo *Inſenſibly* from one act of the Intellect to another upon the ſimple Ideas of Senſation, that we are at length apt to miſtake them for *Originals*; which hath been the Occaſion of that pernicious Error of calling them, and thoſe of Senſation, promiſcuouſly by the common Name of *Ideas*, and treating both as *Equaly* the *Firſt Ground* of Knowledge. Whereas not only theſe, but *All*

3   the

the moſt abſtracted of our complex Notions and Conceptions are, at beſt but a curious Piece of intellectual Workmanſhip; and the *Materials* are no other than the Ideas of *Senſation* for the firſt *Groundwork*, conſidered together with all the *Subſequent Operations* of the Intellect upon them. Inſomuch that the moſt refined and exalted Knowledge, when we come to reſolve it analyticaly into *Simple Ideas*, will be found to end ultimately in that *Senſation* from whence it took its *Riſe*: So true is that Saying of a modern Philoſopher, *Nulla ſunt in Cerebro Veſtigia, nullæ in ipſa mente Species inſculptæ, quæ res ab omni ſenſu remotas exhibeant; atque adeo ſemper huc eſt redeundum.*

HAD we *Simple Original Ideas* of other Objects beyond thoſe of Senſation, we ſhould all indifferently and readily acquieſce in our Opinions about them; a Peaſant would have as *Clear* and *Diſtinct* Ideas of them, of the *Intellect* for Inſtance and of all its Operations; of all the *Paſſions* and *Affections* of the Mind; and of all things *Immaterial* and ſpiritual, as the moſt acute and learned Head. Our Knowledge of all theſe things would then be as *Intuitive*, as our preſent ſimple View of *Senſitive* Ideas in the Imagination is; there would be as rare a *Difference* of Sentiments, as little *Variety* of Judgments, and we ſhould as ſeldom *Diſpute* about them, as we do now about the common Objects of Senſe.

THIS opens to the View of the Understanding a new, and immense Field of what goes properly under the Name of *Knowledge* and *Learning* in the World: For the Intellect is under a Necessity of *Supplying* the Want of original simple Ideas of all things beyond sensible Objects, by the best *Compositions* it can, which are its *Notions* or *Conceptions* of them. These Notions or Conceptions are infinitely varied according to the different *Natural* Sagacity, and *Acquired* Improvement of the Intellect, and the *Diligence* and Sincerity of Men's Minds in the Pursuit of Knowledge; and they are ever more or less *True*, as they approach the *Real Nature* and *Truth* of things. Some Men's Notions come *Short* of this; and others go too far *Beyond* it; some have their Notions of things *More* complex, some *Less*; some have all the Ingredients of these complex Notions ranged more *Closely* and firmly and *Methodicaly* together, so that they become clear, and easy, and distinct; others by leaving them *Loose* and ill compacted, and not rightly *Ranged*, have all their Notions confused and perplex'd, dubious and uncertain. There is no end of these *Complex Notions* or Conceptions of things, nor of their *Differences* and *Agreements* in the Mind; besides that it is not easy to find two Men who have made up to themselves *Exactly* the same complex Notion of any thing: And from hence mostly ariseth that infinite *Variety* of Opi-

nions

nions and *Sentiments* which occasions so many Debates and Controversies, and fills the World with Strife and Contention.

I T should be observed here, that all comprehended under this and the foregoing Head, may be aptly enough called by the Name of *Judicium* or *Judgment*; and when the Mind pronounces upon any of those Ideas simple or compounded, or upon any of these complex Notions or Conceptions by express *Affirmation* or *Negation*, then it becomes a *Proposition*; the Nature of which is varied according to the different *Quantity* or *Quality* of it, as the Schools term it. We are to observe likewise that the Imagination, being the *Storehouse* where all the original Materials are *Reposited* for the Exercise and Employment of the *Intellect*; may be conceived as if it were the *Place* of Acting, and the *Scene* of all its Operations: And it is from the close and intimate Union of the *Imagination* with the *Spiritual* Part of Man, that it is so impregnated with these *Complex Notions*, as to retain them there in that common Repository, together with the Ideas of external Objects obtained at the first. When this is done, the Intellect hath the same absolute despotic Power over *Them*, which it had over the Ideas of *Sensation*; it can *Transpose* and *Separate*, or *Combine* and *Alter* them at Will; It can call for them *When* and in *What order* it pleases, which is *Memory*: If any of these complex Notions

tions are mifflay'd or hid among Heaps, it can
fearch it out; when any one of them is *Defaced*
and even in appearance obliterated, it can *Revive* it again; after it has become dark and
Confufed by time, it can *Brighten* it up anew,
render it clear and diftinct, and lay it up again
at hand for more ready Ufe on future Occafions.

Now tho' what I have defcribed here will
to an attentive and unprejudiced Mind appear
to be true, and the *Real* Progrefs of the Underftanding in its Attainment of Knowledge;
yet perhaps by way of *Anfwer* to all this I may
be asked; But may not a Man of Name and
Character in the World efpecialy for a Vo-
luminous Syftem of Logic and Metaphyfics,
juftly call all thefe *Complex Notions* and Conceptions by the Denomination of *Ideas*, if he
pleafes? I anfwer, No; becaufe a Man is in-
exculable who always ufes *One* and the fame
Term, to exprefs indifferently *Two* things the
moft different in *Nature* that poffibly can be;
and who confounds two things which ought to
be moft carefully and exactly diftinguifhed; the
Ideas of *Senfation*, and thofe *Complex Notions* or
Conceptions which arife from the Operations
of the Intellect upon them: Efpecialy when
the laying down Ideas of *Senfation* and *Reflection*
as *Equaly original*, and equaly the Ground of
all our Knowledge, doth fhamefuly miflead
and *Confound* the Underftanding; under a Pre-

tence

tence and folemn Profeffion of *Helping* it forward, of fetting out its true Bounds and Limits, and defcribing its Progrefs. No Man
fhould take a Liberty fo evidently injurious
not only to Knowledge in *General*, but to that
of *Religion* in particular ; and which leads Men
directly into *Scepticifm* and *Infidelity*, by tend-
ing to fix them in this Opinion, That they can
have no *Knowledge* of things whereof they have
no *Ideas*.   When a Man fets out with an Error fo *Fundamental*, as the blending together into
One, two things fo totaly and intirely *Oppofite*
in Nature ; his Treatife muft neceffarily carry
along with it many *Infinuations* againft the divine revealed Truths and Myfteries of Chriftianity ; of which it is fure we have, properly
fpeaking, no *Ideas* ; tho' we have diftinct *Notions* and *Conceptions* of them in their *Symbols*
and *Reprefentatives*.

C H A P. VI.

*Illation or Inference, or Reafon ftrictly
fo call'd.*

THERE being fuch a wonderful Increafe of Knowledge in the Mind from
the Addition of our complex Notions and
Conceptions, the Intellect naturaly proceeds
from thence to the higheft Operation of it,
which is *Illation* or *Inference*. This in the more
ftrict

ſtrict and limited Senſe of the Word is called *Reaſon*; which is not ſo much employed upon our *Simple* Ideas, or even thoſe which are *Compounded* out of them; as upon our *Complex Notions* and Conceptions. For as the Perception of Senſation, with the after-View of our ſimple original Ideas is a kind of *Intuitive* Knowledge; ſo is that of the *Agreement* or *Diſagreement* of them likewiſe for the moſt Part intuitive; it is moſtly diſcerned at *One* View by a Juxta-Poſition; and they ſeldom require the Application of any *Common Meaſure*, to find out their Differences or Agreements. So fundamentaly falſe is that celebrated Maxim, that *Reaſon fails us where there are no* I D E A S; *and that all our Knowledge conſiſts in a Perception of the Agreement or Diſagreement of our Ideas.* Which Maxim evidently excludes,

1. FIRST, all Knowledge beyond that of Ideas of *Senſation*, and their *Compounds*. There could, according to this, be no Reaſoning or Argumentation upon any of our *Complex Notions* or Conceptions of things; tho' upon them *Chiefly* our reaſoning Faculty is moſt truly and properly employed: For the *Obſcurity*, and *Confuſion*, and *Imperfection*, together with the endleſs *Variety* and *Oppoſition* of Men's *Complex Notions* and Conceptions, is the very Cauſe and true Occaſion of almoſt all our *Reaſoning* and *Argumentation*; whereas the *Simple Apprehenſion* of *Ideas* is much the ſame in all Men, and

this

this occasions almoft a general Confent and Acquiefcence in their Agreements and Difagreements.

2. SECONDLY, it utterly excludes all Degrees of Knowledge in things *Spiritual* and *Immaterial*, of which we have *No Ideas* ; and which are therefore conceived by Subftitution only and *Analogy*, and by making up the beft *Complex Notions* we can out of things Material and Human to *Reprefent* them : Nor is it poffible for us to have any *Intermediate Idea* or a common Meafure between things utterly *Imperceptible*, and *Inconceivable* to us as they are in their *Own Nature* ; that is in other Words, for which we have *No Ideas.* We cannot difcern the *Agreement* or *Difagreement* of *Ideas* where there are *None* ; and confequently according to that *Maxim* we could have no *Knowledge* of fuch things.

3. THIRDLY, It intirely excludes all true *Illation*, or the *Actual* infering one thing from another ; and in effect all Knowledge whatfoever that is not *Intuitive.* Inftead of *Syllogifm* the Author of that Maxim lays down a mere naked *Juxta-Pofition* of Ideas, ranged in this Order for the more ready and convenient View of the Intellect. You muft in your Mind place the two Extremes on each fide ; and the common *Meafure*, or intermediate Idea or Ideas *Between* them, all in a *Row :* And then the Intellect

at

at one *Glance* will difcern, firft how far the *Ex-tremes* agree with the *Intermediate Ideas*; and then how they agree or difagree with *Each o-ther*, without any *Exprefs*, or even *Mental* De-duction or *Illation*. For fays he, *Every Man hath a native Faculty to perceive the Coherence or Incoherence of his Ideas.* And *Thefe are to be feen by the Eye and perceptive Faculty of the Mind.*

BUT if every Man hath a *Native*, that is a *Natural* Faculty of perceiving the Coherence or Incoherence of his Ideas, he would with that native Eye equaly difcern the Coherence or In-coherence of *All*, or of *Any* of his Ideas *Alike*; and there would be no Occafion for any *Inter-mediate* Ideas: For perceiving the Coherence or Incoherence between the *Extremes*, would be as *Natural* to him; as perceiving thofe be-tween *Them*, and any *Intermediate* Ideas.

HOWEVER, to give this intellectual Form of *Seeing* without Argumentation, all the *Play* imaginable; let us fuppofe that the Mind hath a native *Faculty* or *Eye*, for that kind of Per-ception in refpect of the Coherence or Inco-herence of *Some* of its Ideas, and not of *Others*. In this Cafe you muft, according to him, place fome of thofe Ideas, for which you *Have* that native Faculty of Perception, between the Ex-tremes, for the Perception of whofe Coherence or Incoherence you have *No* fuch Faculty: And then the Eye of the Mind will perceive

E e 4 the

the Difference or Agreement between the Extremes *Themselves*; and all *Actual* Deduction or Inference either in the Mind, or in exprefs Words is *Needlefs* and trifling. For that fuppofes the native Eye of the Mind to be very *Dim* and *Weak*, and that the Man wants *Spectacles*; if he hath common Sence he would fee *Without* them, and leave it to the Ignorant to draw *Actual* Confequences.

BUT what is all this unlefs a *Maimed* and *Defective* Syllogifm; a laying down Premifes, and forbidding the Conclufion? In Syllogifm you actualy make either a *Mental* only, or *Exprefs* Application of the *Medius Terminus*, alternately to the two Extremes. No, fays that Author, you fhall only place the intermediate Idea or common Meafure *Between* the Extremes; and then the Eye of the Mind naturaly perceives the Coherence or Incoherence between *Them*, without any fuch *Alternate* Application either in Thought or in Words; and the drawing any *Actual* Confequence in either is *Superfluous*. But I hope it muft be allow'd, that the *Actual* Application of a Meafure to the Extremes muft render the Coherence or Incoherence more *Clear* and *Distinct* to our *Selves*; and that the noting and marking them down by an *Actual* Confequence, muft render them more evident and perfpicuous to *Others*. In both Cafes the Procedure is *Syllogistic*; in this it is full, and exprefs, and *Complete*; whereas
that

that *Juxta-Pofition* is but an half formed *Embrio* of Syllogifm: And it can have no other Tendency but to render the plain, and natural, and receiv'd way of Argumentation by Syllogifm, infinitely more perplexed and *Intricate*; under a fpecious Colour of introducing a Form intirely *New*; or rather a way of clearing up Knowledge without any *Perfect* way of Reafoning or Argumentation at all.

Tho' this is abundantly fufficient; yet to fhew the profound *Trifling* of all that hath been faid in Defence of this *Juxta-Pofition*, let us fuppofe it to be the beft Method of proceeding in refpect of all that are properly call'd *Ideas:* And then ask, what will become of it, when it is to be apply'd to any of our *Complex Notions* and *Conceptions* (efpecialy when they are transferr'd to things fupernatural and fpiritual by *Analogy*) which make up the *Greateft* Part of our Knowledge; and upon which the *Moft* of all our Reafoning or *Argumentation* is employ'd? In *Simple* Ideas Men generaly *Agree*, becaufe they have a *Native* Faculty of perceiving their Coherence or Incoherence,*Without* fuch *Intermediate* Ideas as are required either in complete Syllogifm or in *Juxta-Pofition*. But Mens *Complex Notions* and Conceptions are infinitely *Varied*; they are much lefs certain and determinate; fo that their Coherence or Incoherence cannot be eafily difcerned by the *Naked Eye* of the Mind: And therefore it is

that

that they so often require, not a *Loose* and shambling, but a perfect and *Complete* Form of Syllogism; not a confused and indistinct way of measuring, but such as is performed with more unerring Exactness and Nicety; such as shall render the Coherence or Incoherence *Very* perspicuous and distinguishable to our selves, and undeniable by others.

IN pursuance of this singular Notion he utterly decries and rejects *Syllogism*, as not only *Useless* but *Pernicious* to Knowledge; he says that Men have a full Use of their reasoning Faculties *Without* it; and he allows it only to those who are *Dimsighted*, and cannot without *Spectacles* see that Agreement or Disagreement of Ideas by the *Naked* Eye of the Mind, which he all along glories in. His two chief Objections against it are these,

1. *That it is not an Instrument of attaining Knowledge, but comes after it*, Word it thus and you see the Trifling clearly; It is not an Instrument of attaining *All* Knowledge, but comes after *Some* Knowledge, For no doubt our *Simple* Ideas and their *Compounds* must be supposed *Known*, before we attempt any *Farther* Knowledge by *Inference*; and these, together with their Agreements and Disagreements are for the most part indeed *Intuitively* discernible by the naked Eye of the Mind without *Spectacles*, only by a *Juxta-Position* of them, And thus likewise

wife are many of our *Complex Notions* and Conceptions fo plain and eafy, that there is a general *Confent* about them in the *Main*; or at leaft their material *Agreements* and *Difagreements* are either fo *Apparent* of themfelves, or fo *Small* and of no Confequence, or depend fo much on *Experience*, that the Mind need not be at the trouble of a continual Application of any *Intermediate Notions* to find out their Differences or Agreements: And therefore there is no want of Syllogifm in *Form* in the common Affairs of Life; or in the Councils of Princes; or in Matters merely practical and experimental. And yet it muft be obferved, that even in *Thefe* no Reafoning is juft, which will not eafily fall into the *Syllogiftic* Form; and which will not appear with *More* Strength and Clearnefs in *That* Form than in any *Other*; which fhews it to be the Form of *Nature* as well as *Art*. But if by this Objection he means, that Syllogifm is *Ufelefs*, becaufe it comes after the Knowledge of that very *Particular Point* about which we are reafoning Syllogifticaly; even thus the Affertion is falfe: For it is no fmall Advantage and Ufe of this Form, that it throws thofe Arguments on which our Knowledge of *That Point* is built, into fuch a *Short* and *Clear* Light, as will beft fhew their *Force* both to our felves; and others who want a Conviction in the Cafe.

BUT tho' it fhould not thus far be of any
great

great Ufe; yet it is in fome Meafure *Neceffary* in Matters of *Theory* and Speculation, wherein our Notions and Conceptions of things are more *Complex* and Accumulate, and confequently our View of them more *Confufed* and indiftinct: And wherein the true Size and Proportion of *Ingredients*, in each Notion to be compared, muft firft be afcertained and determined; as well as in that of the *Medius Terminus* or Common Meafure; before any Agreement or Difagreement can appear from an Application of it to the Extremes. And where the carefully removing from them all *Ambiguity* either in the *Conceptions*, or in the *Terms* by which they are expreffed; and paring off every thing *Superfluous* and foreign, is abfolutely neceffary. Here I fay Syllogifm is an excellent *Inftrument* of attaining true Knowledge, by pulling off the Mask from Error, and expofing it in its own naked Deformity; or as the aforementioned Author words it, *By difcovering a Fallacy hid in a Rhetorical Flourifh, or cunningly wrap'd in a fmooth Period; and by ftripping the Abfurdity of the Cover of Wit, and good Language;* and again *By detecting Fallacies concealed in florid, witty, or involved Difcourfes.* To which if we add that it prevents all *Circumlocution* in Difputes, and wandering in a multitude of Words; that it keeps Men *Clofe* to the Subject; and helps to reduce all abftrufe and intricate Matters of Controverfy to one fingle *Point* of Decifion; I think nothing more need be faid to prove it

an

an excellent Inftrument of Reafon and Knowledge: And furely till fome form of Argumentation or Illation is found out which may more
effectualy anfwer all thefe Ends, Syllogifm muft
be allowed to be better than no Form at all.

2. THE fecond and indeed the moft plau-
fible Objection is, that the *Form of Argumentation by Syllogifm is intricate and perplex'd*; that
there is much Difficulty in knowing how many
ways three Propofitions may be put together;
and which of them conclude right, and which
wrong. To which I anfwer, that in order to
argue Syllogifticaly it is not neceffary for a
Man to be acquainted with *All* thofe feveral
ways. The better he is acquainted indeed
with thofe *Modes* and *Figures* which conclude
rightly, the more acute Reafoner he will make.
But a plain Man of good natural Sence, may
with much eafe be brought to argue Syllogifticaly with great Readinefs: Only by firft making him underftand what a *Propofition* is, and
how it is varied according to the different *Quality* and *Quantity* of it; and then by acquaint-
ing him (inftead of the many obfcure and intricate Rules in Logick for finding it out) that
a *Medius Terminus* is nothing but the *Proof or
Reafon* you give for any Affertion. As for inftance; if one were to find out a *Medius Terminus* to prove that *God fhould be worfhiped by
Man*; he need only to think of a *Reafon* why
he ought to be worfhipped by Man. When

3

this Reafon offers itfelf, the whole falls naturaly into a Syllogifm, the Major only whereof is Hypothetic and the Conclufion Categoric,
thus.

IF God be infinitely powerful, wife, and good;
then Man ought to worfhip God.

BUT God is infinitely powerful, wife, and
good.

Therefore, &c.

A PERSON who never looks farther for a
Medius Terminus, than the beft *Reafon* he can
give for the Truth or Falfhood of any Propofition to be proved ; and throws it immediately into that *Hypothetic* Form, which offers of
itfelf as readily as if it were natural ; and ufeth
himfelf to do this in a few Inftances, will come
to argue Syllogifticaly with great Readinefs.

I SHALL obferve, here that as this Form of
Syllogifm which has the major *Hypothetic* is the
moft *Eafy*, and *Natural*, and *Clear* ; fo it is the
Beft : And it hath the Advantage of an *Enthy-
mem* or that which hath only an Antecedent
and Confequent, becaufe the Confequence is in
this laft *Imply'd* and *Prefumed* only ; but is actualy *Expreffed* in the Major of the Hypothetic
Syllogifm; which is ever the ftrongeft and
cleareft way of arguing, if it be but fo form'd
that the Confequence of the Major is too clear
to be denied ; and if it is not fo, it is no Fault
of *Syllogifm*, but of him who makes it.   I

I SHALL give two Inftances of the Ufefulnefs of Syllogifm, in detecting two fundamental *Fallacies cunningly wrap'd up in a long
Series of fmooth Periods, and which have lain
concealed in florid, witty, and involved Difcourfes*;
and in reducing two Matters in Controverfy,
of no fmall Importance, to a fingle Point of
Decifion. The firft lies concealed in this Propofition, *We have Ideas of the Operations of our
Minds by Reflection.* The Falfity of which Propofition will appear by thefe two Syllogifms.

I F the *Operations themfelves,* and the *Ideas*
of thofe Operations, be not within us at the
Same time; then there are no fuch *Ideas of Reflection.*

B U T the Operations themfelves, and the
Ideas of them, are not within us at the fame
time.

Therefore, &c.

T H E Minor is proved thus.

I F there is no *Occafion* or *Neceffity* in Nature for *Both* being together within us at *Once,*
then the Minor is true.

B U T there is no Occafion or Neceffity in
Nature for both being within us at once.

Therefore, &c.

T H I S Minor can never be evaded, 'till it be

fhewn

ſhewn that there is ſome Occaſion or *Neceſſity* in Nature for both the Operations *Themſelves,* and their *Ideas* being together within us at the *Same* time: And if it were poſſible to ſhew that Nature acted ſo much in *Vain*; yet it muſt be afterwards ſhewn, why the Mind views the *Ideas* only by a reflex Act, and not the Operations *Themſelves*; which are ſurely *As much,* if not *More* conſpicuous and diſcernible than any *Idea* of them can be.

BUT that the Force of this Argument may appear to the Admirers of the *Juxta-Poſition* Method, it muſt ſtand thus. *Operations of the Mind*— *Ideas of thoſe Operations*— *Within us at the ſame time*— *No Neceſſity*— *Ideas of Reflection*— And now I hope they ſee clearly *By the Eye and perceptive Faculty of the Mind,* without any help of *Spectacles,* that it is as ridiculous to ſuppoſe both the *Operations* and their *Ideas* to be within us at the ſame time; as to ſuppoſe an *Horſe,* and the *Idea* of an Horſe to be placed together in the Imagination.

THE ſecond fundamental Fallacy lies hidden in this Maxim, *All our Knowledge conſiſts in the Perception of the Agreement or Diſagreement of our Ideas.* Againſt which I argue thus.

IF we have *Knowledge* of things, whereof we have no *Ideas*; then that Maxim is falſe.

BUT

B u t we have Knowledge of things, whereof we have no Ideas.

Therefore &c.

The Minor is proved thus.

I f we have Knowledge of things *Spiritual* and *Immaterial*; we have *Knowledge* of things whereof we have no *Ideas*.

B u t we have *Knowledge* of things spiritual and immaterial.

Therefore &c.

T h e Minor cannot be denied, without denying all *Natural* as well as *Revealed* Religion. Nor can the Confequence of the Major ever be evaded, except by fhewing that we have *Ideas* of things *Imperceptible* and *Incomprehenfible*, which is flat Contradiction in Terms. Nor can it be faid that we have *Complex Ideas* of them, for that is not Sence; tho' *Compound Ideas* is good Sence, and a proper way of fpeaking. We can have no *Knowledge* of things *Immaterial* (whofe very *Exiftence* we infer from the Exiftence of things *Material*) otherwife than by *Complex Notions* and Conceptions, form'd by the Mind from its own various *Operations* upon the *Ideas* of things material and human : And thefe are fo far from giving us any *Idea* of them properly fpeaking, that they are all merely *Analogical Reprefentatives* of them.

Ff

Thus I hope these two grand *Maxims* are fully overthrown; which are the main *Pillars* upon which that whole *Metaphysical* Castle in the Air was erected, that hath been so much the vain and empty *Boast* of this sceptical and unbelieving Age: And surely till these Syllogisms are clearly answered, it must be allow'd, by all Men, to be the greatest Trifle that ever gained a Reputation in the World.

I ought not to close this Head without observing, that as *Brutes* have neither a simple Apprehension and *Intellectual View* of their Ideas; nor a Power of *Compounding* or *Altering* them; nor of raising up to themselves *Complex Notions* or Conceptions, out of any Intellectual Operations exercised upon those Ideas; so much less have they any Power of *Illation* or Consequence, that can be call'd *Reason* in any Degree. For in order to this, they must first have, not only a Power to perform what I have already mentioned; but also a Faculty of *Internal Judgment*, with regard to the *Differences* and *Agreements* of Ideas and Conceptions. And if this be granted them, why should we exclude them from a Power of *Expressing* those Judgments *Externaly*, in *Propositions* of some kind or other; which tho' very obscure and unintelligible to *Us*, yet may be very clear and well understood among *Themselves?* And surely those Men who contend for Brutes having de-

grees

grees of *Reason*, can't forbear fancying that they hear the Oxen *Bellowing* Propositions; the Sheep softly *Bleating* Propositions; and Lyons *Roaring* them out imperiously. But without a Jest, it is very sure that if *Brutes* had any degree of *Reason*, their Sounds would be *Articulate* in Proportion to that degree: They would be the *Voice* and *Speech*, and not the *Noise* only of a Beast; and every Species of Brutes would speak a Language of its own, tho' not so refin'd and articulate as *Greek* and *Latin*. This can never be denied by those, who use it as one Argument of their being rational, that they have *Organs fitted for articulate Sounds:* When at the same time nothing can conclude more strongly against them; for if Brutes have Organs fitted for articulate Sounds, then there is nothing to hinder them from *Speaking*, but the want of some degree of *Reason* within them.

IF Brutes had an *Internal* Perception of the *Agreement* or *Disagreement* of their Ideas, either by a *Juxta-Position* of them, according to the new way of Reasoning; or by the Application of some *Common Measure* to them one after another, where the Agreement or Disagreement is not visible to the Eye of their natural Instinct by a mere *Juxta-Position:* Then it is not unlikely that they would reduce their dim imperfect Affirmations and Negations into some *Form* of Argumentation very like our *Syllogism* (which I hope might in such a Case be of Ser-

vice

vice to *Brutes*, tho' not allow'd fo to *Men*)
As it hath been argued to the great Credit and
Reputation of *Hounds*, that in full Purfuit of
the Game they *Syllogize*, when they are at a
Lofs by the meeting of three different ways.
As extravagant as this is, it doth not come up
to that of a Man's infinuating, that Brutes muft
have fome degree of Reafon, from a long Con-
verfation of an old experienced *Parrot* upon
the Subject of feeding *Poultry*. To this height
of Reafon not much lefs than human, have the
partial Advocates for *Birds* and *Beafts* advanced them; unmercifuly excluding from this
Privilege the whole race of *Fifhes*; which furely
ought to be prefumed as truly rational in their
way, tho' lefs able to *Speak* for themfelves:
When at the fame time they are fuch profeffed Enemies of Mankind, that they bring *Us*
down to the level of Brutes; by maintaining
that *mere Matter* may be endued with a Power
of *Thinking*.

It is very obfervable that thofe who will
not allow *Reafon* (not even that degree of it
which confifts in Illation and *Inference*) to be
the *Diftinguifhing* Character between *Men* and
Brutes; do however place it in *Abftraction* or
the Power of forming *General* Ideas: As if Deduction of Confequences were not a more *Elevated* Work of Reafon, than that of making
the cleareft and moft diftinct Idea or Conception we have of any one *Individual*, ftand in

our

our Mind to *Reprefent* the whole *Kind*; which after all metaphyfical Nicety is the true Meaning of that hard Word. Tho' Brutes for want of *Reafon* cannot do this *Inwardly*, fo as to have thus an *Univerfal Idea* of the *Kind*; yet the Idea of *One Man* or *One Dog* imprefled upon their Imagination, ferves them to diftinguifh all the *Individuals* of the whole Species *Outwardly*, one after another, as the Impreffions of them are made fucceffively upon their *Senfes*: So that thefe Men have unluckily placed the *Diftinguifhing* Character in that particular Inftance of Reafon, wherein Brutes make the *Neareft* Approaches to Man.

WE have now brought the Mind of Man to the utmoft extent of that Knowledge, it can have of Things merely *Temporal*. It had by Nature the fimple original Ideas of *Senfation* only, for a *Groundwork* of all its Knowledge; it hath made various *Tranfpofitions*, *Alterations*, and *Combinations* of them without Number. From obferving the Manner of exerting its own *Operations* upon thofe Ideas, it is come to a very diftinct *Confcioufnefs* of all thofe Operations. Out of *Thefe*, in Conjunction with thofe *Ideas* upon which they operate, it has raifed up to itfelf *Complex Notions* and *Conceptions* without End; and laid them all up in the common *Store-houfe* the *Imagination*; either to remain there as they are, or to undergo any *Farther* Alterations or Combinations, at the ar-

bitrary

bitrary Will and Pleasure of the Intellect. And laftly, it hath increafed all this into an immenfe Fund of *Knowledge*, by that noble Operation of *Deduction* and Confequence ; which in our Condition of Infirmity fupplies the place of *Intuition*, by fathoming with a Line thofe *Depths* where the *Naked* Eye of the Mind cannot fee to the *Bottom* ; and by the Application of a common *Meafure* to fuch *Heights* and *Diſtances*, as it cannot bring *Together* for a fingle View by any *Immediate* and near Comparifon.

THE Mind having thus proceeded to the utmoft Bounds of things merely *Natural*, let us ftop a while here, to behold it at this Stage of its Progrefs ; and to obferve all our *Idea-Mongers* daily loading it with *Fetters* and Shackles, left it fhould make any Attempt to move one Step *Farther*. And yet nothing is plainer than that all hitherto is no more than *Secular* Knowledge ; and that tho' within this Compafs men may arrive to the greateft Infight attainable into all things on *This* Side *Heaven* ; nay tho' they could fee thro' the whole Series and Chain of fecond *Caufes* and their *Effects*, fo that one *Link* of it did not efcape their Obfervation : And could calculate all the Motions of the heavenly Bodies to an Inftant, yet all this is but *Secular* Knowledge ftill ; and if the Mind of Man could exert itfelf no *Farther*, there would not be the leaft room left for any Knowledge of *Religion* natural or revealed.   ACCOR-

ACCORDING to their fundamental Principle, *That if our Words do not ſtand for* IDEAS, *they are Sounds and nothing elſe* ; *that the Mind neither doth nor can extend itſelf farther than* THEY *do* ; *and that where we have no* IDEAS *our Reaſoning Stops, and we are at an end of our Reckoning* ; it is plain that the Mind is tied down altogether to Objects of *Senſation* ; of which only, as we have ſeen, it can properly ſpeaking have *Direct* and *Immediate Ideas* ; and that it can never carry one Thought beyond the fix'd Stars, any more than if all without them were an empty *Void*. Nay this Conſequence from thoſe Principles would be neverthelefs true, tho' we ſhould allow our ſelves to have *Simple* original *Ideas* of the *Operations* of our own *Minds* ; and tho' we ſhould moſt abſurdly call our *Complex Notions* and Conceptions of things here below, by the Name of *Ideas :* For all theſe are ſtill within our ſcanty limited Syſtem ; and will not give us the leaſt *Direct* View over its Bounds ; from whence we might form any one ſuch *Idea*, or even *Complex Notion* or Conception, not only of the real *True Nature*, but even of the *Exiſtence* of any thing in another World, as we have of things *Here* which are within the *Immediate* Reach and Compaſs of Senſe and Reaſon. But much leſs can they help us to any *Direct Idea* or Notion either of the *Exiſtence* of *God*, or of his real *True*

Nature

Nature and *Attributes*; which is the Foundation of all Religion natural and revealed.

THO' the Men, who lay down these Positions, do not *Expresly* or in Profession renounce all *Natural* Religion at least; yet they plainly destroy even *This* by immediate necessary *Consequence*; whilst under Colour of adhering to the strictest Sense, and Reason, and Evidence they lay an *Injurious* and *Unnatural* Restraint upon the Understanding, and tye it down to the Objects or Ideas of *Sensation* only. Insomuch that the unavoidable Effect of that Doctrine in which they would be thought to excel, is plainly the precluding us from all *Knowledge* of any thing beyond this visible Frame, which must therefore be to us the *Universe*: And upon *Their* Principles, our Case must be much the same with that of those homebred ignorant *Peasants*, who cannot be perswaded to *Know* or *Believe* there is any Earth or Sky beyond the Tops of the neighbouring *Mountains*.

CHAP. VII.

We have Knowledge of things, whereof we have no Ideas.

THO' these Men make an open and vain Profession of their Progress even to the *Utmost* Limits of human Understanding; we

must

must however leave them far behind us, and proceed to shew how the Mind comes by the *Knowledge* of things whereof it neither hath, nor can have any *Ideas*.

THE Intellect by the foregoing Operation of *Deduction* or Inference, doth from the Existence of things *Material* and sensible, infer not only the *Possible*, but the *Probable* Existence of things *Immaterial* and imperceptible in *General*; that is, of things whose very *Existence* would have been utterly unknown to the Mind otherwise than by this *Consequence*; and which will always remain unknown otherwise than by *Analogy* whilst we are in this World, both as to their whole *Nature*, and *Manner* of Existence. Wherefore as we neither have, nor can have any such *Perception* or *Idea* of them in any degree as we have of things *Material* and *Human*; so neither is it possible to express them in any *Language* so peculiar to them, that it shall not be *First* more applicable to things whereof we have a *Direct* Perception and *Idea*, or an *Immediate Consciousness*. We can find out no *Proper Terms* for distinguishing, and expressing things utterly *Inconceivable* to us by any *Proper Ideas* or *Direct Conceptions*, as all *Spiritual* Beings are: So that we are under an absolute *Necessity* of *Conceiving* them by such Ideas and Notions as are *Already* in the Mind; and of *Expressing* all our Knowledge of them in such *Words* and Language, as were *Familiar* to us before any

Infe-

Inference at all was made in relation to their Exiftence.

I F we had as *Clear* and *Diſtinct* an *Idea* of the Subſtance or Properties of *Spirit*, as we have of *Bodily* Subſtance or its Properties; the *Exiſtence* of Spirits would be known to us by their *Ideas*, as the Exiſtence of *Matter* is known; and not by any Reaſoning or *Deduction* only from the Exiſtence of things Material: But this is ſo far from being true, that we have no *Idea* at all of the Subſtance or Properties of Spirit. We can diſcern one and the ſame *Bodily* Subſtance with all our five *Senſes*; but we cannot diſcern a pure Spirit by any one of them, or by all of them together.

B u t why have we as *Clear* and *Diſtinct* an *Idea* of *Spiritual* Subſtance, as we have of *Corporeal* Subſtance? Becauſe we are equaly *Ignorant* of *Both*, and can have no *Idea* at all of *Either*; this is a new Method indeed of Arguing. But ſays the celebrated Author of that grand Soloeciſm, We have equaly clear and diſtinct Ideas of their *Qualities*. Suppoſe this were true, how doth it prove that we have *Equaly clear* and *Diſtinct* Ideas of their *Subſtances*; or that we are *Equaly ignorant* of them? But this happens to be as falſe as the other, nay doubly falſe; for we have not as clear and diſtinct *Ideas* of the *Operations* of the *Mind*, as we have of the ſenſible Qualities of *Corporeal* Subſtance.

ftance. We have *Immediate, fimple, original* Ideas of the Qualities of corporeal Subftance, by Impreffion from outward Objects; but there are *No Ideas* within us of the Operations of the Mind; fo that the Operations *Themfelves* are difcerned, and not any *Ideas* inftead of them: And that too no otherwife than by a *Confciouf-nefs* of the Mind's operating from the firft upon Ideas of *Senfation*; and afterwards upon thofe *Compound* Ideas and *Complex Notions* which it raifes up to itfelf out of them.

BUT what is yet more abfurd, granting that we had *As clear* and *Diftinct* Ideas of the Qualities or Operations of our Mind, fuch as *Thinking, Knowing, Doubting*, and *Power of Moving*, as of *Corporeal* Qualities; yet this would give us no Idea either of the Qualities or Sub-ftance of a *Spirit:* For in *Man* thefe are all the joint Operations of *Spirit* and *Matter* in effential *Union* and Conjunction; which can give us no *Ideas* of the Qualities and Ope-rations of a Subftance *Purely immaterial*, and in-tirely *Independent* of Matter. And what is yet worft of all is, that if mere *Matter* is capable of having the Powers of *Thinking, Willing, Knowing, Doubting*, as the aforefaid Author contends; then *Thefe* Properties can give us no Ideas or diftinguifhing *Marks* of things which are *Not* Matter; and which muft confequently be endued with *Knowledge* without that *Think-ing*, which (upon this Suppofition of his) muft either be a Quality *Effential* to Matter, or elfe

Change

Change the very *Essence* of Matter, whenever it
is *Superinduced.*

I SHALL take this Opportunity of remarking here, that I suppose what led the Author
abovementioned into this profound Error of
a *Possibility that Thinking may be superadded to
Matter*; was his not rightly distinguishing between our being capable of *Abstractedly considering* the *Properties* of a Substance, without
considering or regarding at the same time the
Substance *Itself*, which is very possible : And
the having an *Actual Perception or Idea* of any
Essential Properties separately and *Abstractedly*
from the *Substance* itself, which is impossible;
because they cannot in *Their Nature* exist separately from it. We cannot discern, or form
an *Actual Idea* of the essential Properties *Without* the Substance ; but according to common
Sence we are said to discern those Properties
In the Substance, or a Substance *With* such Properties : This is so evident that a plain Man
would laugh at you, if you should tell him that
he did neither taste nor feel the *Substance* of the
Morsel of *Bread* he was eating ; and that for
ought he knew he was chewing only a parcel
of *Properties*, or *Qualities.* This absurd Notion,
I say, of an *Abstraction* utterly *Impossible* (of
which this Author is every where full) led him
into an Opinion of the Possibility of an *Actual
Separation* of an *Essential Property*, from the Essence or *Substance itself*; and into a Belief that
Thinking

Thinking could become a *Superadded Property* of Matter, without fuperadding at the fame time the fpiritual or thinking *Subftance.*

I T is for want of any *Clear* and *Diftinct*, or even *Obfcure* and *Confufed Idea* of Spirit, that we are forced to conceive it by framing to our felves the beft *Complex Notion* we can of an human Mind, and then transferring it by *Analogy* to an unknown *Being.* We do not, as the aforefaid Author defcribes it, form an *Idea* of Spirit by putting together many *Simple Ideas* of the Operations of our Mind, fuch as *Thinking*, *Willing*, *Knowing*, and *Power* of beginning *Motion*, and then by joining thefe in their *Firft* and *Original* Acceptation, and as differing in *Degrees* of Perfection only, to a Subftance of which we have as *Clear* and *Diftinct* an *Idea* as we have of *Body :* But we firft frame to our felves the beft and moft perfect *Complex Notion* we have of an human Mind, from a *Confcioufnefs* of its various Operations upon material Objects or their Ideas ; and then we *Subftitute* this Notion to reprefent *Analogicaly* a Being whofe *Subftance* and *Properties* are of a quite *Different Kind* from ours ; and utterly imperceptible and inconceivable, as they are in their *Own Nature.* The very Reafon of which proceeding of the Underftanding is, becaufe it is *Neceffary* ; for we can have no *Idea* either of the *Real* Properties or *True* Subftance of Angel or Spirit ; and if it were not for this way of
Procefs

Procefs we could neither *Think* nor *Speak* of them.

FOR this fame Reafon it is, that when Men *Attempt* to conceive an Angel by any *Simple Idea*, they do it by that of the moft *Spirituous* Parts of *Matter*, or more vulgarly by that of a *Flying Boy*, or a *Winged Head*; to which they add the beft Conception they have of the Properties of an human Mind : And this they do for want of any *Idea* either of its *Subftance*, or of its inconceivable *Manner* of *Knowledge* without any neceffary Concurrence of material Organs; which is therefore no more performed by *Thinking*, than it is expreffed or communicated by *Speaking*. And accordingly the Language of Revelation often falls in with this more *Vulgar* way of conceiving Angels and Spirits; and fpeaks of the *Tongue*, and *Voice*, and *Food*, and *Mouth*, and *Face*, and *Hand* of an Angel; and the very *Denomination* itfelf is taken from the manner of one Man's *Sending* another about Bufinefs, and originaly denotes a *Meffenger*.

CHAP.

CHAP. VIII.

From the Existence of Things material and human, is infer'd the necessary Existence of God.

FROM thus inferring the *Probable* Existence of immaterial Beings in *General,* which we call *Substances* from our gross Idea of *Matter*; the Intellect by a natural Gradation proceeds to infer the *Necessary* Existence of one immaterial *Supreme Being,* the *First Cause* of all things. Because the Mind perceives it to be a flat Contradiction that the Beings which have been *Produced,* taken all together or singly, should produce *Themselves*; or that they should possibly be produc'd or preserv'd as they are, otherwise than by the infinite Power and Wisdom of an *Intelligent Agent:* Which first Cause must be *Without* Beginning; since it is likewise flat Contradiction that he should have made himself.

WITH this plain, and necessary, and obvious Inference it is, that after the utmost Reach of the Understanding in the Knowledge of things *Natural* and merely *Human,* the Mind enters upon a glorious Scene of Action intirely *New*; and upon a very *Different* manner of exerting and exercising all its Operations over again.

Not

Not by employing itself *Here* as it did *Before*, upon any *Direct* and *Immediate Ideas*, such as it had of things *Natural* and *Senfible*; nor upon any *Obfcure* Glimmering and *Imperfect Ideas* of things *Supernatural* and *Imperceptible*; or then raising up to itself *Complex Notions* and Conceptions from obferving its own various ways of *Operating* upon *Such Ideas*; or laftly by making any Inferences and Deductions, in relation to *Such* Notions and Conceptions. No, but by choofing out the *Cleareft* and moft diftinct *Notions* and Conceptions we have *Already* formed, *Originaly* for the Operations and Perfections of our own Mind; and when they are put together into one complex Notion or Conception, properly and *Immediately* for the Mind of *Man*; then by *Subftituting* that very Notion or Conception fo formed for the Supreme Being; and what was a *Direct* and *Immediate* Conception before, becomes thus afterwards a *Mediate, Indirect,* and *Analogical* Reprefentation of that incomprehenfible Being, for whom we can have no *Direct* Conception or Idea. Thus it is that, as the fimple Ideas of *Senfation* only are the whole Foundation and firft Materials of all Knowledge merely Natural and Human; fo fome of thofe *Complex Notions* and Conceptions raifed up from the immediate Operations of the Mind upon *Them*, do become a *New* Foundation, and *Secondary* Set of Materials for the whole Superftructure of all *Religion*, as well Natural as *Reveal'd*.

THE Method by which the aforementioned Author says we frame a *Complex Idea* of *God*, is by putting together the *Simple Ideas* we have from *Reflection*, of those Qualities and Powers which we find it better to *Have* than to be *Without*, such as the *Idea* we have of *Knowledge* (which is perform'd by *Thinking*) together with the *Ideas* of all the other most perfect *Operations* and Properties of an human *Intellect* and *Will*; as also the *Ideas* of all the commendable *Affections* of the Mind; and then *Enlarging* all these without Bounds, in their *Original* Acceptation, and in *Degree* only, by adding the *Idea* of *Infinity* to each of them: And likewise by adding Ideas even of *Sensation*, such as those of *Existence*, *Duration*, and *Extension*; and *Enlarging* them also to that Vastness to which *Infinity* can extend them.

IN which Doctrine, besides the false and groundless Supposition of our having *Ideas* of *Reflection*, as *Simple* and *Original* as those of *Sensation*; and the Absurdity of calling it one *Complex*, instead of one *Compounded Idea* of many simple Ideas put together, which is a confused and indistinct way of speaking: And also his supposing us here to have an *Idea* of *Infinity*, which we express by a *Negative* because we have *No* Idea of it; to pass these over I say, which ought not to be passed over; there are two fundamental Errors in that Doctrine.

G g   THE

THE firſt conſiſts in furniſhing out this *Idea* of God as he calls it, by *Enlarging* thoſe Operations and Affections of our Mind, in Conjunction with the Ideas of *Senſation* beforementioned, even to *Infinity:* Which is in truth and reality no other than extending and aggravating ſo many *Infirmities* (even at the beſt) of our human Nature, and carrying them on to a boundleſs *Degree*, till they are *Monſtrous* beyond all Imagination. The *Beſt* and moſt perfect, and indeed the *Only Proper* Conception we have of *Knowledge*, is that which is perform'd by *Thinking* and the various Modes of it; which is the Action of *Matter* as well as *Spirit* operating together in eſſential *Union:* It is a *Gradual* and *Succeſſive* Operation, and all the Modes of it expreſs their own *Eſſential Imperfection*; ſuch as *Reaſoning, Inferring, Doubting, Deliberating, Judging*. So that when we apply to God *Infinite Knowledge*, we ought to be ſo far from attributing it to him as improved in *Degree* only, that to render it worthy of him, we muſt neceſſarily abſtract from the whole *Kind*, and *Nature*, and *Manner* of our Knowing; and remove from him all *Thinking* with the various Modes of it, as an eſſential *Imperfection* of our compounded Humanity. When we apply the Word *Knowledge* to God, it imports an infinite *Inconceivable Perfection; Anſwerable* to our imperfect manner of Knowledge by *Thinking:* And yet when we ſay *God knows*, we we fpeak as much *Solid Truth*, as when we fay *Man knows*; only with this Difference, that by the *Former* we mean an infinite inconceivable Perfection of the Divinity; by the *Latter* we exprefs the infirm State and Condition of our Humanity. And thus it is for want of *Any Idea* of that divine Perfection, and of any more *Proper Term* to exprefs it, that we ufe the Words *Knowledge* and *Thinking* in common both for God and Man.

Again, the beft Idea or Conception we have of *Power*, is from Strength of *Body*, or a *Mighty Arm*; from a Multitude of Men difciplined for *War*; or the moving our Body by *Willing* it. The beft Conception we have of *Goodnefs*, is that which confifts in the *Informing* our *Underftandings* in Matters of Duty; rectifying our *Wills*; reftraining and regulating our *Paffions* and *Affections*; and in Benevolence from one *Man* towards *Another*. The only *Idea* or Conception we have of *Exiftence*, is of that of *Corporeal* Subftance, as of a Pebble or of a Fly; or at beft of Matter and Spirit in effential *Union*. Nor can this any way be *Enlarged* or improved, but by enlarging the *Object* which exifts to an immenfe and boundlefs Size; or by *Multiplying* the Beings of the fame Kind which do exift. If it is faid, that the Idea of Exiftence may be enlarged by our Idea of *Duration*, or by the Continuance of that Exiftence; this itfelf neceffarily implying *Succeffion*, is ano-

ther

ther *Imperfection* of the Creature altogether unworthy of God. Our Idea of *Extenfion*, which we have from *Space* or *Body*; and our *Only* Perception of *Pleafure* and *Happinefs*, which we have from a *Confcioufnefs* of the Gratification of our *Appetites*, and *Paffions*, and *Defires*, are likewife altogether *Unworthy* of God.

THUS we fee what an *Unnatural* hideous Compofition is made up for our Notion of *God*, by enlarging or improving even our *Beft* Ideas and *Choiceft* Conceptions, in *Degree* alone, as far as we can extend them towards Infinity; and how it is highly *Injurious* to his Majefty and Excellency to apply any of thofe Words, with their *Proper* and *Original* Ideas or Conceptions, to his *Incomprehenfible* Perfections. This is plainly no other than putting together fo many *Infinite Imperfections* of the *Creature*, to make up our complex Notion of the infinitely *Perfect Creator.* Nay tho' we could fuppofe all thofe preceding Inftances to be real *Perfections* in us, and *So far* not unworthy of God; yet the very Addition of *Infinity* to each of them, would intirely alter their *Nature*, and render them Perfections of quite another *Kind*; for nothing that is *Finite*, can be of the fame *Kind* with that which is *Infinite.*

THE fecond Error yet more grofs, and more *Pernicious* in its Confequences, confifts in his fuppofing, that by putting together the *Simple*

Simple Ideas, we are faid to have, of the *Ope-rations* and *Affections* of our own *Mind*; and thofe Ideas of *Senfation* beforementioned, we come by as *Direct* and *Immediate* a Conception, or *Idea* as he calls it, of *God,* as we have of the *Mind* itfelf; nay by as clear and diftinct an Idea of his very Subftance, as we have of the Subftance of a *Fly* or a *Pebble.* This is in Purfuance of that de-teftably falfe Maxim, *That we have no Knowledge beyond our fimple Ideas:* But the truth is perfectly the Reverfe, for by that means we come by a *Me-diate* only and *Indirect Notion* or Conception of God; and fuch as exhibits to us nothing of the *Re-ality* of his *True Nature, Subftance,* or *Attributes* as they are *In themfelves*; in the Attainment of which Conception, the Intellect proceeds thus. It firft frames to itfelf as clear and diftinct a *Complex Notion* as it can of the Mind of *Man,* by uni-ting and combining all its own moft perfect Operations into one: This Notion or Concep-tion, already formed, and *Originaly* apply'd to *Our felves,* is attributed in the whole, as well as in every part of it, to a *Being* or Subftance *Incomprehenfible*; and then becomes an *Analo-gical Reprefentation* only, of the *Real,* internal and infinite Perfections of the divine Nature; of which we have not the leaft *Imperfect, Ob-fcure,* or glimmering Perception or *Idea.*

WE are fo far from having any *Direct* and *Immediate Ideas* of the Exiftence, and Prope-ties or Attributes of *God*; or any *Clear* and *Di-*

ftinct

ſtinct Idea of his *Subſtance*, that we have no *Idea at all* of them : For *His* manner of Exiſtence we conceive as well as we can by our *Own*; and we come to the *Knowledge* of it, not by any ſuch immediate *Conſciouſneſs* as we have of our own; but by Conſequence and *Deduction* firſt, and afterwards by *Revelation*. His *Attributes* we conceive by the Operations, and Properties, and Affections of our Mind; and the only *Idea* we can form of his *Immaterial Subſtance*, is from that of the moſt ſpirituous *Corporeal* Subſtance, tho' theſe two are directly *Oppoſite* and incompatible,

THUS we ſee, as I obſerved before, that our immediate conſcious *Conceptions* of the *Mind*, and all its *Operations*; together with all Ideas of *Senſation*; and the Terms expreſſing them, in their *Firſt* and *Proper* Acceptation, muſt be *Removed* from the divine Nature as ſo many *Imperfections*, not only of the *Creature*, but of a Creature of a very low and *Inferior* Degree: And whenever they are transfer'd to the Divinity, it muſt be by *Analogy* only. Infomuch that the ſame Operations which being put together in the *Strict* and *Proper* Acceptation of the Terms expreſſing them, make up the complex Notion of *Our Mind*; when transfer'd to the divine Nature, ʒo denote ſo many infinite *Unknown Perfectiovs*; and are the very Ingredients which make up our Complex Notion of *God*. Now becauſe

the

the Intellect so *Naturaly* and insensibly falls into this way of conceiving him, we may reasonably from thence conclude, that there must be such a secret Parity of Reason, and *Correspondent Analogy* between the Operations of our Mind, and the infinite Perfections of God; that it renders all our Conceptions and *Moral* Reasonings concerning him, as *Solid* and *True*, as if they did *Directly* and *Immediately* exhibit to us the *Reality* of his internal Nature.

Thus it is that the Intellect infers and concludes that this supreme Being, whom it calls by the Name *God*, the first Cause of all things, must have all *Absolute* and *Consummate* Perfections in himself; but such as are altogether *Incomprehensible*, and infinitely beyond any Conception of ours: Which it therefore describes mostly by *Negative* Terms; and those of them which are express'd in *Positive* Terms, being no other than the natural Perfections of the *Creature*, it concludes must be *Imperfections* when attributed in their *Literal* and *Proper* Acceptation to him who is altogether *Supernatural*, and the *Creator* of them all. So that none of those Perfections, even the *Greatest* of an human Mind, can be spoken of him, so as to express his infinitely perfect *Nature* and *Attributes*: Nor indeed any otherwise than as they are transfer'd to him by way of Representation only, and *Analogy*; and as they denote and *Symbolize* some real *Correspondent*

Per-

Perfections of the Divinity, whereof ours are but so many distant, imperfect, and transient Images.

As God is realy and intirely of another *Kind*, in *Essence* and *Substance*, from all his Creatures; so likewise the Intellect concludes that his manner of *Existence*, together with his *Attributes*, must be not only different in *Degree* of Perfection, but necessarily of quite another *Kind* from those of the most glorious Beings of the Creation; and much more from those of our human Nature, who are perhaps in the lowest Rank of intelligent Agents. But since there can be no *Perfection* in the Creature, any otherwise than as it bears *Some* Resemblance or Similitude of him, who is the Fountain of it all; then all *Intelligent* Creatures especialy must be more or less perfect, as they bear a greater or less Semblance and *Analogy* with his infinite incomprehensible Perfections: And consequently all their Notions and *Conceptions* of the Divine Being must be more or less sublime, exalted, and exact; in Proportion to that Resemblance which their *Own* essential Perfections bear to his, who is the *Standard* of all Perfection.

CHAP.

CHAP. IX.

From the Exiſtence of God, and the ſeveral Relations he bears to Mankind, the ſpeculative Knowledge of natural Religion is infer'd.

FROM thus inferring the neceſſary Exiſtence, and infinite Perfection of God, as he is *Abſolutely* in himſelf; the Intellect naturaly proceeds to the more particular Conſideration of the ſeveral *Relations* he bears to us, and we to him: And as we think and ſpeak of all his eſſential Perfections when more *Abſolutely* conſider'd, by Correſpondence and *Analogy* with thoſe Perfections, which are natural or acquired in *Our ſelves*; ſo we conceive all thoſe *Relations* likewiſe under the Semblance and *Analogy* of ſuch as we bear to *One another*.

FIRST we conceive him as our *Maker*; and becauſe we have no *Idea* of producing a thing into Being no part of which exiſted before; therefore we conceive it by that of a *Man's* making a Statue, or any other Work of Art: And to this *Inconceivable* Operation of infinite Power we affix the peculiar Name *Creation*, to diſtinguiſh it from the *Literal* Sence of the Word *Making*, which is forming any Work of Art out of *Pre-exiſtent* Materials, of which we
have

have a clear and diſtinct *Idea*.   It is in this *General* Sence only that God was ſtiled *Father*, both by Jews and Heathen.

A G A I N we conceive him as our *Governor*. In which Conception both the *Idea* and the *Word* by which it is expreſſed, are borrowed from thoſe of an earthly Monarch: As our Notion of the *Manner* of his governing the *Univerſe* is, from the Conceptions we have formed to our ſelves of the beſt *Human Polity*, and the manner of ruling a *Temporal* Kingdom, of which we have a clear and diſtinct Conception; but how God governs the Univerſe we know not. His *Providence* is originaly conceived, from the previous Notion we have of that commendable Care, and Forecaſt, and Contrivance we obſerve among *Men* for providing all things convenient, and good, and neceſſary for the *Publick*.   Thus again we conceive God as our *Defender*, and call him ſo, from the Notion we have firſt formed of one *Man*'s defending another from any Aſſault or impending Danger, by his *Wiſdom*, or *Strength* of Body, or military Force. We ſtile and conceive Him our *Deliverer* from the ſecret Malice of evil Men, and the inviſible Power of the Spirits of Darkneſs; from that *Viſible* Help, and Aſſiſtance, and Kindneſs whereby one *Man* reſcues another out of the Hands of his inveterate Enemy.   And we conceive him the inviſible *Diſpoſer* of all things, from the *Viſible* Diſtribution of *Worldly*
Happi-

Happiness, or Riches, and Honours, and Preferments in the State. So likewise it is by the same *Analogy* that he is stiled our *King* and *Lord*, from that Conception we have in the Mind of a *Temporal Prince*, surrounded with all the Insigns of Power, and Majesty, and royal Grandeur.

THE last Relation of the Supreme Deity to Mankind I shall mention is, that of our *Judge*. This Term, together with the Notion annexed to it, is taken originaly from that we have of a Man's sitting upon a Bench for the Tryal of Criminals, and pronouncing an *Impartial* Sentence of Absolution or Condemnation according to the Forms in our Courts of Judicature: Or from a just *Prince's* Examination and Inquiry into the Inclinations and Behaviour of his Subjects, and his *Equal* Distribution of *Rewards* and *Punishments* according to their Merits or Demerits.

FROM this last mentioned Relation of the Supreme Cause to us, as his Creatures endued with that *Freedom of Will*, and Liberty of Acting in every instance of Duty, this way or directly the contrary, and that *Power* of *Disobeying* which we experience in our selves; the Intellect infers the Necessity of a future State of *Rewards* and *Punishments* in another World. This it doth by a plain and natural Consequence from the unequal Distribution of Providence

vidence fo vifible in *This* Life; even to that Degree that the moft immoral Men are often the moft Profperous; perhaps that they may have all the Reward of a partial Obedience, and of a *Mix'd* and *Imperfect* Virtue here: And that the ftricteft Obfervers of the Light of Nature are Sufferers by it in their Fortune efpecialy, and too often in Reputation and Character; that they may have a more full Compenfation and Reward of a *Sincere* Virtue and Obedience hereafter. Nay and from obferving that temporal *Profperity* hath an Aptnefs and *Tendency* to make Men Tranfgreffors; and that *Adverfity* on the contrary is apt to make corrupt and wicked Men reflect and *Reform*; which cannot be fuppofed of any true and *Genuine* Rewards and Punifhments for Virtue or Vice from the Supreme Being.

FROM the Confideration of thofe feveral Relations of *God* to *Mankind*, naturaly follow the feveral mutual and correfpondent Relations of *Us* towards *Him*; as being his peculiar *Property*, and *Creatures*, and *Subjects*, and *Children*, in the fame wide and extenfive Acceptation of that Term, in which God is ftiled *Father* by the Light of *Nature* only. Hence again immediately arife all the Duties of Natural or Moral Religion; for a Foundation of which we are to poffefs our Minds with the higheft Opinion, and Veneration, and Love of God we are capable of doing from the Operations

tions of our own Minds, and from all the Perfections in the vifible Part of the Creation. We are to conceive him as a Being altogether fo *Incomprehenfible*, that we come by the Knowledge of his very *Exiftence* by Deduction only and Confequence; and not from any *Direct* Conception or Idea we can have of his real Nature itfelf; and are therefore obliged, for want of better, to think and fpeak of him in the moft exalted Conceptions and Expreffions, whereby we think and fpeak of our felves, or of the moft glorious Objects in Nature. As we neceffarily infer in *General* that he muft have all confummate and infinite Perfection; and yet find we can have no direct Conception or Idea of any *Particular* Perfections as they fubfift in his *Real Nature*; fo we neceffarily afcribe to him all the particular Perfections of our own rational Nature: Thefe we call his Attributes, becaufe they are only *Attributed* to him; that is transfer'd from *Man* to *God*, and from *Earth* to *Heaven*; and do by Semblance and *Analogy* only reprefent and exprefs the inconceivable, but *Real* however, and *Correfpondent* Perfections of the Divinity.

HERE it is worth while to ftop a little, and obferve how great an Ingredient *Faith* is, even in a merely *Moral* Religion; I mean that Faith which neceffarily includes an Affent of the Mind to the *Truth* and *Reality* of things utterly *Incomprehenfible*, and of the Nature
whereof

whereof we can have no Conception or Idea, otherwise than by Semblance and *Analogy* with the things of this World; whether we come to the Knowledge of their *Exiflence* by Reafon or Revelation. It is of this *Faith* the Apoftle fays, that without it *It is impoffible to pleafe God*; and he inftances in a Point of *Natural* Religion, *For he that cometh to God muft believe that he is; and that he is a Rewarder of them that diligently feek him.* Which Character of a *Rewarder* is founded upon his Power, and Wifdom, and Goodnefs; and upon the reft of his Divine Attributes that are *Themfelves* all Objects of *Faith* according to the Apoftle's Definition of it, *Faith is the Subftance of things hoped for:* Which Subftance is in this. Life reprefented in Types and Images; fo that we Hope for things in another World whereof we have here no *Direct* Perception or Idea. *The Evidence of things not feen,* that is either by the *Direct* Eye of Body or Mind; but *Clearly* and *Diftinctly* conceived and underftood in their Types and *Reprefentatives:* In which we have a full Proof and Evidence of the true Subftance and *Real Exiflence* of the *Antitypes,* tho', as they are in themfelves, they be now utterly inconceivable. Thus the Sum and Import of this Definition of the Apoftle's is, that the things of another World are now the *Immediate* Objects of our *Knowledge* and *Faith,* only in their Types and Reprefentatives; and the *Mediate* Objects of *Both,* as to their *True Nature* and *Subftance* and

I   Reality.

Reality. So far is *Faith* from being confined to the *Mysteries* of the *Gospel*, that it was of the very Essence of Religion from the Days of *Abel*; and the most noble Acts of Faith were exerted by *Him*, and by *Enoch*, and *Noah*, and *Abraham*, and the succeeding Patriarchs, and *Moses*, before any of the inspired Writings appeared in the World.

C H A P. X.

The Practical Duties of Natural Religion, infer'd from that Speculative Knowledge.

FROM Matters of *Faith*, the Intellect proceeds to infer all those *Practical* Duties of Natural Religion founded on the inconceivable *Perfections* of the Divine Nature, and the several *Relations* it bears to Mankind ; all which require from us suitable Returns of *Fear* and *Love*, of *Honour* and *Gratitude* ; and of *Obedience* to all the Dictates of *Right Reason :* Which are the *Laws* of Nature, that is of *God* who hath endued us with that *Reason*, and with *Freedom of Will*, and Power for the Observance of those Laws. These Laws of Nature are unavoidably divided first, into Religious *Worship* both of Body and Mind to be paid to *God alone*, as to the only Object of Worship among *Invisible Beings*. Secondly, into a becoming and equitable

table

table Treatment of our *Fellow Creatures*, in all Inftances of Behaviour; which Branch of Duty, from the manifold Corruption and Obfcurity in which it was involved under uninlightned Reafon among Jews and Heathens, is now reduced with Clearnefs and Certainty to one univerfal Rule of Action, *What foever ye would that Men fhould do unto you, do ye alfo unto them:* So that upon an imaginary Change of Condition and Circumftances with any other Perfon, it is almoft impoffible to err in Judgment unlefs thro' *Perverfnefs* and Partiality. And laftly into the feveral Duties owing to *Our felves*, with regard to our *Private* Happinefs and Perfection; the Sum of which confifts in the Reftraining our *Appetites*, and the Regulation of our *Paffions* according to *Reafon*.

THE Intellect having, in the Series and Order before defcribed, attain'd at length to a commendable Knowledge of the Exiftence of *God*, and of his *Attributes*; and of the feveral *Relations* which he bears to Mankind; which are the Foundations of *Faith* in him, and of Divine *Worfhip*; together with that of all other *Practical* Duties in Religion merely *Moral*, has gone the whole length of its Chain, and cannot by its own *Natural* Powers take one Step farther. Here then we are arrived at the *Utmoft* Limits of human Underftanding, fet out by God and Nature; fuch as are utterly Impaffable, and never to be furmounted by the

I   utmoft

utmoft Efforts, and higheft Flights of *Unin-lightened* Senfe and Reafon.

ACCORDINGLY here it is, that all the Oppofers of *Revelation* fet up their *Standard*; where they labour with all their Force and Artifice, to guard and defend thefe *Frontiers* of theirs; by hindering all *Attempts* of the Mind to obtain any Degree of *Supernatural* Knowledge, which might be *Conveyed* from *Heaven* over thofe fcanty Bounds, to the Side of Nature. They will not fuppofe any Knowledge necef-fary to Religion, beyond the *Immediate* Reach of thofe Faculties interwoven with our Frame; or which cannot be attained by the fame *Un-affifted* and uninterrupted Method of Proceeding, and continued Chain of Confequences, by which the Mind of Man attains to any *Other* kind of Knowledge merely *Temporal* and Human. Their Perfuafion is, that neither the *Mind* nor *Confcience* has any thing to do with things, whereof Men, without any immediate Light from *Heaven*, cannot form to themfelves fome *Direct Idea* or *Conception* : Such reveal'd Truths they call a *Knowledge* without any Kind of *Ideas*; and a *Faith* without *Knowledge*; both which they efteem *Unreafonable* in *God* to require, and altogether *Impracticable* and unneceffary in refpect of *Man*.

THIS would have been a very juft way of Arguing, if Man had continued in that Frame
and

and Temper of Body and Mind wherein he
was firft made: But we are now, not as the
Hypothefis of thofe Men moft abfurdly fuppofes, in an original *Healthy* State of Nature;
but in one which is new and fuperinduc'd, and
altogether *Preternatural.* We find by fad Experience that we labour under a broken and
crazy Conftitution, with great Dimnefs of Sight
in our *Underftanding*; Crookednefs in our *Will*;
Diftortion in all the *Paffions* and *Affections* of
the inferior Soul; together with Corruption
and Pollution in all the *Appetites* of the Body.
In this Condition our mere Moralifts would
have the *Purblind* fickly Mind of Man judge
for itfelf; and work out a *Cure* intirely upon
the Strength of its *Own* Judgment, without
the leaft *Advice* or Help from *Heaven.*

THEIR fatal Error is, that they infift
wholly on the Light of *Nature* alone, in this
Unnatural State of Mind; and will choofe to
fee with no other than this obfcure, uncertain,
expiring Light; which was fo near being *Ex-
tinguifh'd*, that it could never have recover'd
without being *Kindled* anew from *Above.* So
that all their Boafts of *Natural* Religion only,
exclufive of *Revelation*, is but glorying in their
Shame : And vainly magnifying that Weaknefs
of the Underftanding, by which it is in the very
Condition of the Man in the Gofpel, *Who faw
Men as Trees walking* when his Eyes were but
half open'd; and which render'd it utterly un-
    2   able

able of itself to contribute any thing to its
own Cure; and therefore necessarily required
Discipline, and Regimen, and a Physician of
Souls. We were so far from being able of *Our
selves* to form any true Judgment upon the sufficient Means and Method of our *Recovery*, by
the Light of Nature; that it could not have
helped us even to any account of the true Cause
of our *Distemper*; and of that fatal Step by which
we were plunged into this deplorable State of
Blindness and Corruption: Which all Men
have ever bewail'd, but could never account
for without Revelation; from whence alone
we learn that it was not our *Original* Frame,
as we first came out of the Hands of God.
Here therefore we are to fix our Foot, for e-
vincing the absolute *Necessity* of some immediate express *Revelation* from Heaven; and must
lay it down as a certain Truth, in Opposition
to what is *Suppos'd* and *Insinuated* by the Mag-
nifiers of *Mere Reason*. That Mankind, in its
Present State of Degeneracy, is to be consider'd;
not in Possession of the Divine Laws *Fair* and
Legible, as they were originaly written on the
Tables of our *Heart* by the *Finger* of *God*; and
still remaining *Whole* and *Intire:* But as they
are *Broken* to Pieces, and *Shatter'd*; like those
lively *Emblems* of them which *Moses*, fill'd with
just Indignation, dashed against the Stones.
So that the whole Sum of all our Knowledge
in Religion merely *Natural*, is nothing more
Now, than the *Poor Remains* of the *First* Tran-

script;

script ; and only some *Few*, *Imperfect*, and *Uncertain* Hints recover'd by the laborious *Gathering* up, and *Piecing* of the *Fragments*.

C H A P. XI.

The Necessity, and Manner of Revelation.

HERE we are come at length to the *Utmost Advancement* of human Understanding, and the highest *Elevation* of the Mind of Man by *Divine Revelation*; whereby it is raised above itself, and above all things in this World, to take a *Clear* and *Delightful* Prospect of another ; whereof it had but a very *Obscure* uncertain View before. This opens to the Mind, all at once, a *New* and immense Scope, and spacious Scene of solid and substantial Knowledge : From which all the Adversaries of *Reveal'd* Religion unhappily preclude themselves, as from a kind of *Utopia* or *Fairy Land*, wherein all is mere *Dream* and *Vision* ; where Men must leave their *Reason* behind them at their first Entrance ; and give a Loose to the groundless and extravagant Amusements of a warm *Imagination*. In this they are so fix'd and positive, that they ever insinuate the Term REVELATION to import nothing more than *Ignorance* and *Superstition*. But their not discerning the absolute *Necessity* of Revelation, is a sad Effect and Consequence of that *Blindness* of their Understanding, which it was intended

2   to

to *Heal* and inlighten : And Men are never in a more *Deplorable* Condition, than when they remain altogether *Infenfible* in a *Mortal* Diftemper ; and cannot be perfuaded they ftand in need of any *Cure* or Remedy.

THAT the native Powers and Faculties of the whole Man were all out of Order and miferably broken and corrupted, the wifeft of the *Heathens* were thoroughly fenfible, and fadly lamented : And that all this proceeded from a *Voluntary* Act of his own, and not from any *Fatal Neceffity*, or *Pofitive Decree* and immediate Interpofition of Almighty Power, we are informed by Scripture. Now, after Man had funk into fuch a Condition of Infirmity and Corruption, as to be utterly unable to extricate himfelf; or to make any *Effectual* Attempt towards the Recovery of his original Frame and Temper of true *Wifdom* and *Innocence :* That unnatural Change and Degeneracy muft neceffarily have either always *Continued*, and have been unavoidably *Increafed* by Cuftom and Habit thro' every Generation ; or there muft have been fome Help or Remedy from *Without*. There could be no Alteration for the better of this daily declining State, and languifhing Condition of the Soul, from *Within* ; *Nature* had no *Strength* left to *Work* off the Diftemper, which proceeded from a mortal and deadly *Poifon*, greedily fwallowed by our firft Parents thro' a fatal Difobedience and In-

H h 3   advertency;

advertency; being treacheroufly handed out to them for the higheft *Cordial*, by the common Enemy of their whole Race. The *Antidote* or *Remedy* was paft all *Human* Art or Prefcription; and that it could be adminiftred by *Infinite Wifdom* alone is plain, fince the *Operation* muft have been according to the Nature and Difpofition of a *Free Agent:* The *Healing*, as well as the *Corruption* muft have been intirely *Voluntary*; and the *Means* of our Recovery muft have been altogether adapted to that perfeft *Freedom* of *Will* with which we were created, and without which we could not be either truly *Virtuous* or *Holy*; and confequently without our *Own* voluntary Concurrence, we could never be *Reftor'd* in any Degree to our primitive Frame and Conftitution.

SINCE therefore the *Freedom* of our *Will* was to be continued whole and *Inviolable*, thro' all the Difpenfations of God towards Mankind for our Recovery; there was no reafonable or *Conceivable* Way of effecting this, but by Application of proper Help and Affiftance to the *Natural Powers* and Faculties of the *Mind:* And particularly to the *Underftanding*, before there could be any room for the fecret Operation of the Spirit of God upon that of Man, for influencing the *Will*. This was to be performed, not by any *Sudden* actual *Illumination* of it *All at once*; as Blindnefs is cur'd in the Body, when it is the immediate Refult of Almighty

mighty Power (for we might as well suppose God, after the Fall, to have first reduced Man to *Nothing*, and then to have made him over again a *New Creature* in a *Literal* Sence) But by *Information* or *Revelation* from *Without*, of such Instances of *Knowledge* as were necessary to enable us to become *New Creatures* in a truly *Evangelical* Sence; and which it was impossible for us to attain by any *Inward* Light or Strength of Reason. And accordingly this Divine Information was begun in the first Promise of the *Seed of the Woman* which was to *Break the Serpent's Head*; and this was continualy *Enlarged* and clear'd up farther in succeeding Ages by *New* Revelations, as the *Gradual* Corruption and Exigencies of Mankind requir'd.

THUS our Understanding is assisted, and inlightned with the Knowledge of things *Supernatural* and *Spiritual*; after the same Manner it is with that of things *Temporal* and *Human*. The Knowledge and Experience of *Other Men* convey'd to us by *Information*, makes up the greatest Part of our *Secular* Knowledge; which we do not take up *Implicitly*, but render it properly *Our own* by the Exercise of our *Reason*, in judging and determining upon the *Credibility* of every thing we give our Assent to upon the Testimony of others. And we have the same *Full* and *Free* Use of our *Reason*, in judging and determining concerning the Credibility of every thing which comes to us by *Di-*

vine

vine Information; which goes by the Name of *Revelation*, to diftinguifh it from that which is *Human*. So that nothing can be more ground-lefs and abfurd, than the general and firm Per-fuafion of all our modern *Infidels* and *Freethink-ers*; That no *Information* hath or can come to us from *God*, as well as from *Man*; and that fuch as we hold to come from *Him*, requires a blind and *Implicit* Affent of the Mind, with-out a thorough Examination and Conviction of *Reafon*.

A s it is thus evident that the Underftanding may be, and is enlightened by *External Infor-mation* in Matters of Religion; fo it appears to the plaineft Reafon, that all fuch *Informa-tions* or *Revelations* muft be convey'd in the *Lan-guage* of *Men*, who are made the *Inftruments* of them all; and by the *Mediation* and *Subftitu-tion* of fuch natural and *Human Ideas* and *Con-ceptions*, for the expreffing of which the Words and Terms of that Language were *Originaly* accommodated. It is not reafonable to ima-gine that this fhould be performed by giving us any Faculties intirely *New*; or by any to-tal *Alteration* of thofe we *Already* have; for this would be a kind of *Second Creation*, and not any *Information* or *Revelation*. And it is as unreafonable to think, that this fhould be performed by exhibiting *Internaly* to the Mind of Man any *Obfcure*, or *Faint*, or *Glimmering Ideas* of things *Supernatural*, as they are *In themfelves*;

themselves ; for we are by Nature as unquali-
fy'd for any, even the leaft Degree of *Such* a
Perception of them, as we are for *Clear* and *Di-*
ſtinct Ideas of that *Real Eſſence:* Beſides that upon
Such a Suppoſition, all that *Knowledge* and *Faith*
which is founded on *Revelation*, muſt of Neceſſity
be *Equaly confuſed*, and *Dubious*, and *Obſcure.*

No, *Divine* Information gives us no *New*
Faculties of Perception, but is adapted to
thoſe we *Already have* ;   nor doth it exhibit to
the *Immediate* View of the Intellect *Any*, the
Leaſt glimmering Idea of things purely ſpiritual,
intirely abſtracted from all *Senſation* or any Dependence upon it: But it is altogether performed by the *Intervention* and Uſe of thoſe
Ideas which are *Already* in the Mind ; firſt conveyed to the Imagination from the Impreſſion
of external Objects upon the Organs of *Senſa-*
tion; then variouſly *Alter'd* and diverſify'd by
the Intellect ; and afterwards by its Operations
of *Judgment* and *Illation*, wrought up into an
endleſs Variety of *Complex Notions* and *Concep-*
tions; which takes in the whole Compaſs of
our merely temporal and *Secular* Knowledge.
Now, all this is transfer'd from *Earth* to *Hea-*
ven, by way of *Semblance* and *Analogy:* So that
the *Ideas* ſimple and compound ;   the *Complex*
Notions and *Conceptions* ;   the *Thoughts* and *Rea-*
ſonings; the *Sentiments* and *Apprehenſions* ;   the
Imaginations, and *Paſſions*, and *Affections* of an
Human Mind ; together with the *Language* and
Terms

Terms by which we exprefs them, become *Sub-*
fervient to all the real Ends and Purpofes of
Revelation. The *Terms* together with the *Con-*
ceptions apply'd to things *Supernatural* and Spiritual, are the *Same* which are in common
Ufe for things *Temporal* and *Human*; but the
Application is *New* and *Holy*; they are only
confecrated to a *Divine Ufe* and Signification:
They are fo far fanctifyed and to be reverenced
as they are thus appropriated to *Religion*; to
the *Reprefentation* of the intrinfick Nature and
Attributes of *God*; and to the glorious, and *O-*
therwife ineffable *Myfteries* of the Gofpel.

THIS Operation of *Subftituting* thofe Ideas
and complex Notions which are *Natural* and
Familiar to us, for the Reprefentation of things
Supernatural and in themfelves *Incomprehenfible*
(which we fall into fo infenfibly, that we do
not eafily diftinguifh between the *Literal*, and
Analogical Acceptation of thofe Terms by which
we exprefs them) is the higheft and moft valuable Privilege of the Intellect. It is this which
gives it full Scope for the Contemplation of
heavenly Objects; which extends its Dimen-
fions; and fo dilates all the Powers and Faculties of the Mind, that it takes in the immenfe
Creation with all its glorious Inhabitants; and
even *God* himfelf, and all his *Attributes*. By
this it comes to a folid and *Real Knowledge*
of things, whereof it can have no *Direct* Conception or Idea; and is enabled to judge and
deter-

determine, to difcufs and argue, to make fure and certain Deductions and Conclufions; and form to itfelf Axioms, and Rules, and Precepts concerning things far removed out of the *Immediate* Reach of all its natural Capacities; and by this they become the Objects of our Fear and Love, Faith and Hope, and of all the Paffions and Affections of a human Soul. In fhort this is the very way by which all *Intercourfe* is kept up between *God* and *Man*; and whereby he lets himfelf *Down* to our prefent Condition of Infirmity, in all his Revelations.

THUS we contemplate things *Supernatural* and *Spiritual*, not by looking directly *Upward* for any *Immediate View* of them; but as we behold the heavenly Bodies, by cafting our Eyes *Downward* to the *Water*. Which tho' it exhibits to us nothing of the *Real Nature* and *True Subftance* of the Firmament, with all its Furniture of radiant and delightful Objects; yet affords us fuch a *Goodly Appearance* and *Lively Reprefentation* of them, that a Perfon (fuppofed never to have feen thofe celeftial Luminaries *Themfelves*; but convinced that there *May* be a true *Similitude*, and *Proportion*, and *Correfpondency* between the *Refemblances* and the *Reality*) would have Notions and Conceptions of the things unfeen, not only *Juft* and *True :* But fo *Clear* likewife and *Diftinct*, that he wou'd from thence infer their *Neceffary Exiftence* ; admire their Splendor, and Beauty, and Ufe ;

and

and reafon upon them, to all *Moral* Intents and Purpofes, with as much folid *Truth* and *Reality* as he could upon thofe things whereof he had either *Direct Ideas*, or an *Immediate Confcioufnefs*; and nothing would be more ridiculous in him, than to draw any *Exact Parallel* between the *Real Nature* and effential *Properties* of the *Types* and *Antitypes*.

THO' this kind of Knowledge is by Semblance only and *Analogy*, yet we have a firm Dependence upon the Wifdom and *Veracity* of God (who formed us to his own *Image* and Likenefs) for fuch a juft *Refemblance*, and *Proportion*, and *Correfpondency* between thofe Types which are natural, and the fupernatural Antitypes, as renders that Knowledge *Solid* and *Real*; the *Faith* that is built upon it, *Certain* and *Firm*; and our *Hope* well grounded and *Sure*. And then only we are in danger of running into Error and Delufion, and may be *Fataly* deceived, when we either turn it into mere *Metaphor* and *Allufion* only; or when we *Strain* that Analogy, by which we conceive things fpiritual, to an *Undue* and *Literal* Comparifon with things natural and human, and in fuch Inftances as never were *Intended* by the Wifdom of God; or laftly, when we begin to imagine, that we have in any degree a *Direct* or *Immediate* Perception of things *Supernatural.*

THE

THE Mind of Man, while it keeps within its own proper *Sphere*, acts with Freedom and Security; but when it strives to exert itself beyond its *Native* Powers and Faculties, then it finks into Weakness and Infirmity; and is ever liable to endless Mistake and Error. It hath no *Direct* Perception, or *Immediate* Consciousness beyond things sensible and human. So that in all its noblest Efforts and most lofty *Flights*, it must ever have a steady *Eye* to the *Earth* from whence it took its Rise; and always consider that it mounts upward with *Borrowed* Wings: For when once it presumes upon their being of its own *Natural* growth, and attempts a *Direct* Flight to the heavenly Regions; then it falls *Headlong* to the Ground, where it lies *Groveling* in Superstition, or Infidelity.

F I N I S.

Printed by JAMES BETTENHAM.

M3